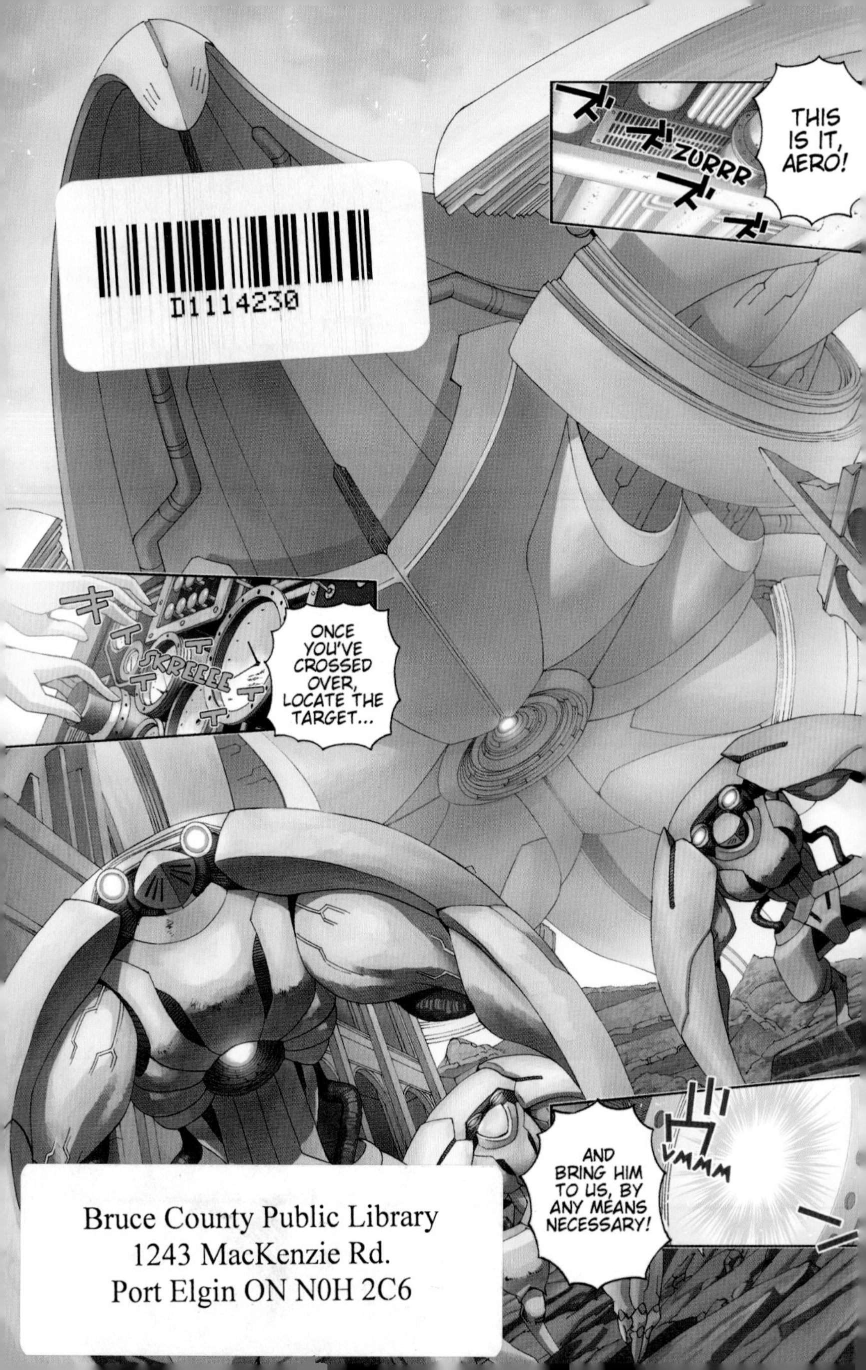
THIS IS IT, AERO!
ZURRR
ONCE YOU'VE CROSSED OVER, LOCATE THE TARGET...
SKREEEE
AND BRING HIM TO US, BY ANY MEANS NECESSARY!
VMMM

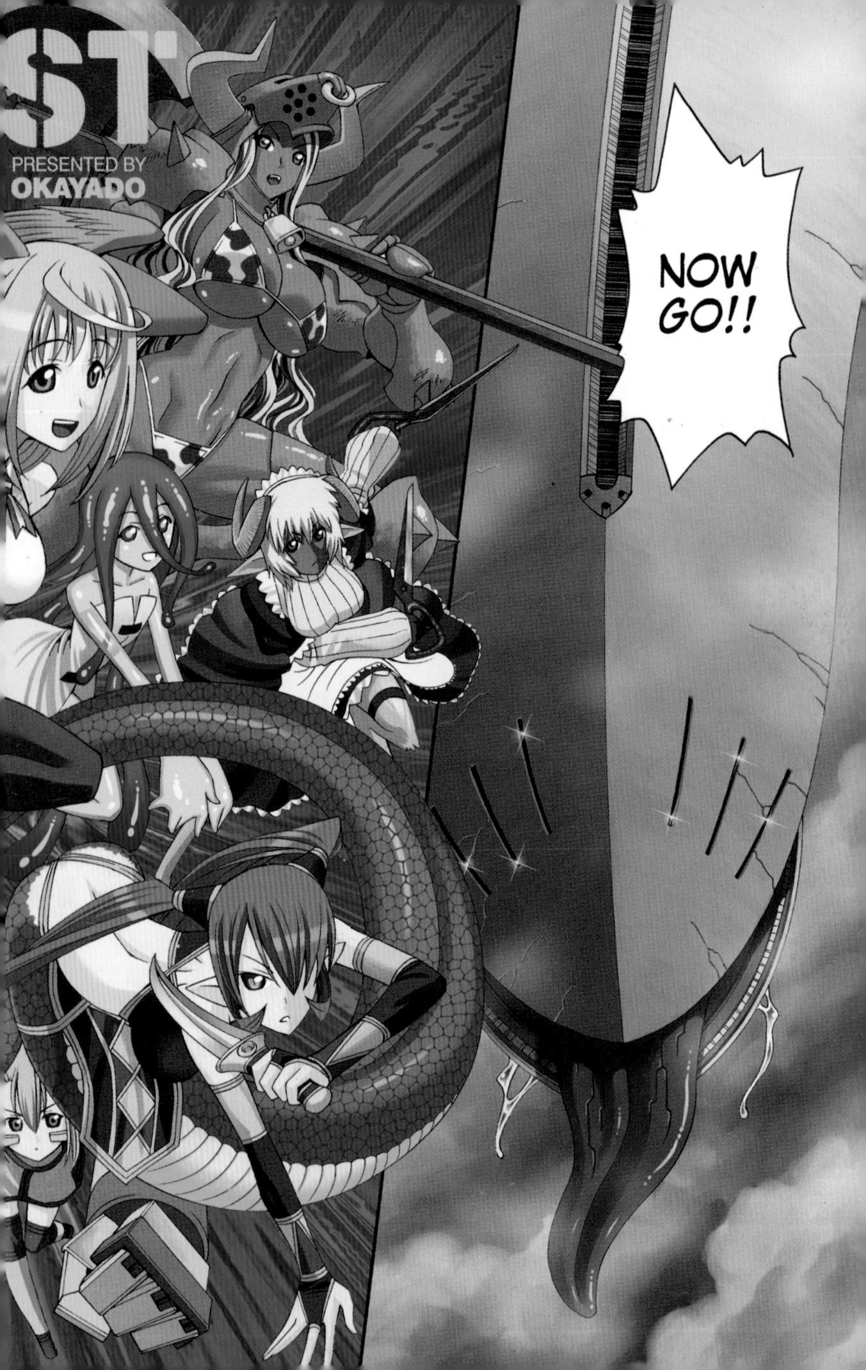
ST
PRESENTED BY
OKAYADO
NOW GO!!

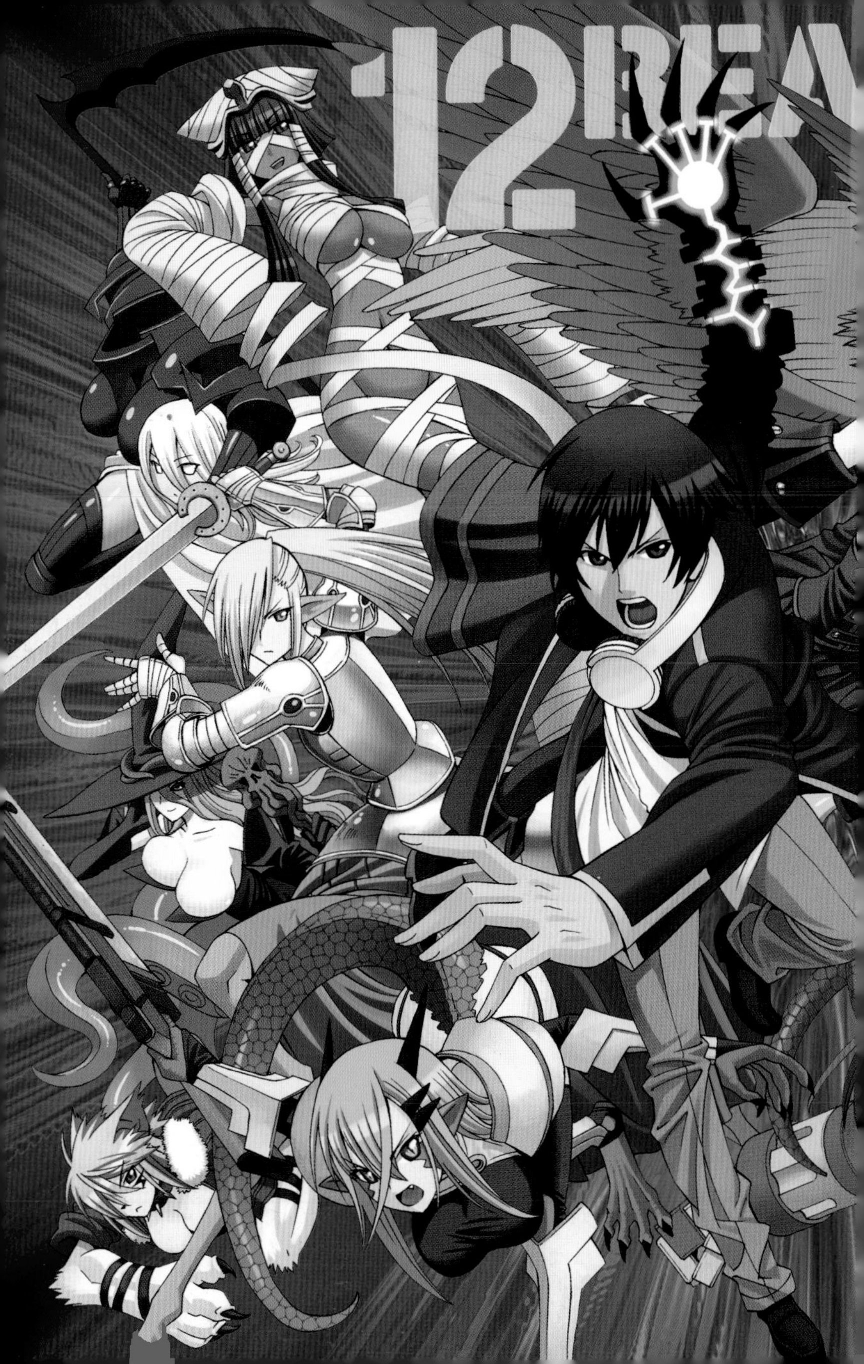
12BEA

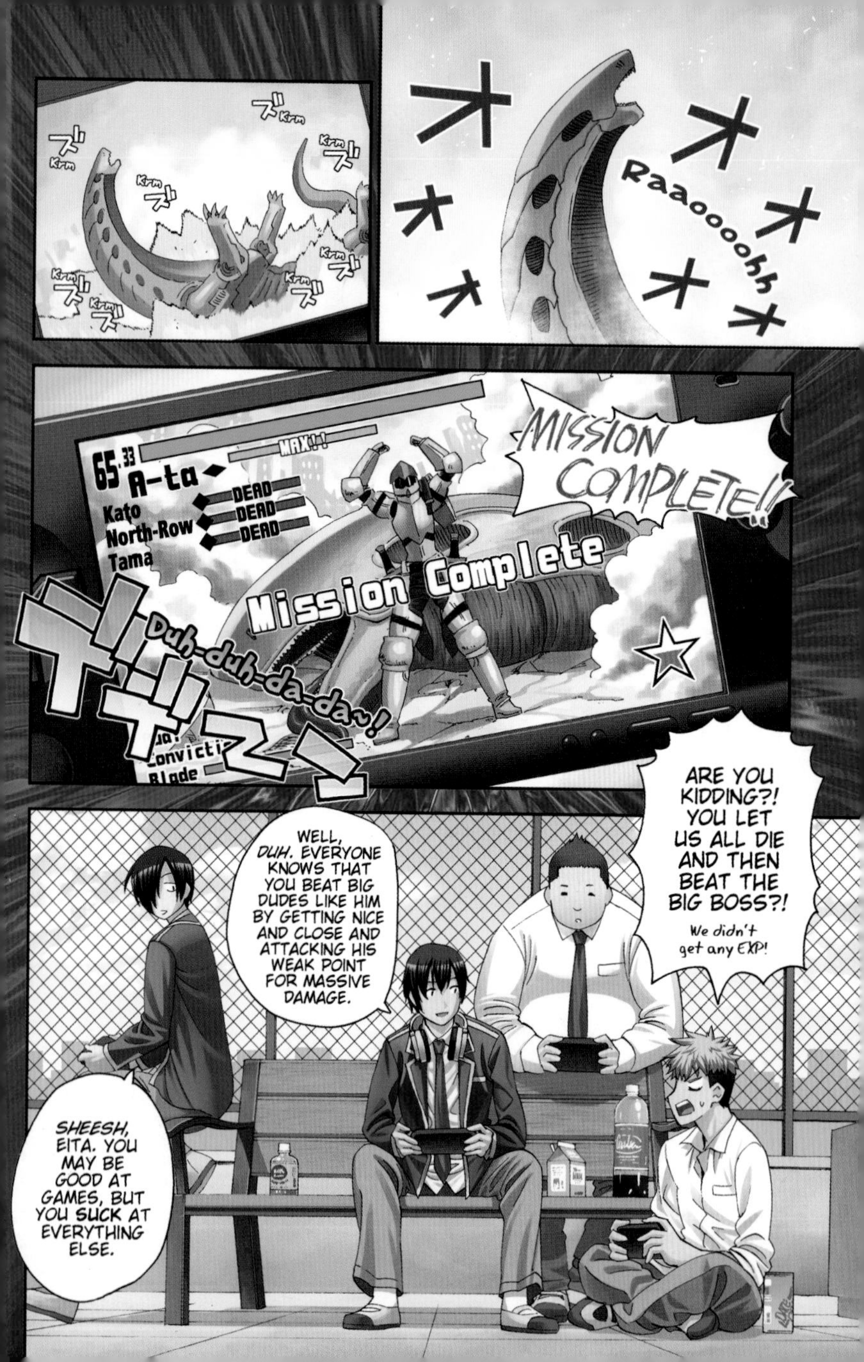
Raaooooohh
Krm
MISSION COMPLETE!!
65.33
A-ta
MAX!!!
Kato
North-Row
Tama
DEAD
DEAD
DEAD
Mission Complete
Duh-duh-da-da~!
Blade
ARE YOU KIDDING?! YOU LET US ALL DIE AND THEN BEAT THE BIG BOSS?!
We didn't get any EXP!
WELL, DUH. EVERYONE KNOWS THAT YOU BEAT BIG DUDES LIKE HIM BY GETTING NICE AND CLOSE AND ATTACKING HIS WEAK POINT FOR MASSIVE DAMAGE.
SHEESH, EITA. YOU MAY BE GOOD AT GAMES, BUT YOU SUCK AT EVERYTHING ELSE.

# Chapter 1: Secret Agent Ninja Apprentice

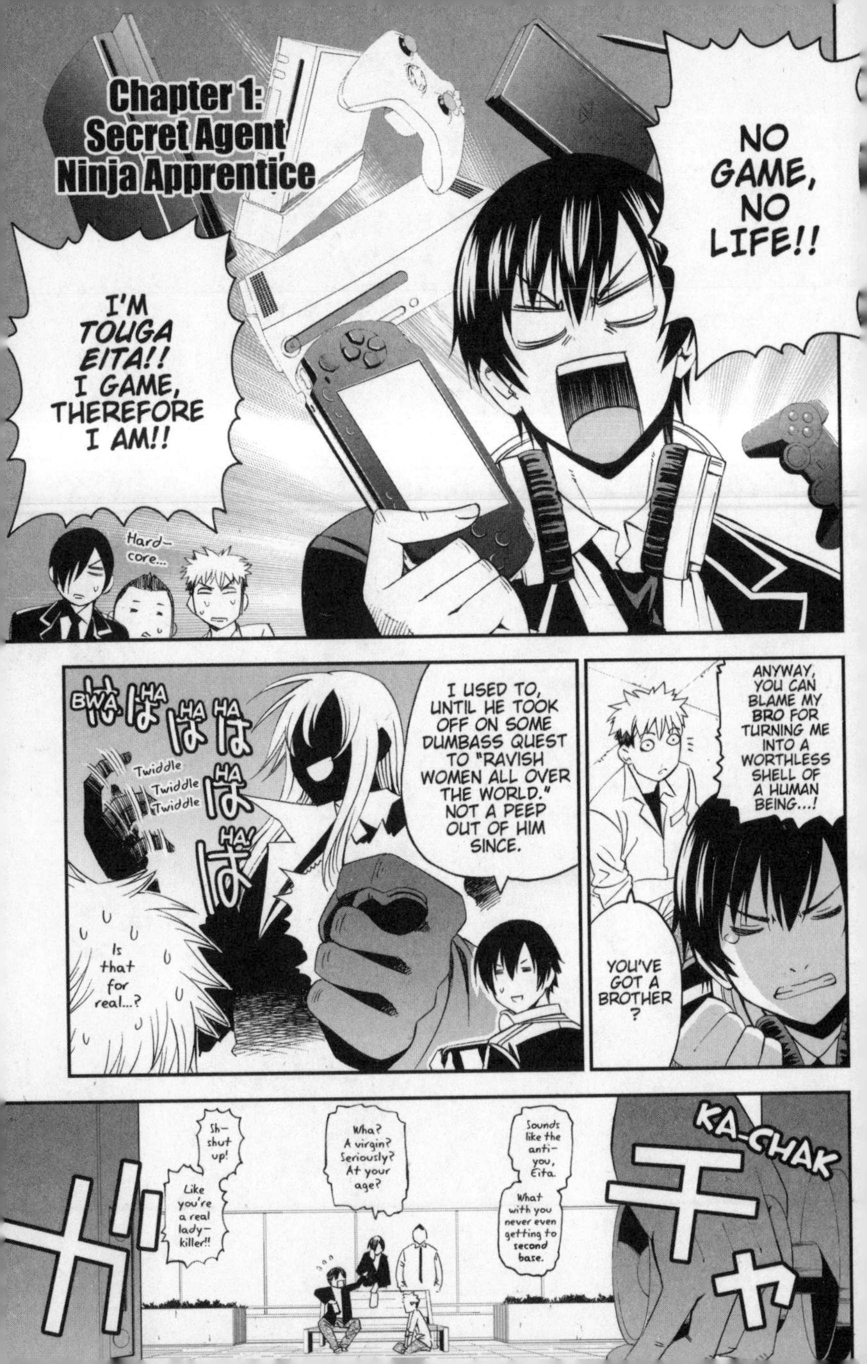
NO GAME, NO LIFE!!
I'M TOUGA EITA!! I GAME, THEREFORE I AM!!
Hard-core...
ANYWAY, YOU CAN BLAME MY BRO FOR TURNING ME INTO A WORTHLESS SHELL OF A HUMAN BEING...!
YOU'VE GOT A BROTHER?
I USED TO, UNTIL HE TOOK OFF ON SOME DUMBASS QUEST TO "RAVISH WOMEN ALL OVER THE WORLD." NOT A PEEP OUT OF HIM SINCE.
BWAHAHAHAHA!
Twiddle Twiddle Twiddle
Is that for real...?
KA-CHAK
Sounds like the anti-you, Eita.
What with you never even getting to second base.
Wha? A virgin? Seriously? At your age?
Sh-shut up!
Like you're a real lady-killer!!

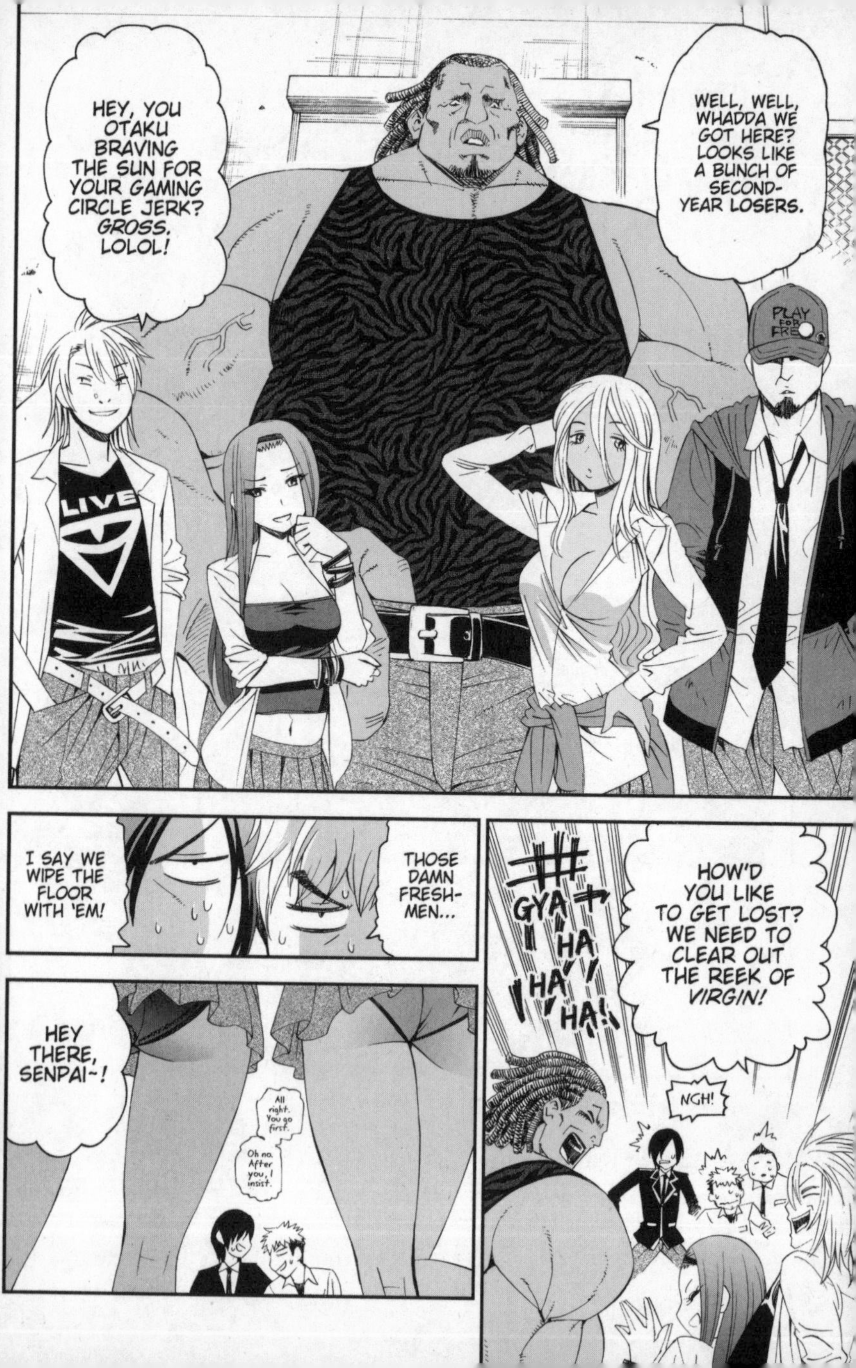
WELL, WELL, WHADDA WE GOT HERE? LOOKS LIKE A BUNCH OF SECOND-YEAR LOSERS.
HEY, YOU OTAKU BRAVING THE SUN FOR YOUR GAMING CIRCLE JERK? GROSS. LOLOL!
LIVE
HOW'D YOU LIKE TO GET LOST? WE NEED TO CLEAR OUT THE REEK OF VIRGIN!
GYA HA HA HA!!
NGH!
THOSE DAMN FRESHMEN...
I SAY WE WIPE THE FLOOR WITH 'EM!
HEY THERE, SENPAI~!
All right. You go first.
Oh no. After you, I insist.

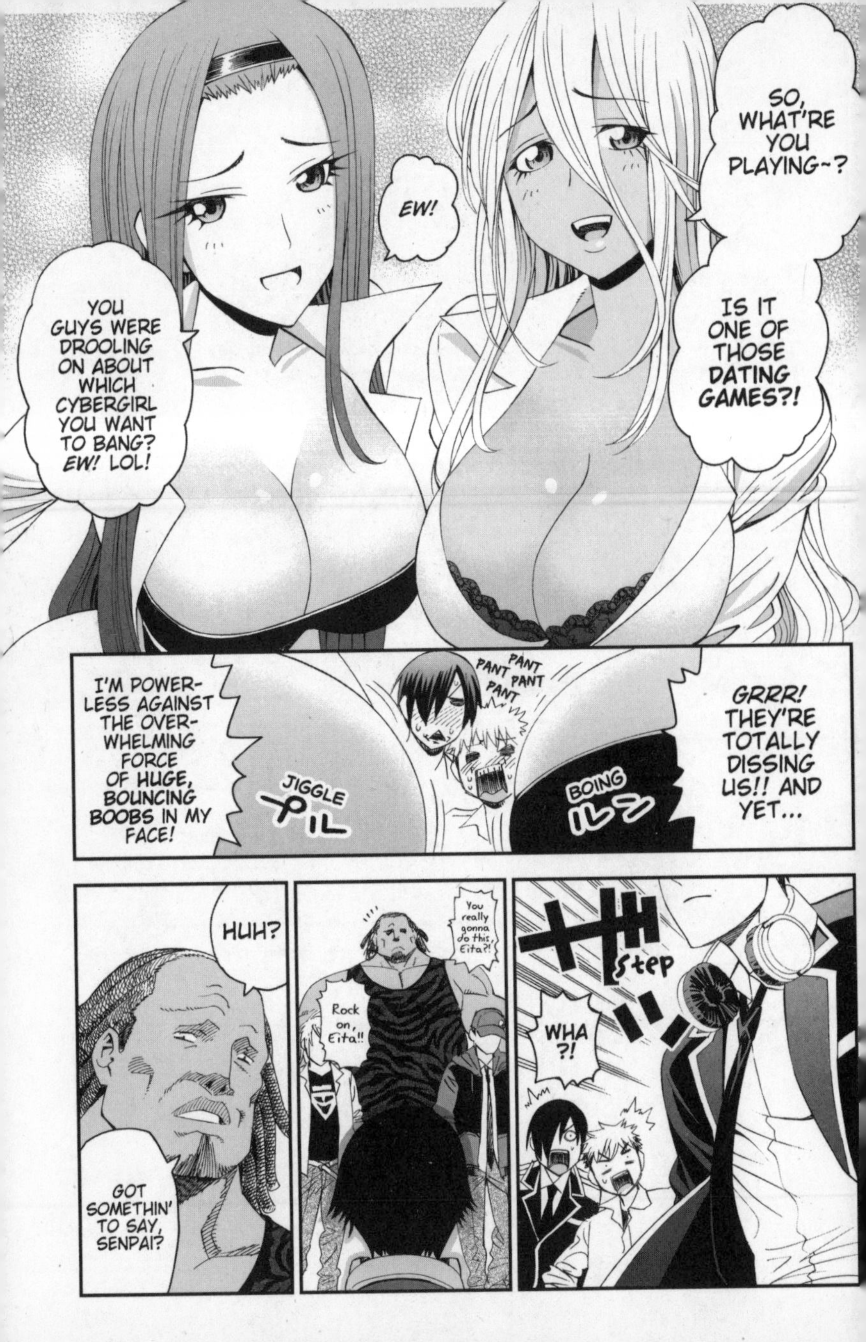
SO, WHAT'RE YOU PLAYING~?
IS IT ONE OF THOSE DATING GAMES?!
EW!
YOU GUYS WERE DROOLING ON ABOUT WHICH CYBERGIRL YOU WANT TO BANG? EW! LOL!
GRRR! THEY'RE TOTALLY DISSING US!! AND YET...
PANT PANT PANT PANT
BOING
JIGGLE
I'M POWER-LESS AGAINST THE OVER-WHELMING FORCE OF HUGE, BOUNCING BOOBS IN MY FACE!
step
WHA ?!
You really gonna do this, Eita?!
Rock on, Eita!!
HUH?
GOT SOMETHIN' TO SAY, SENPAI?

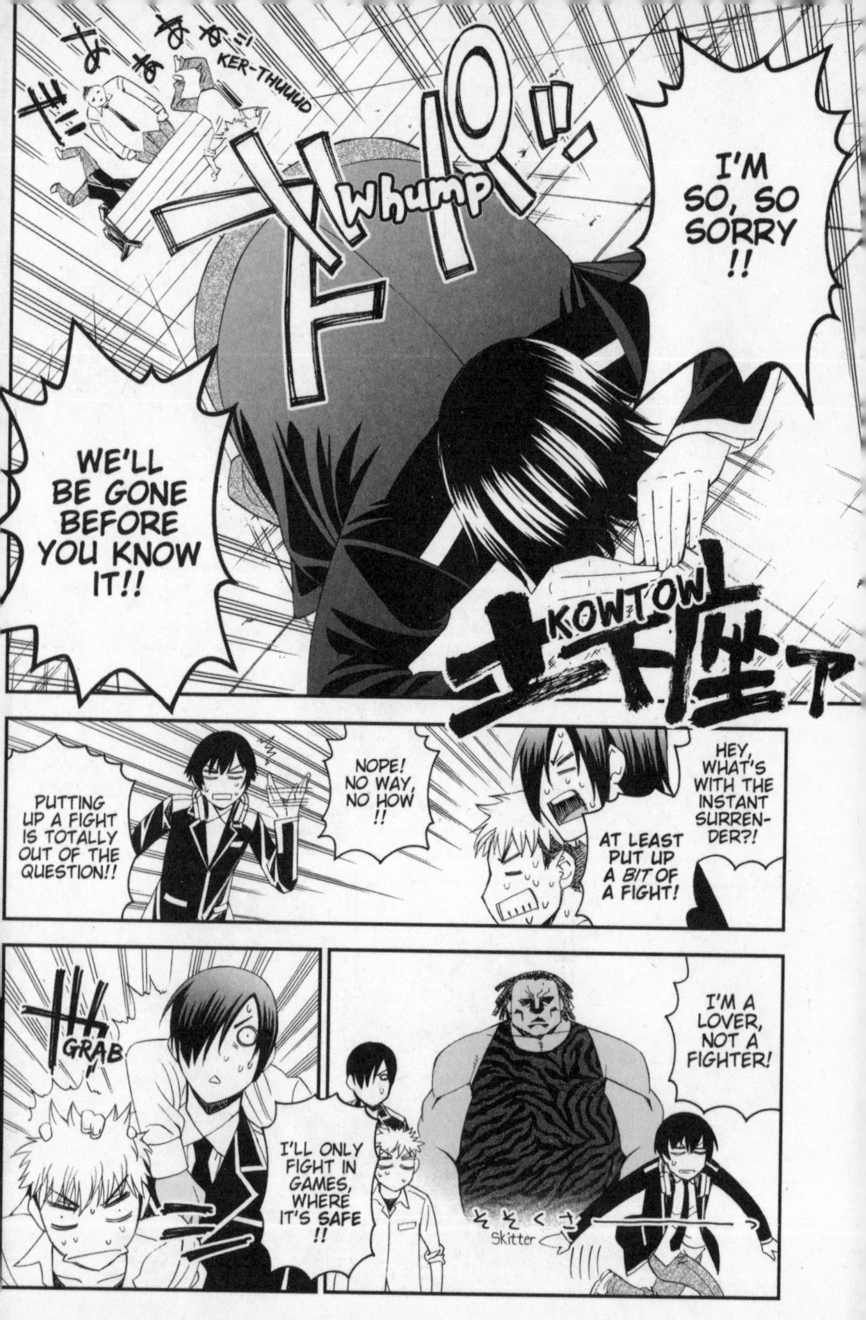
I'M SO, SO SORRY!!
Whump
KER-THUUUD
WE'LL BE GONE BEFORE YOU KNOW IT!!
KOWTOW
土下座ア
HEY, WHAT'S WITH THE INSTANT SURREN-DER?!
AT LEAST PUT UP A BIT OF A FIGHT!
NOPE! NO WAY, NO HOW!!
PUTTING UP A FIGHT IS TOTALLY OUT OF THE QUESTION!!
I'M A LOVER, NOT A FIGHTER!
I'LL ONLY FIGHT IN GAMES, WHERE IT'S SAFE!!
そそくさ
Skitter
GRAB

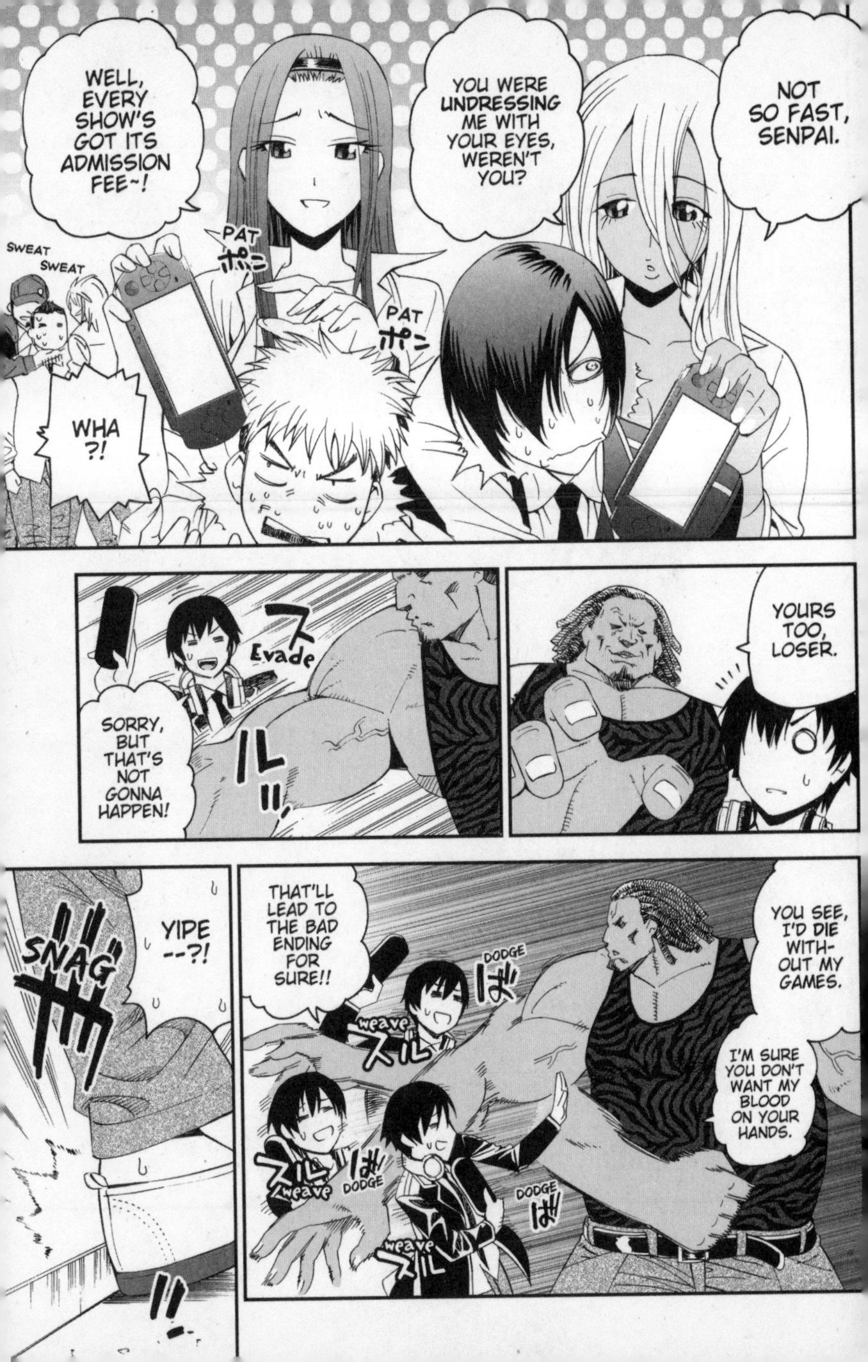

NOT SO FAST, SENPAI.
YOU WERE UNDRESSING ME WITH YOUR EYES, WEREN'T YOU?
PAT
PAT
WELL, EVERY SHOW'S GOT ITS ADMISSION FEE~!
WHA?!
SWEAT SWEAT
YOURS TOO, LOSER.
Evade
SORRY, BUT THAT'S NOT GONNA HAPPEN!
YOU SEE, I'D DIE WITH-OUT MY GAMES.
I'M SURE YOU DON'T WANT MY BLOOD ON YOUR HANDS.
THAT'LL LEAD TO THE BAD ENDING FOR SURE!!
DODGE
weave
DODGE
weave
DODGE
weave
YIPE --?!
SNAG

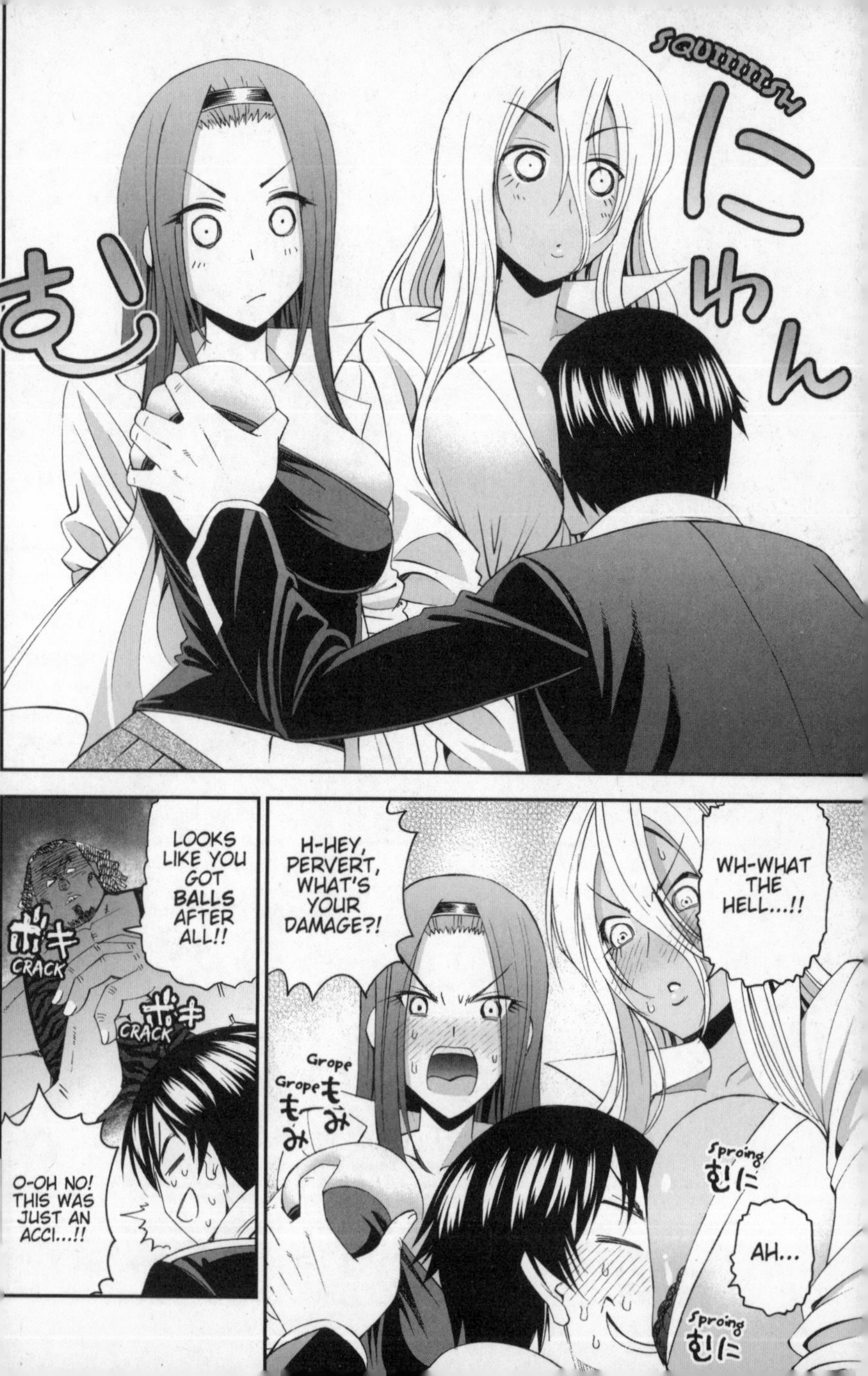

SQUIIIIISH
にゅん
WH-WHAT THE HELL...!!
H-HEY, PERVERT, WHAT'S YOUR DAMAGE?!
Grope もみ
Grope もみ
Sproing むに
AH...
Sproing むに
LOOKS LIKE YOU GOT BALLS AFTER ALL!!
ボキ CRACK
ボキ CRACK
O-OH NO! THIS WAS JUST AN ACCI...!!

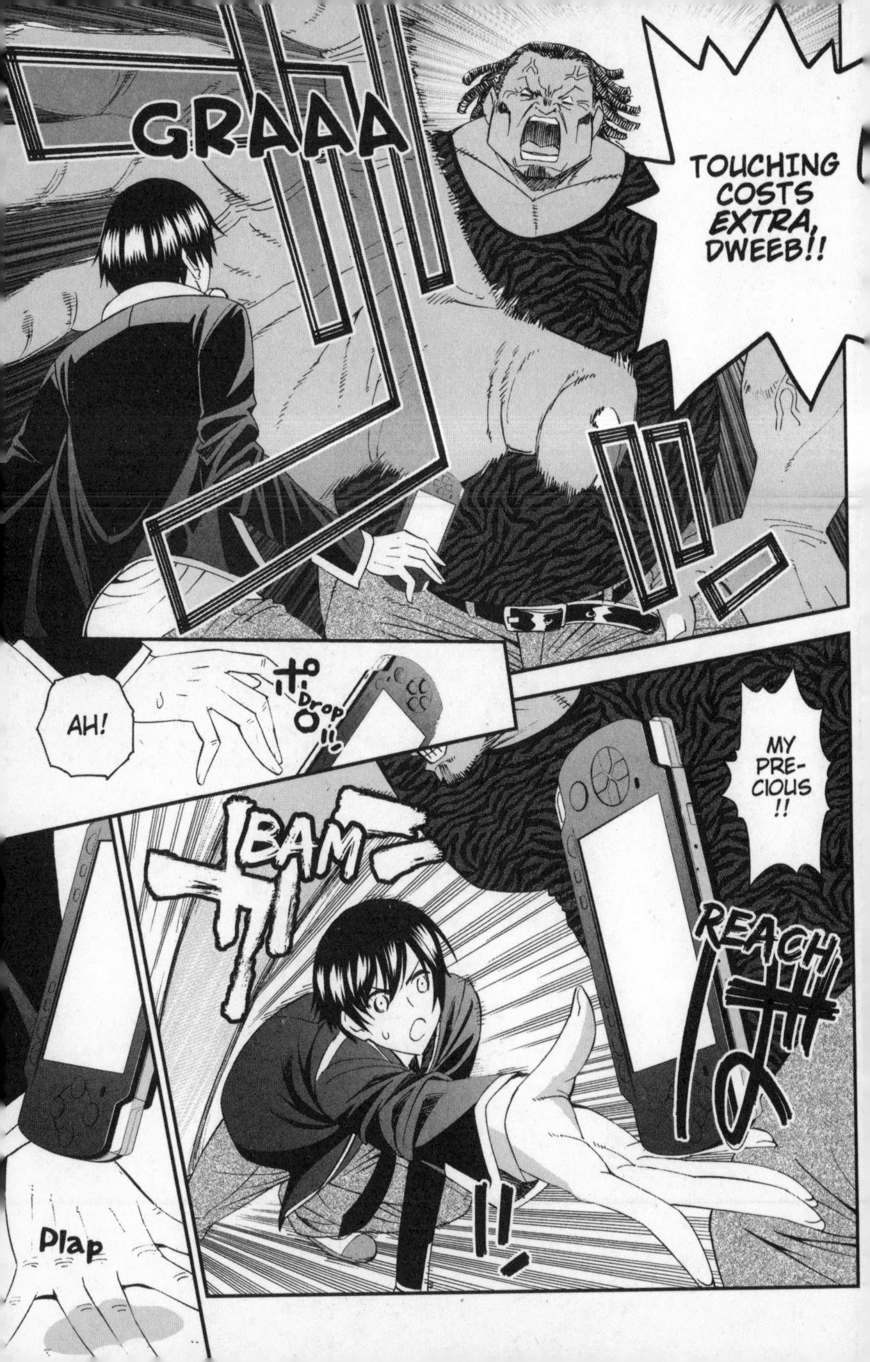
TOUCHING COSTS EXTRA, DWEEB!!
GRAAA
Drop
AH!
MY PRE-CIOUS!!
REACH
BAM
!!
Plap

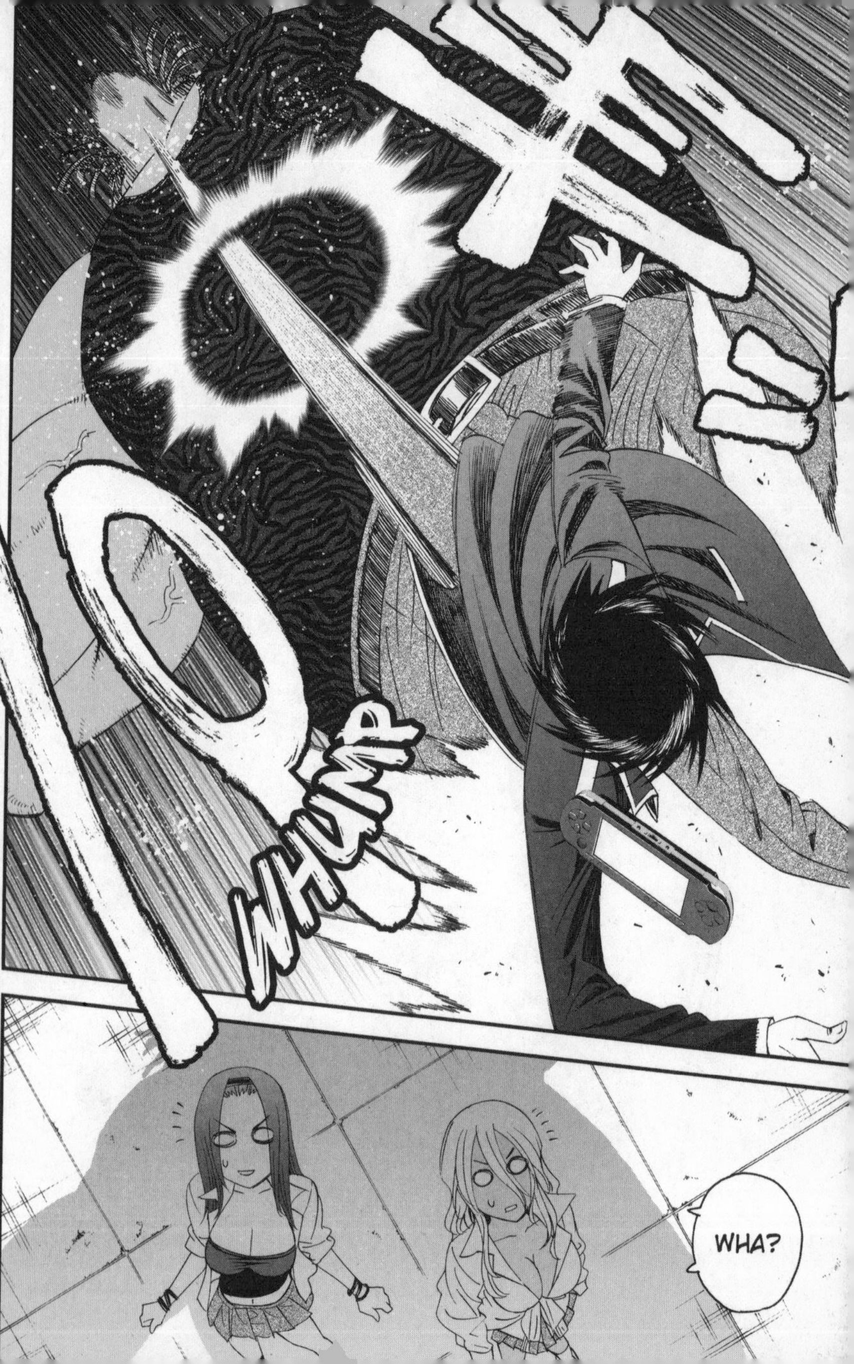
WHUMP
WHA?

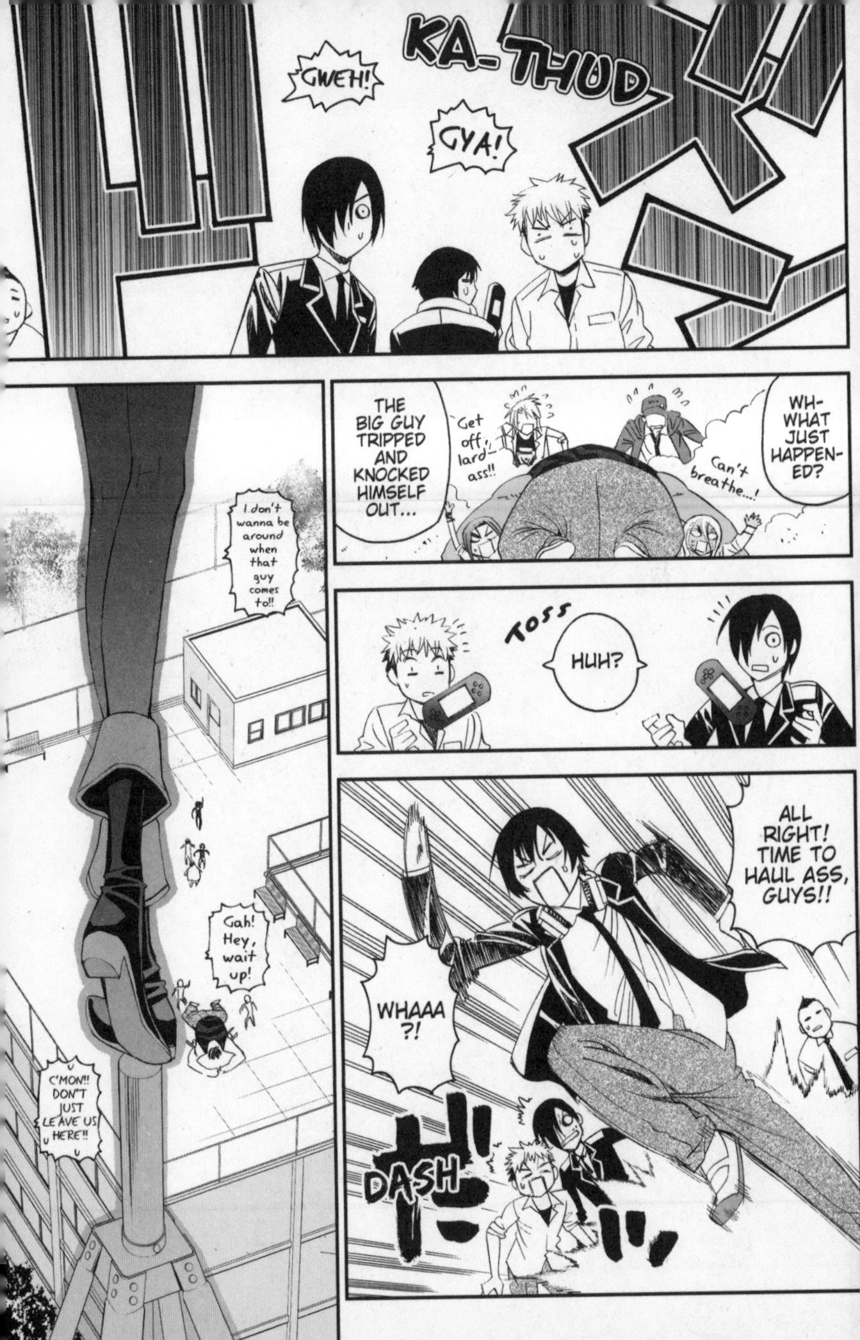
KA-THUD
GWEH!
GYA!
WH-WHAT JUST HAPPEN-ED?
Can't breathe...!
Get off, lard-ass!!
THE BIG GUY TRIPPED AND KNOCKED HIMSELF OUT...
TOSS
HUH?
ALL RIGHT! TIME TO HAUL ASS, GUYS!!
WHAAA?!
DASH
I don't wanna be around when that guy comes to!!
Gah! Hey, wait up!
C'MON!! DON'T JUST LEAVE US HERE!!

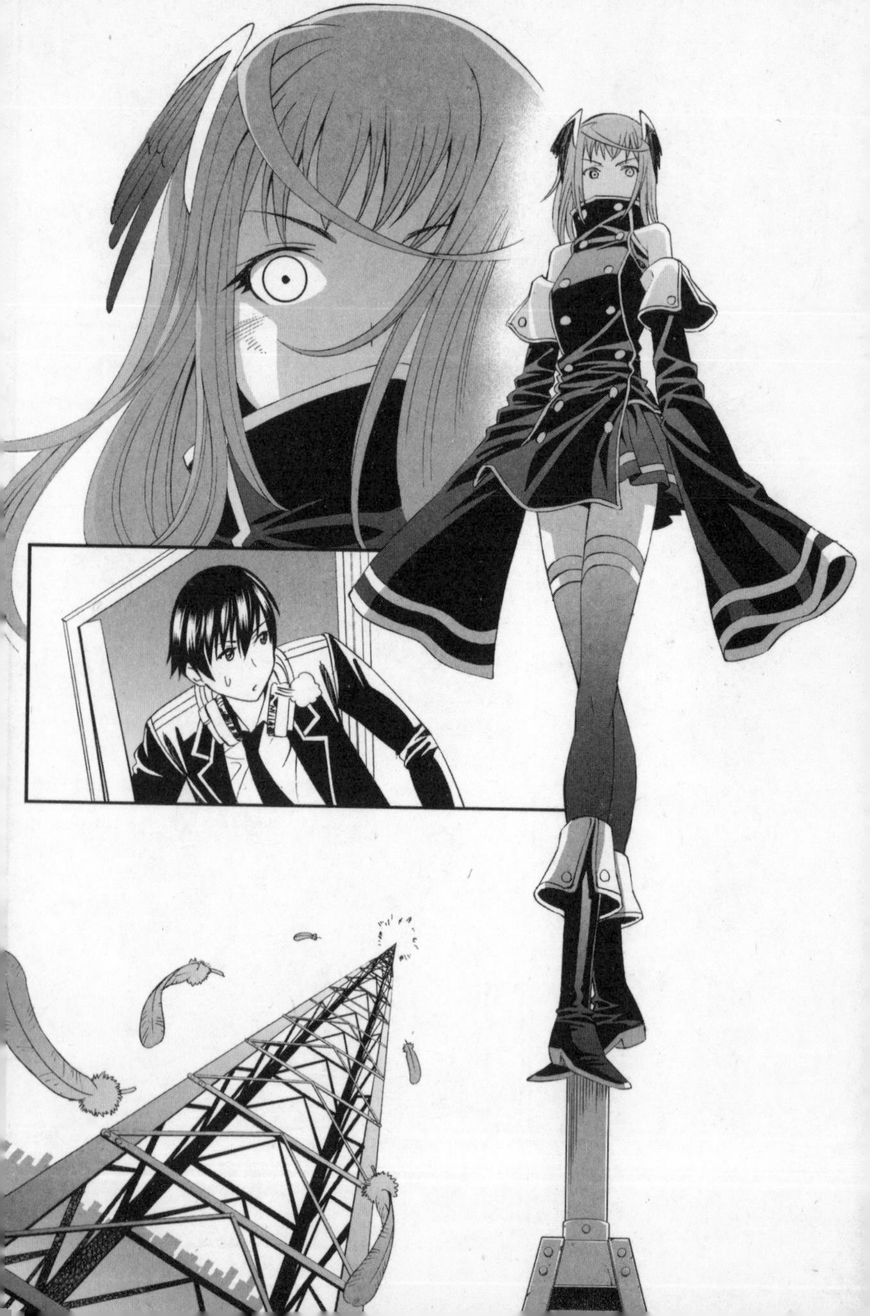

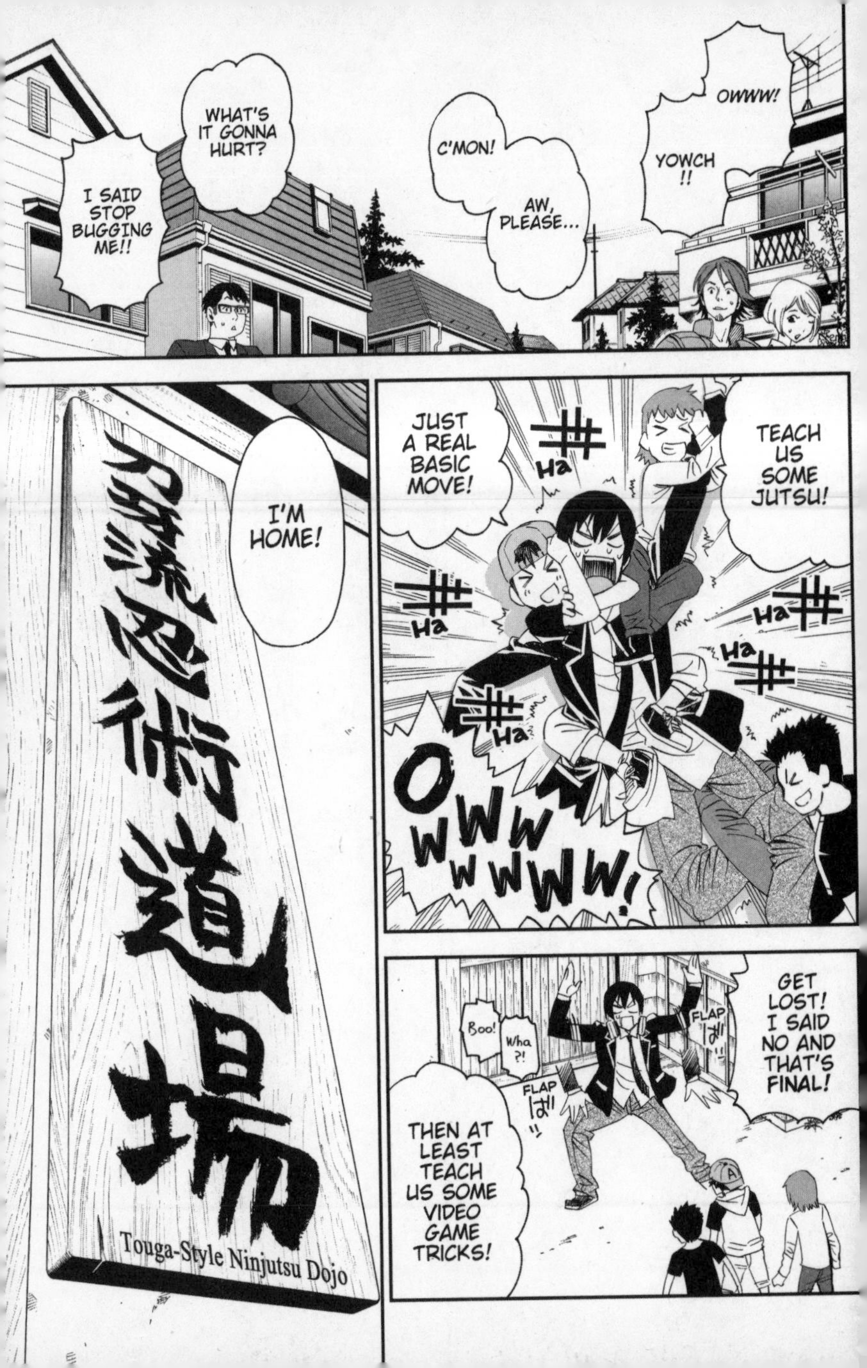
OWWW!
YOWCH!!
C'MON!
AW, PLEASE...
WHAT'S IT GONNA HURT?
I SAID STOP BUGGING ME!!
TEACH US SOME JUTSU!
JUST A REAL BASIC MOVE!
Ha
Ha
Ha
Ha
Ha
OWWWWWWWWW!
GET LOST! I SAID NO AND THAT'S FINAL!
FLAP
Wha?!
Boo!
THEN AT LEAST TEACH US SOME VIDEO GAME TRICKS!
FLAP
I'M HOME!
Touga-Style Ninjutsu Dojo

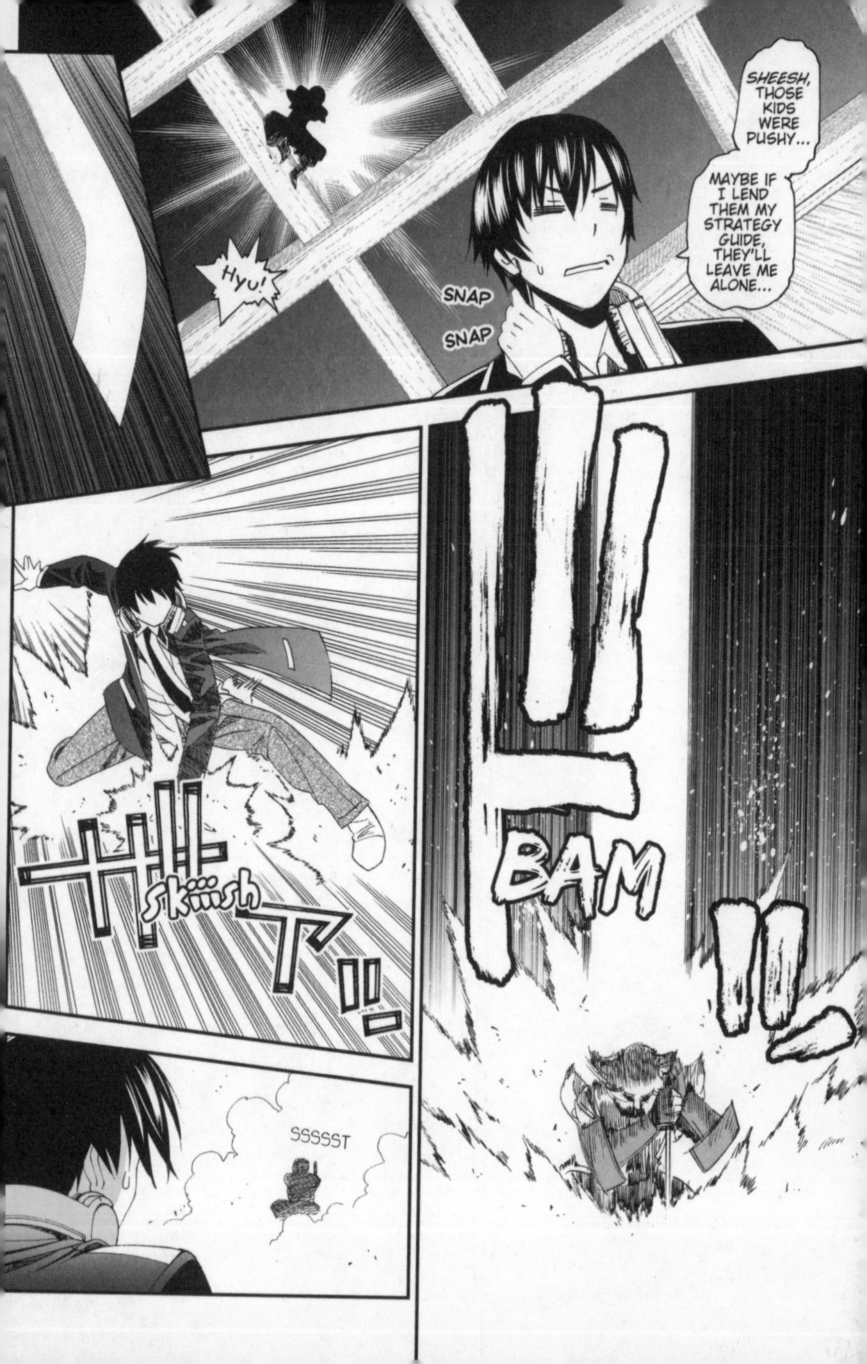
SHEESH, THOSE KIDS WERE PUSHY...
MAYBE IF I LEND THEM MY STRATEGY GUIDE, THEY'LL LEAVE ME ALONE...
SNAP
SNAP
Hyu!
BAM
skiiish
SSSSST

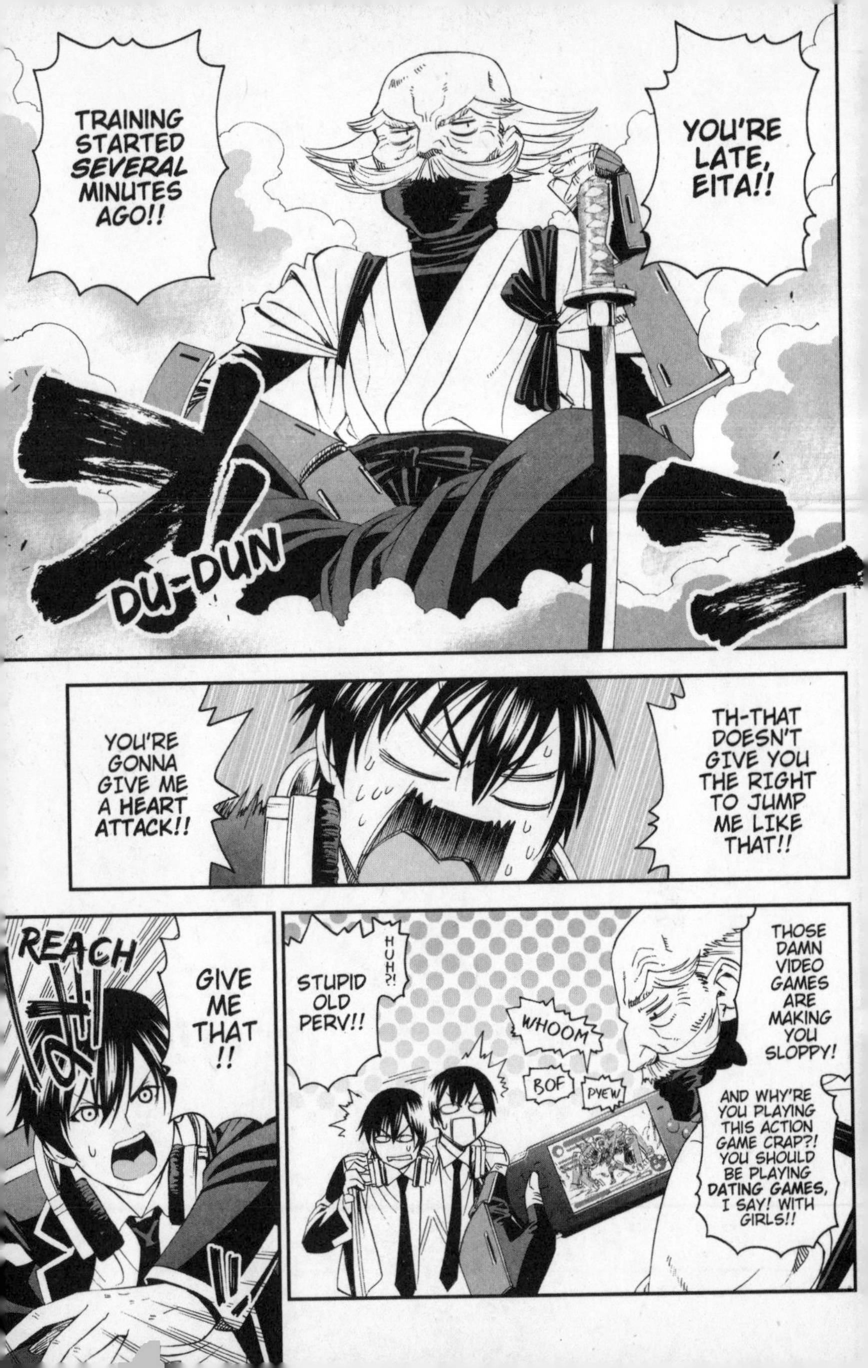
YOU'RE LATE, EITA!!
TRAINING STARTED SEVERAL MINUTES AGO!!
DU-DUN
TH-THAT DOESN'T GIVE YOU THE RIGHT TO JUMP ME LIKE THAT!!
YOU'RE GONNA GIVE ME A HEART ATTACK!!
THOSE DAMN VIDEO GAMES ARE MAKING YOU SLOPPY!
AND WHY'RE YOU PLAYING THIS ACTION GAME CRAP?! YOU SHOULD BE PLAYING DATING GAMES, I SAY! WITH GIRLS!!
WHOOM
BOF
PYEW
HUH?!
STUPID OLD PERV!!
REACH
GIVE ME THAT!!

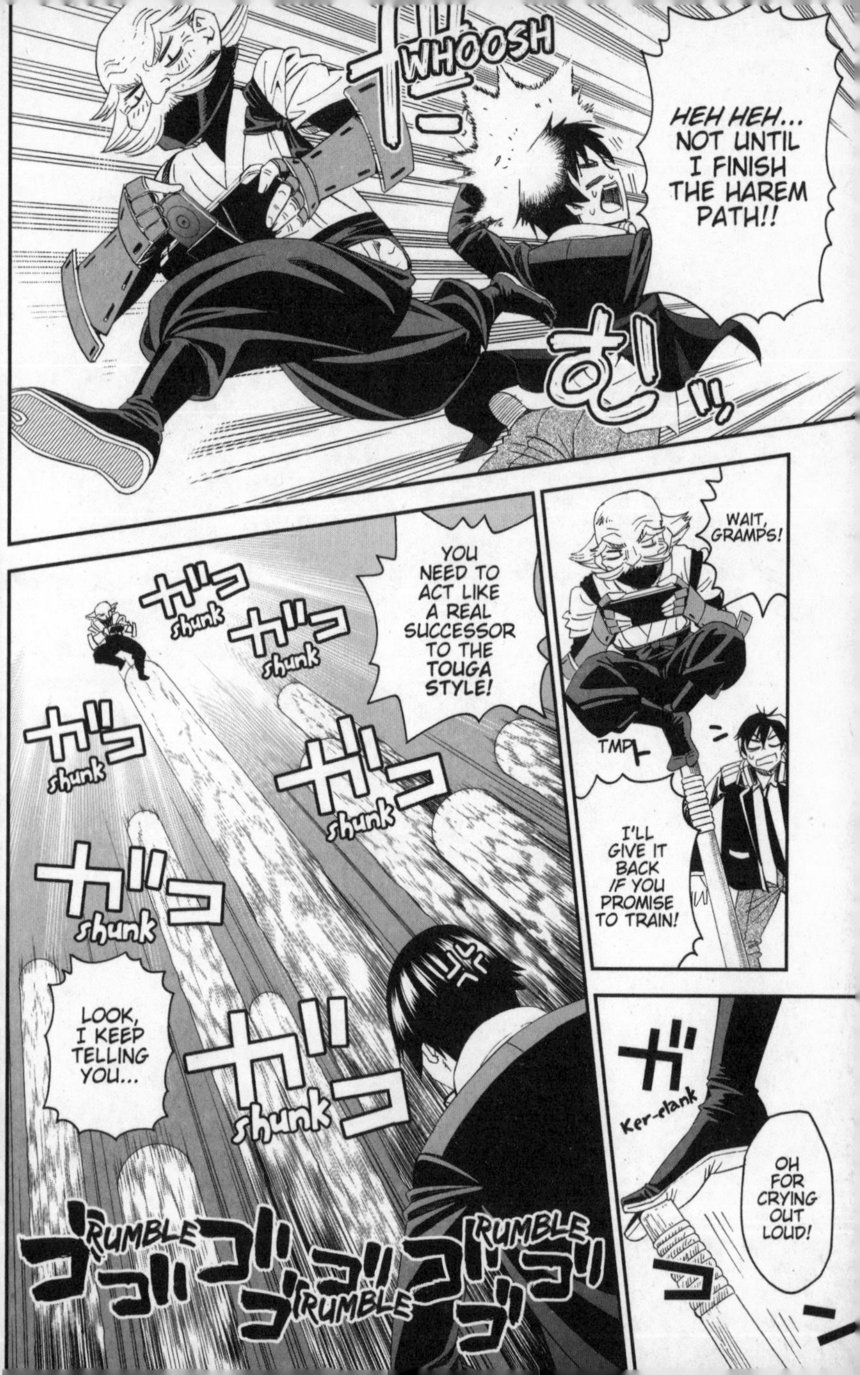
WHOOSH
HEH HEH... NOT UNTIL I FINISH THE HAREM PATH!!
WAIT, GRAMPS!
TMP
I'LL GIVE IT BACK IF YOU PROMISE TO TRAIN!
Ker-clank
OH FOR CRYING OUT LOUD!
YOU NEED TO ACT LIKE A REAL SUCCESSOR TO THE TOUGA STYLE!
shunk
shunk
shunk
shunk
shunk
shunk
LOOK, I KEEP TELLING YOU...
RUMBLE
RUMBLE
RUMBLE

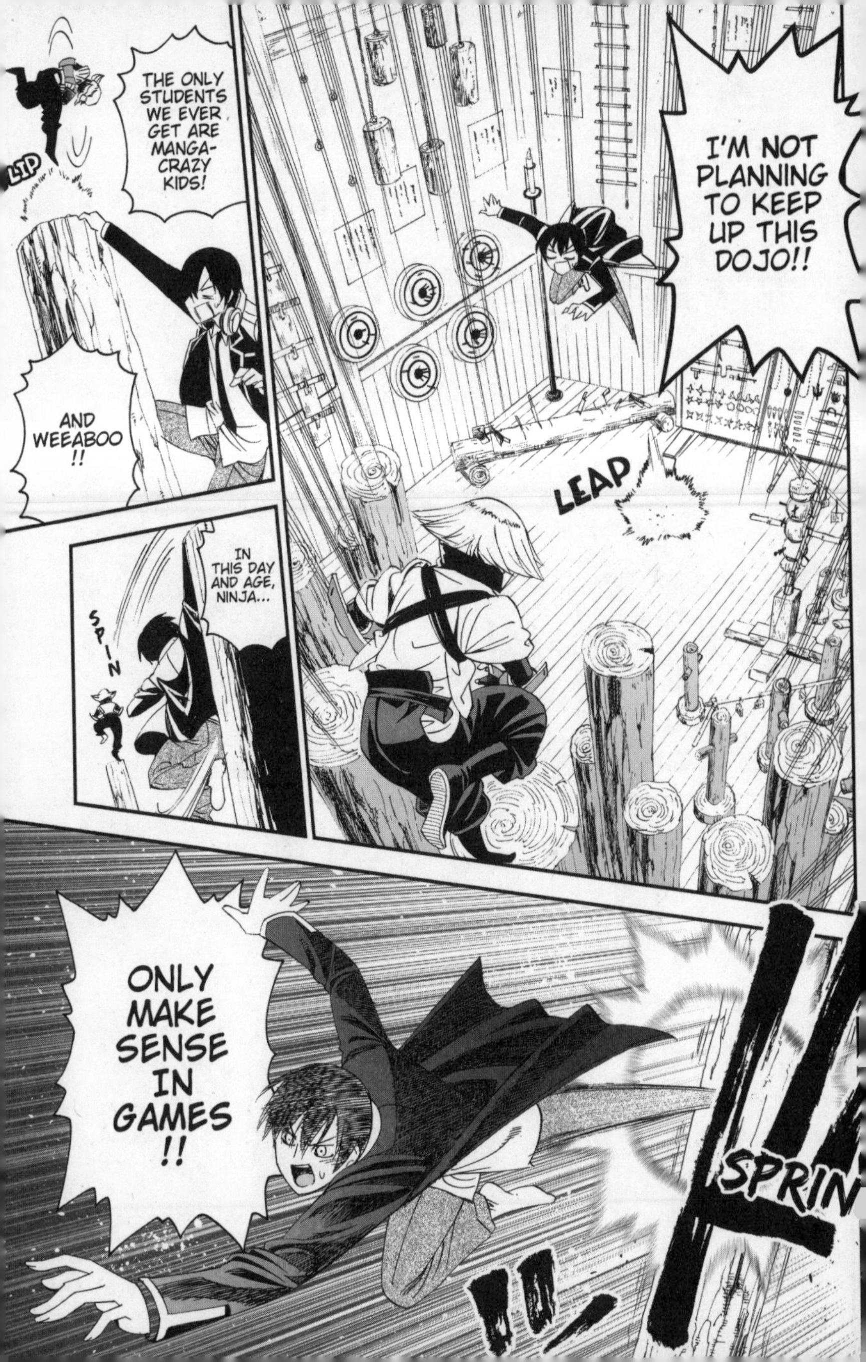
I'M NOT PLANNING TO KEEP UP THIS DOJO!!
LEAP
THE ONLY STUDENTS WE EVER GET ARE MANGA-CRAZY KIDS!
LIP
AND WEEABOO !!
IN THIS DAY AND AGE, NINJA...
SPIN
ONLY MAKE SENSE IN GAMES !!
SPRIN

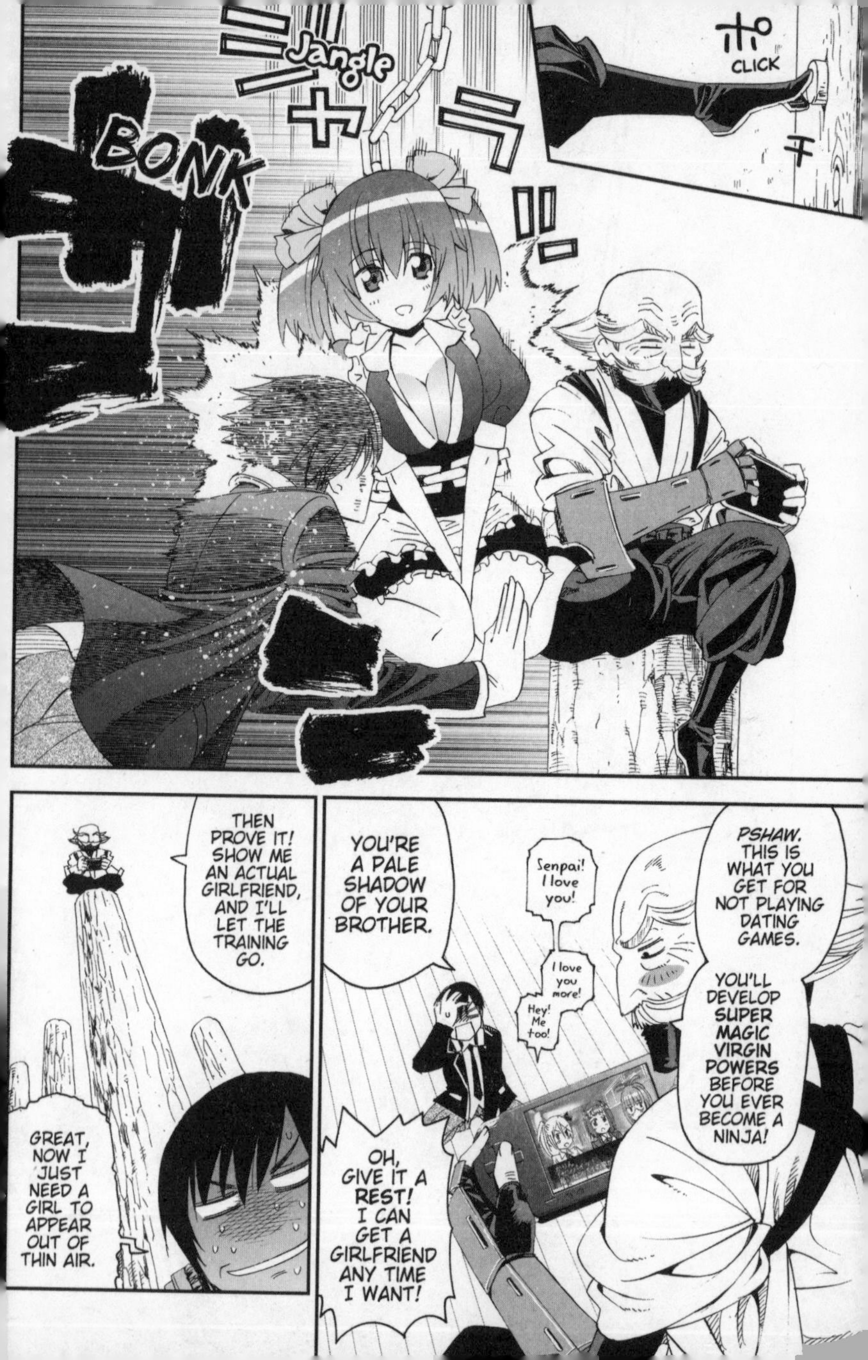
CLICK
Jangle
BONK
PSHAW. THIS IS WHAT YOU GET FOR NOT PLAYING DATING GAMES.
Senpai! I love you!
I love you more!
Hey! Me too!
YOU'LL DEVELOP SUPER MAGIC VIRGIN POWERS BEFORE YOU EVER BECOME A NINJA!
YOU'RE A PALE SHADOW OF YOUR BROTHER.
OH, GIVE IT A REST! I CAN GET A GIRLFRIEND ANY TIME I WANT!
THEN PROVE IT! SHOW ME AN ACTUAL GIRLFRIEND, AND I'LL LET THE TRAINING GO.
GREAT, NOW I JUST NEED A GIRL TO APPEAR OUT OF THIN AIR.

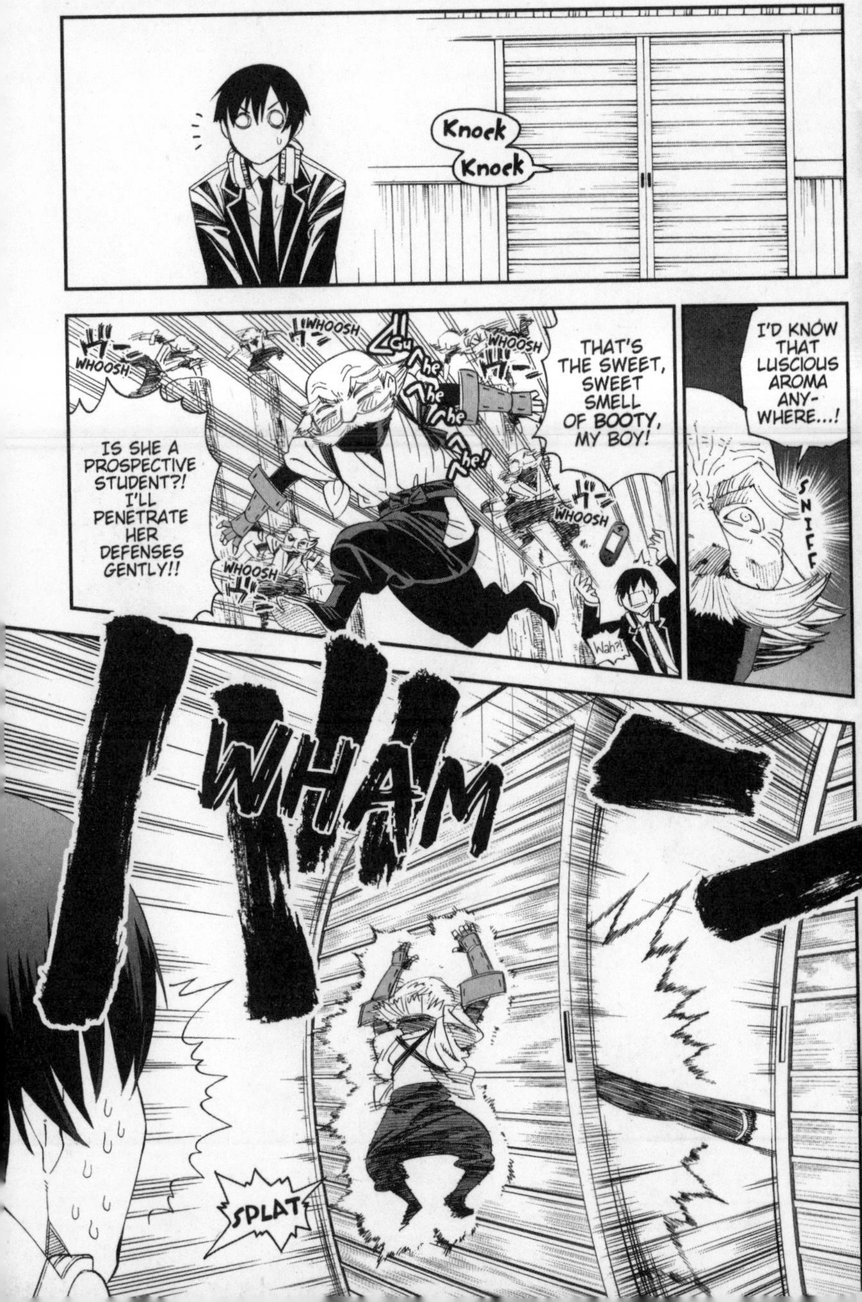
Knock
Knock
I'D KNOW THAT LUSCIOUS AROMA ANY-WHERE...!
SNIFF
THAT'S THE SWEET, SWEET SMELL OF BOOTY, MY BOY!
WHOOSH
Gu he he he he!
WHOOSH
WHOOSH
WHOOSH
IS SHE A PROSPECTIVE STUDENT?! I'LL PENETRATE HER DEFENSES GENTLY!!
WHOOSH
Wah?!
WHOOSH
WHAM
SPLAT

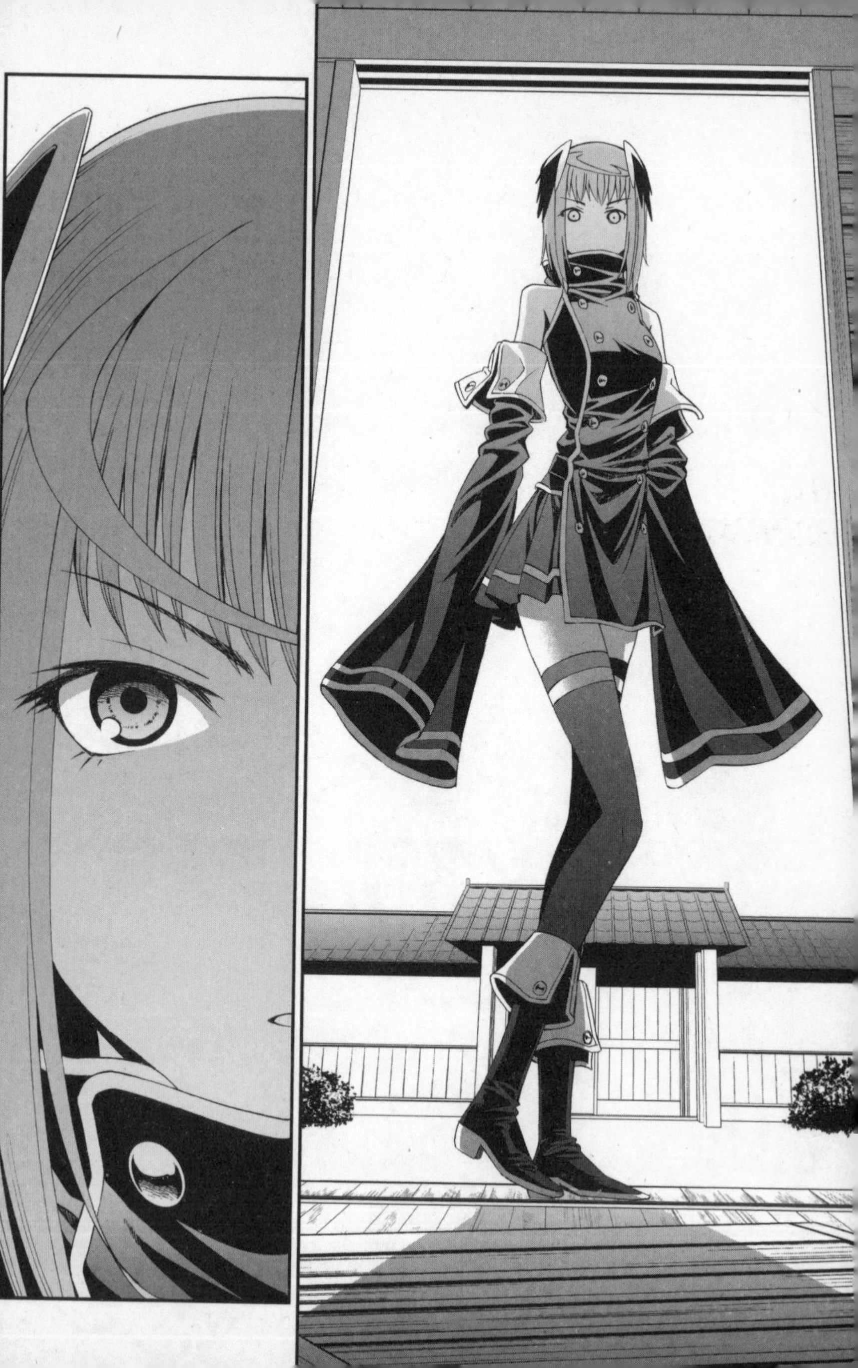

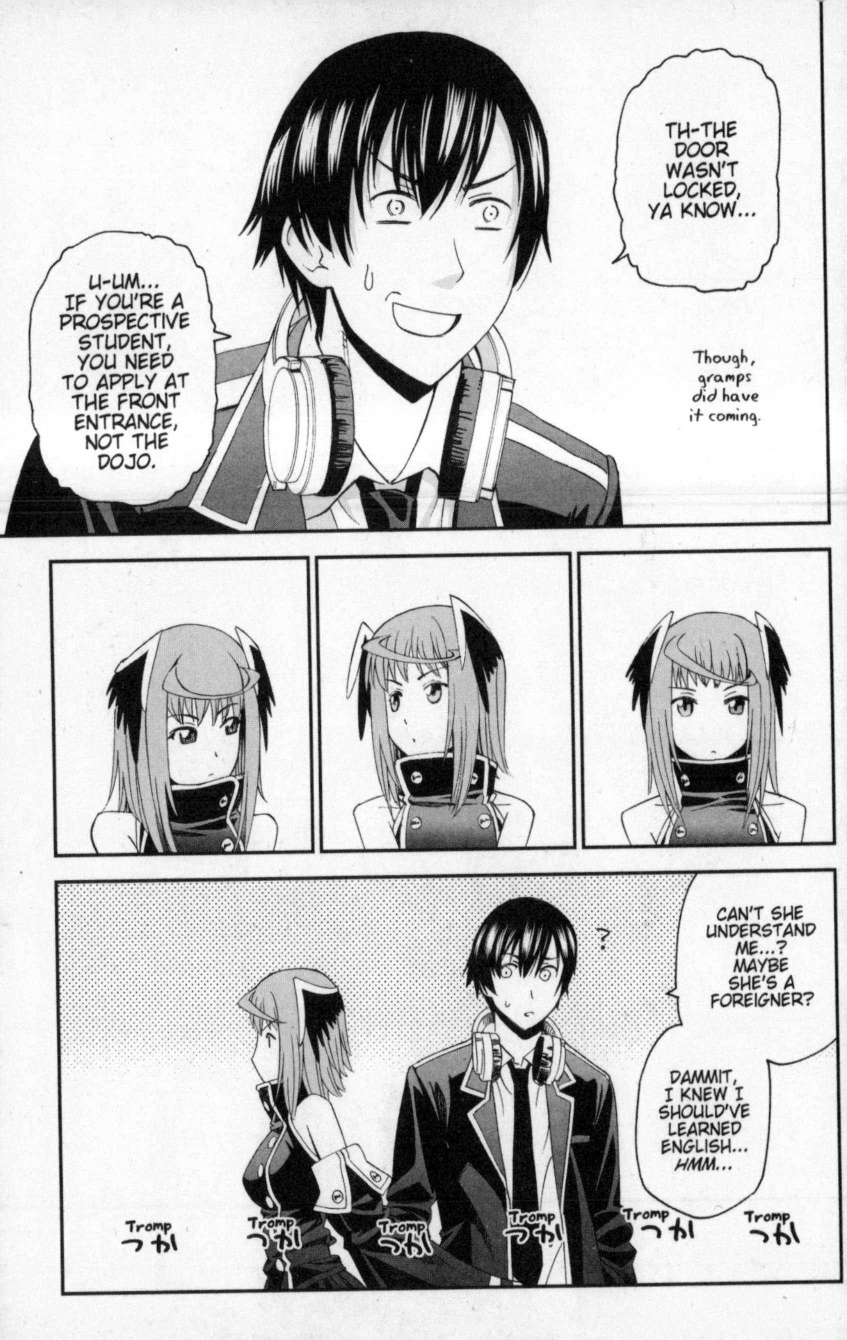
TH-THE DOOR WASN'T LOCKED, YA KNOW...
Though, gramps did have it coming.
U-UM... IF YOU'RE A PROSPECTIVE STUDENT, YOU NEED TO APPLY AT THE FRONT ENTRANCE, NOT THE DOJO.
CAN'T SHE UNDERSTAND ME...? MAYBE SHE'S A FOREIGNER?
DAMMIT, I KNEW I SHOULD'VE LEARNED ENGLISH... *HMM...*
?
Tromp つか
Tromp つか
Tromp つか
Tromp つか
Tromp つか
Tromp つか

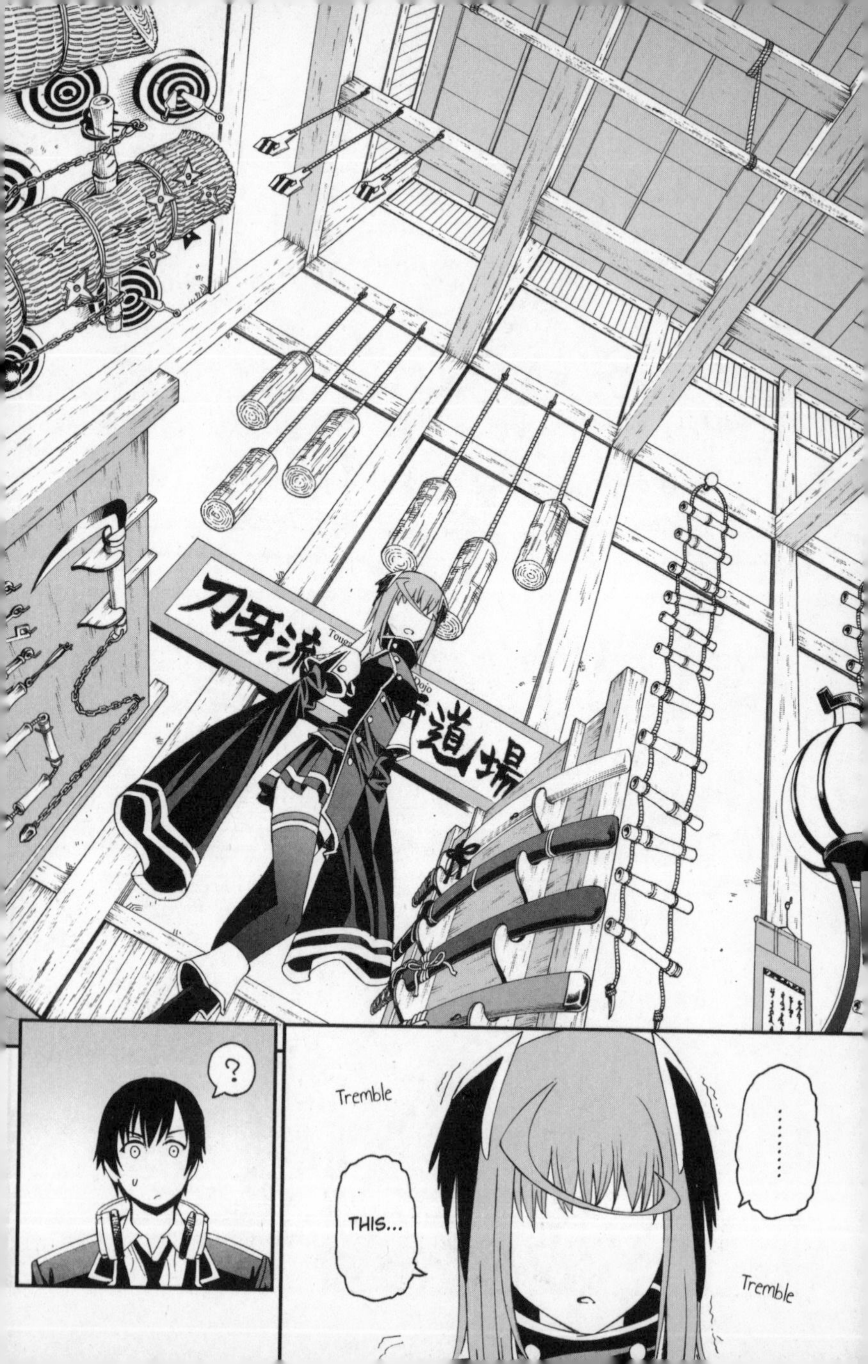
刀牙流
Touga
Dojo
道場
Tremble
......
THIS...
Tremble
?

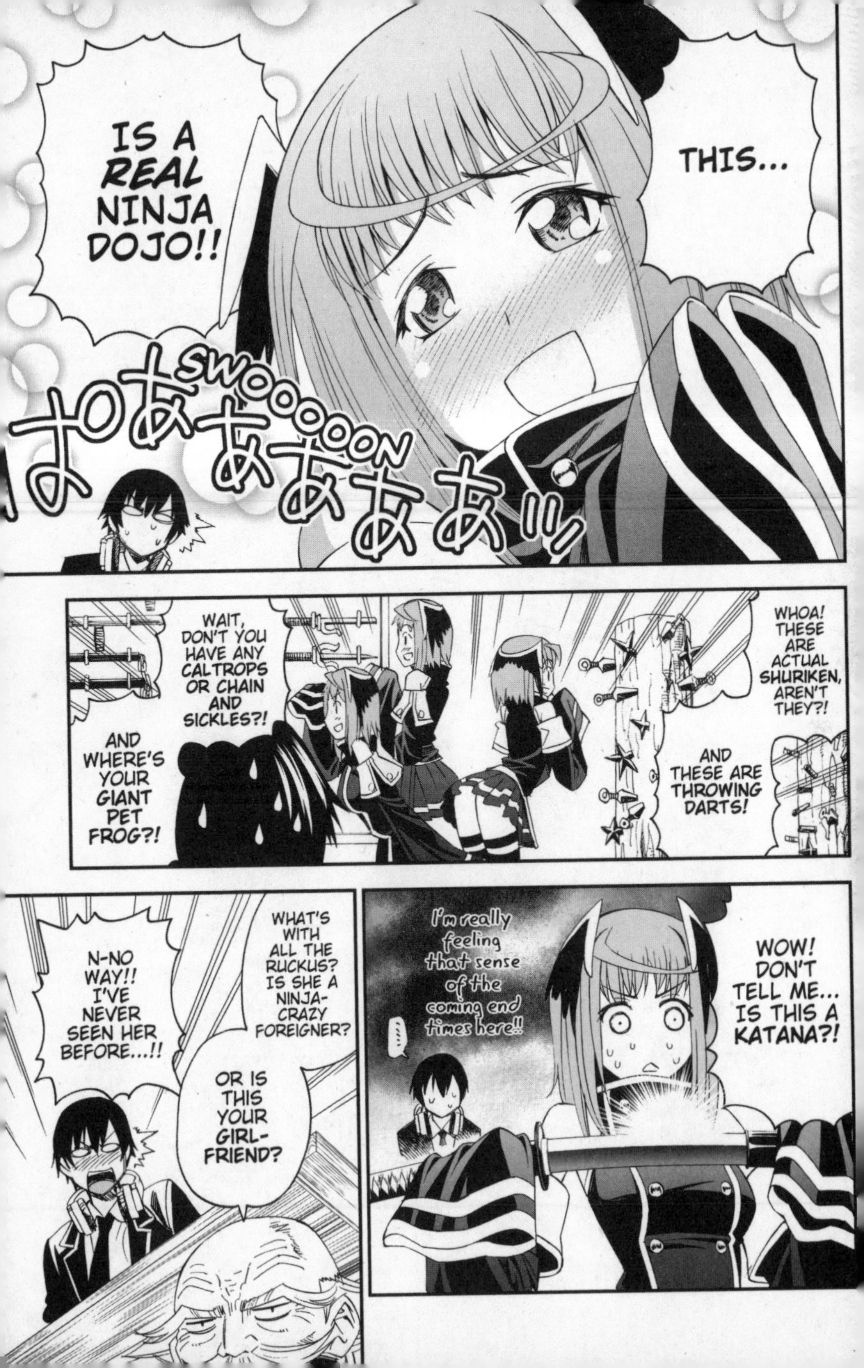
THIS...
IS A *REAL* NINJA DOJO!!
SWOOOOOON
はあああああッ
WHOA! THESE ARE ACTUAL SHURIKEN, AREN'T THEY?!
AND THESE ARE THROWING DARTS!
WAIT, DON'T YOU HAVE ANY CALTROPS OR CHAIN AND SICKLES?!
AND WHERE'S YOUR GIANT PET FROG?!
WOW! DON'T TELL ME... IS THIS A KATANA?!
I'm really feeling that sense of the coming end times here!!
......
WHAT'S WITH ALL THE RUCKUS? IS SHE A NINJA-CRAZY FOREIGNER?
OR IS THIS YOUR GIRL-FRIEND?
N-NO WAY!! I'VE NEVER SEEN HER BEFORE...!!

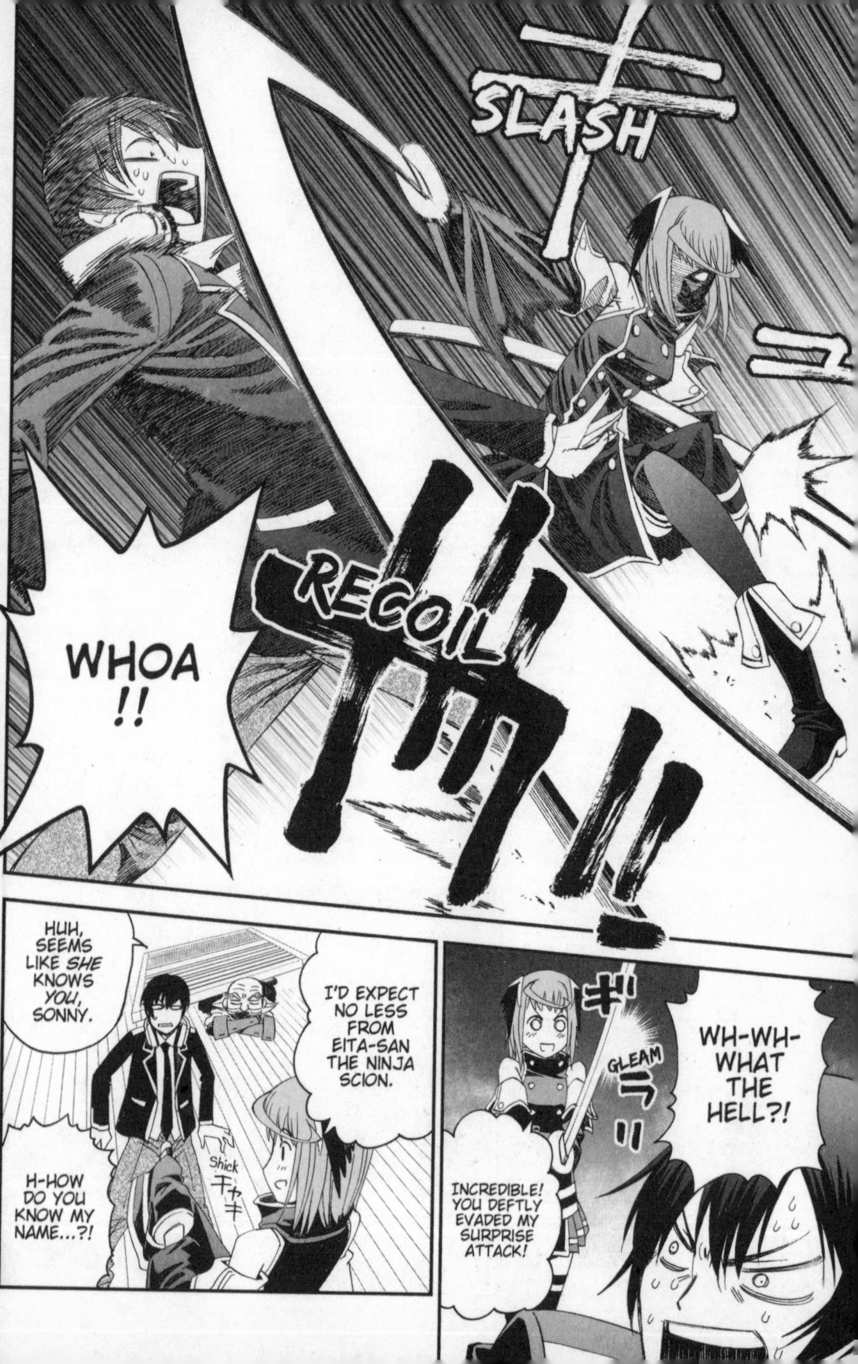
SLASH
RECOIL
WHOA!!
WH-WH-WHAT THE HELL?!
GLEAM
INCREDIBLE! YOU DEFTLY EVADED MY SURPRISE ATTACK!
I'D EXPECT NO LESS FROM EITA-SAN THE NINJA SCION.
HUH, SEEMS LIKE *SHE* KNOWS *YOU*, SONNY.
Shick
H-HOW DO YOU KNOW MY NAME...?!

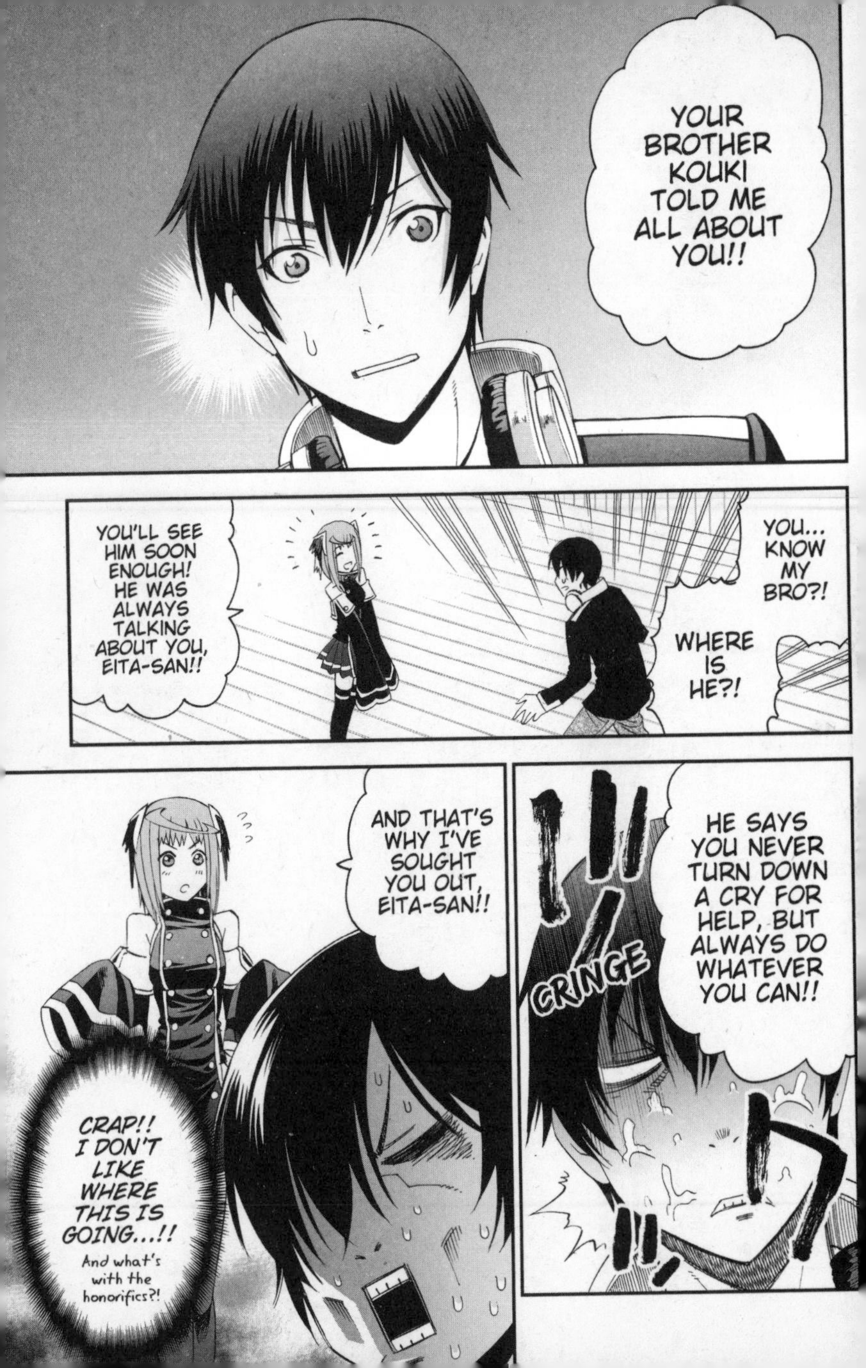
YOUR BROTHER KOUKI TOLD ME ALL ABOUT YOU!!
YOU... KNOW MY BRO?!
WHERE IS HE?!
YOU'LL SEE HIM SOON ENOUGH! HE WAS ALWAYS TALKING ABOUT YOU, EITA-SAN!!
HE SAYS YOU NEVER TURN DOWN A CRY FOR HELP, BUT ALWAYS DO WHATEVER YOU CAN!!
CRINGE
AND THAT'S WHY I'VE SOUGHT YOU OUT, EITA-SAN!!
CRAP!! I DON'T LIKE WHERE THIS IS GOING...!!
And what's with the honorifics?!

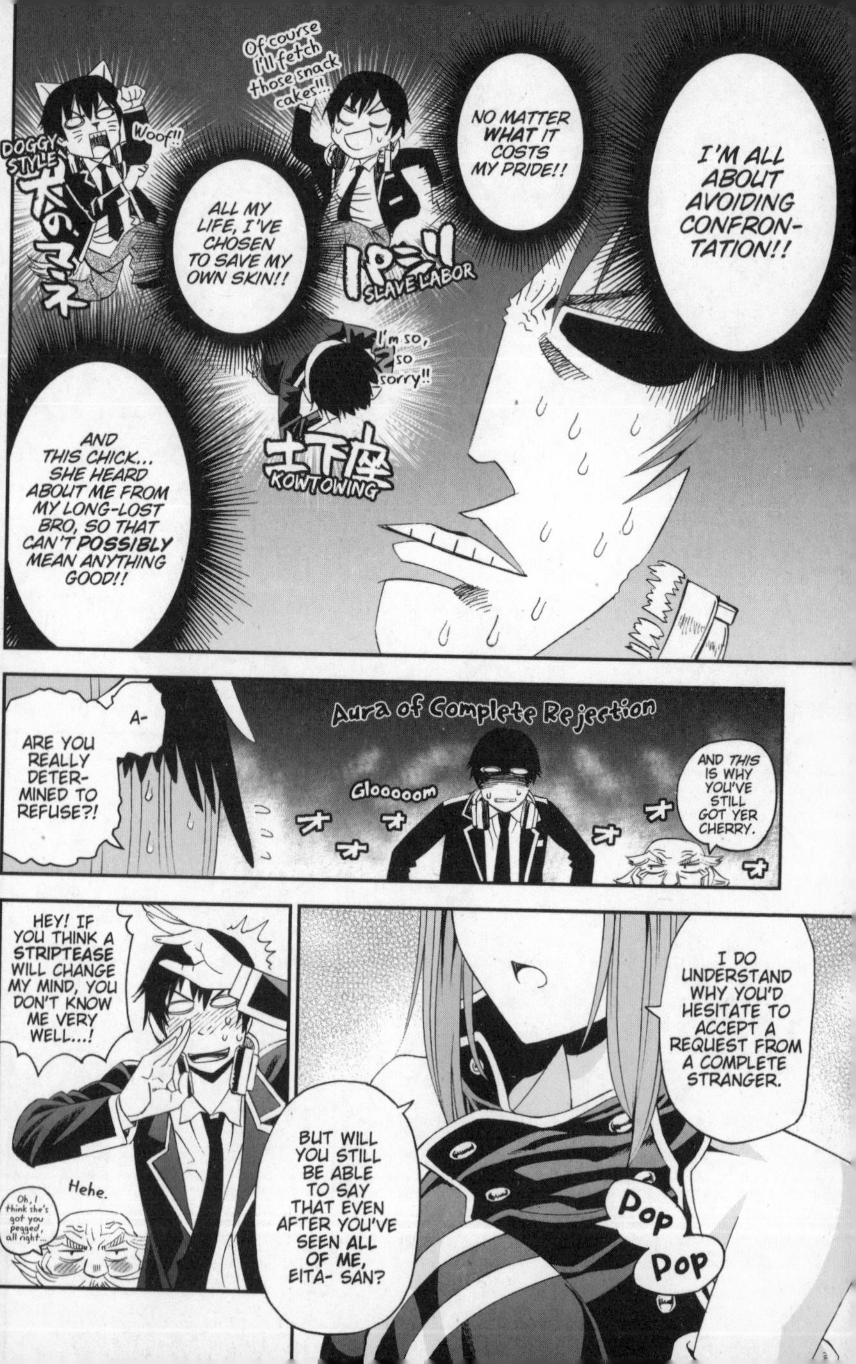
I'M ALL ABOUT AVOIDING CONFRON-TATION!!
NO MATTER WHAT IT COSTS MY PRIDE!!
Of course I'll fetch those snack cakes!!!
SLAVE LABOR
ALL MY LIFE, I'VE CHOSEN TO SAVE MY OWN SKIN!!
Woof!!
DOGGY STYLE 犬のマネ
I'm so, so sorry!!
土下座 KOWTOWING
AND THIS CHICK... SHE HEARD ABOUT ME FROM MY LONG-LOST BRO, SO THAT CAN'T POSSIBLY MEAN ANYTHING GOOD!!
AND THIS IS WHY YOU'VE STILL GOT YER CHERRY.
Aura of Complete Rejection
Glooooom
A-
ARE YOU REALLY DETER-MINED TO REFUSE?!
I DO UNDERSTAND WHY YOU'D HESITATE TO ACCEPT A REQUEST FROM A COMPLETE STRANGER.
BUT WILL YOU STILL BE ABLE TO SAY THAT EVEN AFTER YOU'VE SEEN ALL OF ME, EITA- SAN?
Pop
Pop
HEY! IF YOU THINK A STRIPTEASE WILL CHANGE MY MIND, YOU DON'T KNOW ME VERY WELL...!
Hehe.
Oh, I think she's got you pegged, all right...

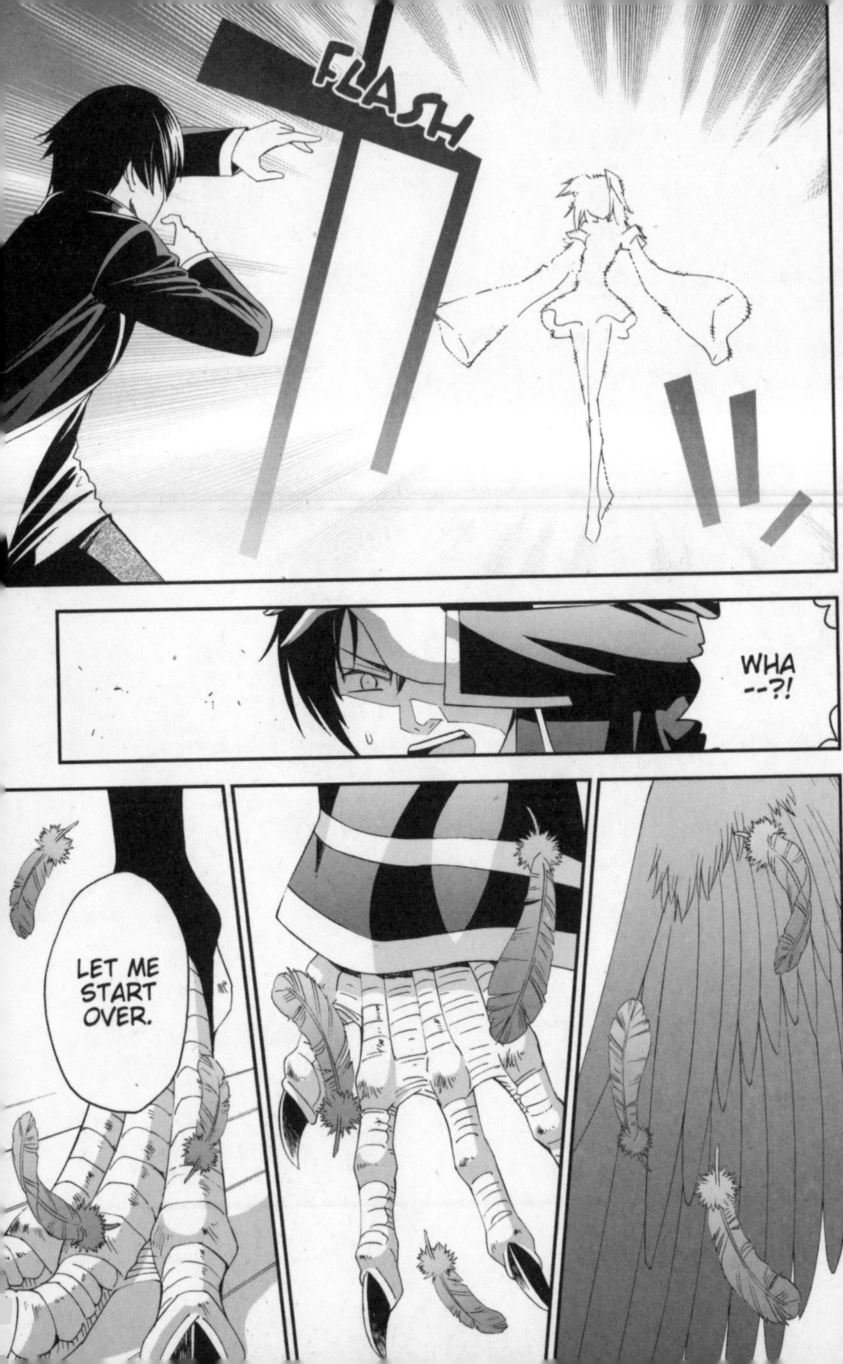
FLASH
WHA--?!
LET ME START OVER.

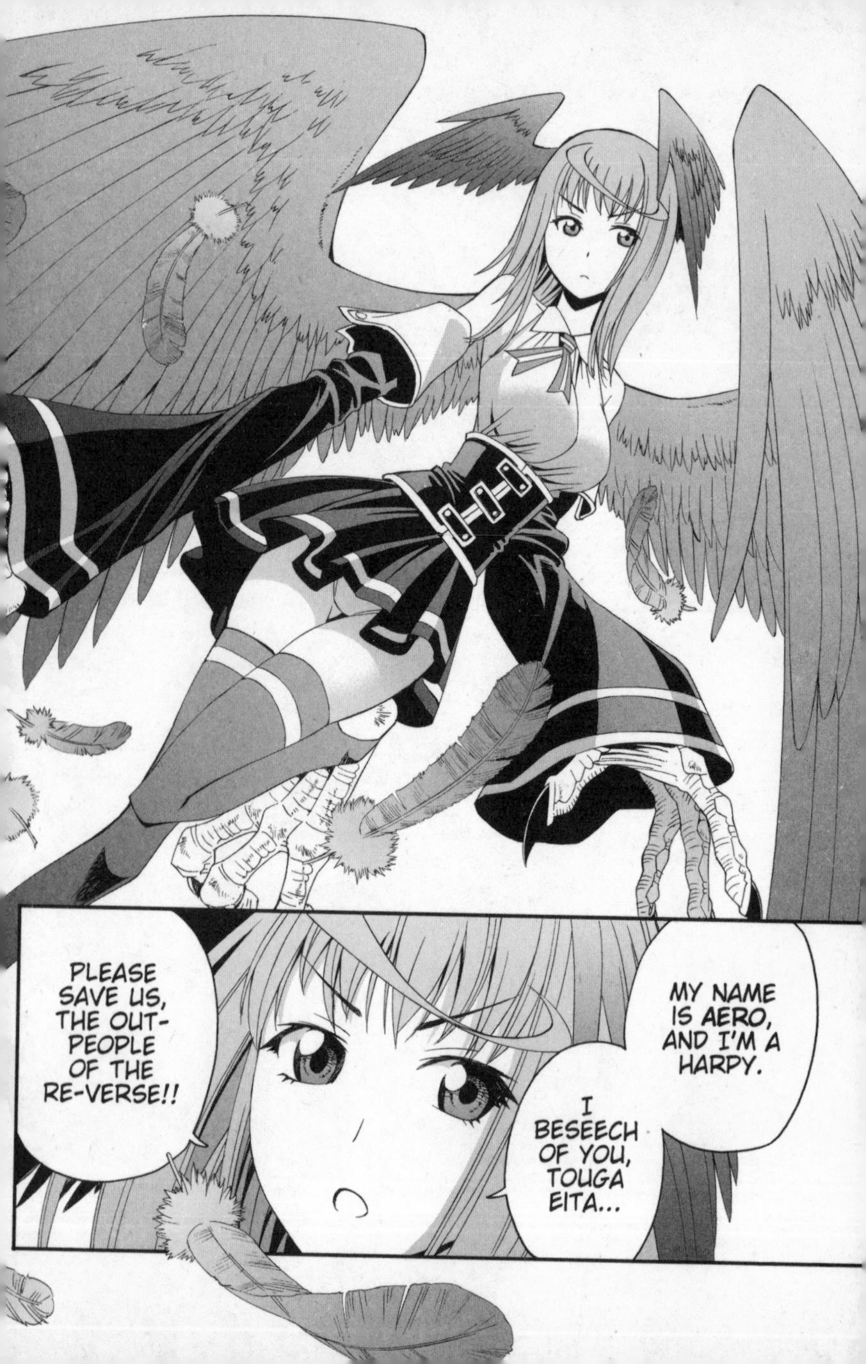
MY NAME IS AERO, AND I'M A HARPY.
I BESEECH OF YOU, TOUGA EITA...
PLEASE SAVE US, THE OUT-PEOPLE OF THE RE-VERSE!!

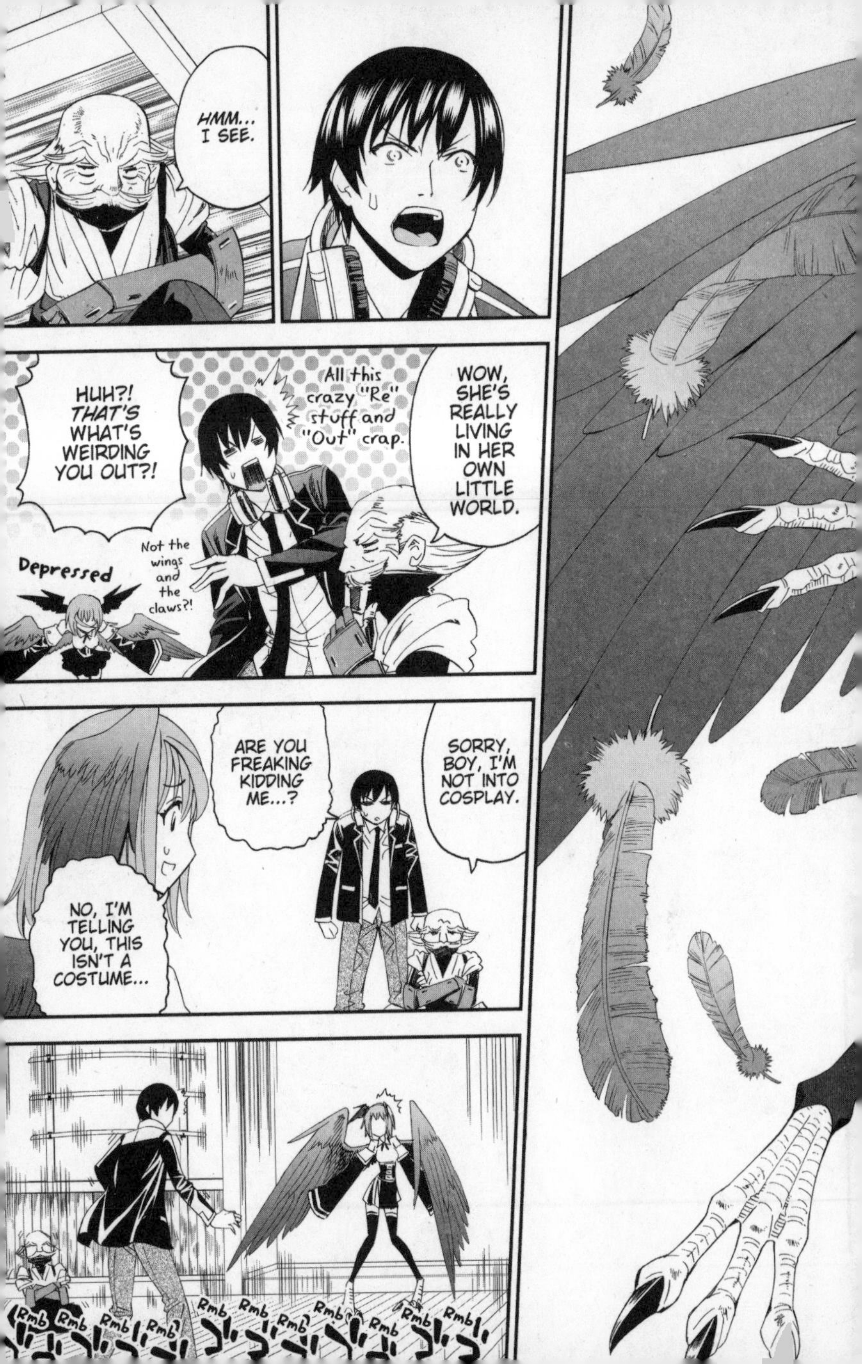
HMM... I SEE.
WOW, SHE'S REALLY LIVING IN HER OWN LITTLE WORLD.
All this crazy "Re" stuff and "Out" crap.
HUH?! THAT'S WHAT'S WEIRDING YOU OUT?!
Not the wings and the claws?!
Depressed
SORRY, BOY, I'M NOT INTO COSPLAY.
ARE YOU FREAKING KIDDING ME...?
NO, I'M TELLING YOU, THIS ISN'T A COSTUME...
Rmb Rmb Rmb Rmb Rmb Rmb Rmb Rmb Rmb Rmb Rmb Rmb

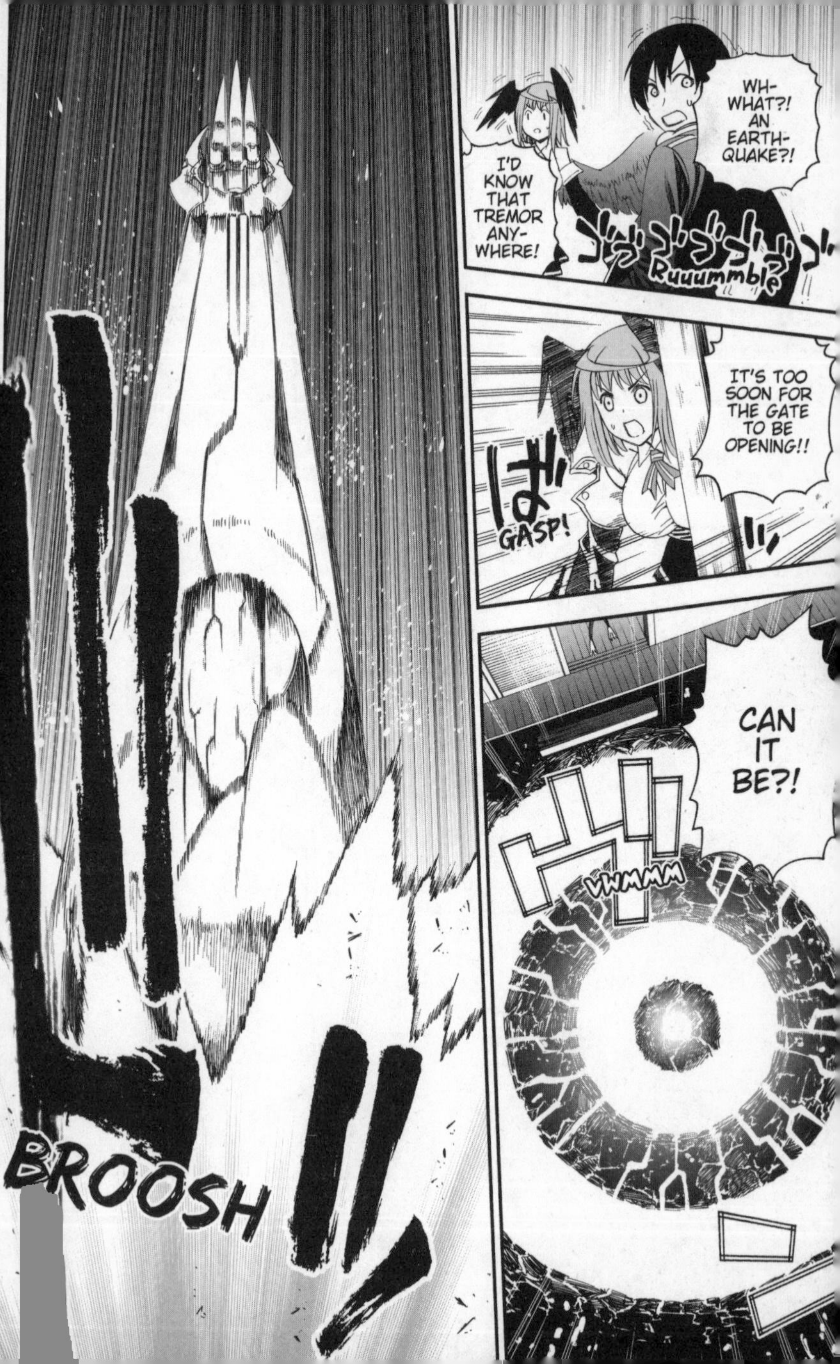
WH- WHAT?! AN EARTH-QUAKE?!
I'D KNOW THAT TREMOR ANY-WHERE!
Ruuummble
IT'S TOO SOON FOR THE GATE TO BE OPENING!!
GASP!
CAN IT BE?!
VWMMM
BROOSH

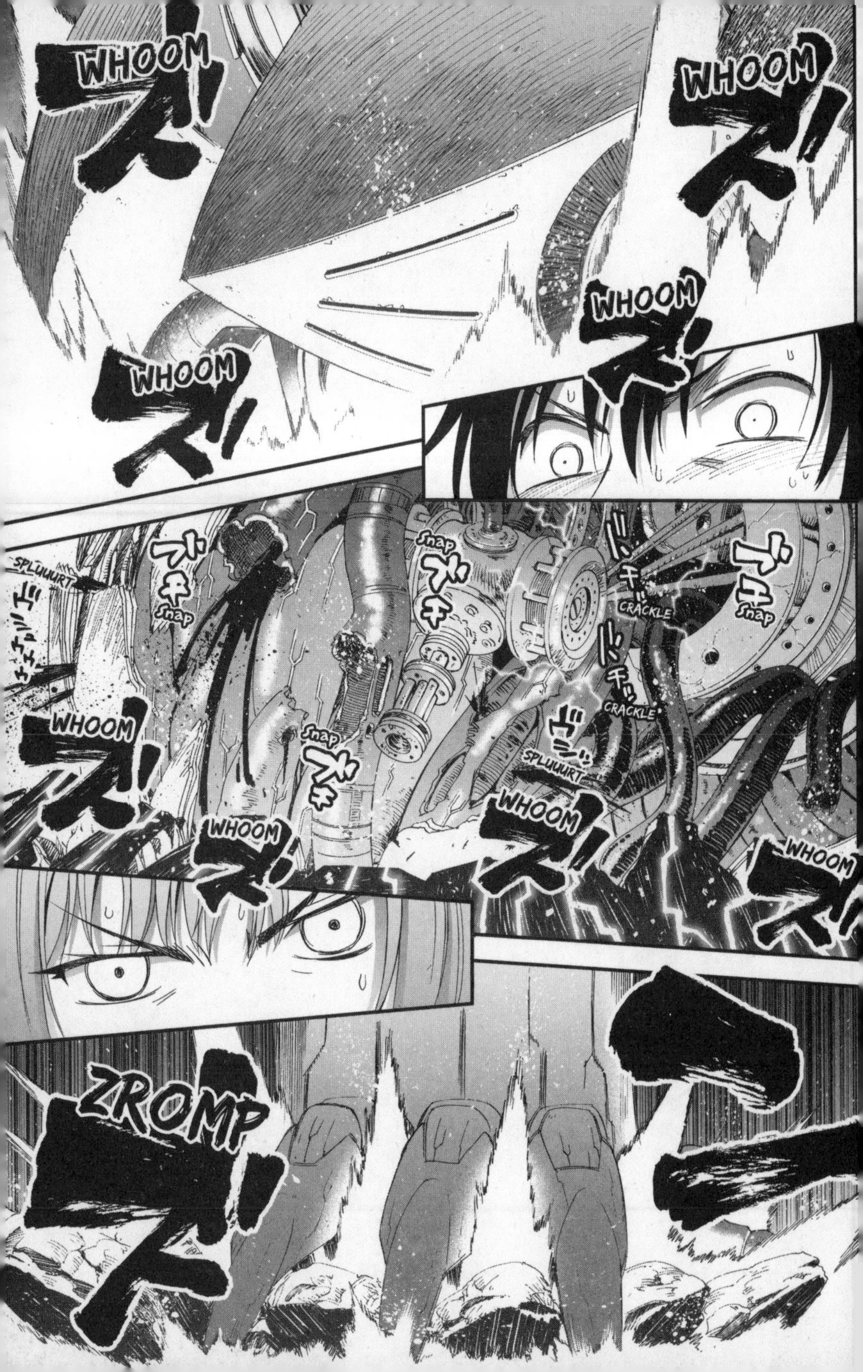
WHOOM
WHOOM
WHOOM
WHOOM
Snap
CRACKLE
CRACKLE
SPLUUURT
Snap
Snap
Snap
SPLUUURT
WHOOM
WHOOM
WHOOM
WHOOM
ZROMP

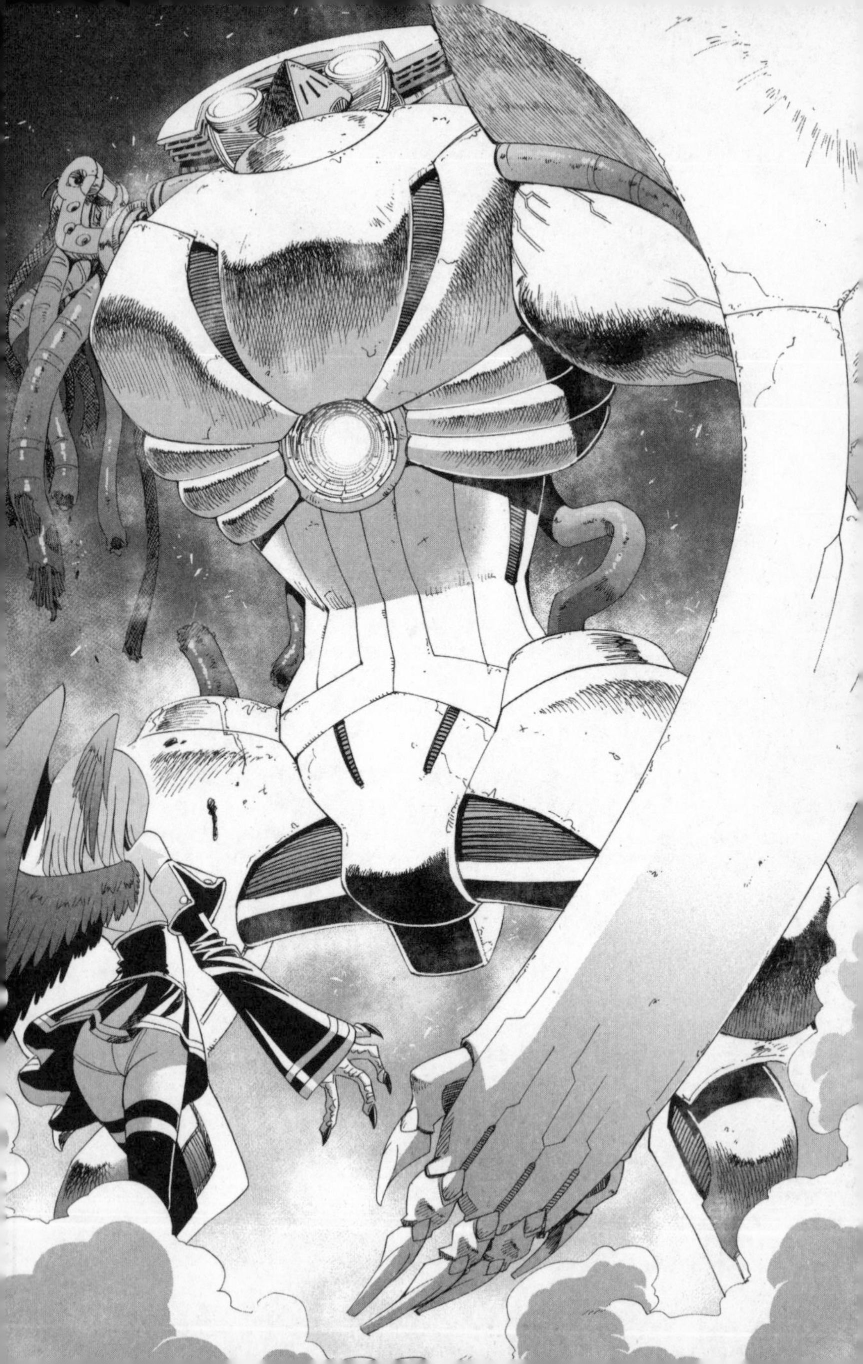

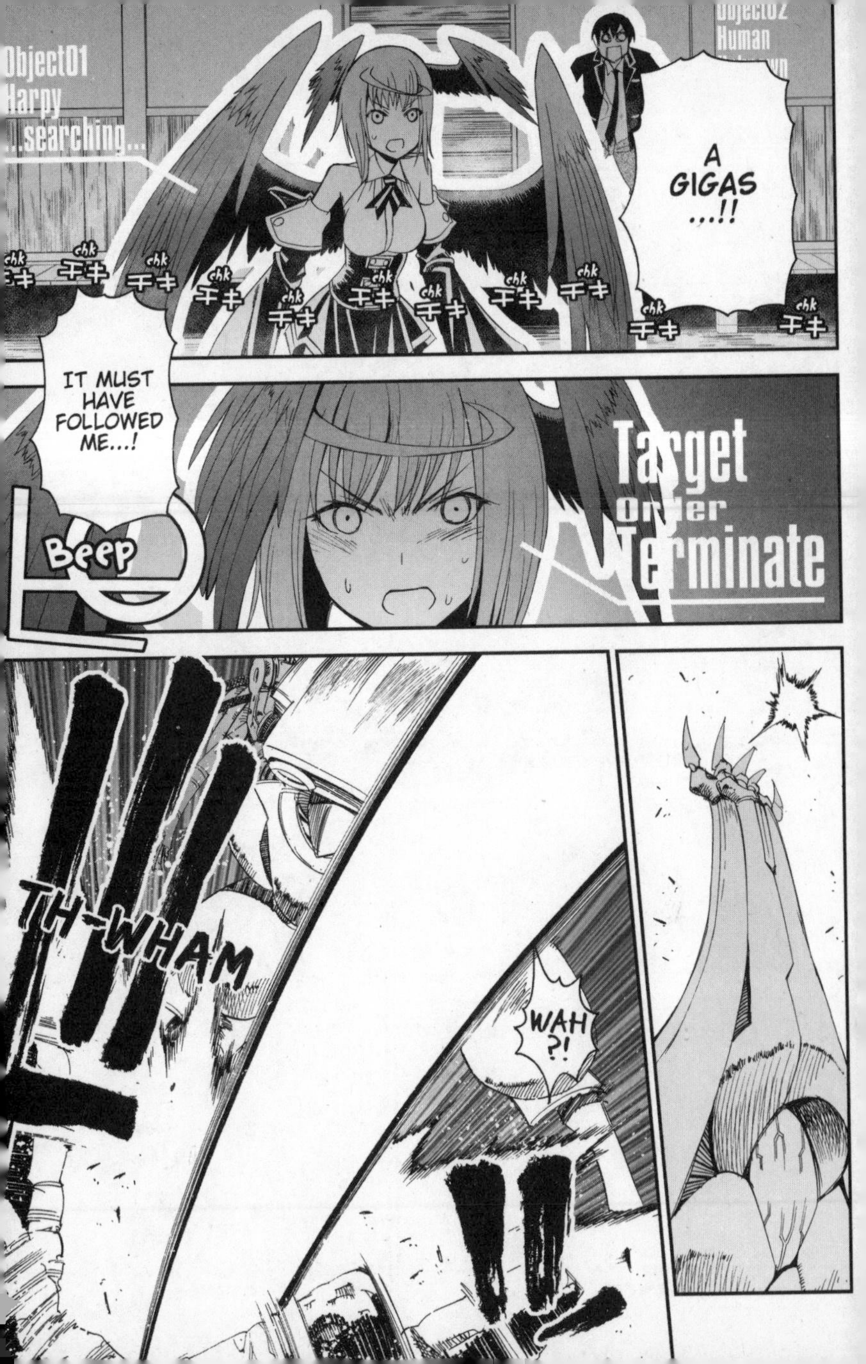
Object02
Human
A GIGAS ...!!
Object01
Harpy
...searching...
chk
chk
chk
chk
chk
chk
chk
chk
chk
chk
chk
IT MUST HAVE FOLLOWED ME...!
Target
Order
Terminate
Beep
WAH ?!
TH-WHAM

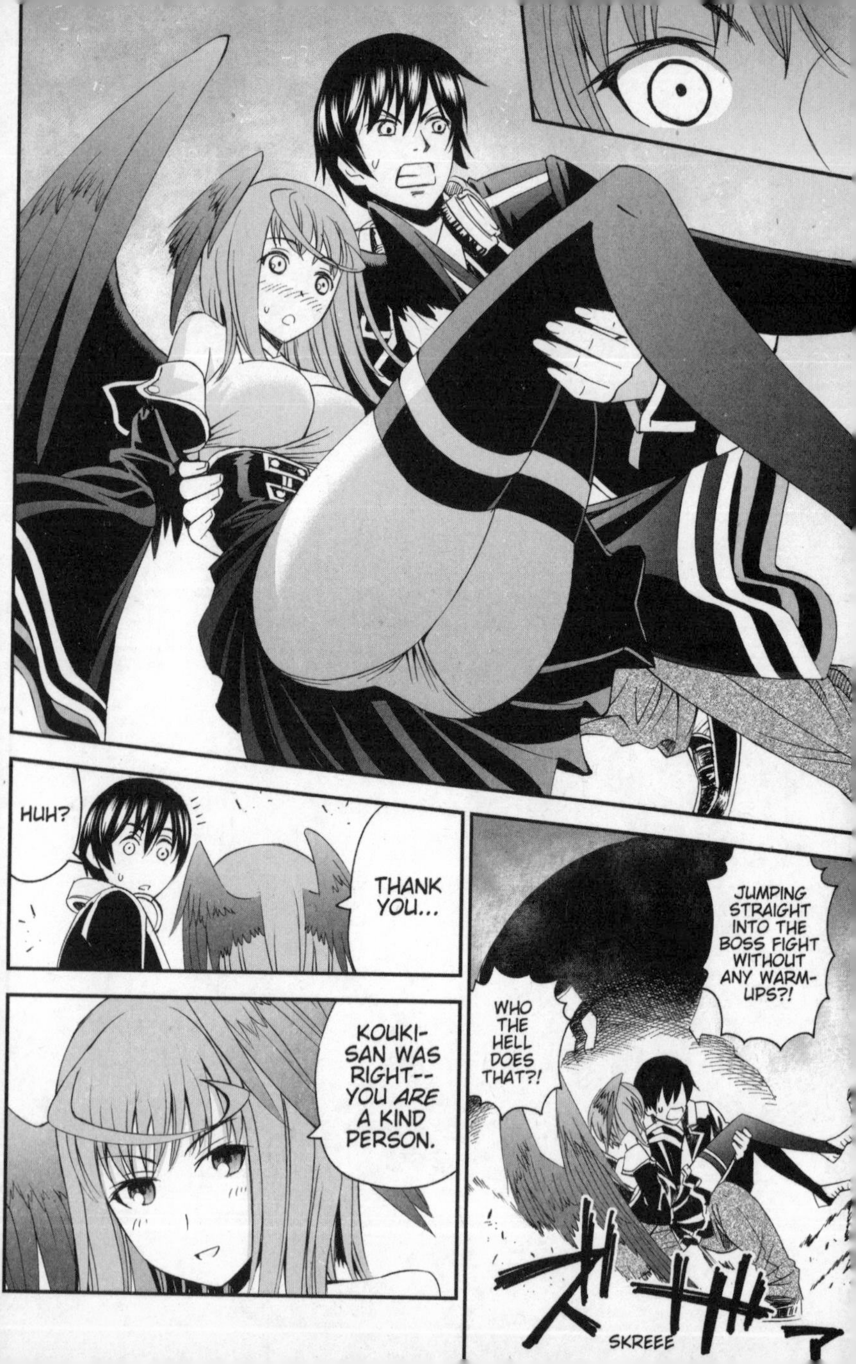
JUMPING STRAIGHT INTO THE BOSS FIGHT WITHOUT ANY WARM-UPS?!
WHO THE HELL DOES THAT?!
SKREEE
THANK YOU...
HUH?
KOUKI-SAN WAS RIGHT-- YOU *ARE* A KIND PERSON.

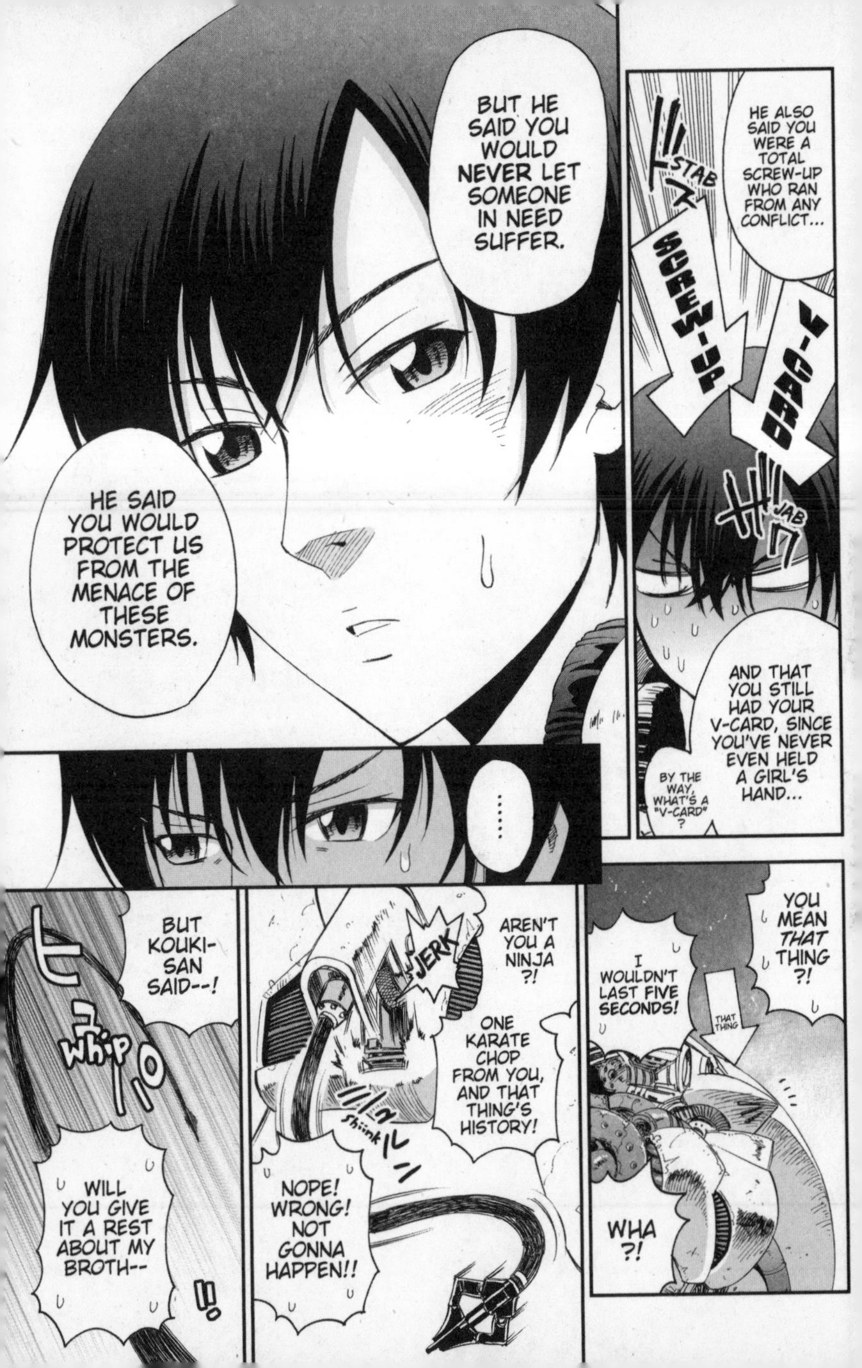
HE ALSO SAID YOU WERE A TOTAL SCREW-UP WHO RAN FROM ANY CONFLICT...
STAB
SCREW-UP
V-CARD
JAB
AND THAT YOU STILL HAD YOUR V-CARD, SINCE YOU'VE NEVER EVEN HELD A GIRL'S HAND...
BY THE WAY, WHAT'S A "V-CARD"?
BUT HE SAID YOU WOULD NEVER LET SOMEONE IN NEED SUFFER.
HE SAID YOU WOULD PROTECT US FROM THE MENACE OF THESE MONSTERS.
......
YOU MEAN *THAT* THING?!
I WOULDN'T LAST FIVE SECONDS!
THAT THING
WHA?!
AREN'T YOU A NINJA?!
JERK
ONE KARATE CHOP FROM YOU, AND THAT THING'S HISTORY!
shiink
NOPE! WRONG! NOT GONNA HAPPEN!!
BUT KOUKI-SAN SAID--!
whip
WILL YOU GIVE IT A REST ABOUT MY BROTH--
!!

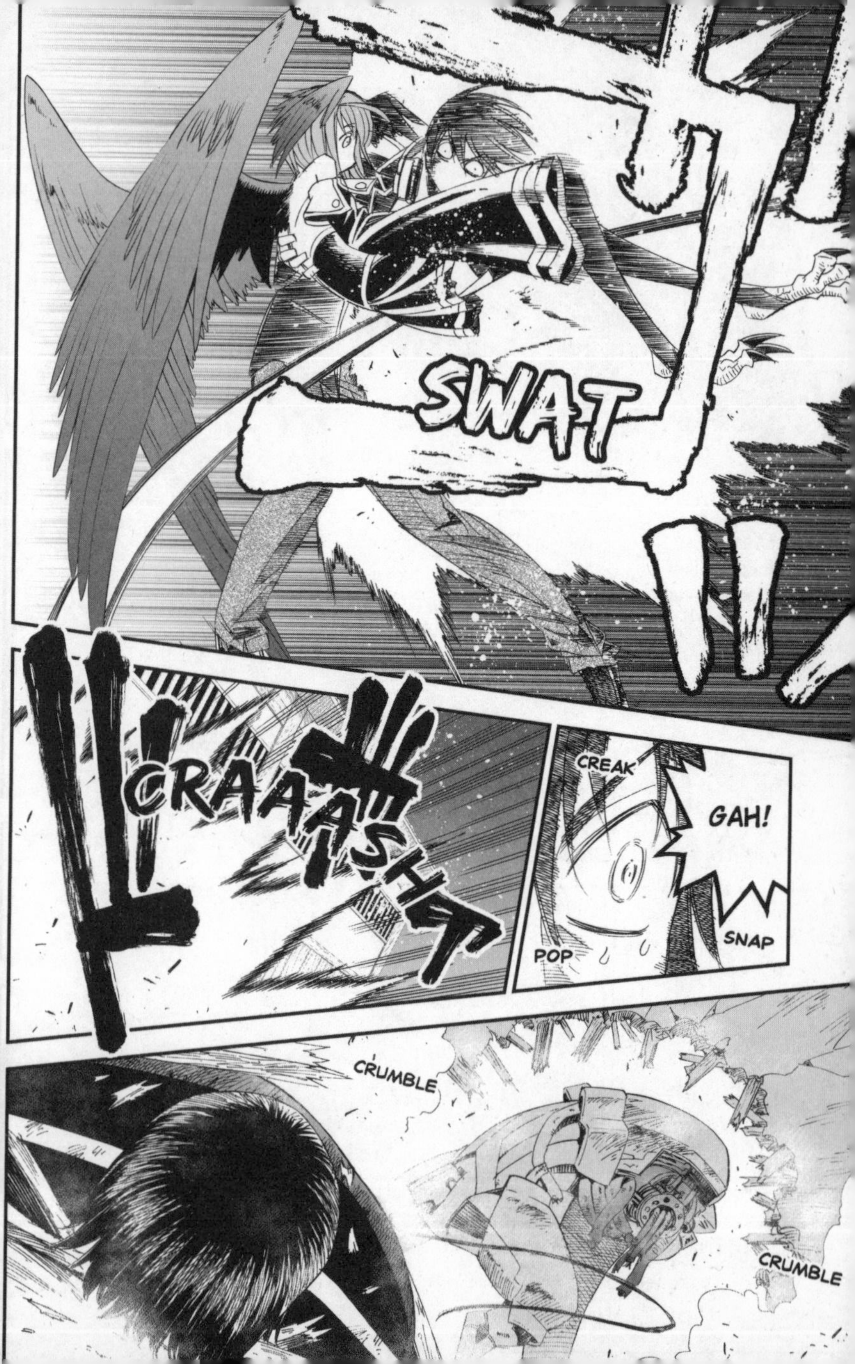
SWAT
CREAK
GAH!
SNAP
POP
CRAAASH
CRUMBLE
CRUMBLE

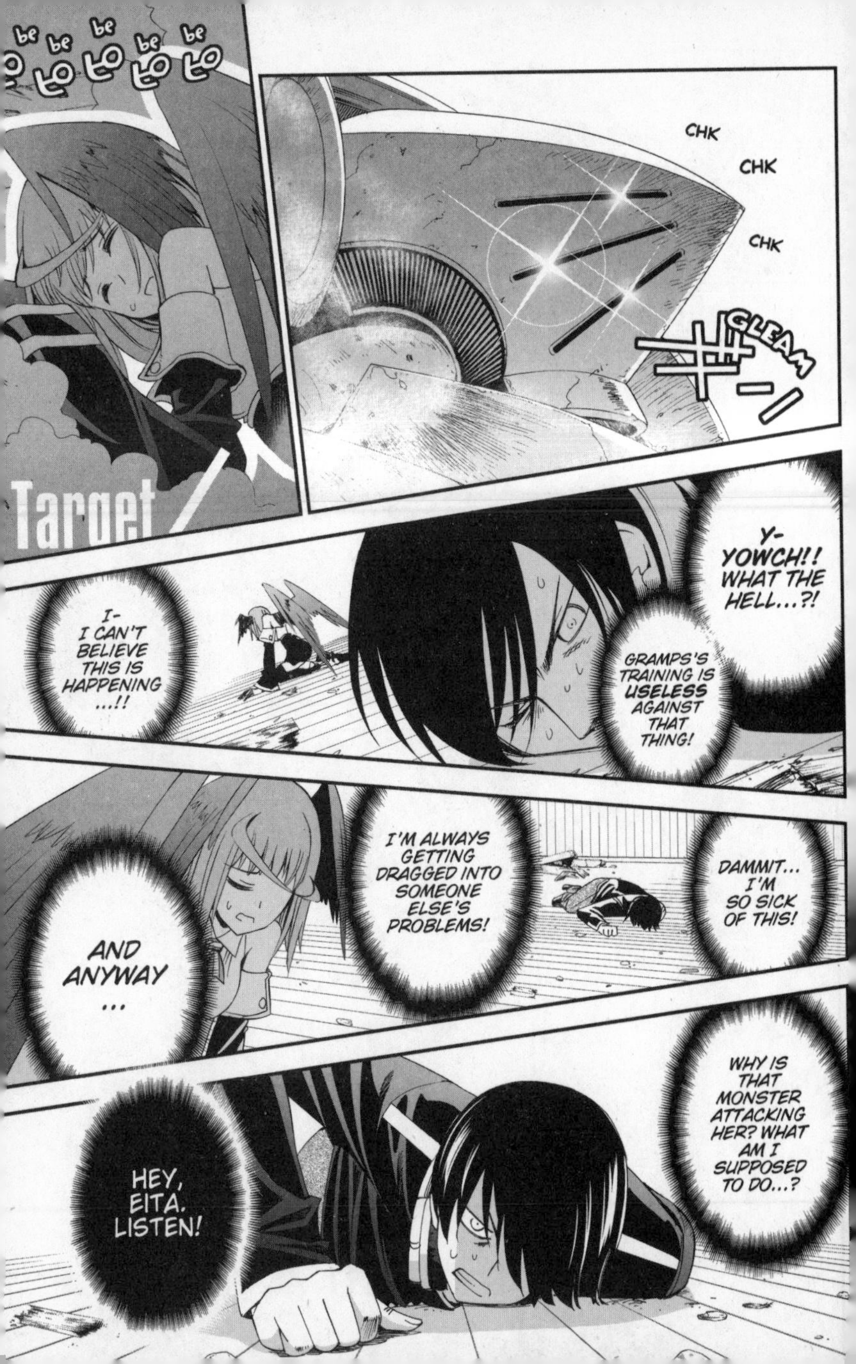
CHK
CHK
CHK
GLEAM
be be be be be
Target
Y-YOWCH!! WHAT THE HELL...?!
GRAMPS'S TRAINING IS USELESS AGAINST THAT THING!
I- I CAN'T BELIEVE THIS IS HAPPENING...!!
DAMMIT... I'M SO SICK OF THIS!
I'M ALWAYS GETTING DRAGGED INTO SOMEONE ELSE'S PROBLEMS!
AND ANYWAY...
WHY IS THAT MONSTER ATTACKING HER? WHAT AM I SUPPOSED TO DO...?
HEY, EITA. LISTEN!

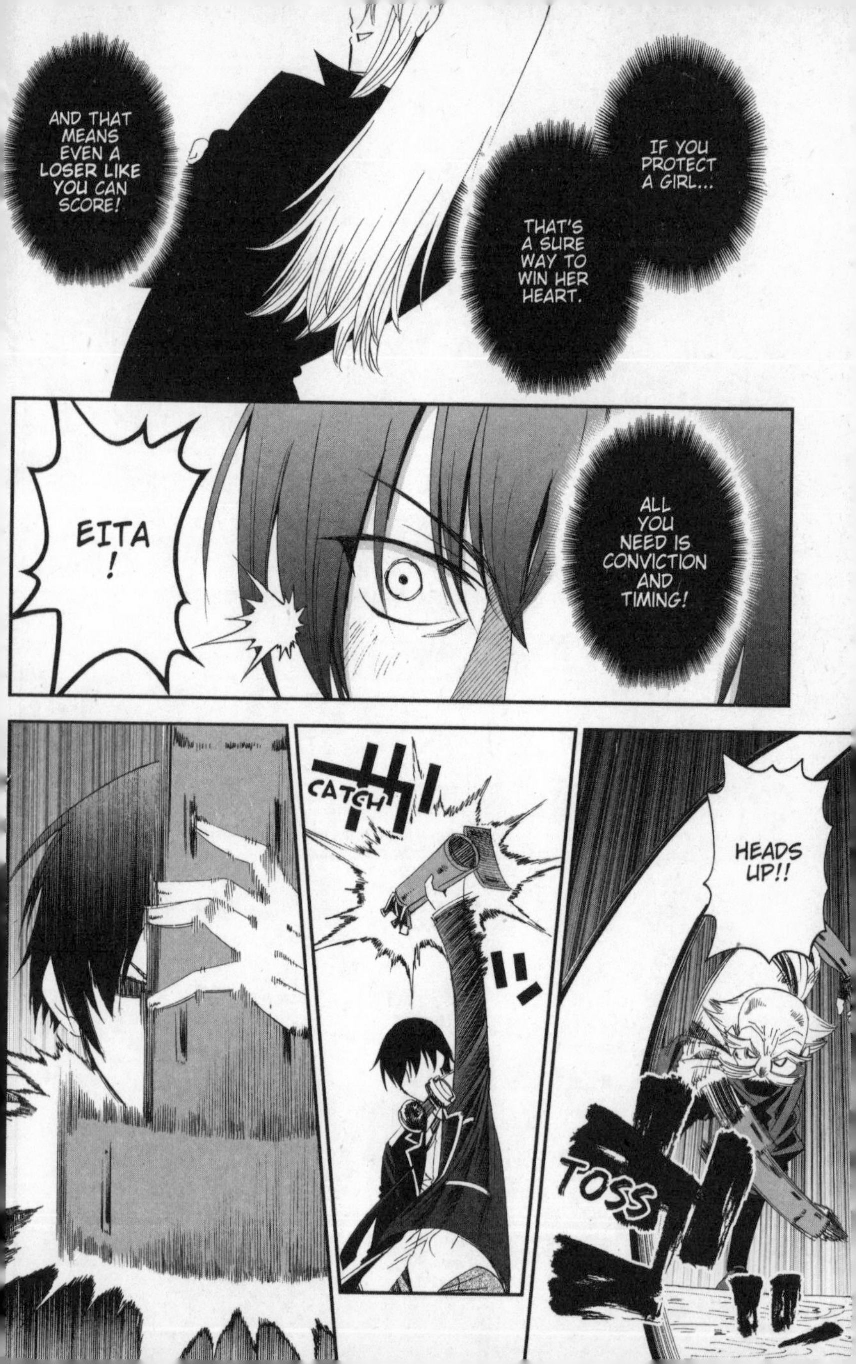
IF YOU PROTECT A GIRL...
THAT'S A SURE WAY TO WIN HER HEART.
AND THAT MEANS EVEN A LOSER LIKE YOU CAN SCORE!
ALL YOU NEED IS CONVICTION AND TIMING!
EITA!
HEADS UP!!
TOSS
CATCH

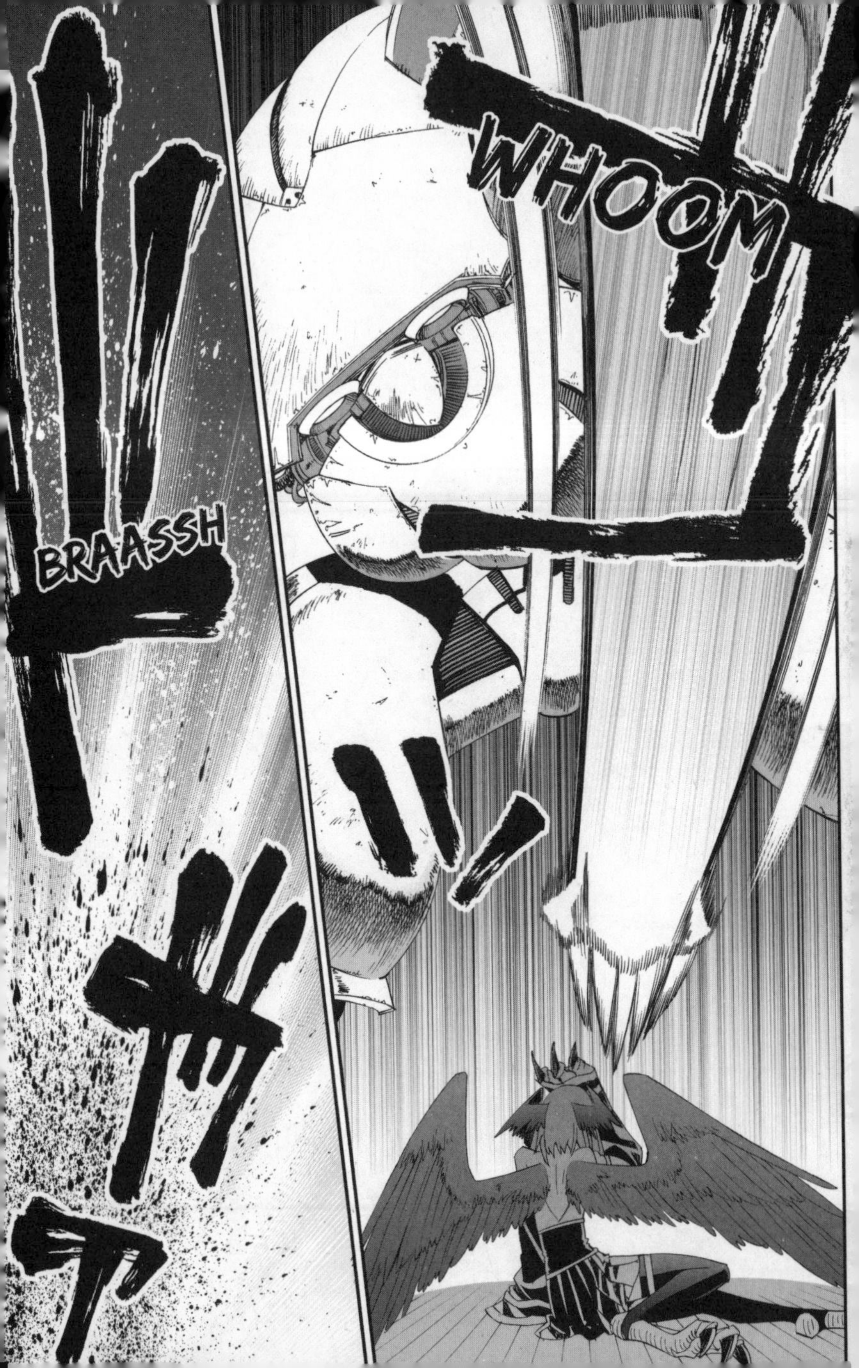
WHOOM
BRAASSH

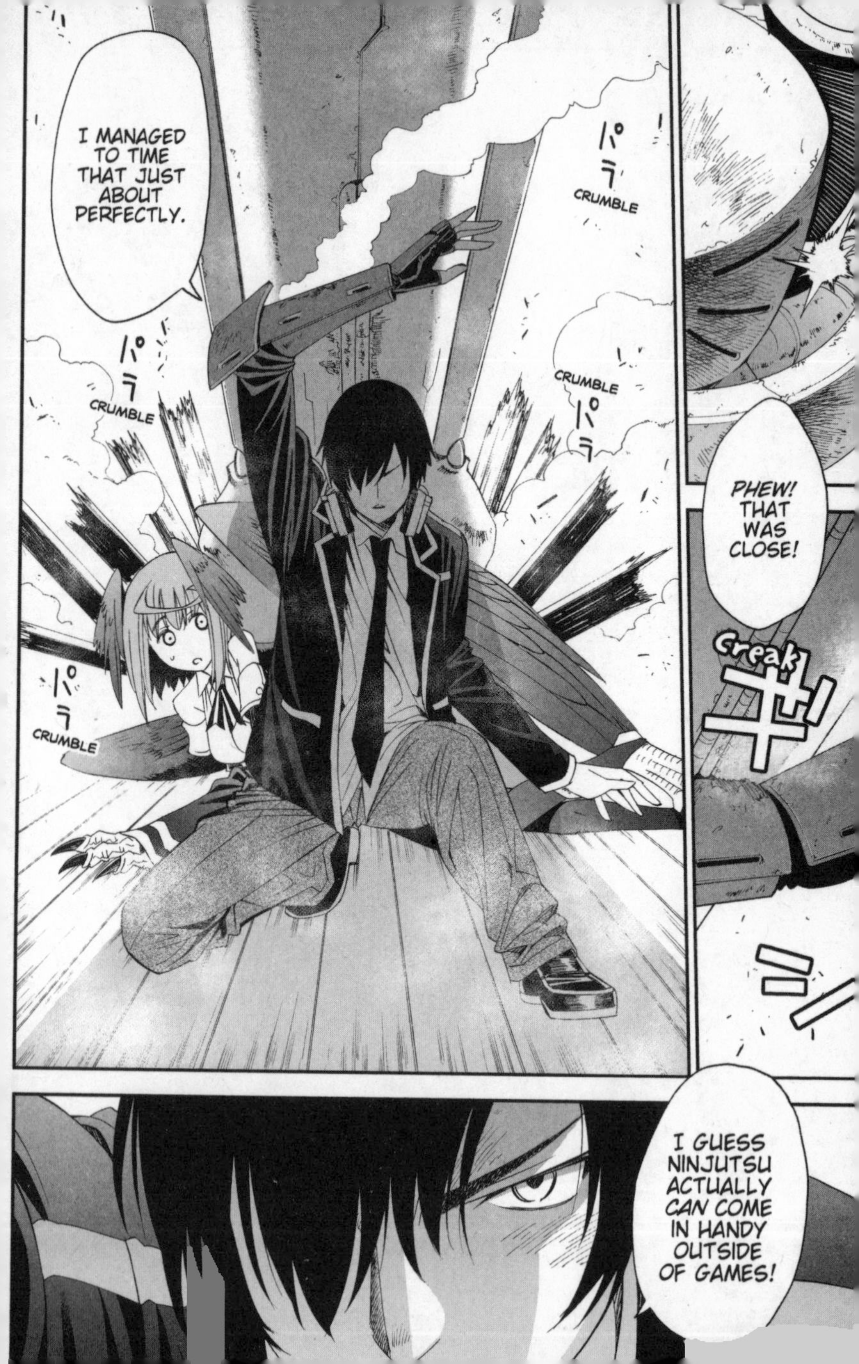
PHEW! THAT WAS CLOSE!
Creak
ギ
I MANAGED TO TIME THAT JUST ABOUT PERFECTLY.
パラ
CRUMBLE
CRUMBLE
パラ
パラ
CRUMBLE
パラ
CRUMBLE
I GUESS NINJUTSU ACTUALLY CAN COME IN HANDY OUTSIDE OF GAMES!

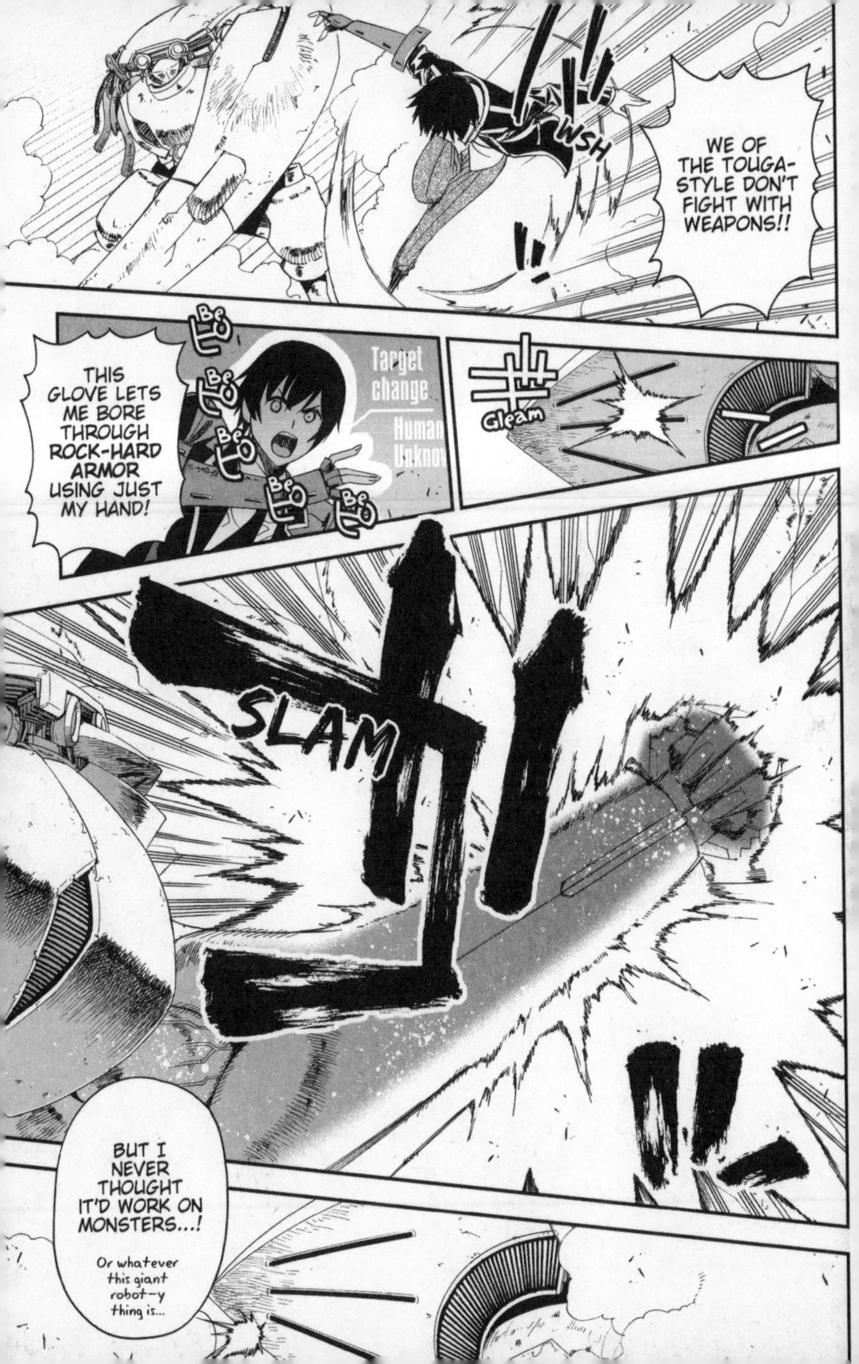
WSH
WE OF THE TOUGA-STYLE DON'T FIGHT WITH WEAPONS!!
Gleam
Target change
Human
THIS GLOVE LETS ME BORE THROUGH ROCK-HARD ARMOR USING JUST MY HAND!
SLAM
BUT I NEVER THOUGHT IT'D WORK ON MONSTERS...!
Or whatever this giant robot—y thing is...

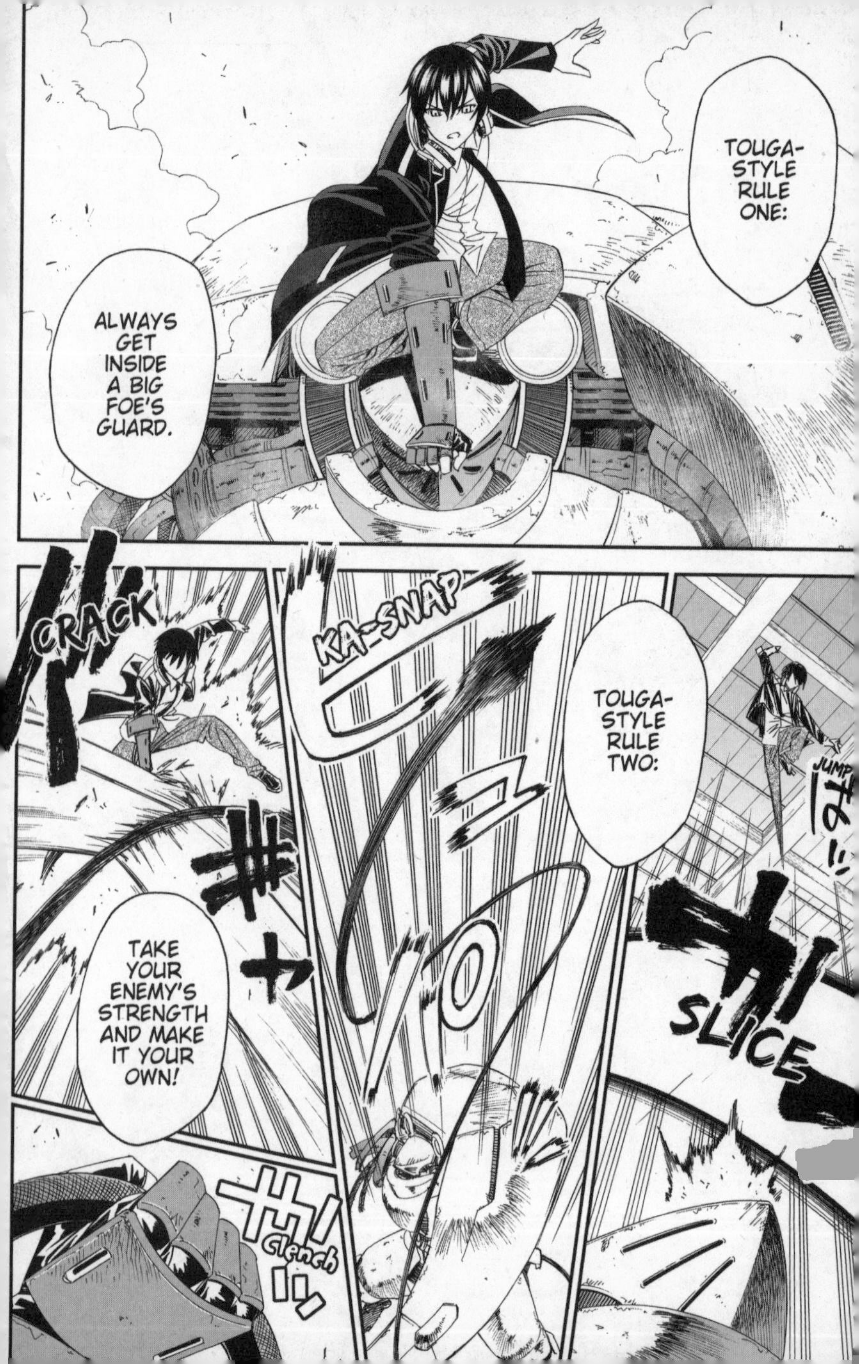
TOUGA-STYLE RULE ONE:
ALWAYS GET INSIDE A BIG FOE'S GUARD.
TOUGA-STYLE RULE TWO:
JUMP
SLICE
KA-SNAP
CRACK
TAKE YOUR ENEMY'S STRENGTH AND MAKE IT YOUR OWN!
Clench

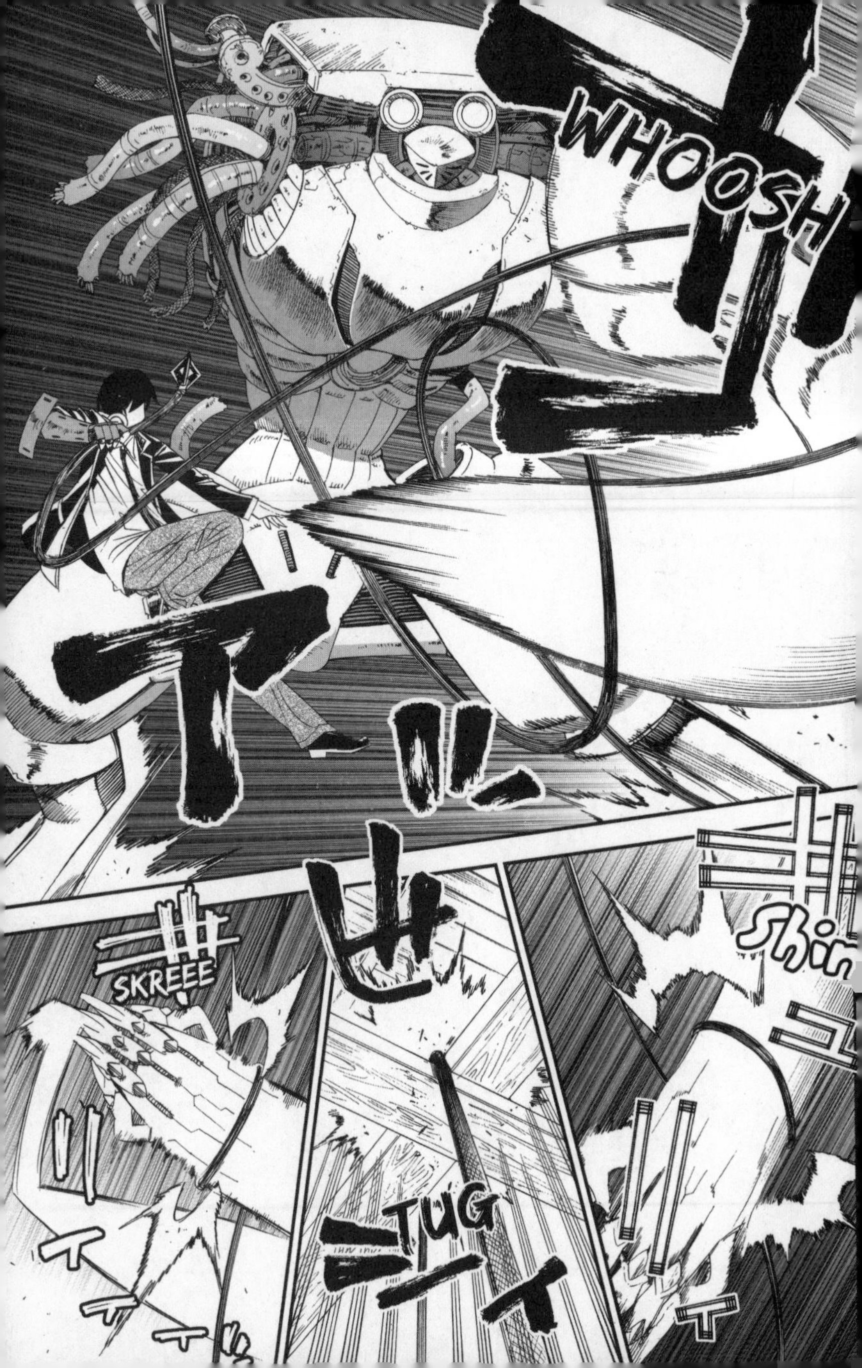
WHOOSH
Shin
TUG
SKREEE

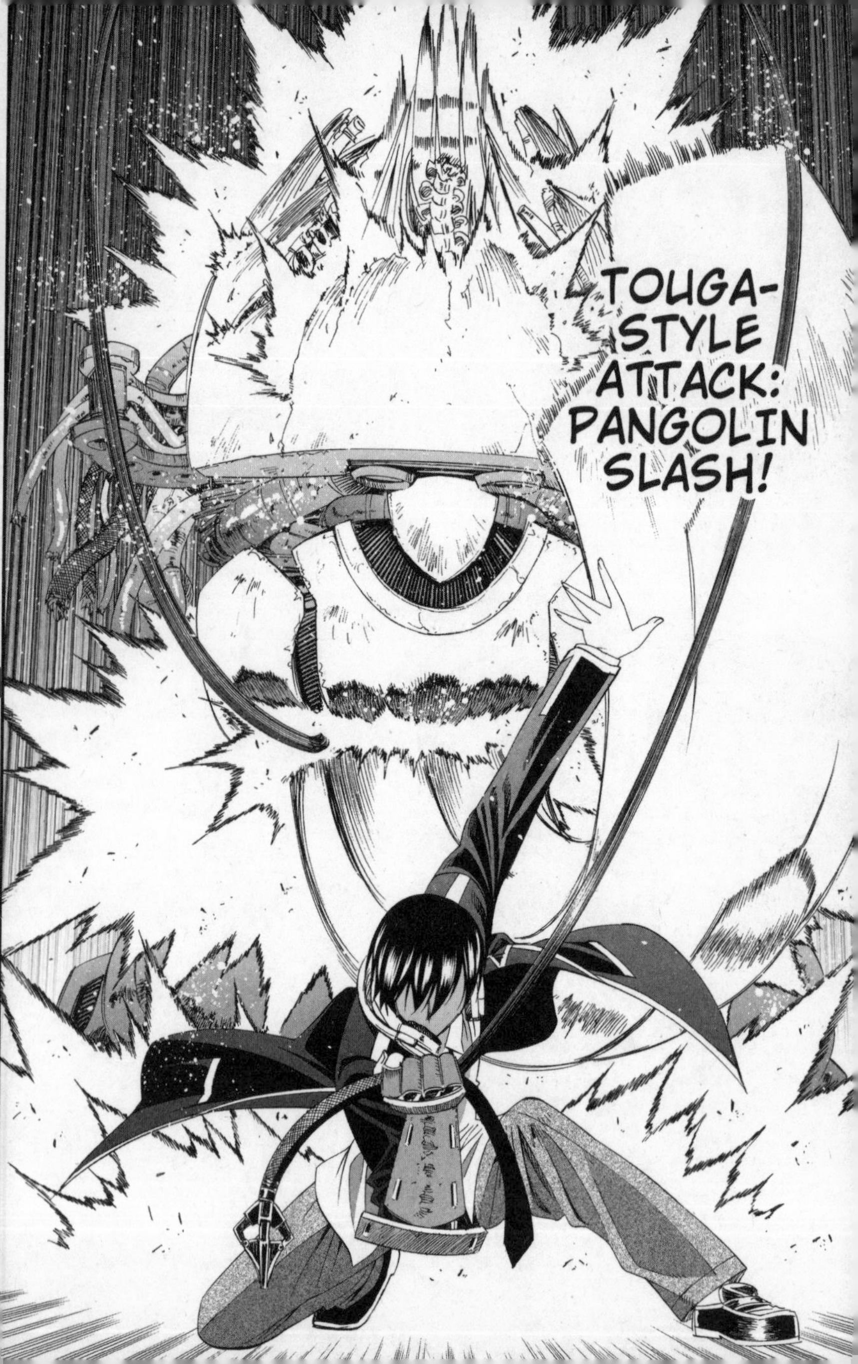
TOUGA-STYLE ATTACK: PANGOLIN SLASH!

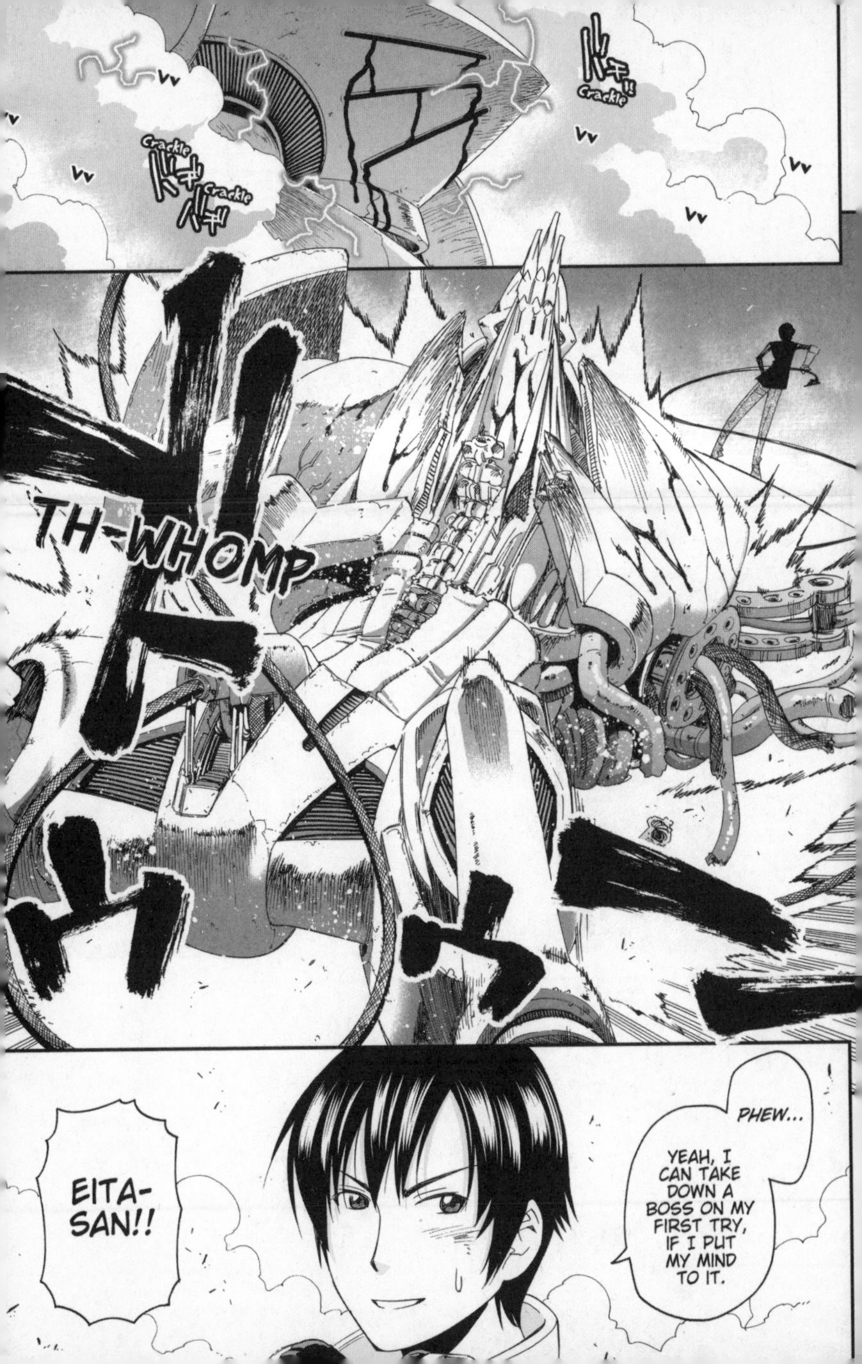
Crackle
Crackle
Crackle
TH-WHOMP
PHEW...
YEAH, I CAN TAKE DOWN A BOSS ON MY FIRST TRY, IF I PUT MY MIND TO IT.
EITA-SAN!!

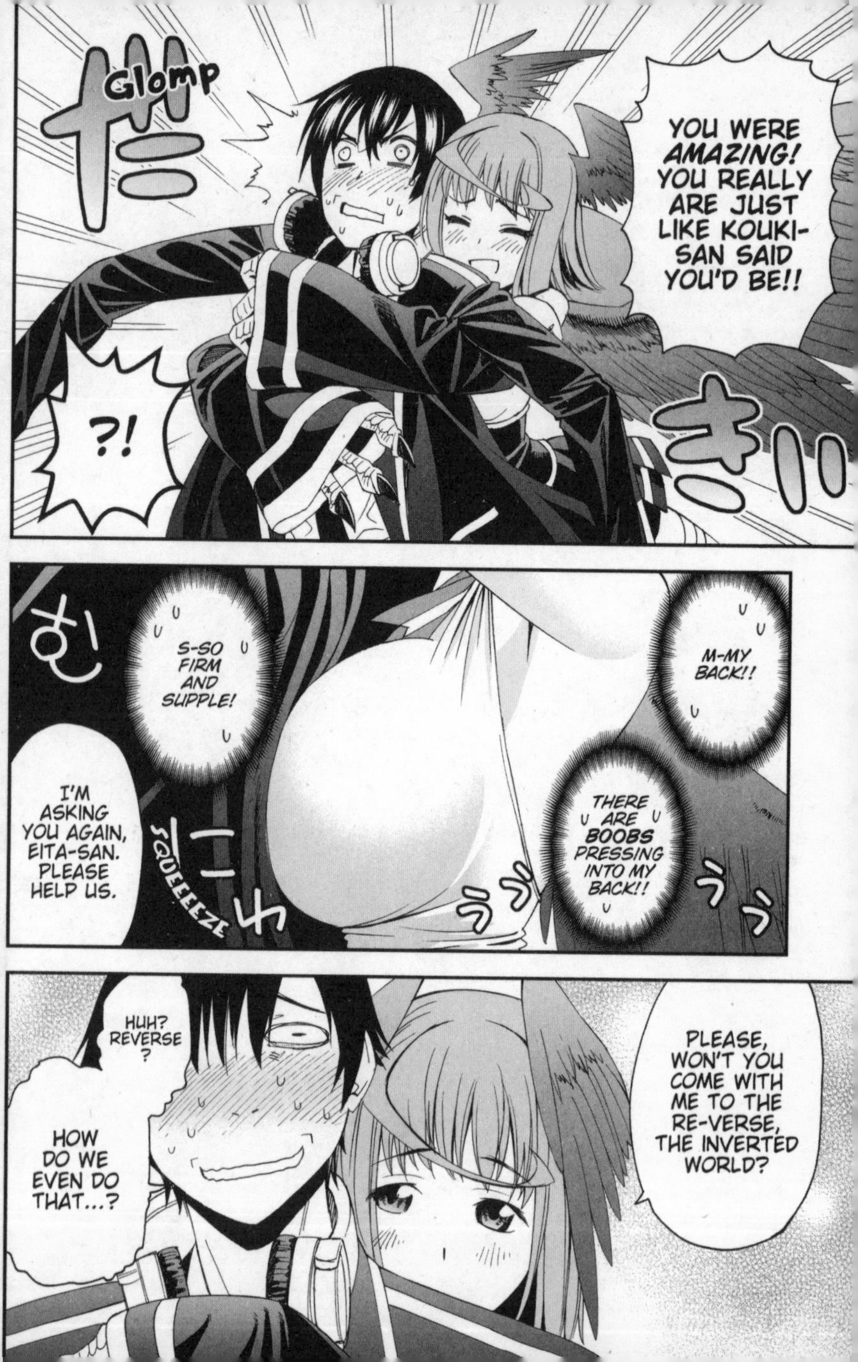
YOU WERE AMAZING! YOU REALLY ARE JUST LIKE KOUKI-SAN SAID YOU'D BE!!
Glomp
?!
M-MY BACK!!
S-SO FIRM AND SUPPLE!
THERE ARE BOOBS PRESSING INTO MY BACK!!
I'M ASKING YOU AGAIN, EITA-SAN. PLEASE HELP US.
SQUEEEEEZE
PLEASE, WON'T YOU COME WITH ME TO THE RE-VERSE, THE INVERTED WORLD?
HUH? REVERSE ?
HOW DO WE EVEN DO THAT...?

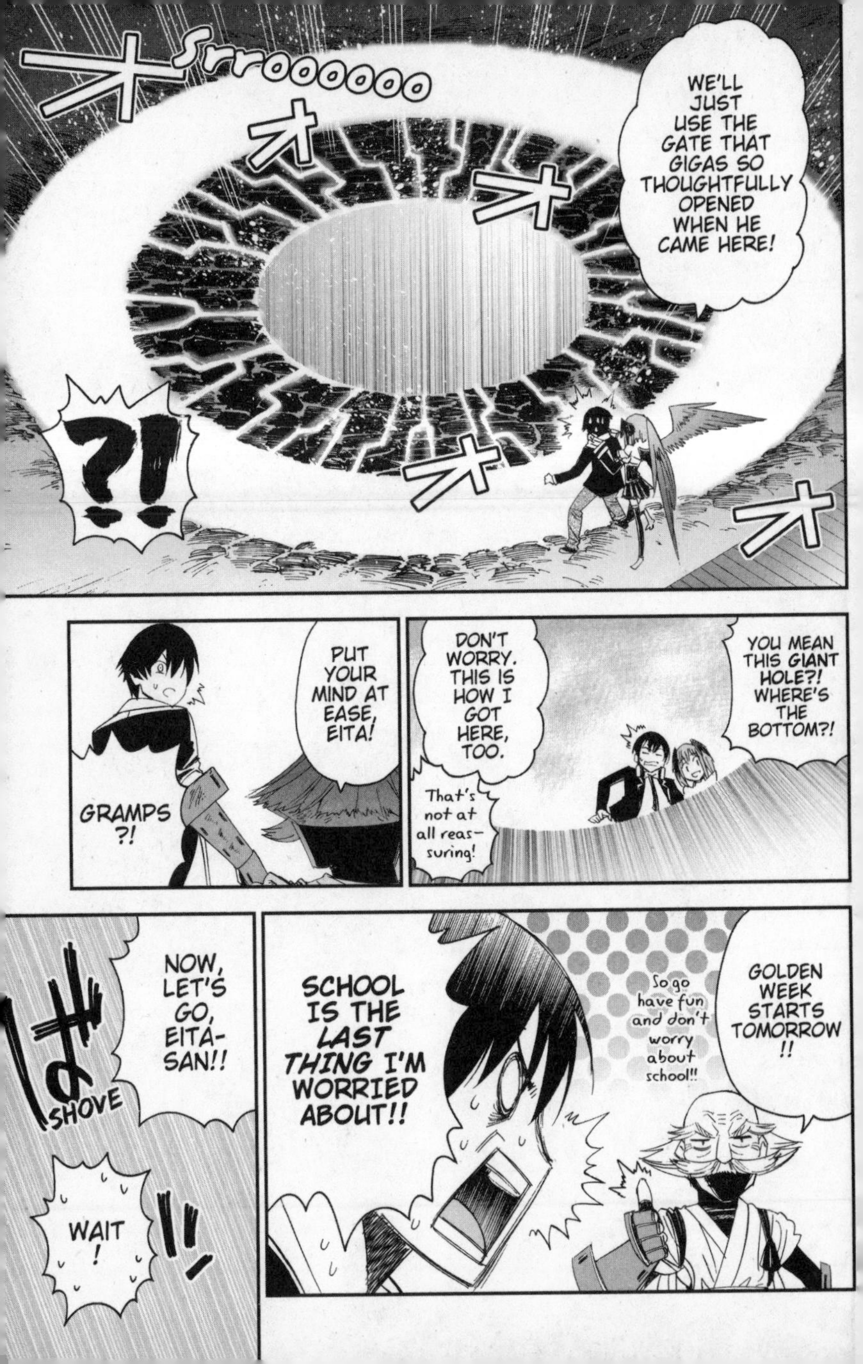

オ
Srroooooo
オ
オ
オ
オ
WE'LL JUST USE THE GATE THAT GIGAS SO THOUGHTFULLY OPENED WHEN HE CAME HERE!
?!
YOU MEAN THIS GIANT HOLE?! WHERE'S THE BOTTOM?!
DON'T WORRY. THIS IS HOW I GOT HERE, TOO.
That's not at all reas-suring!
PUT YOUR MIND AT EASE, EITA!
GRAMPS?!
GOLDEN WEEK STARTS TOMORROW!!
So go have fun and don't worry about school!!
SCHOOL IS THE *LAST THING* I'M WORRIED ABOUT!!
NOW, LET'S GO, EITA-SAN!!
SHOVE
WAIT!

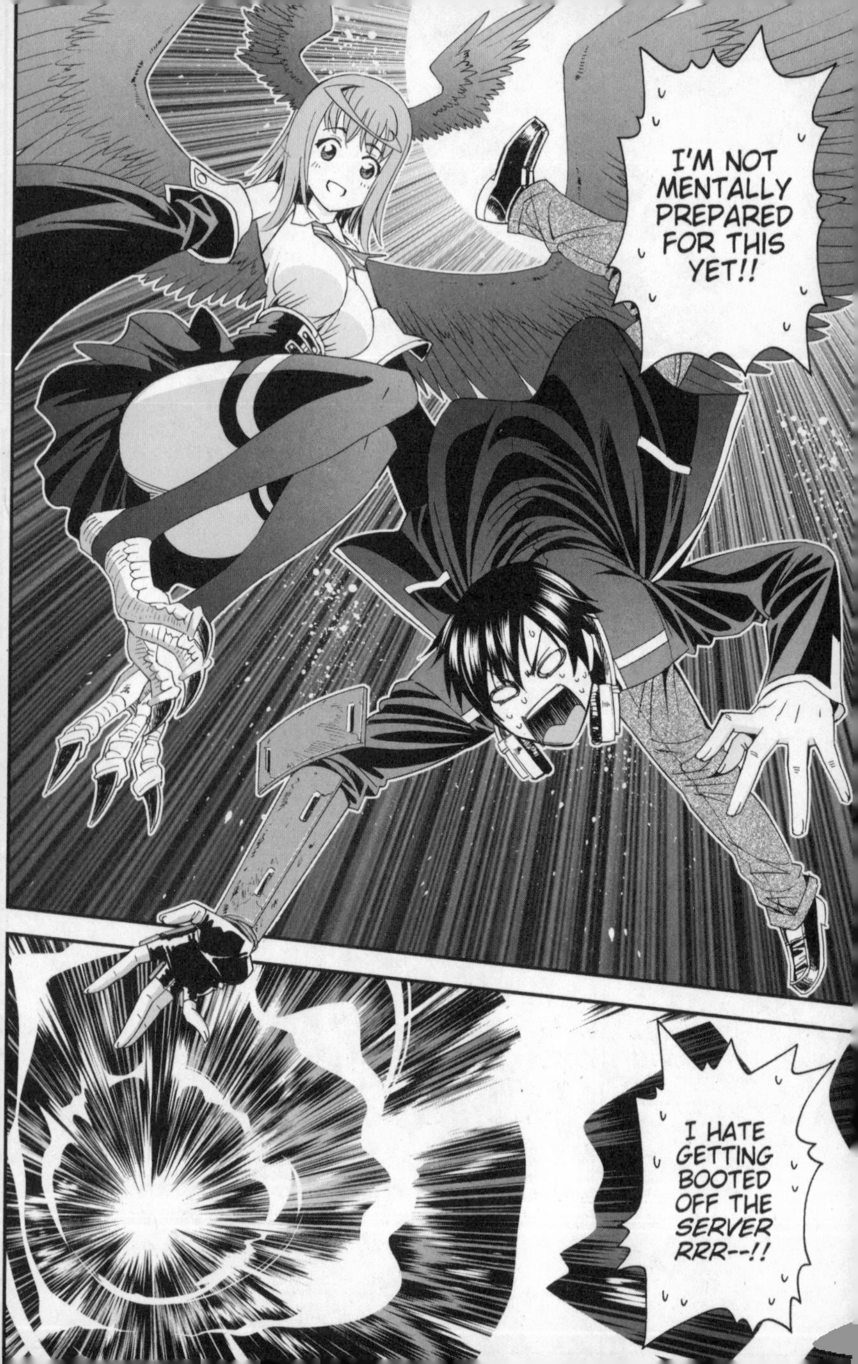
I'M NOT MENTALLY PREPARED FOR THIS YET!!
I HATE GETTING BOOTED OFF THE SERVER RRR--!!

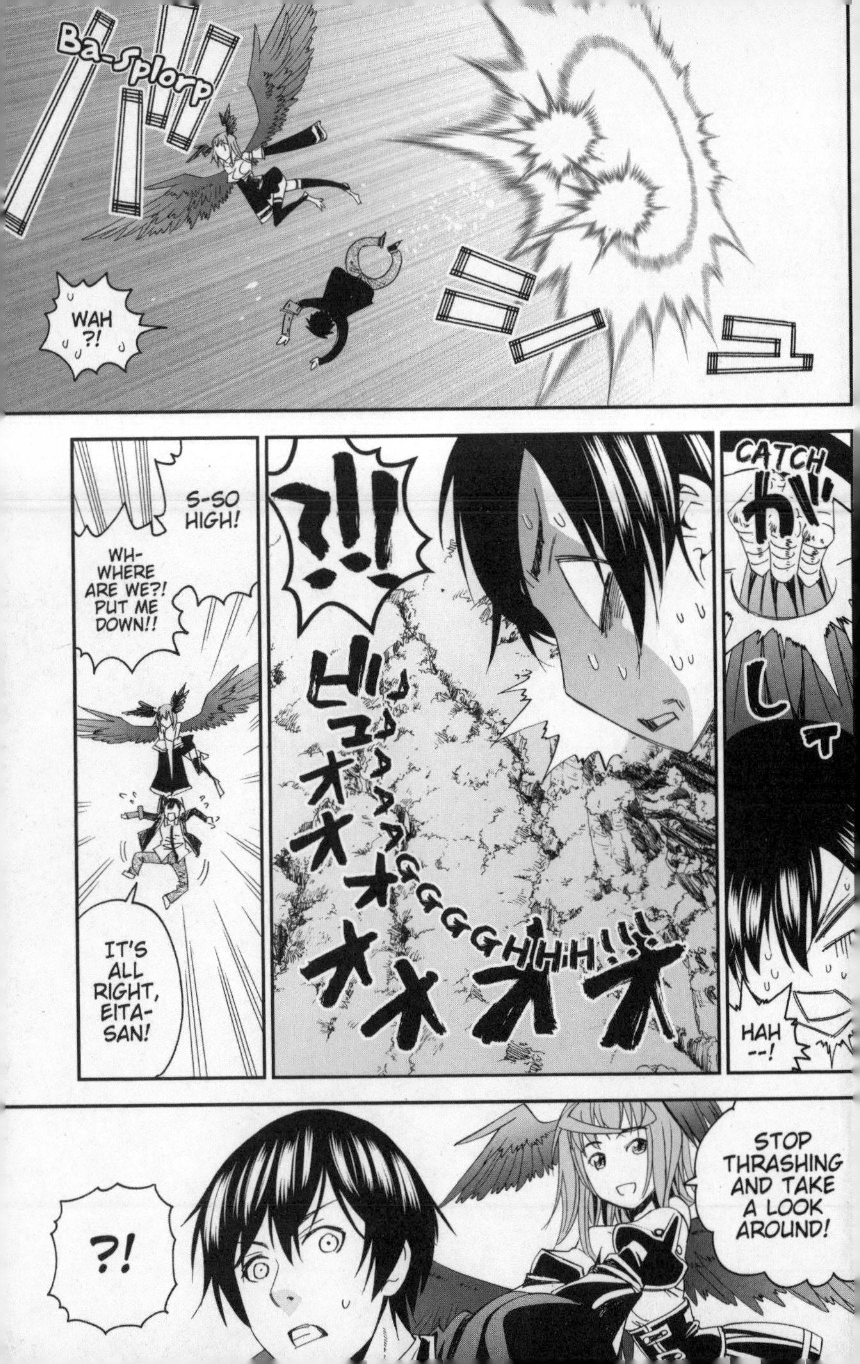
Ba-Splorp
WAH ?!
CATCH
HAH --!
?!!
HIAAAAAGGGGGHHH!!
S-SO HIGH!
WH-WHERE ARE WE?! PUT ME DOWN!!
IT'S ALL RIGHT, EITA-SAN!
STOP THRASHING AND TAKE A LOOK AROUND!
?!

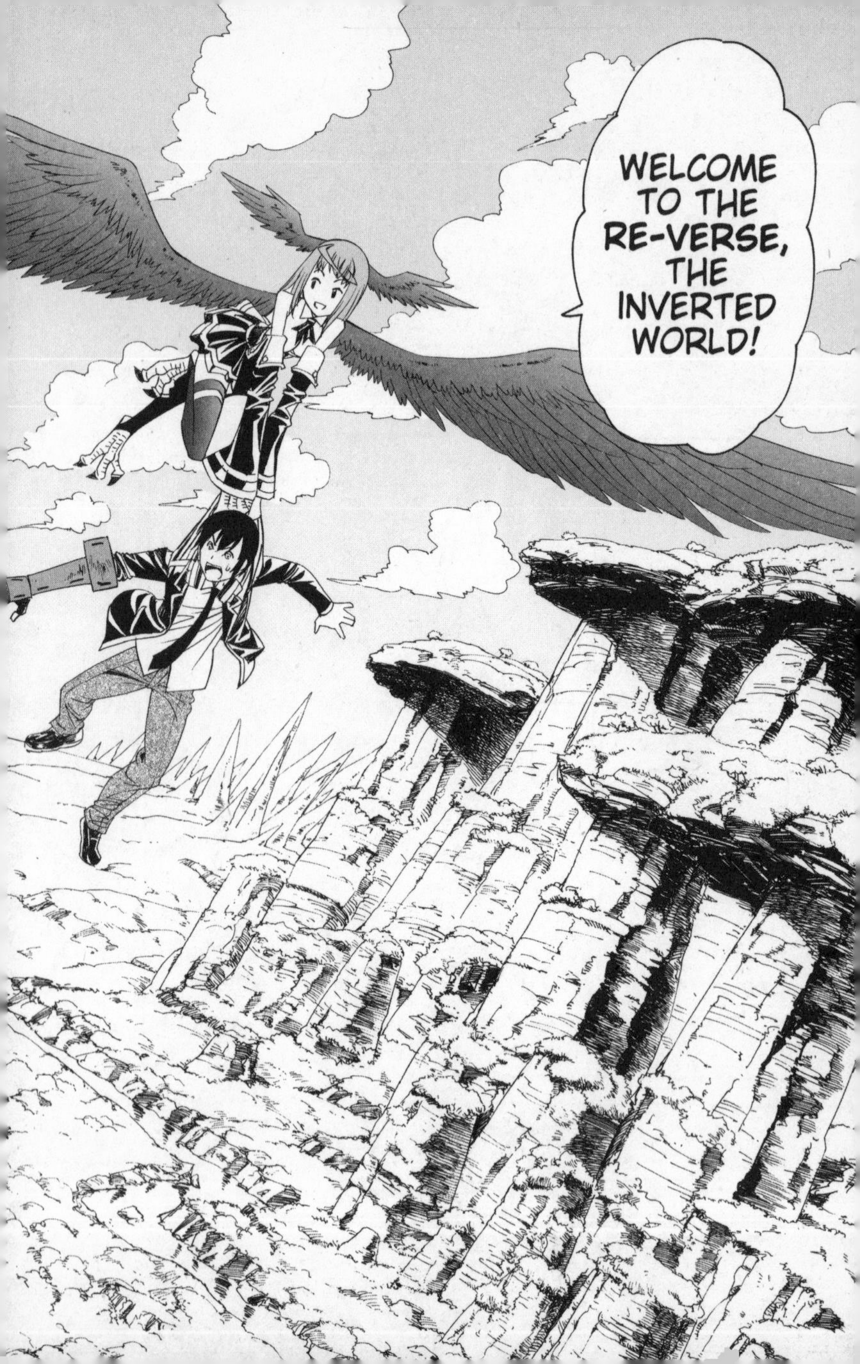
WELCOME TO THE RE-VERSE, THE INVERTED WORLD!

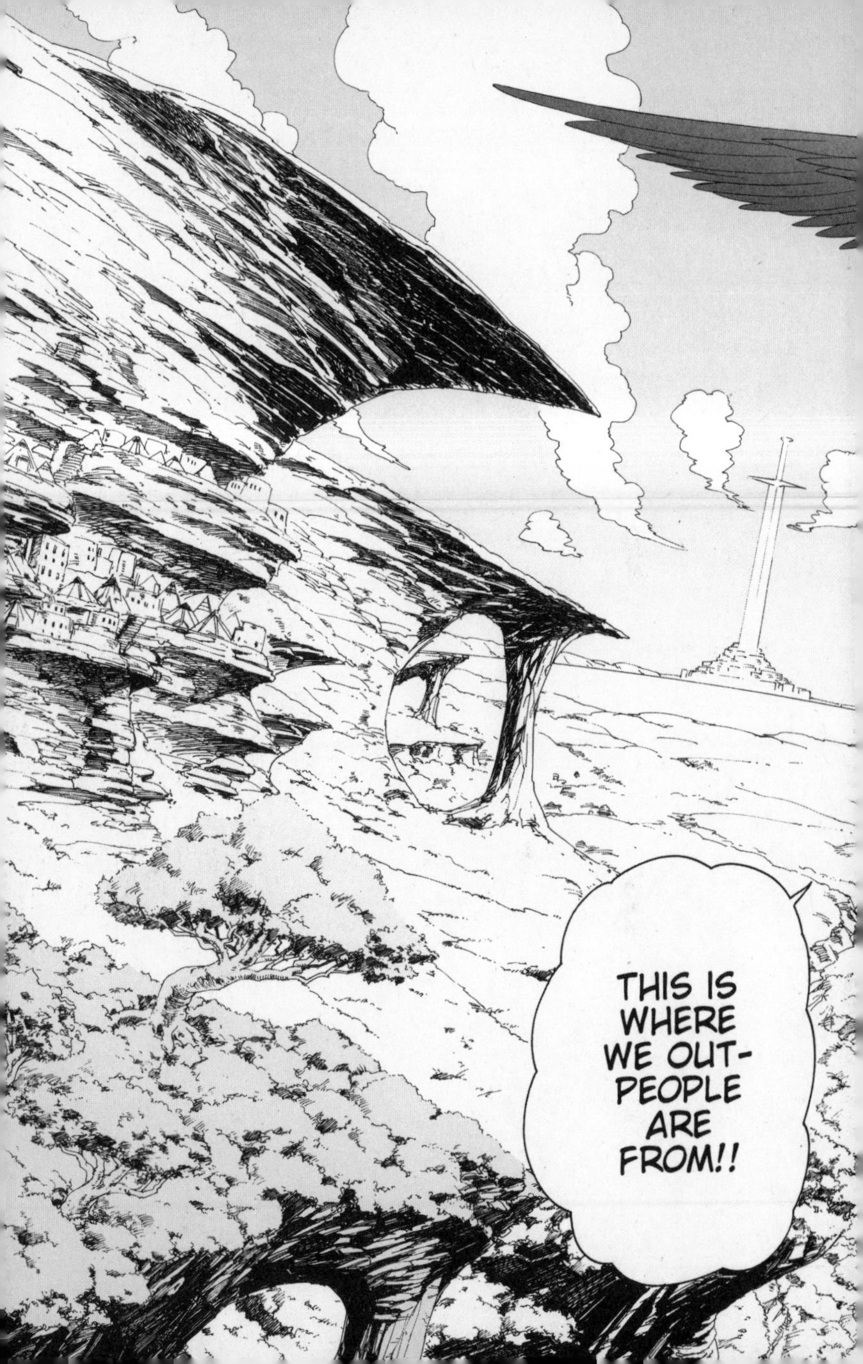
THIS IS WHERE WE OUT-PEOPLE ARE FROM!!

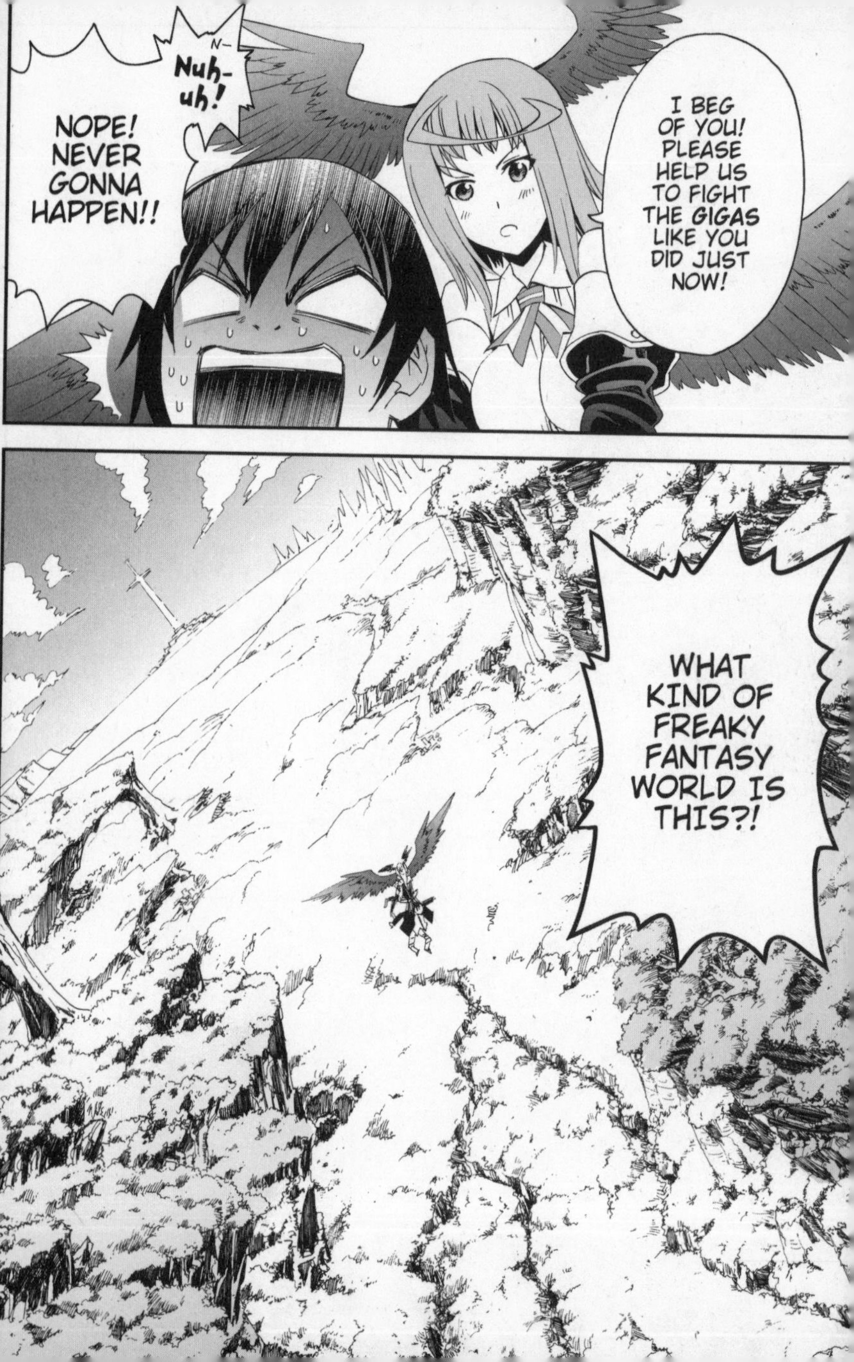
I BEG OF YOU! PLEASE HELP US TO FIGHT THE GIGAS LIKE YOU DID JUST NOW!
N— Nuh-uh!
NOPE! NEVER GONNA HAPPEN!!
WHAT KIND OF FREAKY FANTASY WORLD IS THIS?!

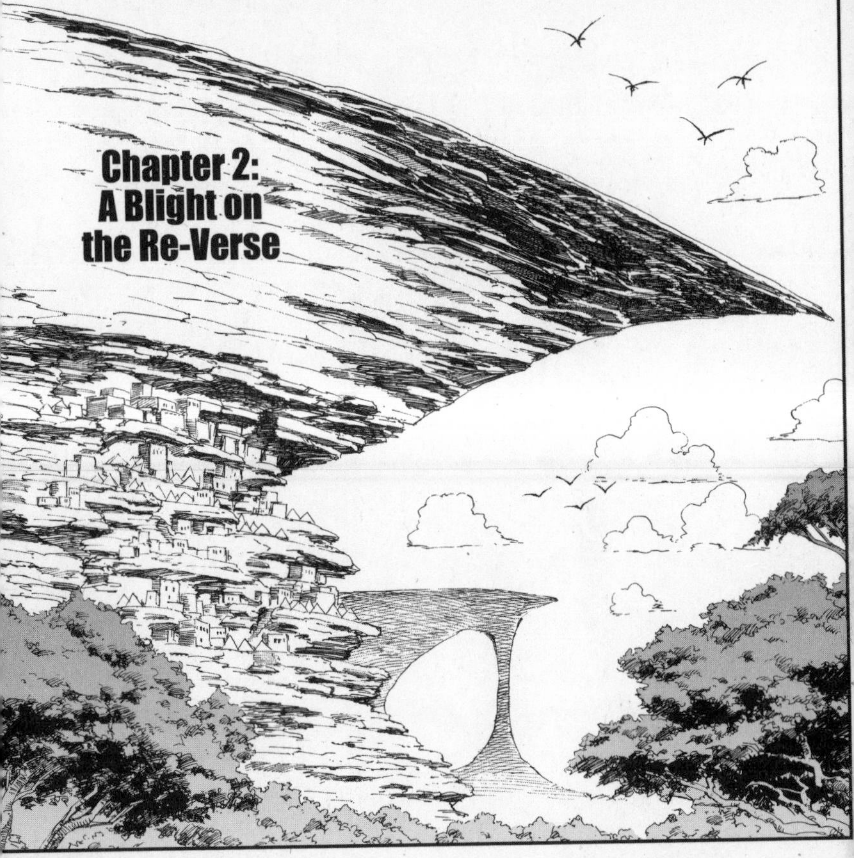
Chapter 2:
A Blight on
the Re-Verse
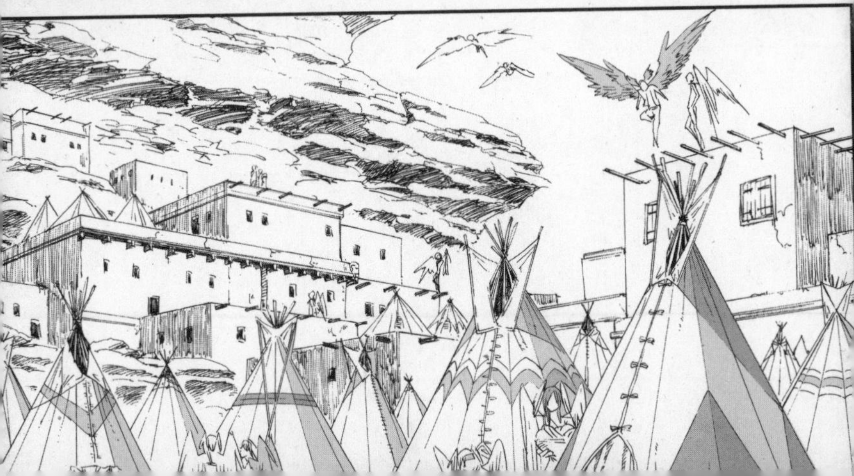

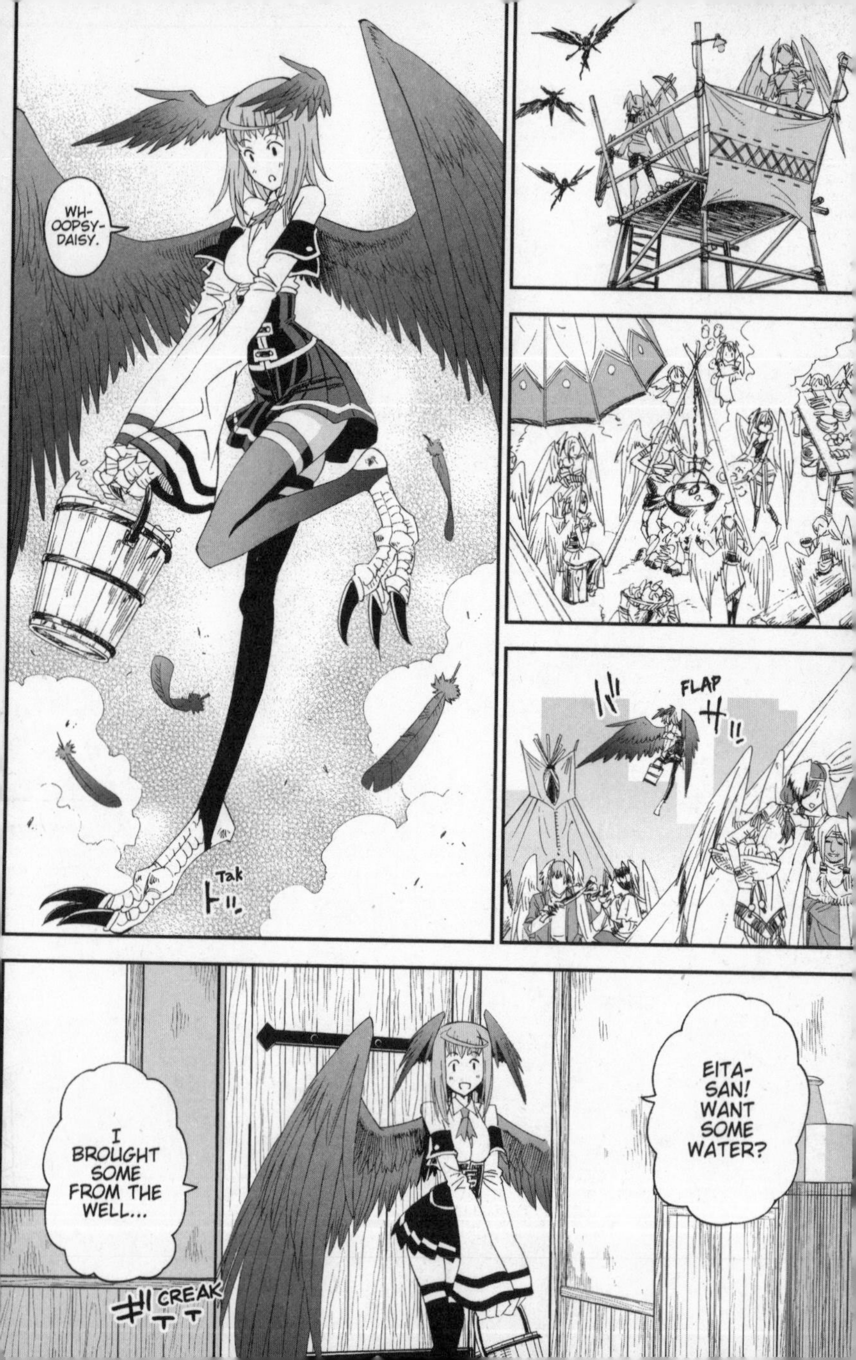
FLAP
WH- OOPSY- DAISY.
Tak
EITA- SAN! WANT SOME WATER?
I BROUGHT SOME FROM THE WELL...
CREAK

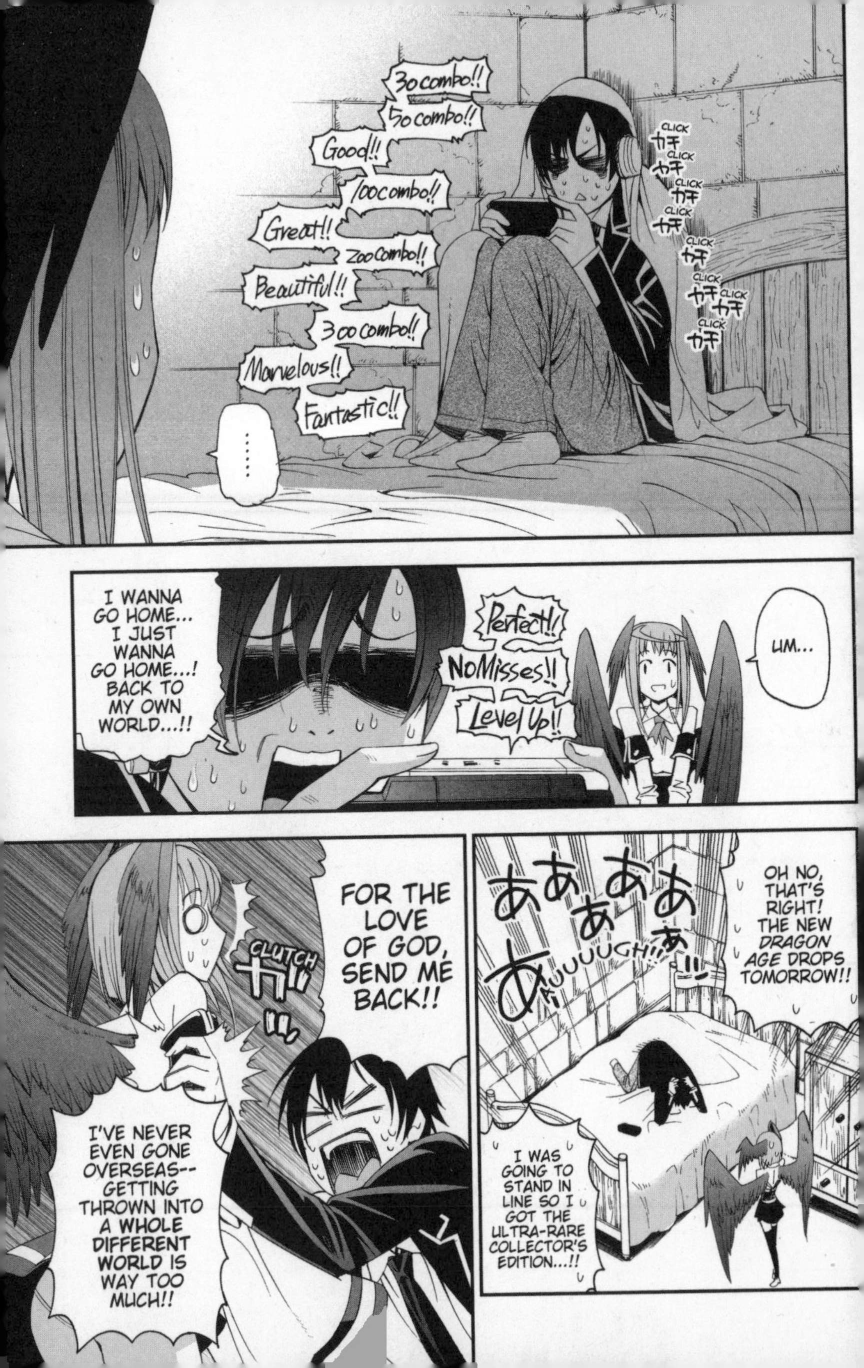

CLICK
カチ
CLICK
カチ
CLICK
カチ
CLICK
カチ
CLICK
カチ
CLICK
カチ
CLICK
カチ
CLICK
カチ
30 combo!!
50 combo!!
Good!!
100 combo!!
Great!!
200 combo!!
Beautiful!!
300 combo!!
Marvelous!!
Fantastic!!
......
UM...
Perfect!!
No Misses!!
Level Up!!
I WANNA GO HOME... I JUST WANNA GO HOME...! BACK TO MY OWN WORLD...!!
OH NO, THAT'S RIGHT! THE NEW DRAGON AGE DROPS TOMORROW!!
ああああああ
UUUUGH!!
I WAS GOING TO STAND IN LINE SO I GOT THE ULTRA-RARE COLLECTOR'S EDITION...!!
FOR THE LOVE OF GOD, SEND ME BACK!!
CLUTCH
ガッ
I'VE NEVER EVEN GONE OVERSEAS-- GETTING THROWN INTO A WHOLE DIFFERENT WORLD IS WAY TOO MUCH!!

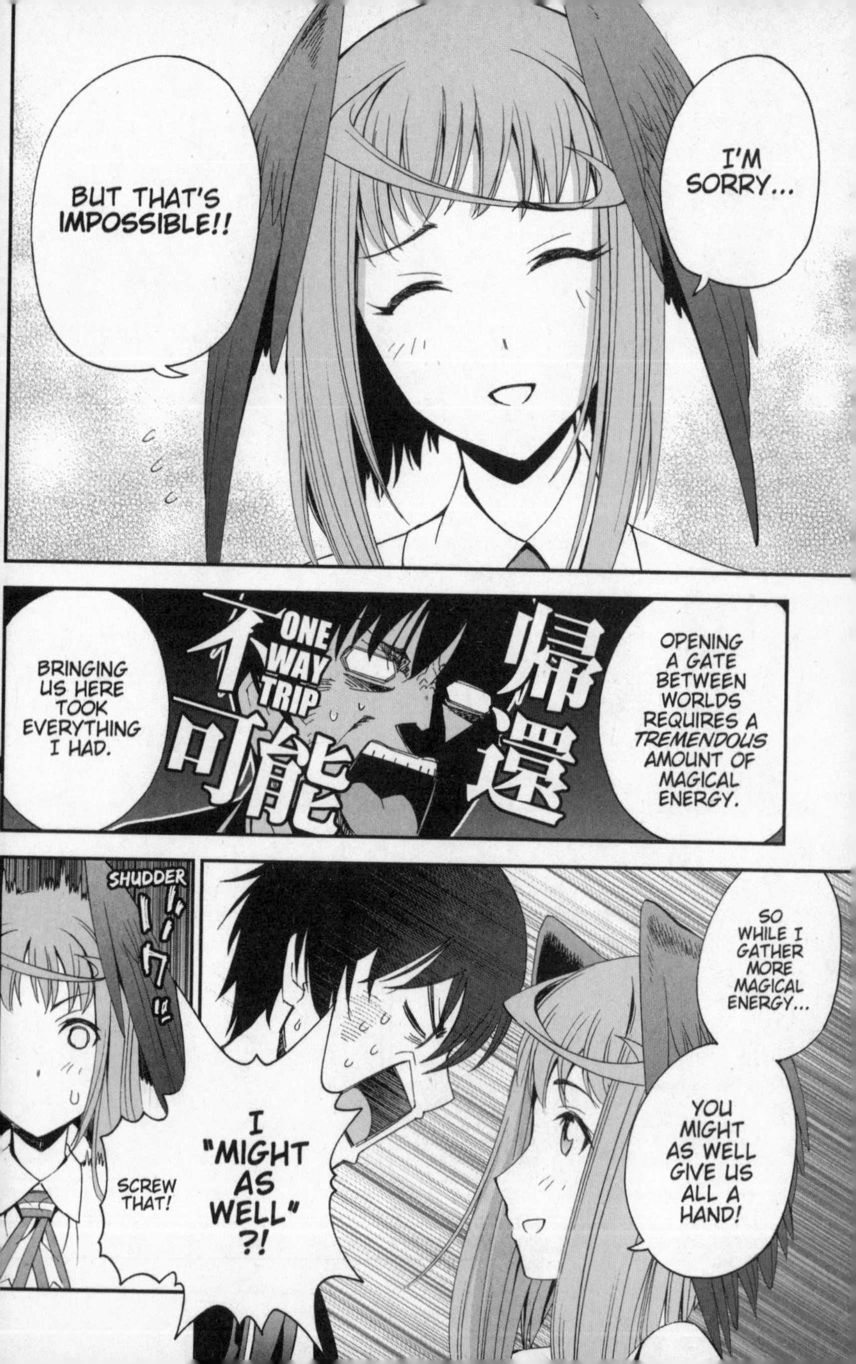
I'M SORRY...
BUT THAT'S IMPOSSIBLE!!
OPENING A GATE BETWEEN WORLDS REQUIRES A *TREMENDOUS* AMOUNT OF MAGICAL ENERGY.
帰還不可能
ONE WAY TRIP
BRINGING US HERE TOOK EVERYTHING I HAD.
SO WHILE I GATHER MORE MAGICAL ENERGY...
YOU MIGHT AS WELL GIVE US ALL A HAND!
I "MIGHT AS WELL" ?!
SCREW THAT!
ビクッ!!
SHUDDER

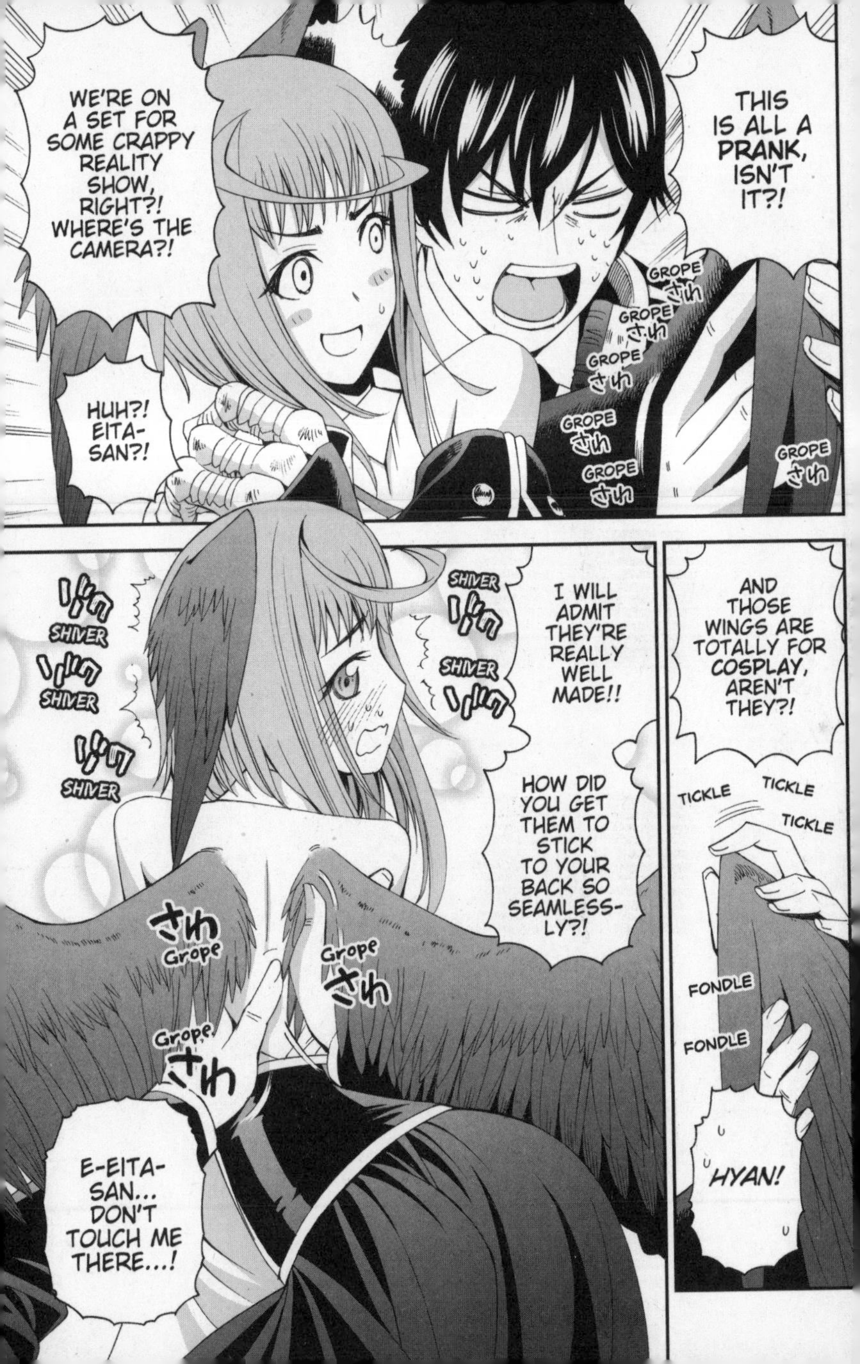
THIS IS ALL A PRANK, ISN'T IT?!
GROPE さわ
GROPE さわ
GROPE さわ
GROPE さわ
GROPE さわ
GROPE さわ
WE'RE ON A SET FOR SOME CRAPPY REALITY SHOW, RIGHT?! WHERE'S THE CAMERA?!
HUH?! EITA-SAN?!
AND THOSE WINGS ARE TOTALLY FOR COSPLAY, AREN'T THEY?!
TICKLE
TICKLE
TICKLE
FONDLE
FONDLE
HYAN!
I WILL ADMIT THEY'RE REALLY WELL MADE!!
HOW DID YOU GET THEM TO STICK TO YOUR BACK SO SEAMLESS-LY?!
SHIVER
SHIVER
SHIVER
SHIVER
SHIVER
SHIVER
さわ Grope
Grope さわ
Grope さわ
E-EITA-SAN... DON'T TOUCH ME THERE...!

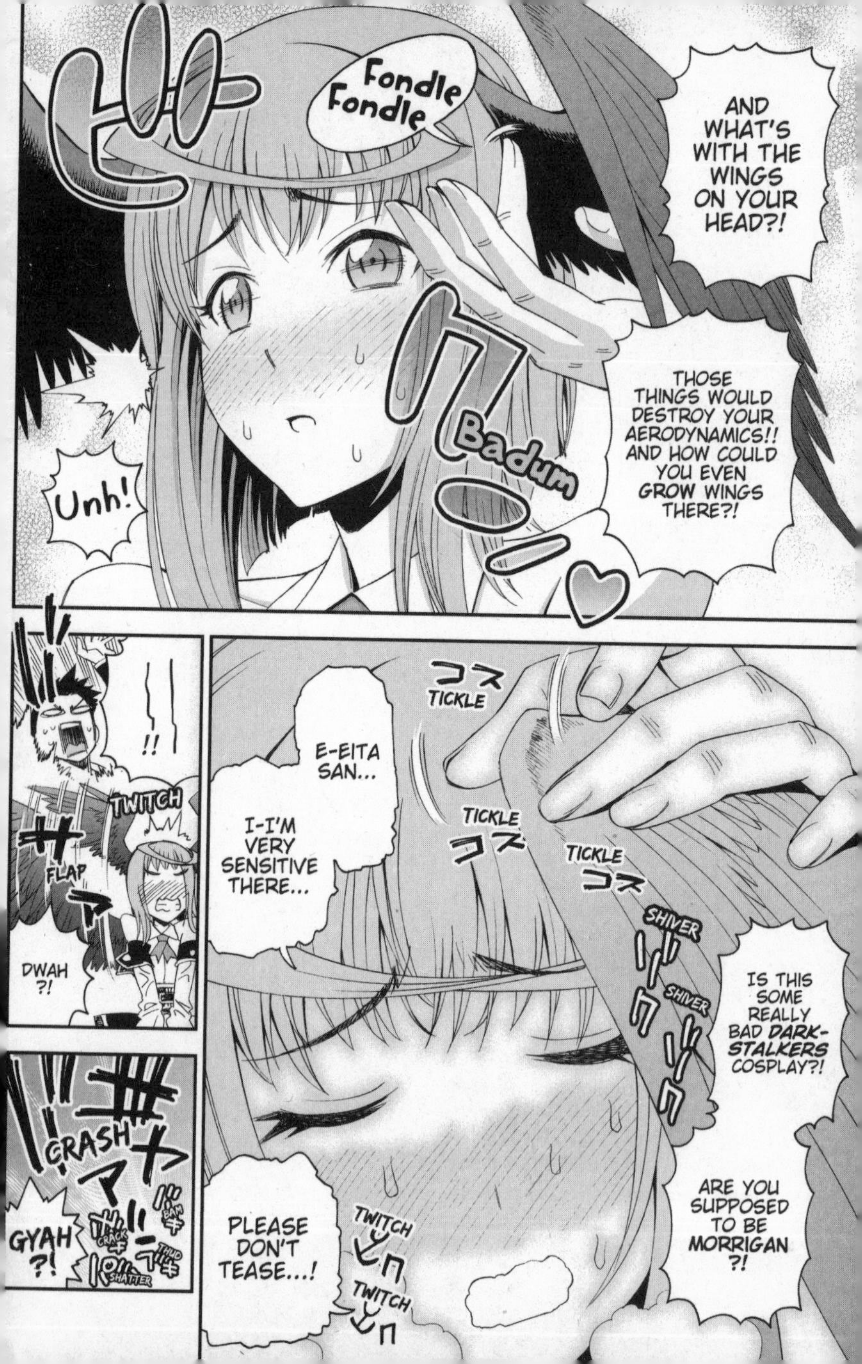
AND WHAT'S WITH THE WINGS ON YOUR HEAD?!
Fondle Fondle
THOSE THINGS WOULD DESTROY YOUR AERODYNAMICS!! AND HOW COULD YOU EVEN GROW WINGS THERE?!
Badum
Unh!
コス
TICKLE
E-EITA SAN...
I-I'M VERY SENSITIVE THERE...
TICKLE
コス
TICKLE
コス
SHIVER
SHIVER
IS THIS SOME REALLY BAD DARK-STALKERS COSPLAY?!
ARE YOU SUPPOSED TO BE MORRIGAN ?!
PLEASE DON'T TEASE...!
TWITCH
TWITCH
!!
TWITCH
FLAP
DWAH ?!
CRASH
BAM
CRACK
THUD
SHATTER
GYAH ?!

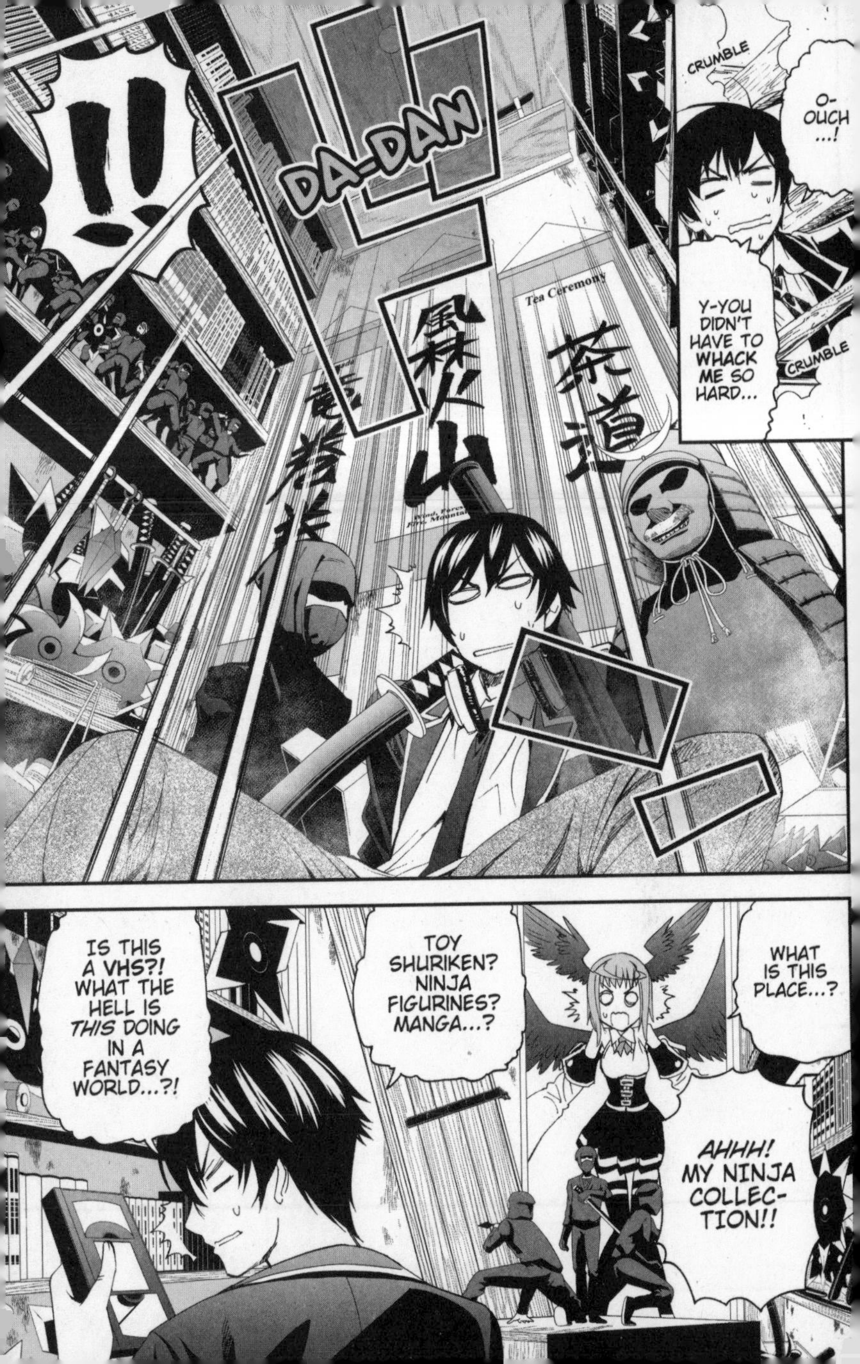
CRUMBLE
O-OUCH...!
Y-YOU DIDN'T HAVE TO WHACK ME SO HARD...
CRUMBLE
!!
DA-DAN
Tea Ceremony
茶道
風林火山
WHAT IS THIS PLACE...?
AHHH! MY NINJA COLLECTION!!
TOY SHURIKEN? NINJA FIGURINES? MANGA...?
IS THIS A VHS?! WHAT THE HELL IS *THIS* DOING IN A FANTASY WORLD...?!

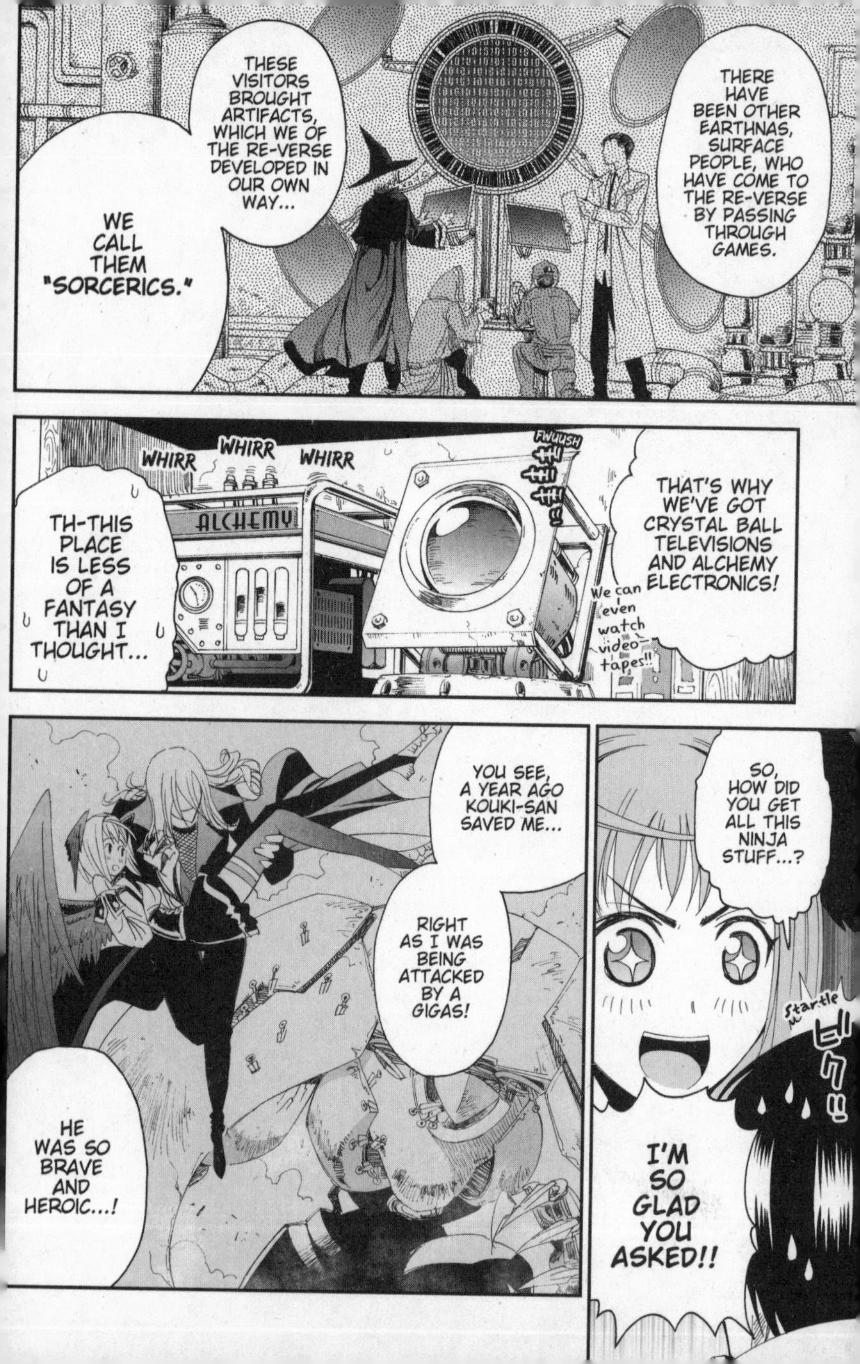
THERE HAVE BEEN OTHER EARTHNAS, SURFACE PEOPLE, WHO HAVE COME TO THE RE-VERSE BY PASSING THROUGH GAMES.
THESE VISITORS BROUGHT ARTIFACTS, WHICH WE OF THE RE-VERSE DEVELOPED IN OUR OWN WAY...
WE CALL THEM "SORCERICS."
FWUUSH
THAT'S WHY WE'VE GOT CRYSTAL BALL TELEVISIONS AND ALCHEMY ELECTRONICS!
We can even watch videotapes!!
ALCHEMY
WHIRR
WHIRR
WHIRR
TH-THIS PLACE IS LESS OF A FANTASY THAN I THOUGHT...
SO, HOW DID YOU GET ALL THIS NINJA STUFF...?
startle
I'M SO GLAD YOU ASKED!!
YOU SEE, A YEAR AGO KOUKI-SAN SAVED ME...
RIGHT AS I WAS BEING ATTACKED BY A GIGAS!
HE WAS SO BRAVE AND HEROIC...!

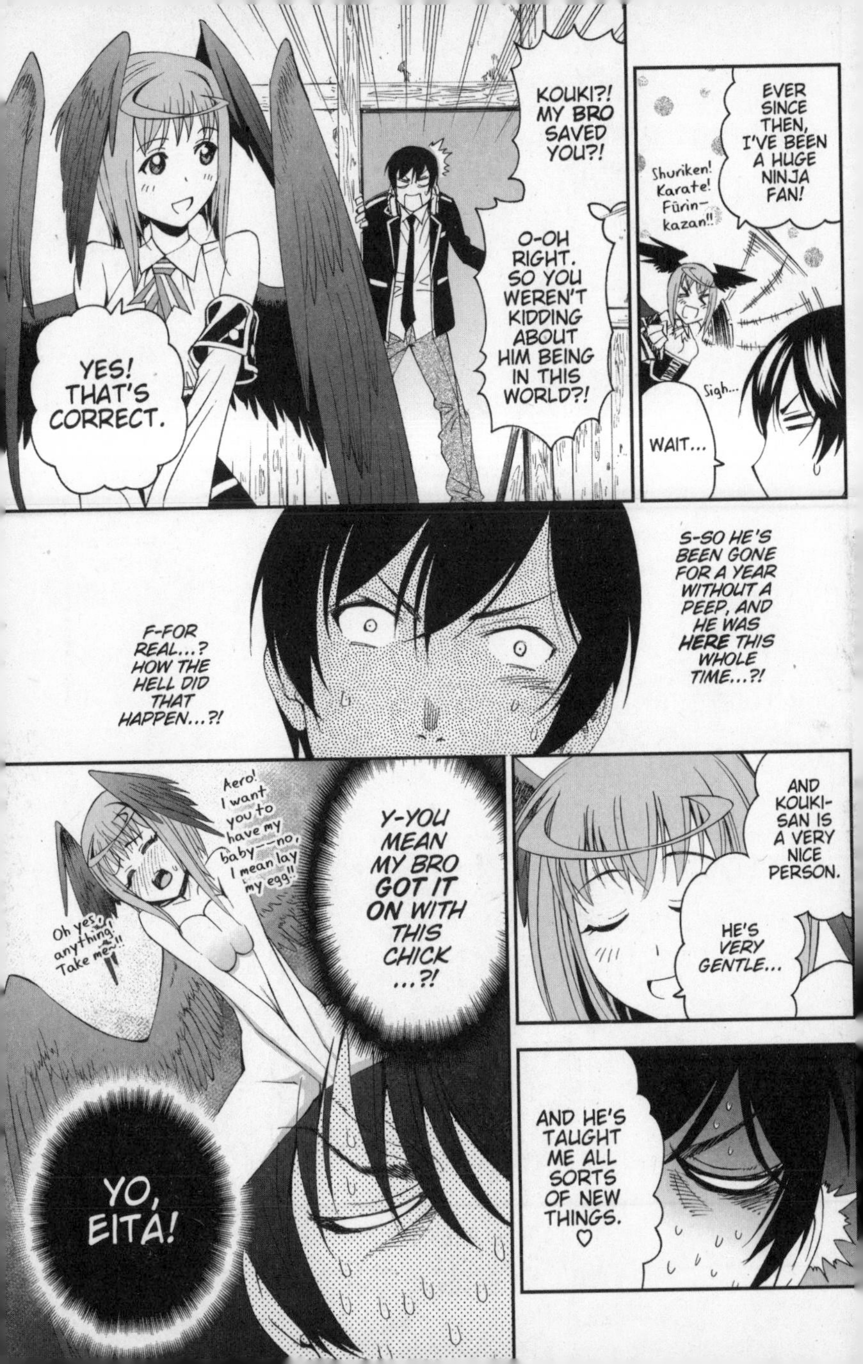
EVER SINCE THEN, I'VE BEEN A HUGE NINJA FAN!
Shuriken! Karate! Fūrin-kazan!!
Sigh...
WAIT...
KOUKI?! MY BRO SAVED YOU?!
O-OH RIGHT. SO YOU WEREN'T KIDDING ABOUT HIM BEING IN THIS WORLD?!
YES! THAT'S CORRECT.
S-SO HE'S BEEN GONE FOR A YEAR WITHOUT A PEEP, AND HE WAS HERE THIS WHOLE TIME...?!
F-FOR REAL...? HOW THE HELL DID THAT HAPPEN...?!
AND KOUKI-SAN IS A VERY NICE PERSON.
HE'S VERY GENTLE...
AND HE'S TAUGHT ME ALL SORTS OF NEW THINGS. ♡
Y-YOU MEAN MY BRO GOT IT ON WITH THIS CHICK...?!
Aero! I want you to have my baby--no, I mean lay my egg!!
Oh yes, anything! Take me~!!
YO, EITA!

GRAA AAAR GH?!

TRAUMA トラウマ

YOUR CLASS IDOL SURE WAS SWEET!!

AND I'M NOT JUST TALKING ABOUT HER FACE!!

SO HE'S COCK-BLOCKING ME IN THIS WORLD TOO, HUH...?!

?

Droop...

AUGH! THAT BASTARD! HE'S MANAGED TO BEAT ME TO EVERY GIRL I'VE EVER WANTED!!

......

WOW, I REALLY AM IN ANOTHER WORLD, AREN'T I?

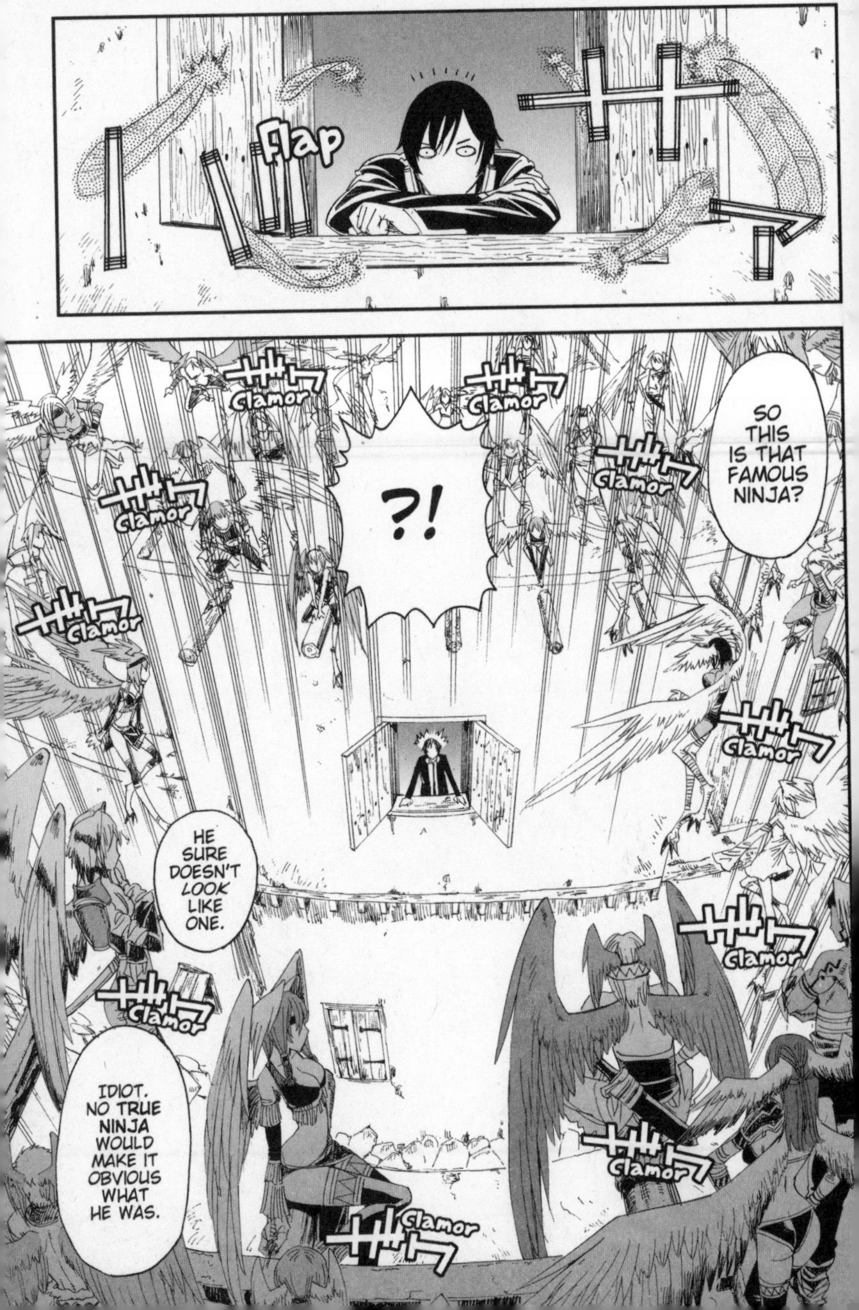
Flap
Clamor
Clamor
SO THIS IS THAT FAMOUS NINJA?
Clamor
?!
Clamor
Clamor
Clamor
Clamor
HE SURE DOESN'T LOOK LIKE ONE.
Clamor
Clamor
Clamor
IDIOT. NO TRUE NINJA WOULD MAKE IT OBVIOUS WHAT HE WAS.
Clamor

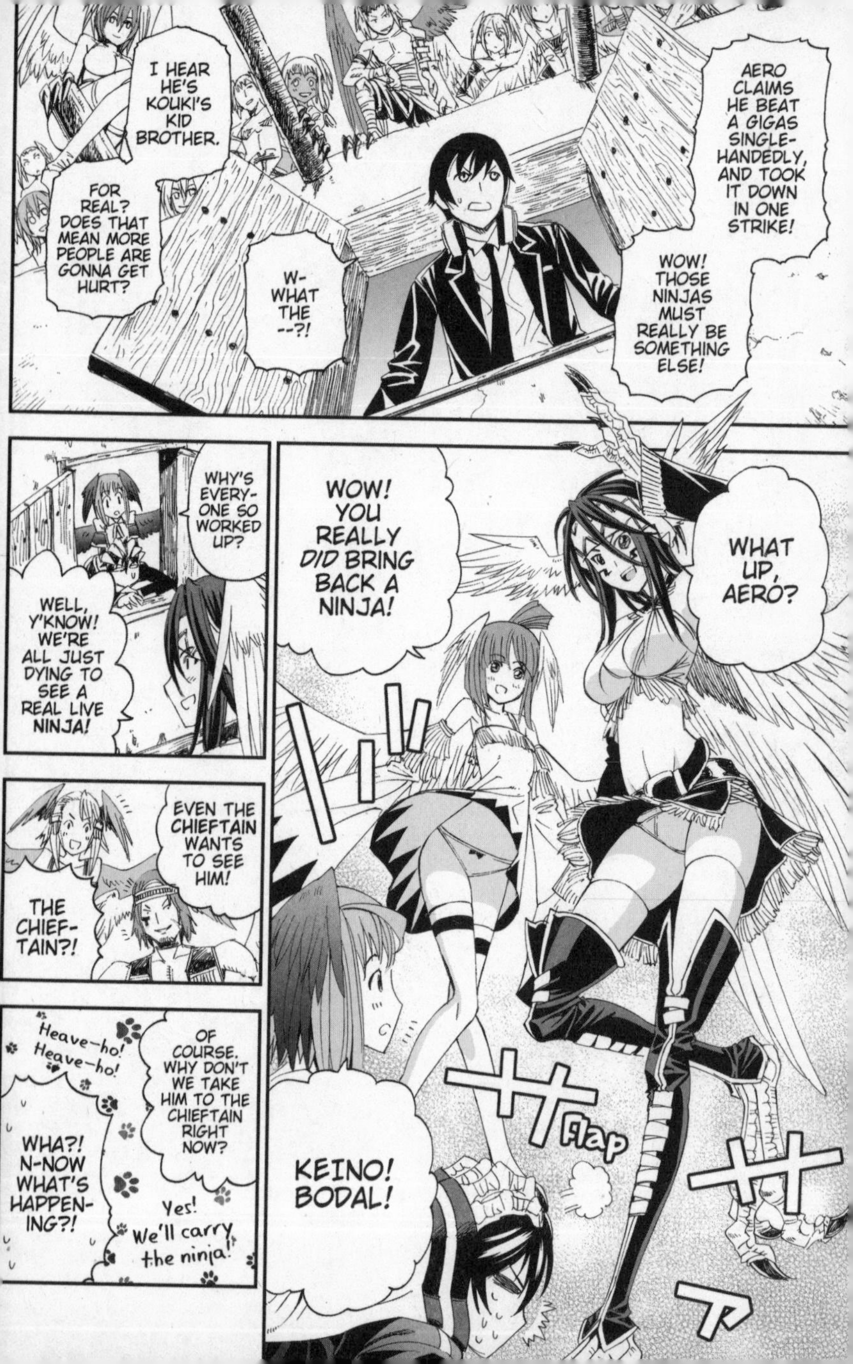
AERO CLAIMS HE BEAT A GIGAS SINGLE-HANDEDLY, AND TOOK IT DOWN IN ONE STRIKE!
WOW! THOSE NINJAS MUST REALLY BE SOMETHING ELSE!
I HEAR HE'S KOUKI'S KID BROTHER.
FOR REAL? DOES THAT MEAN MORE PEOPLE ARE GONNA GET HURT?
W-WHAT THE --?!
WHAT UP, AERO?
WOW! YOU REALLY *DID* BRING BACK A NINJA!
Flap
KEINO! BODAL!
WHY'S EVERYONE SO WORKED UP?
WELL, Y'KNOW! WE'RE ALL JUST DYING TO SEE A REAL LIVE NINJA!
EVEN THE CHIEFTAIN WANTS TO SEE HIM!
THE CHIEF-TAIN?!
OF COURSE. WHY DON'T WE TAKE HIM TO THE CHIEFTAIN RIGHT NOW?
Heave-ho! Heave-ho!
WHA?! N-NOW WHAT'S HAPPEN-ING?!
Yes! We'll carry the ninja!

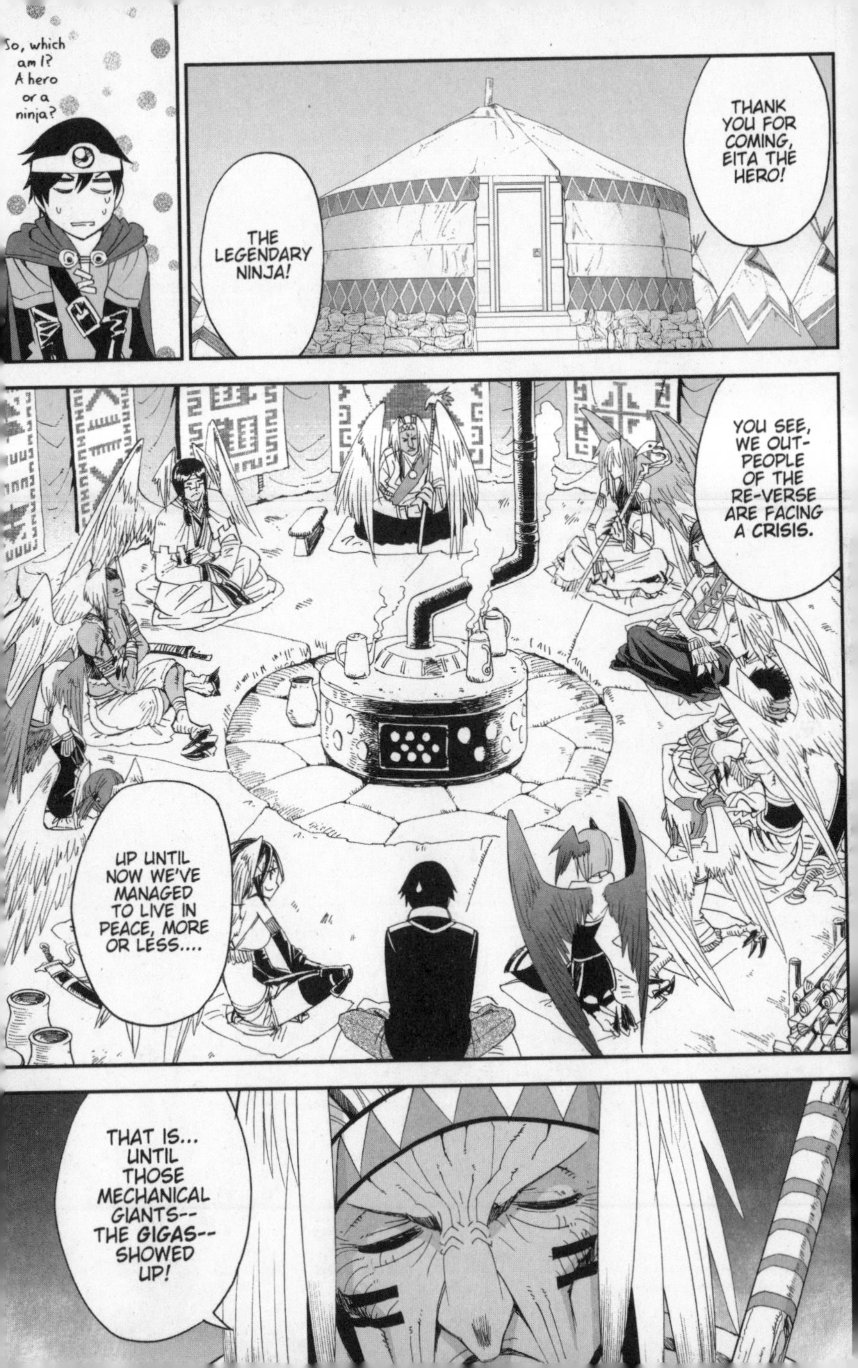
THANK YOU FOR COMING, EITA THE HERO!
THE LEGENDARY NINJA!
So, which am I? A hero or a ninja?
YOU SEE, WE OUT-PEOPLE OF THE RE-VERSE ARE FACING A CRISIS.
UP UNTIL NOW WE'VE MANAGED TO LIVE IN PEACE, MORE OR LESS....
THAT IS... UNTIL THOSE MECHANICAL GIANTS-- THE GIGAS-- SHOWED UP!

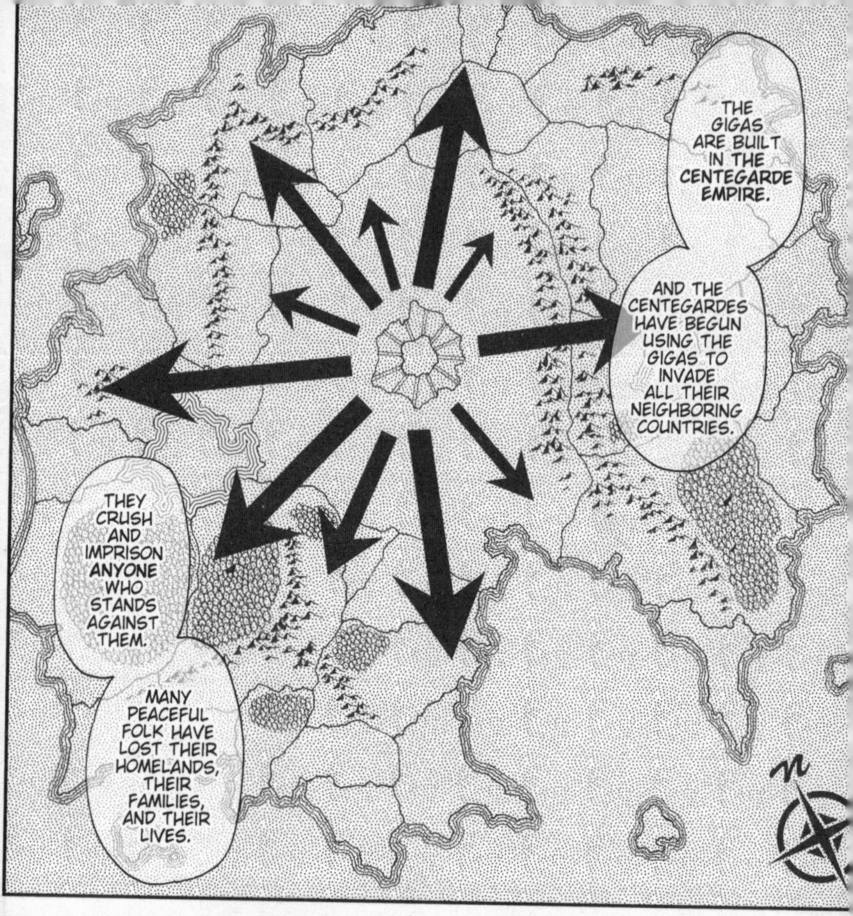
THE GIGAS ARE BUILT IN THE CENTEGARDE EMPIRE.
AND THE CENTEGARDES HAVE BEGUN USING THE GIGAS TO INVADE ALL THEIR NEIGHBORING COUNTRIES.
THEY CRUSH AND IMPRISON ANYONE WHO STANDS AGAINST THEM.
MANY PEACEFUL FOLK HAVE LOST THEIR HOMELANDS, THEIR FAMILIES, AND THEIR LIVES.

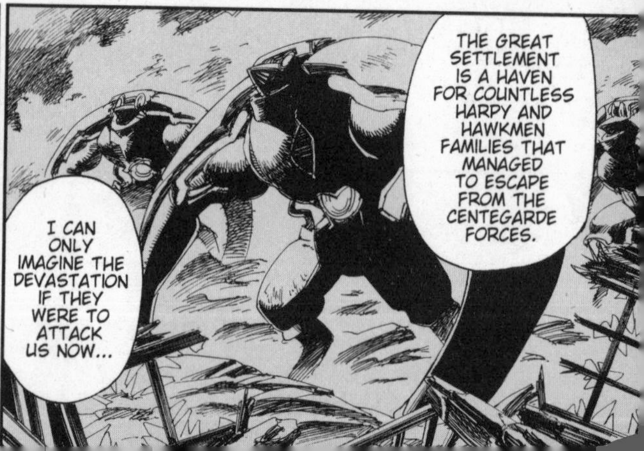
THE GREAT SETTLEMENT IS A HAVEN FOR COUNTLESS HARPY AND HAWKMEN FAMILIES THAT MANAGED TO ESCAPE FROM THE CENTEGARDE FORCES.
I CAN ONLY IMAGINE THE DEVASTATION IF THEY WERE TO ATTACK US NOW...

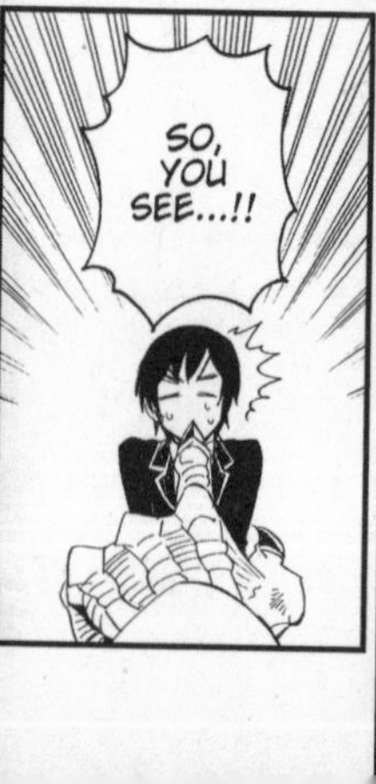
SO, YOU SEE...!!

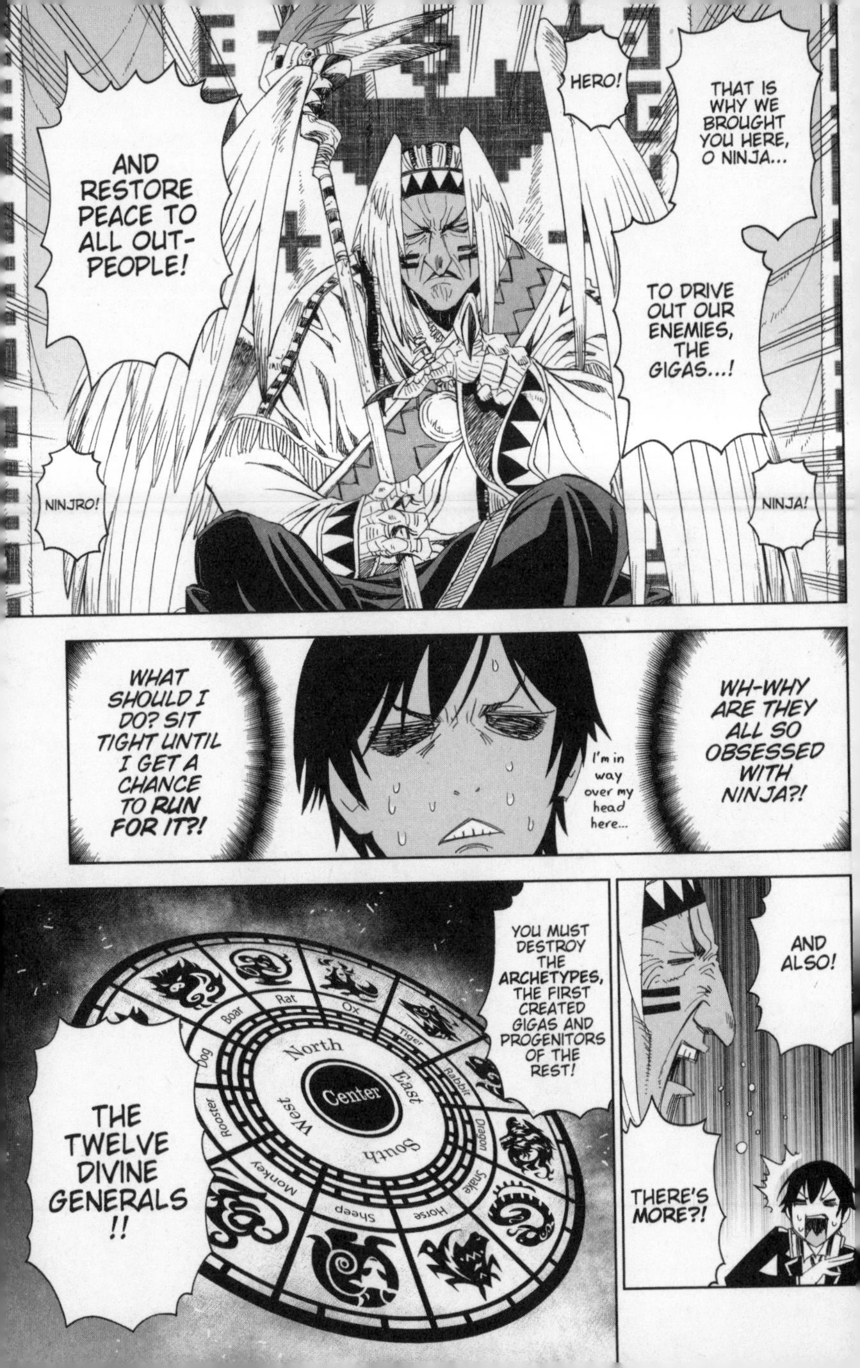

THAT IS WHY WE BROUGHT YOU HERE, O NINJA...
HERO!
TO DRIVE OUT OUR ENEMIES, THE GIGAS...!
AND RESTORE PEACE TO ALL OUT-PEOPLE!
NINJA!
NINJRO!
WH-WHY ARE THEY ALL SO OBSESSED WITH NINJA?!
I'm in way over my head here...
WHAT SHOULD I DO? SIT TIGHT UNTIL I GET A CHANCE TO RUN FOR IT?!
AND ALSO!
THERE'S MORE?!
YOU MUST DESTROY THE ARCHETYPES, THE FIRST CREATED GIGAS AND PROGENITORS OF THE REST!
THE TWELVE DIVINE GENERALS!!
Center
North
East
South
West
Rat
Ox
Tiger
Rabbit
Dragon
Snake
Horse
Sheep
Monkey
Rooster
Dog
Boar

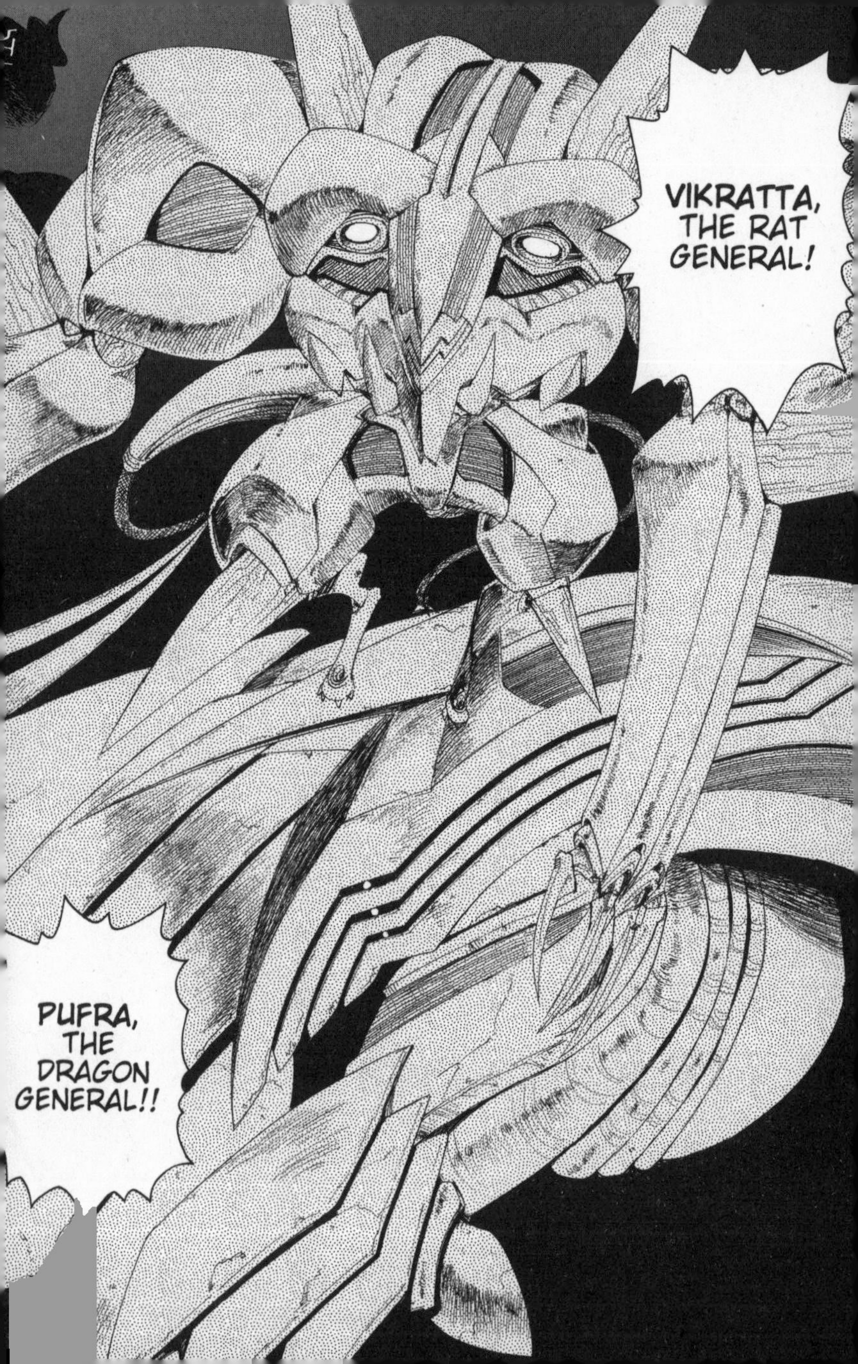
VIKRATTA, THE RAT GENERAL!
PUFRA, THE DRAGON GENERAL!!

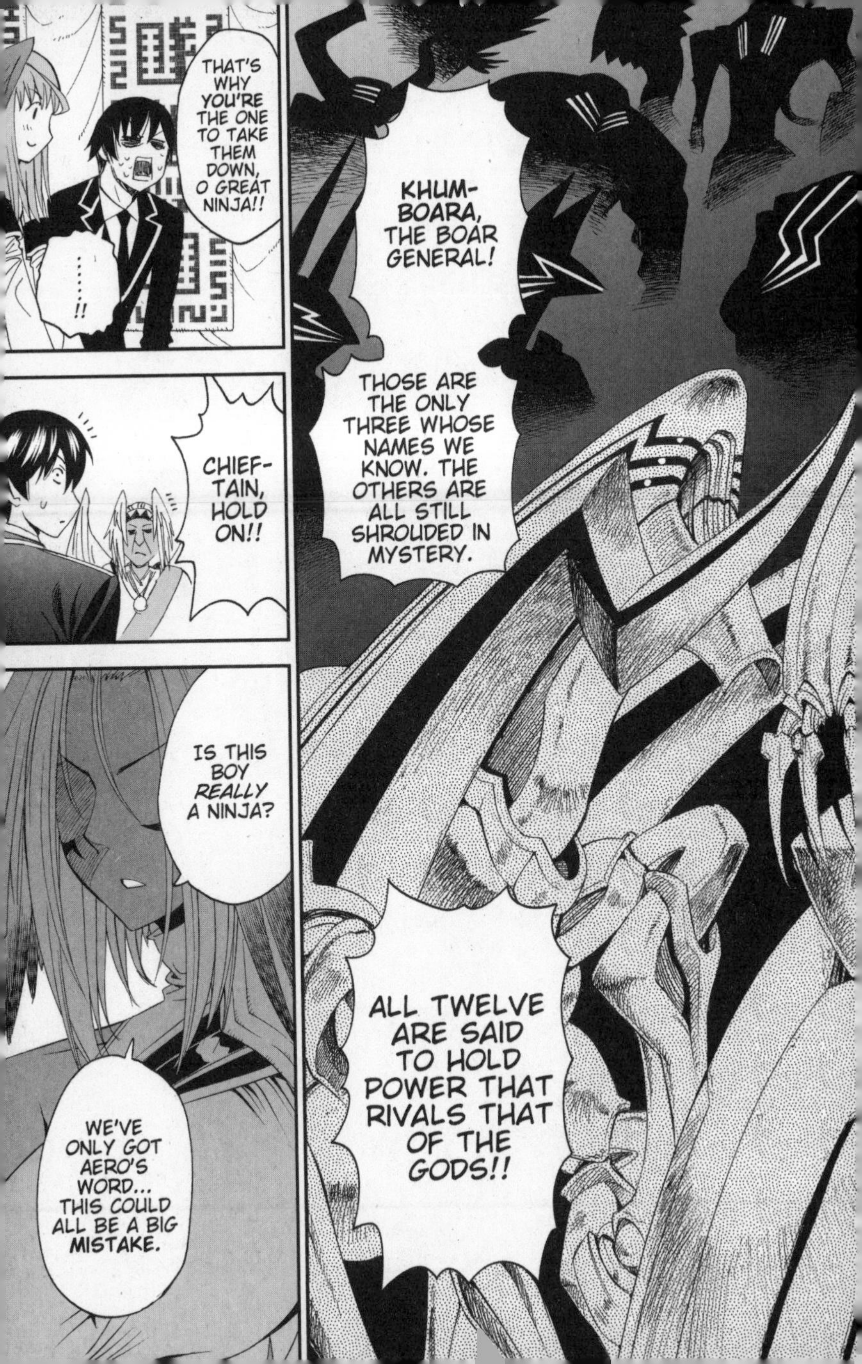
KHUM-BOARA, THE BOAR GENERAL!
THOSE ARE THE ONLY THREE WHOSE NAMES WE KNOW. THE OTHERS ARE ALL STILL SHROUDED IN MYSTERY.
ALL TWELVE ARE SAID TO HOLD POWER THAT RIVALS THAT OF THE GODS!!
THAT'S WHY YOU'RE THE ONE TO TAKE THEM DOWN, O GREAT NINJA!!
......!!
CHIEF-TAIN, HOLD ON!!
IS THIS BOY REALLY A NINJA?
WE'VE ONLY GOT AERO'S WORD... THIS COULD ALL BE A BIG MISTAKE.

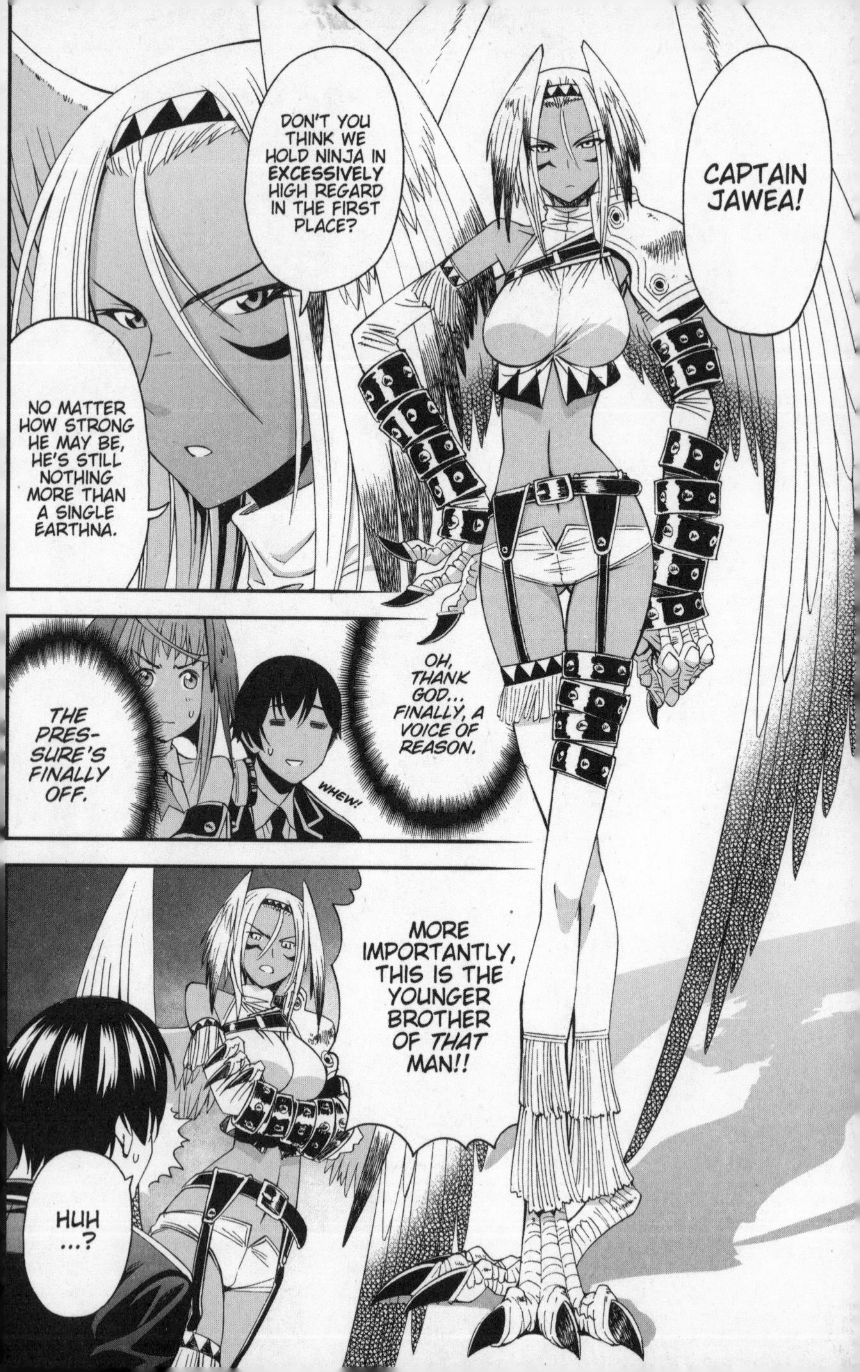
CAPTAIN JAWEA!
DON'T YOU THINK WE HOLD NINJA IN EXCESSIVELY HIGH REGARD IN THE FIRST PLACE?
NO MATTER HOW STRONG HE MAY BE, HE'S STILL NOTHING MORE THAN A SINGLE EARTHNA.
OH, THANK GOD... FINALLY, A VOICE OF REASON.
THE PRES-SURE'S FINALLY OFF.
WHEW!
MORE IMPORTANTLY, THIS IS THE YOUNGER BROTHER OF *THAT* MAN!!
HUH ...?

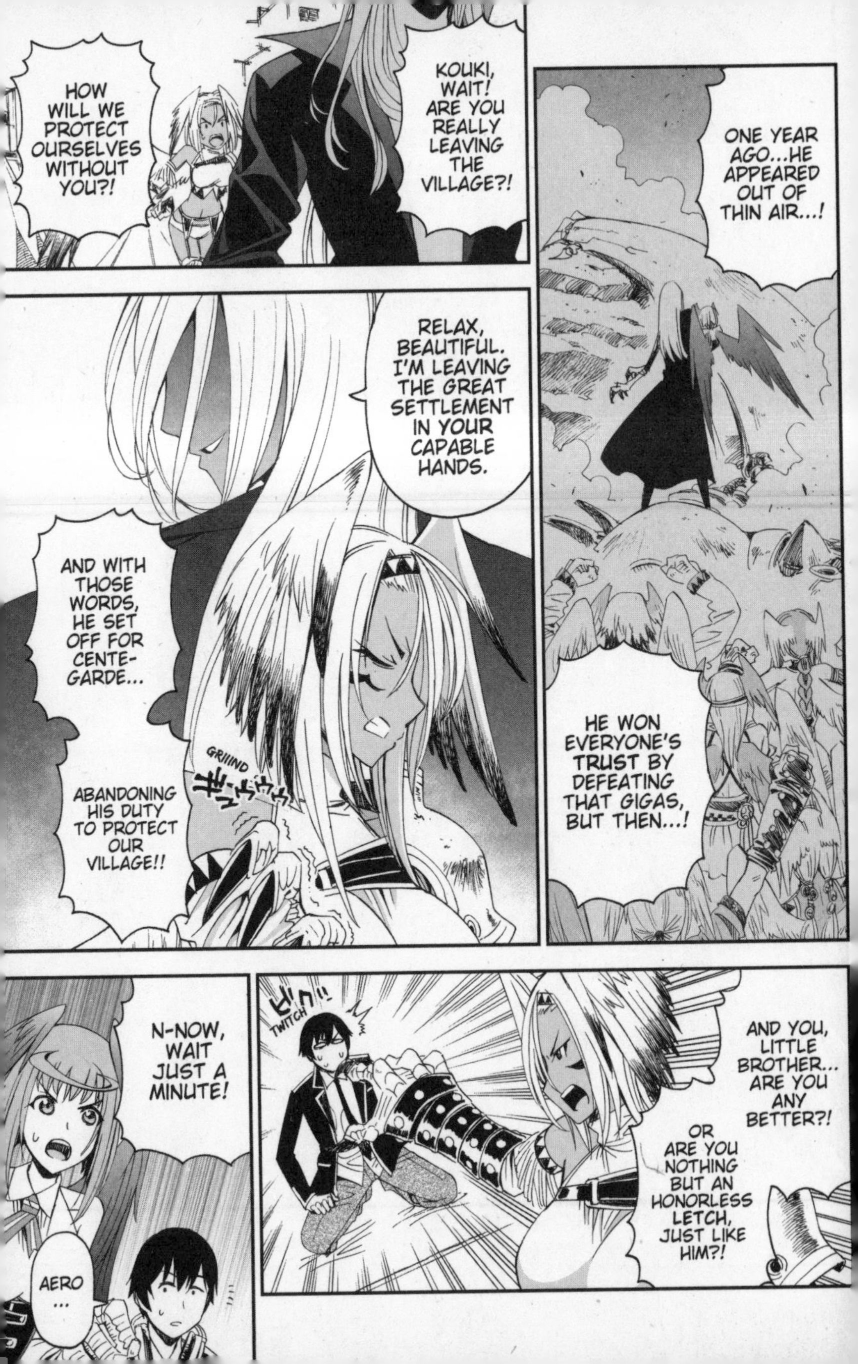
ONE YEAR AGO...HE APPEARED OUT OF THIN AIR...!
HE WON EVERYONE'S TRUST BY DEFEATING THAT GIGAS, BUT THEN...!
KOUKI, WAIT! ARE YOU REALLY LEAVING THE VILLAGE?!
HOW WILL WE PROTECT OURSELVES WITHOUT YOU?!
RELAX, BEAUTIFUL. I'M LEAVING THE GREAT SETTLEMENT IN YOUR CAPABLE HANDS.
AND WITH THOSE WORDS, HE SET OFF FOR CENTE-GARDE...
GRIIND
ABANDONING HIS DUTY TO PROTECT OUR VILLAGE!!
TWITCH
AND YOU, LITTLE BROTHER... ARE YOU ANY BETTER?!
OR ARE YOU NOTHING BUT AN HONORLESS LETCH, JUST LIKE HIM?!
N-NOW, WAIT JUST A MINUTE!
AERO ...

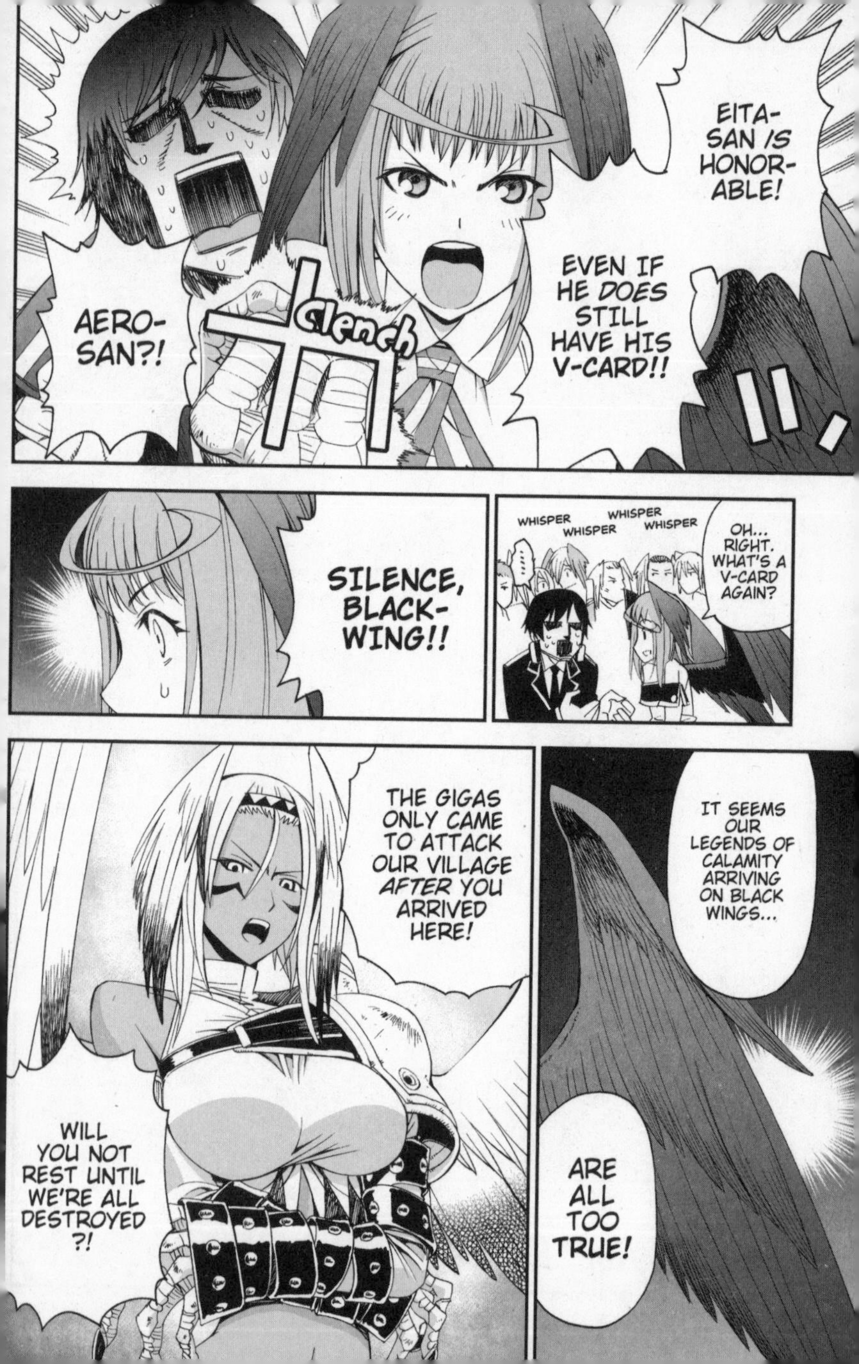
EITA-SAN *IS* HONORABLE!
EVEN IF HE *DOES* STILL HAVE HIS V-CARD!!
Clench
AERO-SAN?!
OH... RIGHT. WHAT'S A V-CARD AGAIN?
WHISPER WHISPER WHISPER WHISPER
SILENCE, BLACK-WING!!
IT SEEMS OUR LEGENDS OF CALAMITY ARRIVING ON BLACK WINGS...
ARE ALL TOO TRUE!
THE GIGAS ONLY CAME TO ATTACK OUR VILLAGE *AFTER* YOU ARRIVED HERE!
WILL YOU NOT REST UNTIL WE'RE ALL DESTROYED?!

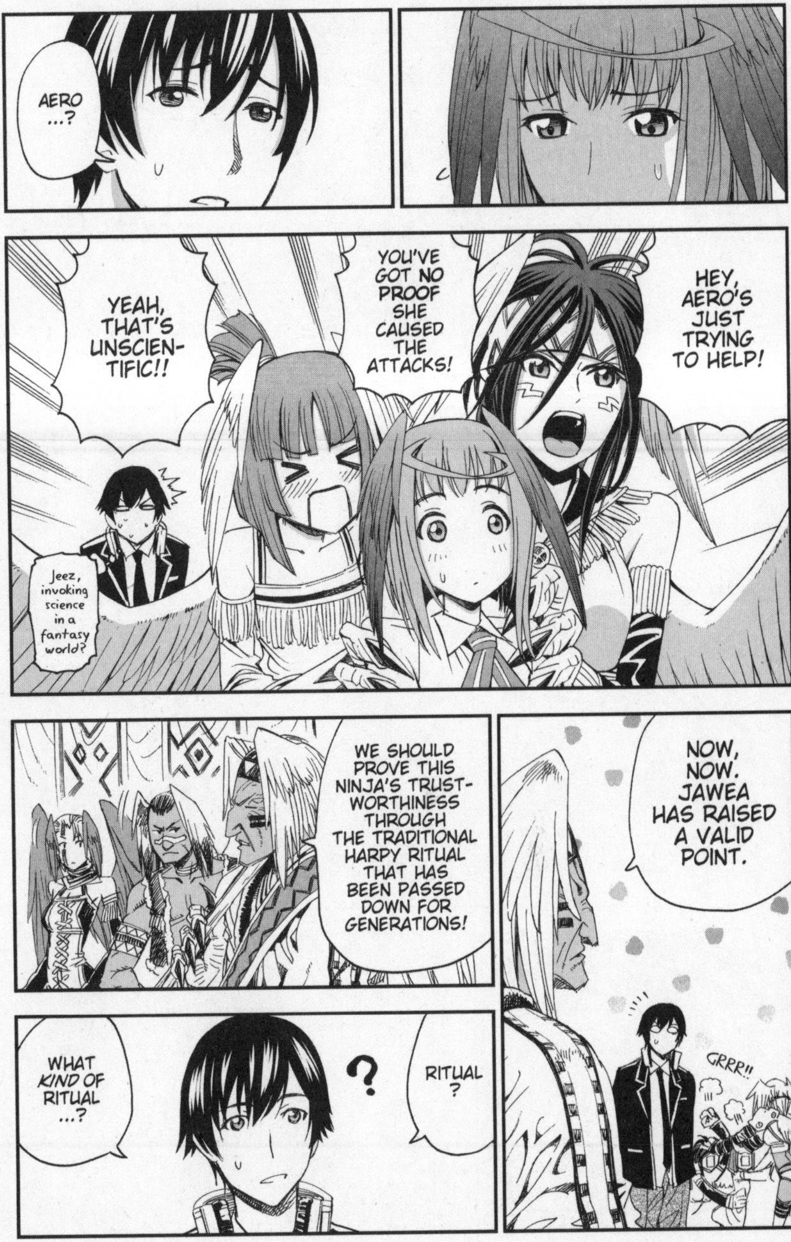
AERO ...?
HEY, AERO'S JUST TRYING TO HELP!
YOU'VE GOT NO PROOF SHE CAUSED THE ATTACKS!
YEAH, THAT'S UNSCIENTIFIC!!
Jeez, invoking science in a fantasy world?
NOW, NOW. JAWEA HAS RAISED A VALID POINT.
GRRR!!
WE SHOULD PROVE THIS NINJA'S TRUST-WORTHINESS THROUGH THE TRADITIONAL HARPY RITUAL THAT HAS BEEN PASSED DOWN FOR GENERATIONS!
RITUAL?
?
WHAT KIND OF RITUAL ...?

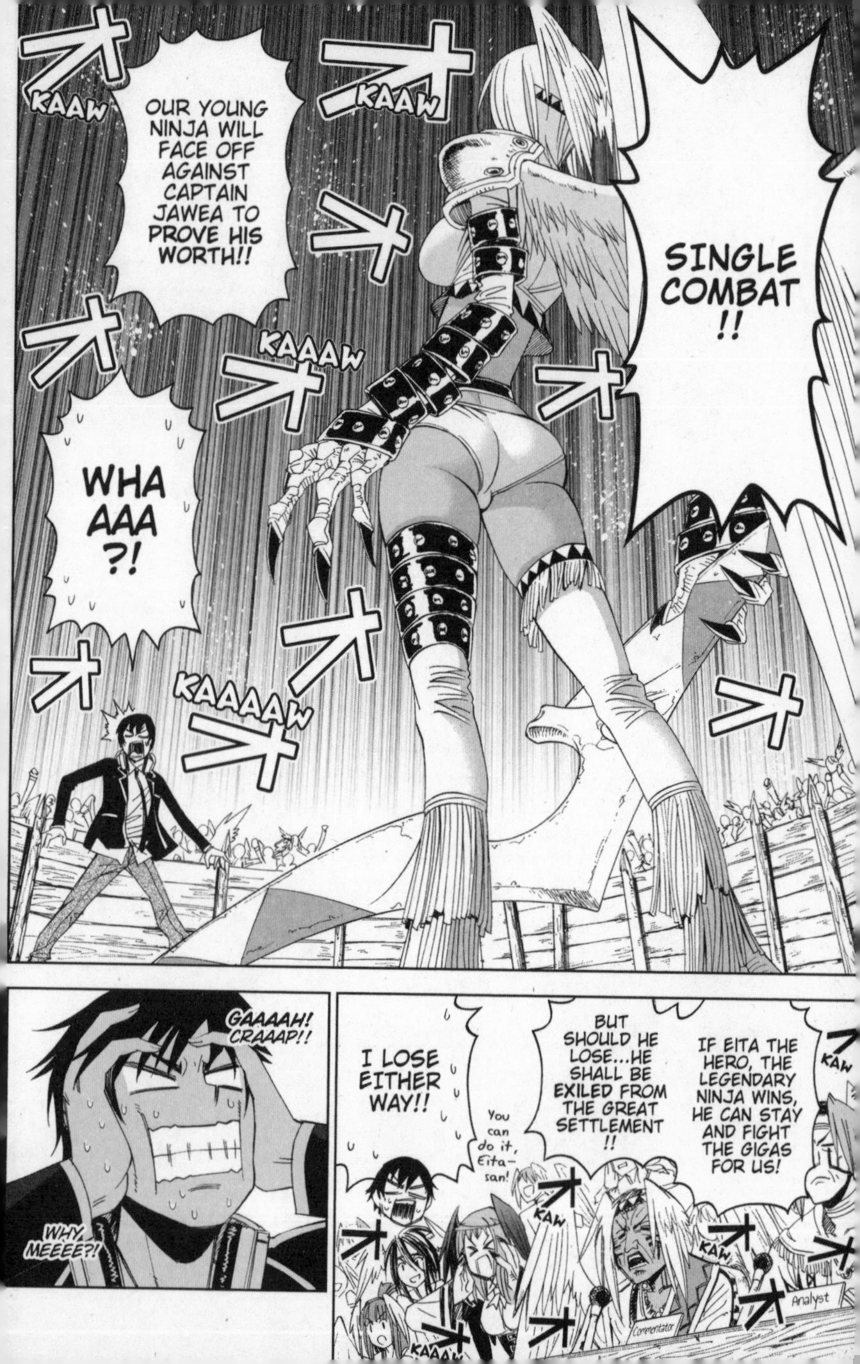
KAAW
KAAW
OUR YOUNG NINJA WILL FACE OFF AGAINST CAPTAIN JAWEA TO PROVE HIS WORTH!!
SINGLE COMBAT !!
KAAAW
WHA AAA ?!
KAAAAAW
KAW
IF EITA THE HERO, THE LEGENDARY NINJA WINS, HE CAN STAY AND FIGHT THE GIGAS FOR US!
BUT SHOULD HE LOSE...HE SHALL BE EXILED FROM THE GREAT SETTLEMENT !!
I LOSE EITHER WAY!!
You can do it, Eita-san!
KAW
KAW
Analyst
Commentator
GAAAAH! CRAAAP!!
WHY MEEEE?!

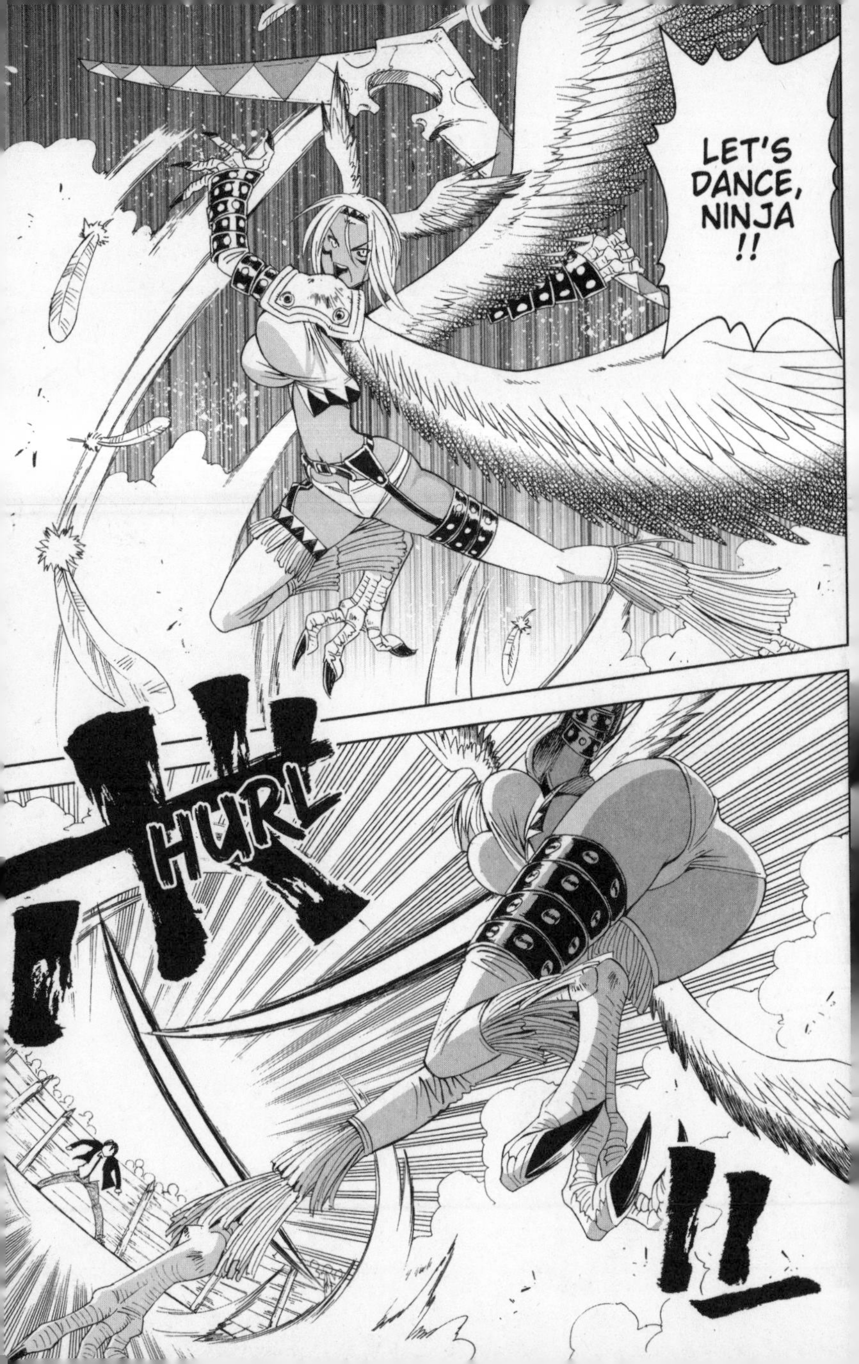
LET'S DANCE, NINJA !!
HURL

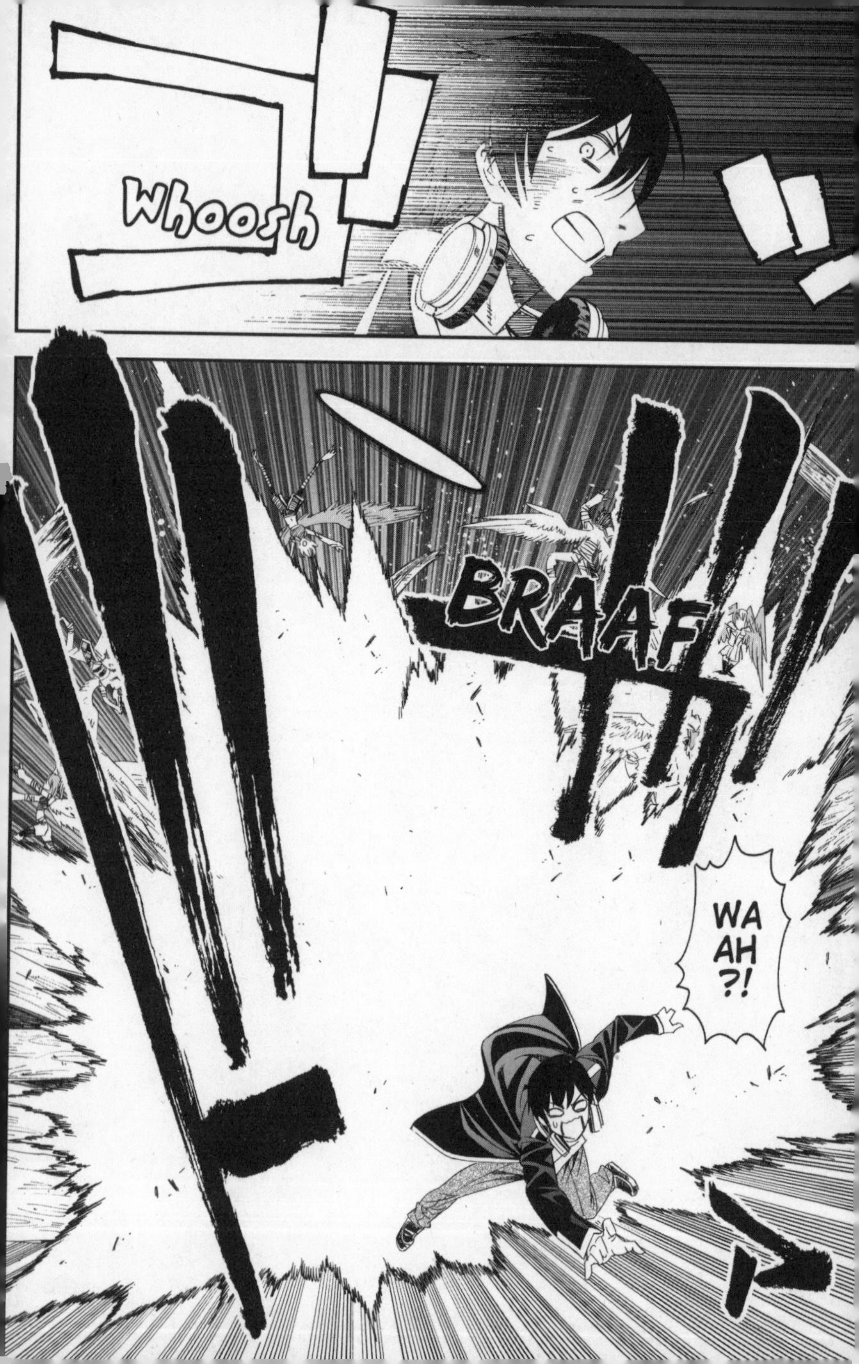
Whoosh
BRAAF
WAAH?!

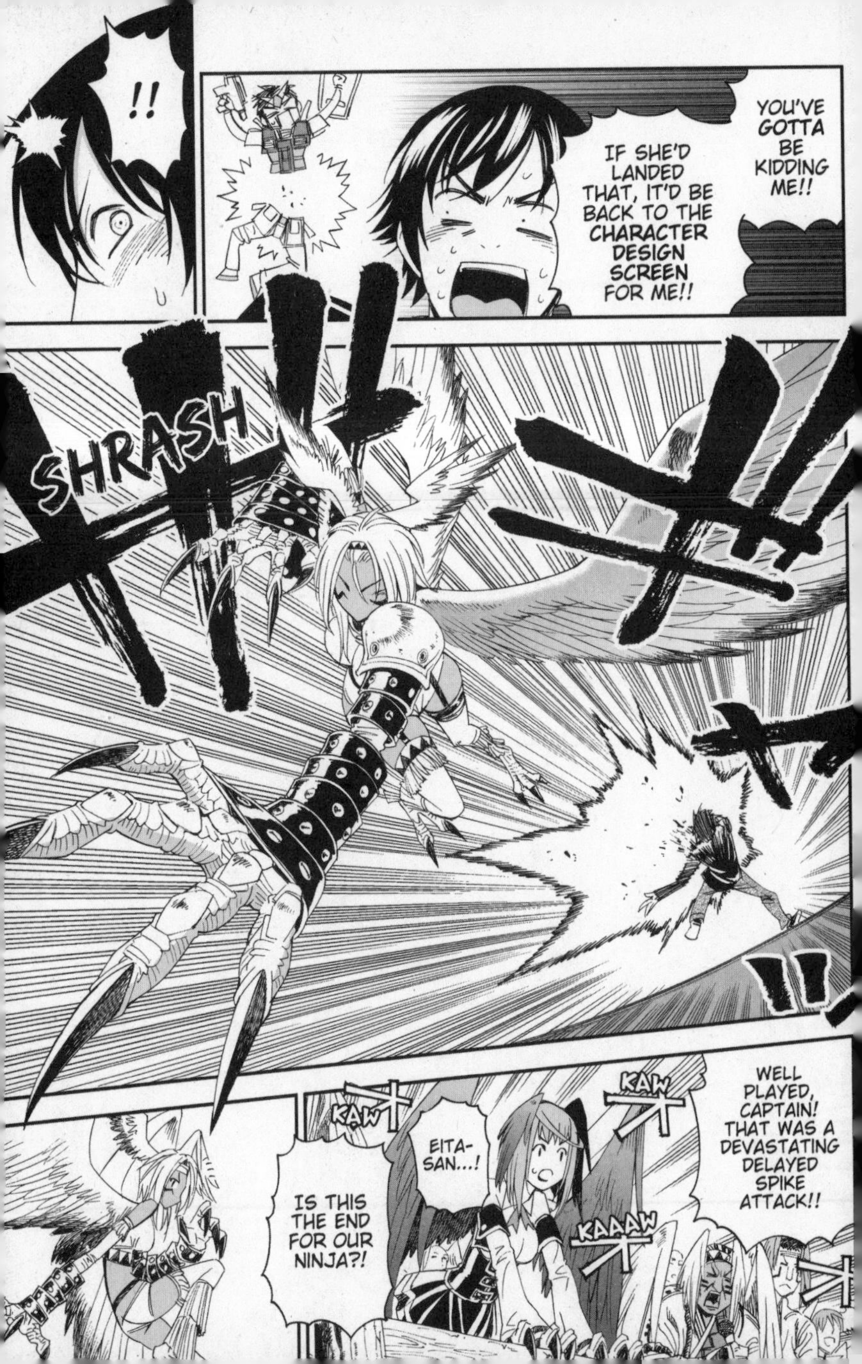
YOU'VE GOTTA BE KIDDING ME!!
IF SHE'D LANDED THAT, IT'D BE BACK TO THE CHARACTER DESIGN SCREEN FOR ME!!
!!
SHRASH
!!
KAW
WELL PLAYED, CAPTAIN! THAT WAS A DEVASTATING DELAYED SPIKE ATTACK!!
KAW
EITA-SAN...!
KAAAW
IS THIS THE END FOR OUR NINJA?!

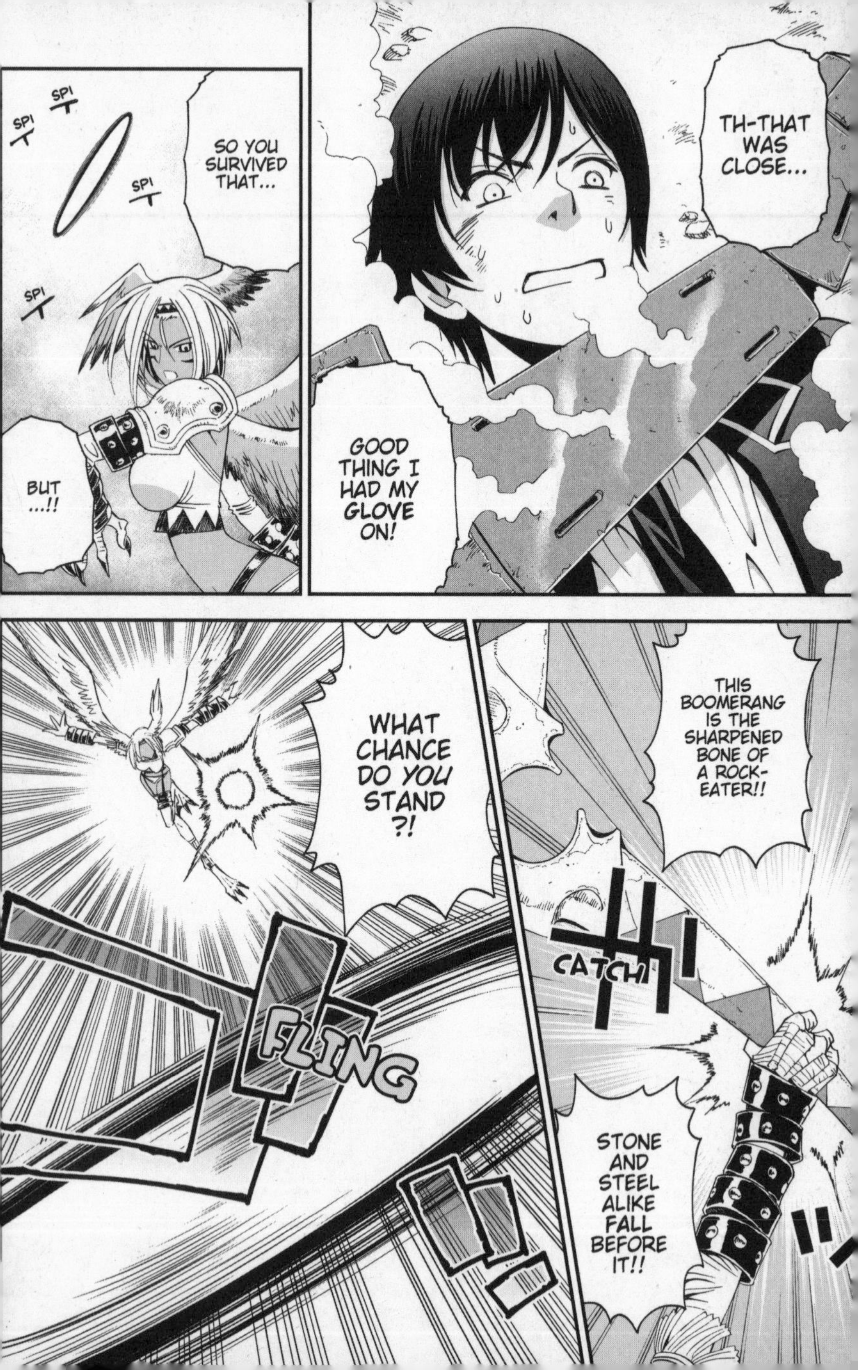
TH-THAT WAS CLOSE...
GOOD THING I HAD MY GLOVE ON!
SPI
SPI
SO YOU SURVIVED THAT...
SPI
SPI
BUT ...!!
THIS BOOMERANG IS THE SHARPENED BONE OF A ROCK-EATER!!
CATCH
STONE AND STEEL ALIKE FALL BEFORE IT!!
WHAT CHANCE DO YOU STAND ?!
FLING

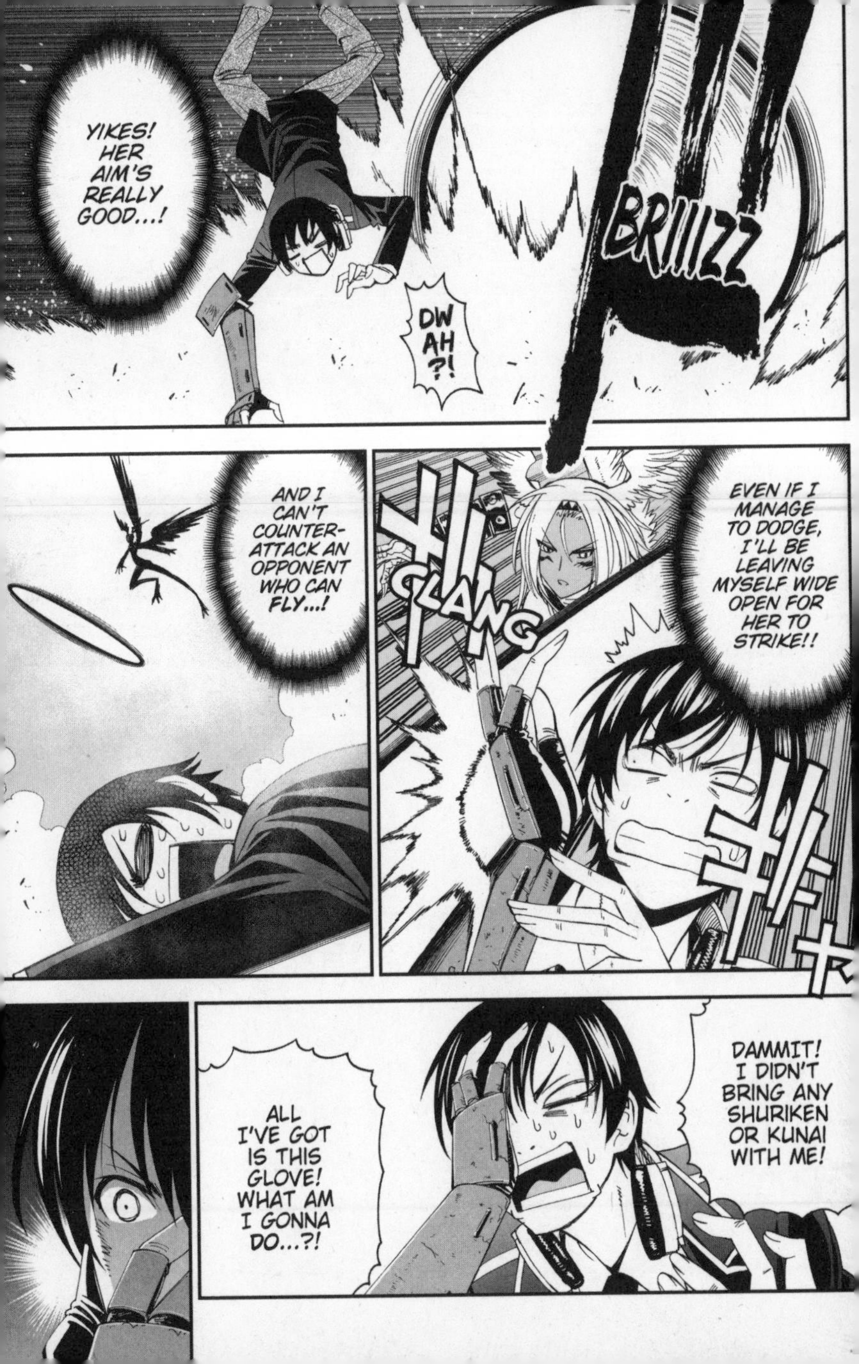
BRIIIZZ
DW AH?!
YIKES! HER AIM'S REALLY GOOD...!
EVEN IF I MANAGE TO DODGE, I'LL BE LEAVING MYSELF WIDE OPEN FOR HER TO STRIKE!!
CLANG
AND I CAN'T COUNTER-ATTACK AN OPPONENT WHO CAN FLY...!
DAMMIT! I DIDN'T BRING ANY SHURIKEN OR KUNAI WITH ME!
ALL I'VE GOT IS THIS GLOVE! WHAT AM I GONNA DO...?!

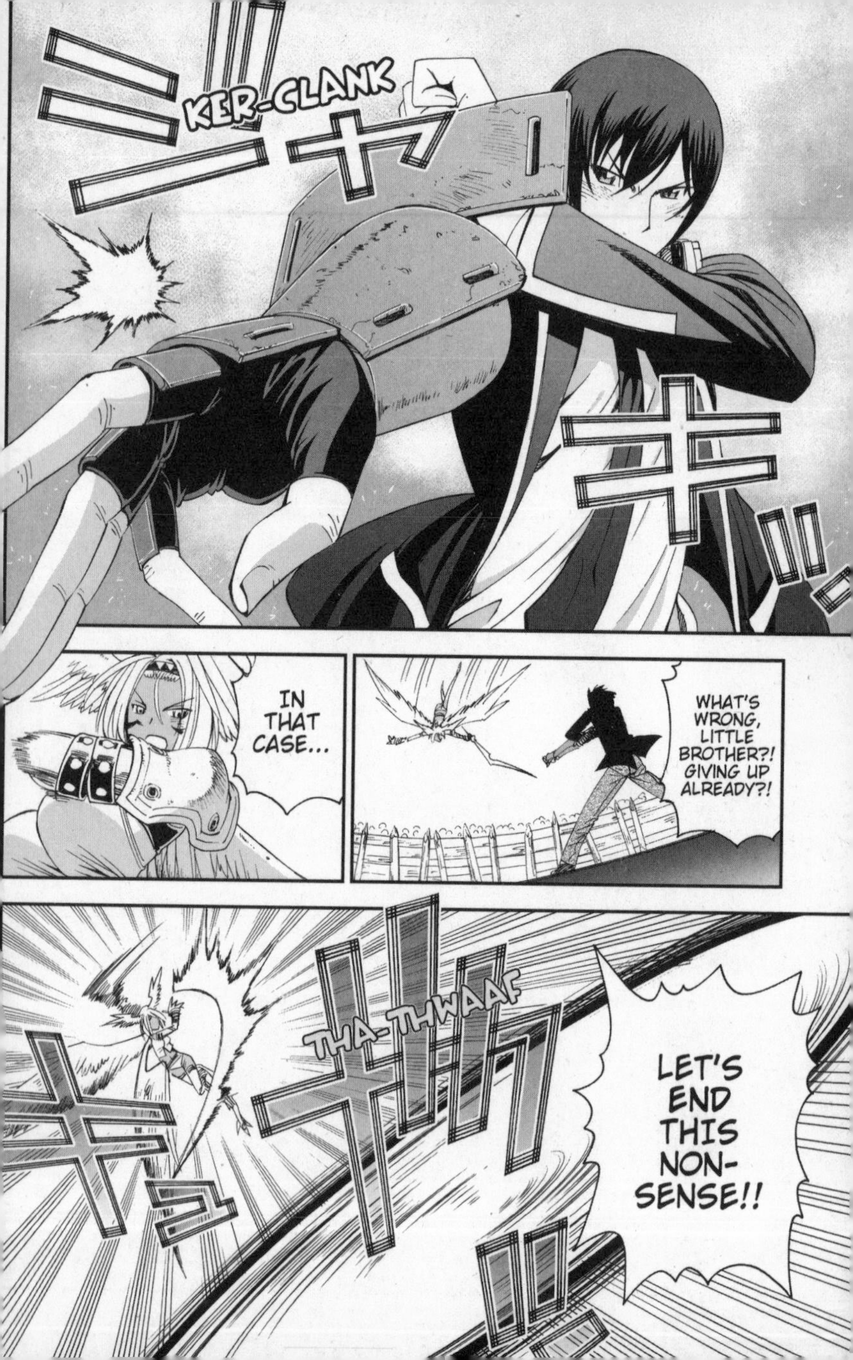
KER-CLANK
WHAT'S WRONG, LITTLE BROTHER?! GIVING UP ALREADY?!
IN THAT CASE...
LET'S END THIS NON-SENSE!!
THA-THWAAF

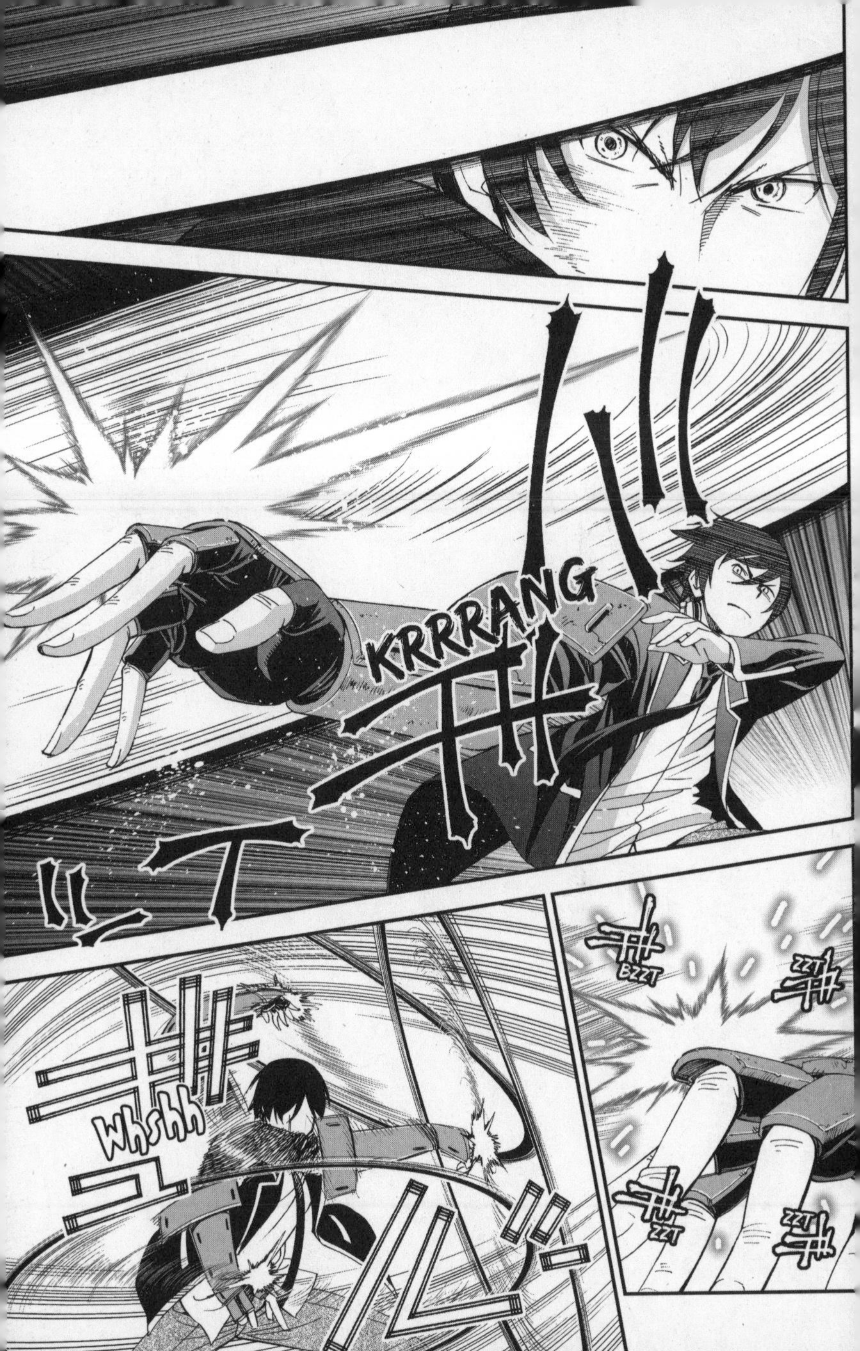
KRRRANG
ZZT
BZZT
ZZT
ZZT
Whshh

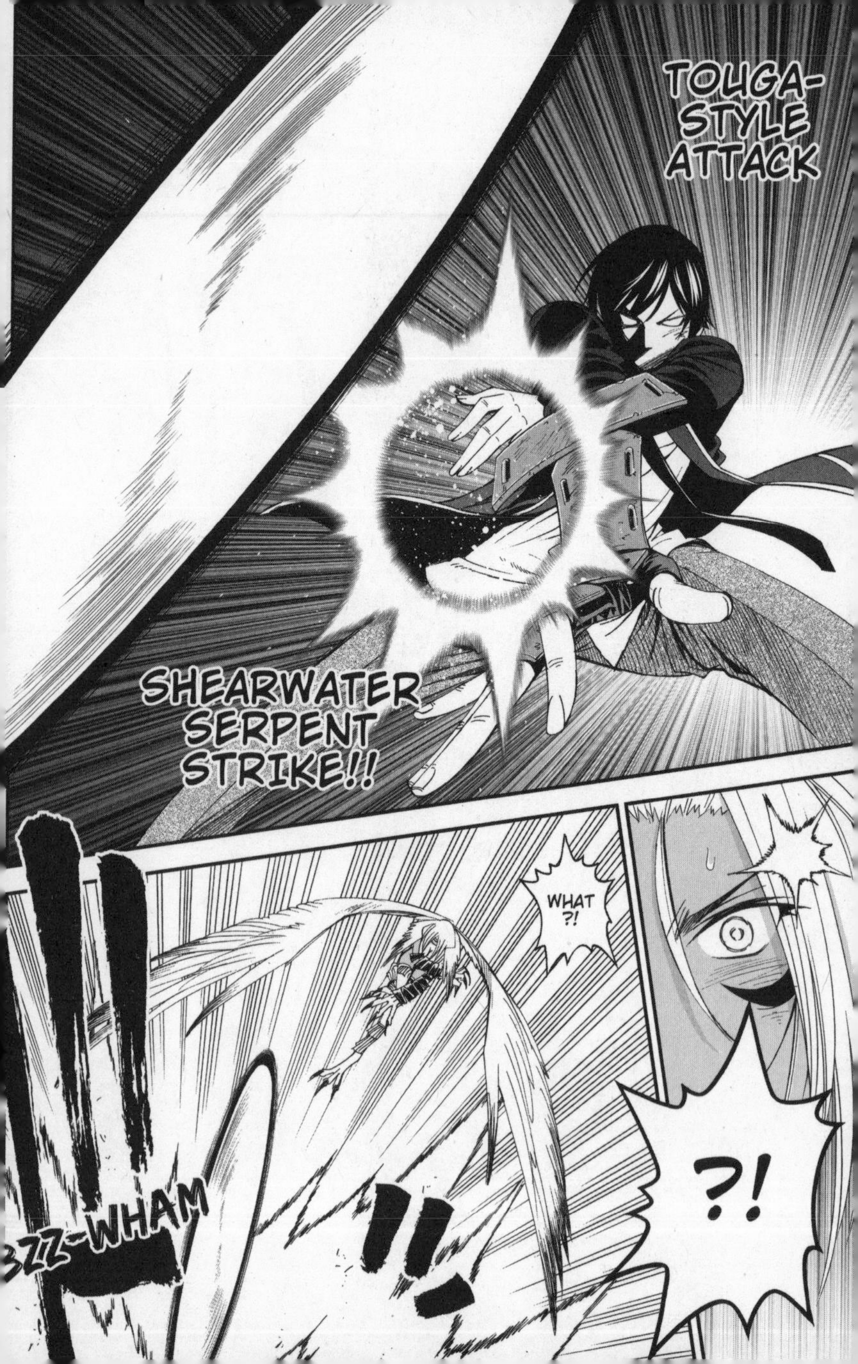
TOUGA-STYLE ATTACK
SHEARWATER SERPENT STRIKE!!
WHAT ?!
?!
ZZ-WHAM
!!

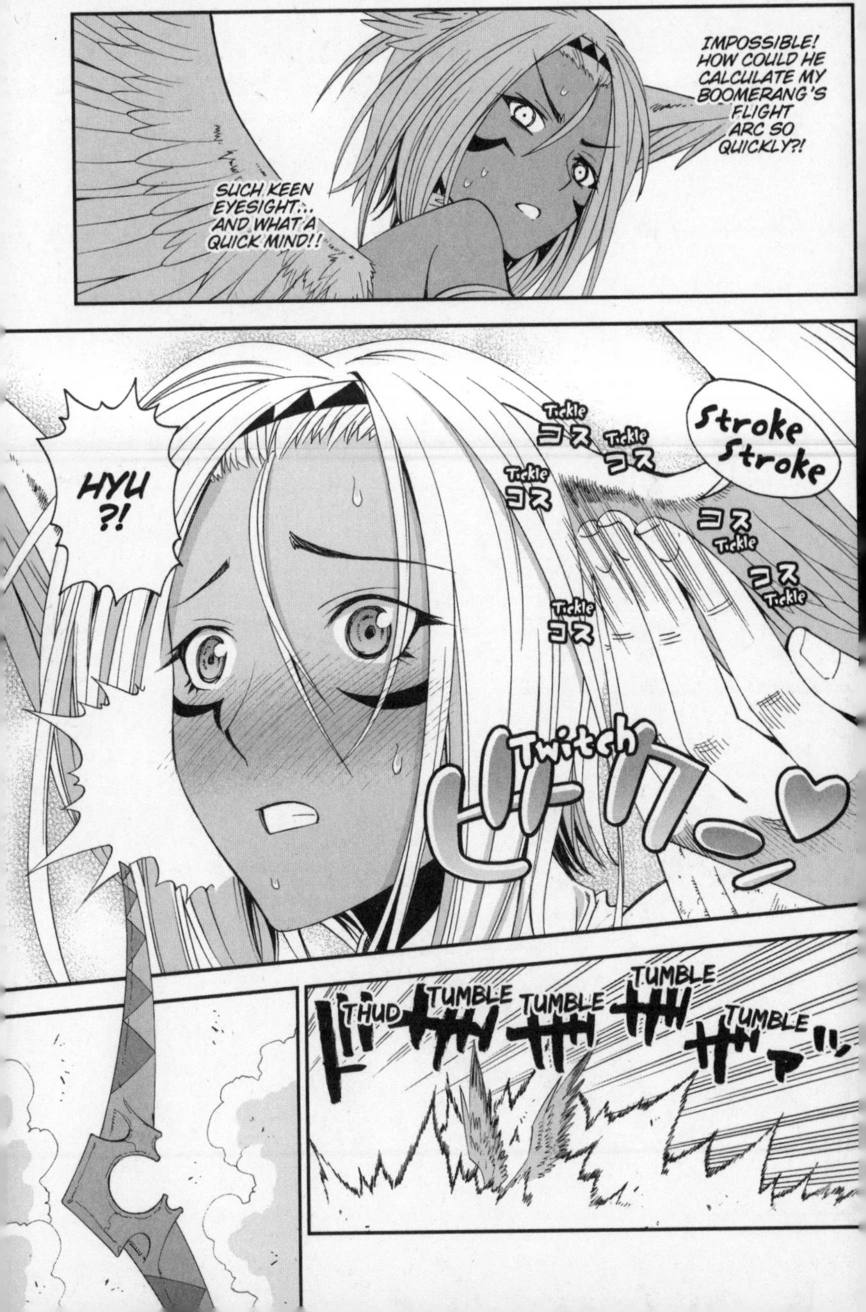

IMPOSSIBLE! HOW COULD HE CALCULATE MY BOOMERANG'S FLIGHT ARC SO QUICKLY?!
SUCH KEEN EYESIGHT... AND WHAT A QUICK MIND!!
Stroke Stroke
Tickle コス
Tickle コス
Tickle コス
Tickle コス
Tickle コス
Tickle コス
Twitch
HYU ?!
THUD
TUMBLE
TUMBLE
TUMBLE
TUMBLE

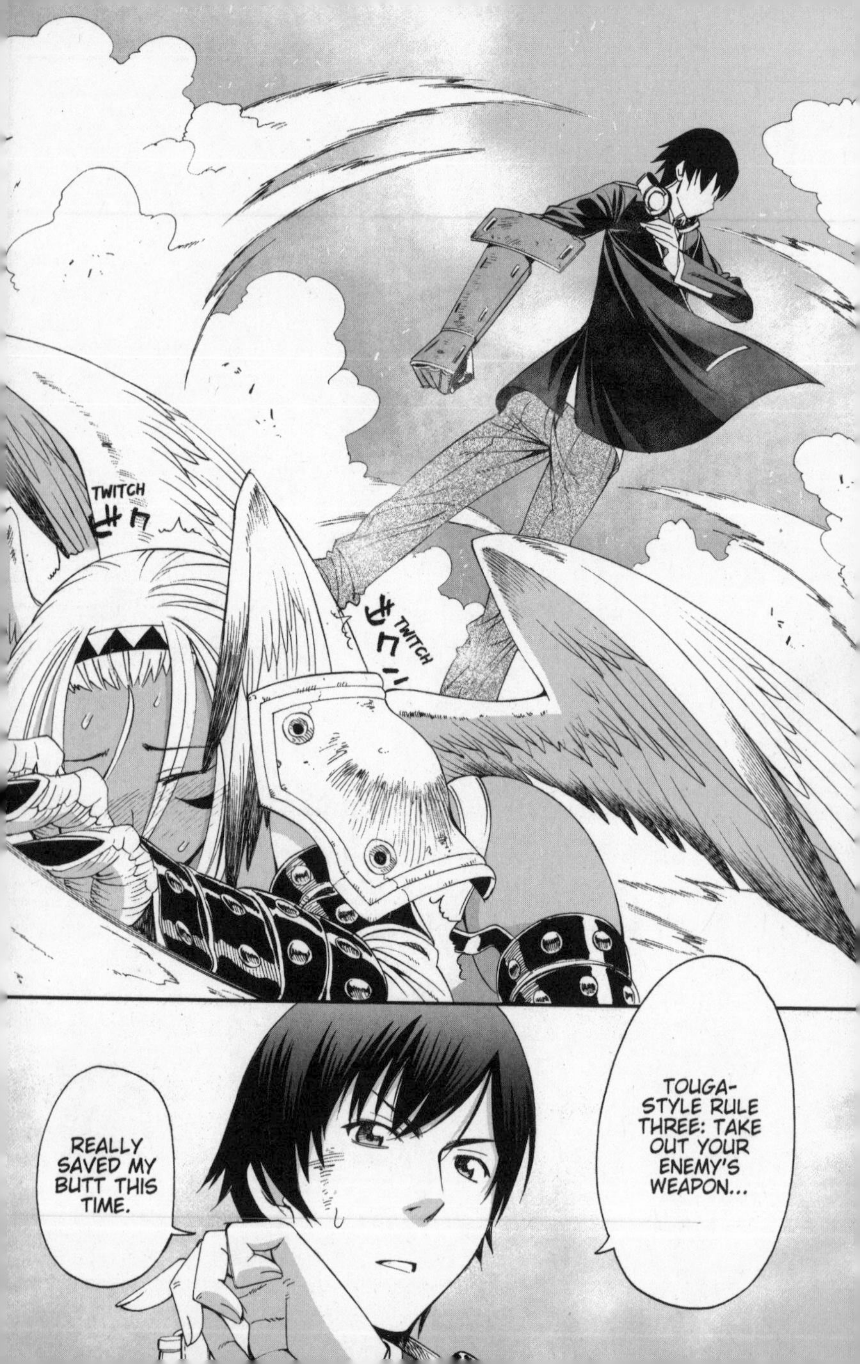
TWITCH
TWITCH
TOUGA-STYLE RULE THREE: TAKE OUT YOUR ENEMY'S WEAPON...
REALLY SAVED MY BUTT THIS TIME.

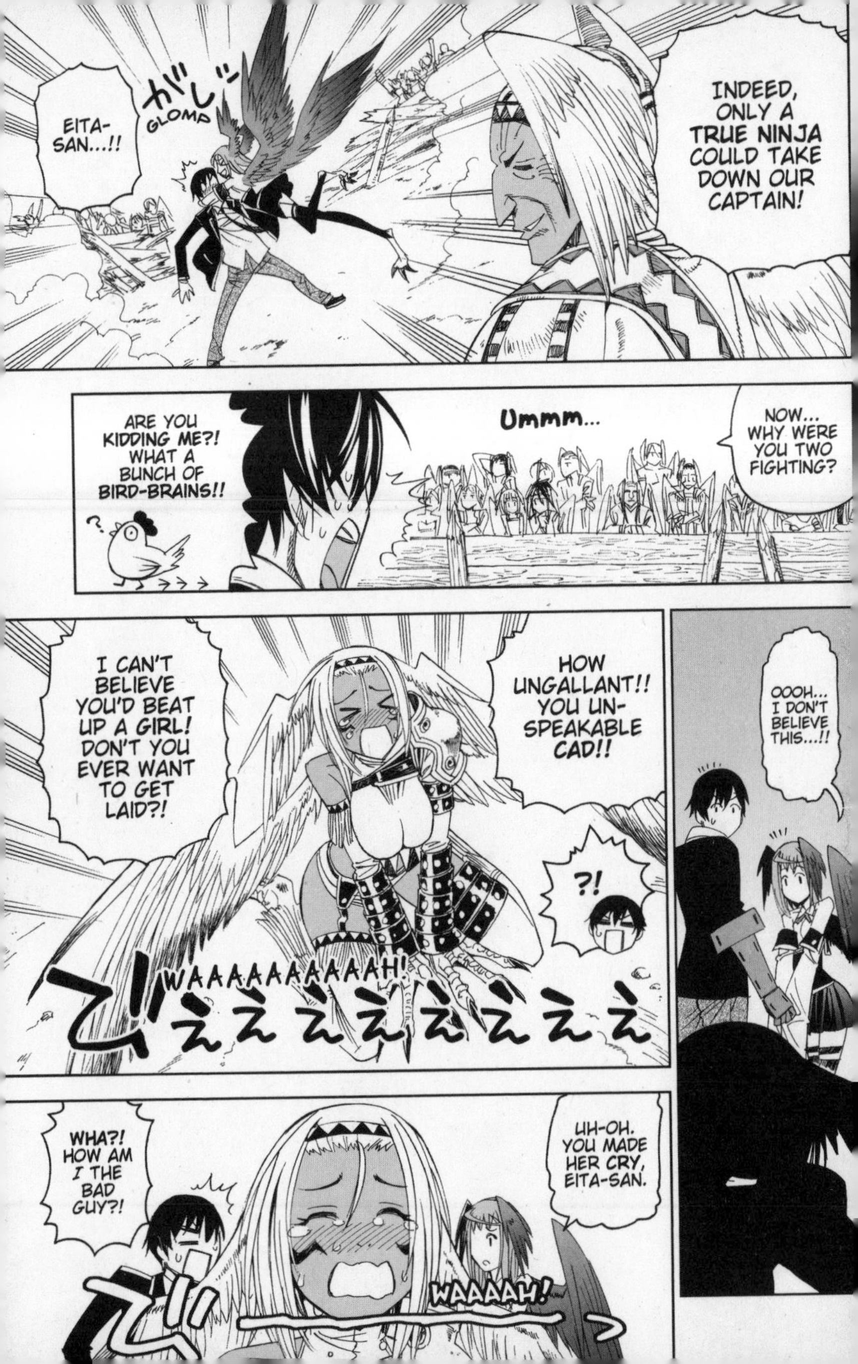
INDEED, ONLY A TRUE NINJA COULD TAKE DOWN OUR CAPTAIN!
GLOMP
EITA-SAN...!!
NOW... WHY WERE YOU TWO FIGHTING?
Ummm...
ARE YOU KIDDING ME?! WHAT A BUNCH OF BIRD-BRAINS!!
OOOH... I DON'T BELIEVE THIS...!!
HOW UNGALLANT!! YOU UN-SPEAKABLE CAD!!
I CAN'T BELIEVE YOU'D BEAT UP A GIRL! DON'T YOU EVER WANT TO GET LAID?!
?!
WAAAAAAAAAAH!
UH-OH. YOU MADE HER CRY, EITA-SAN.
WHA?! HOW AM I THE BAD GUY?!
WAAAAH!

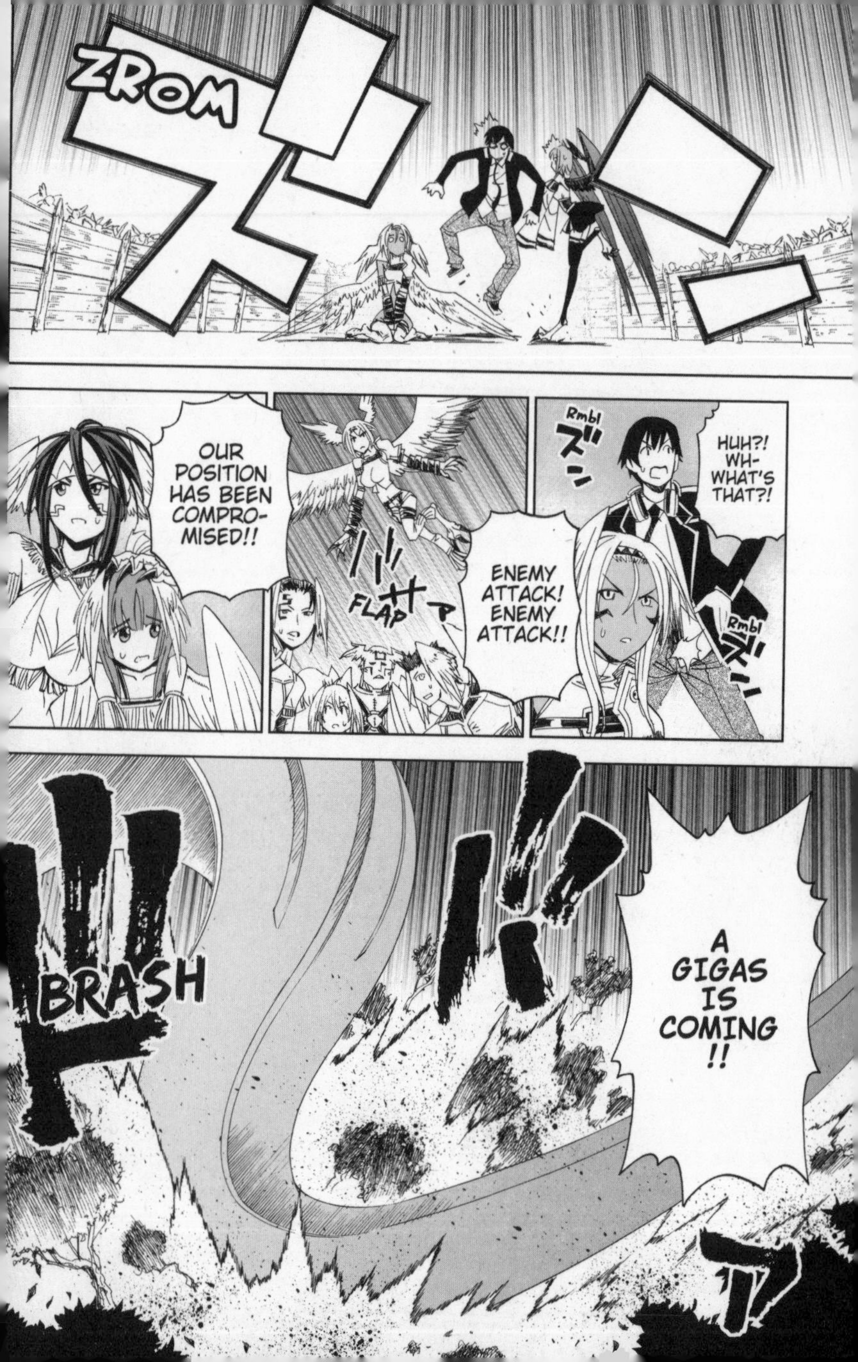
ZROM
Rmbl
HUH?! WH-WHAT'S THAT?!
Rmbl
ENEMY ATTACK! ENEMY ATTACK!!
FLAP
OUR POSITION HAS BEEN COMPRO-MISED!!
A GIGAS IS COMING!!
BRASH

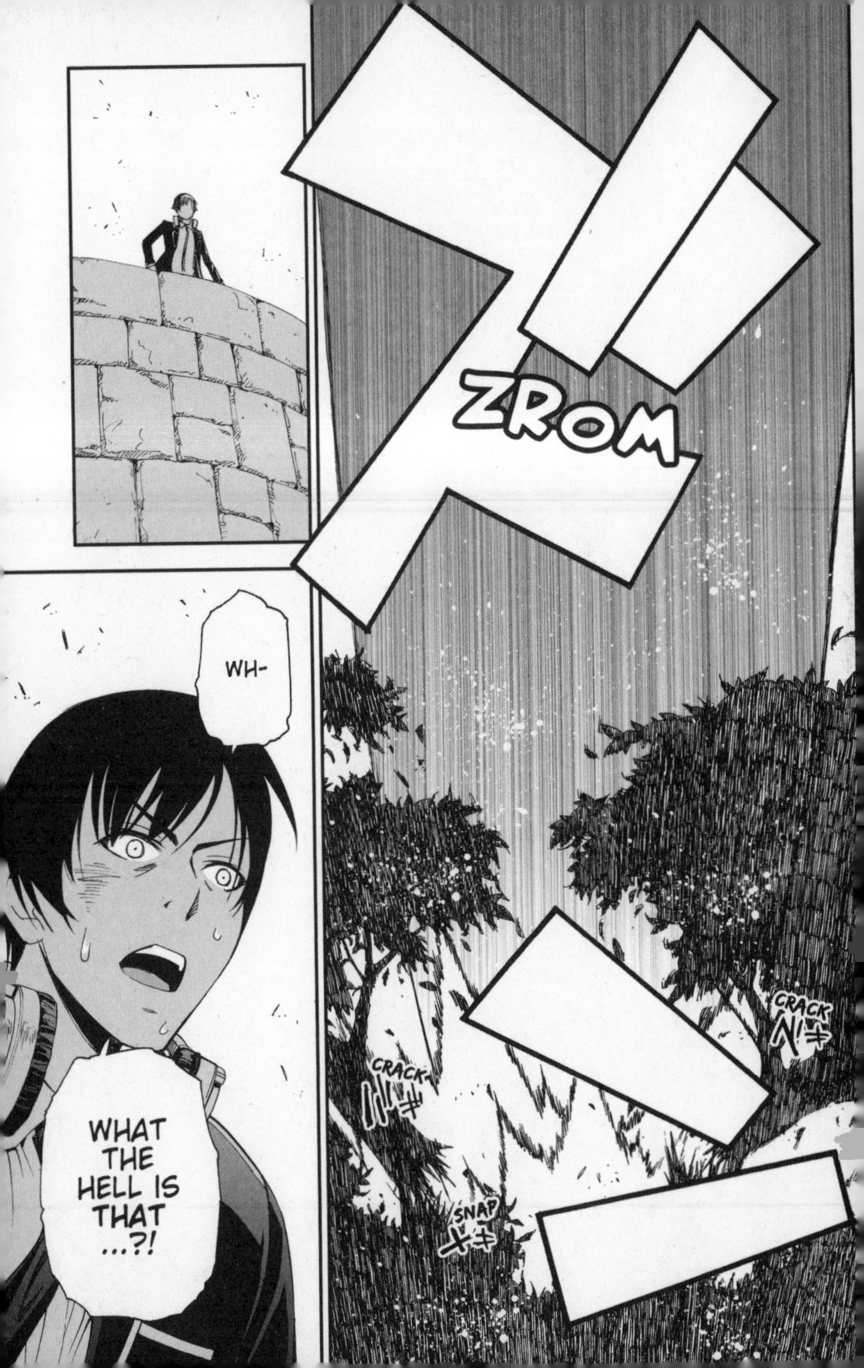
ZROM
CRACK
CRACK
SNAP
WH-
WHAT THE HELL IS THAT ...?!

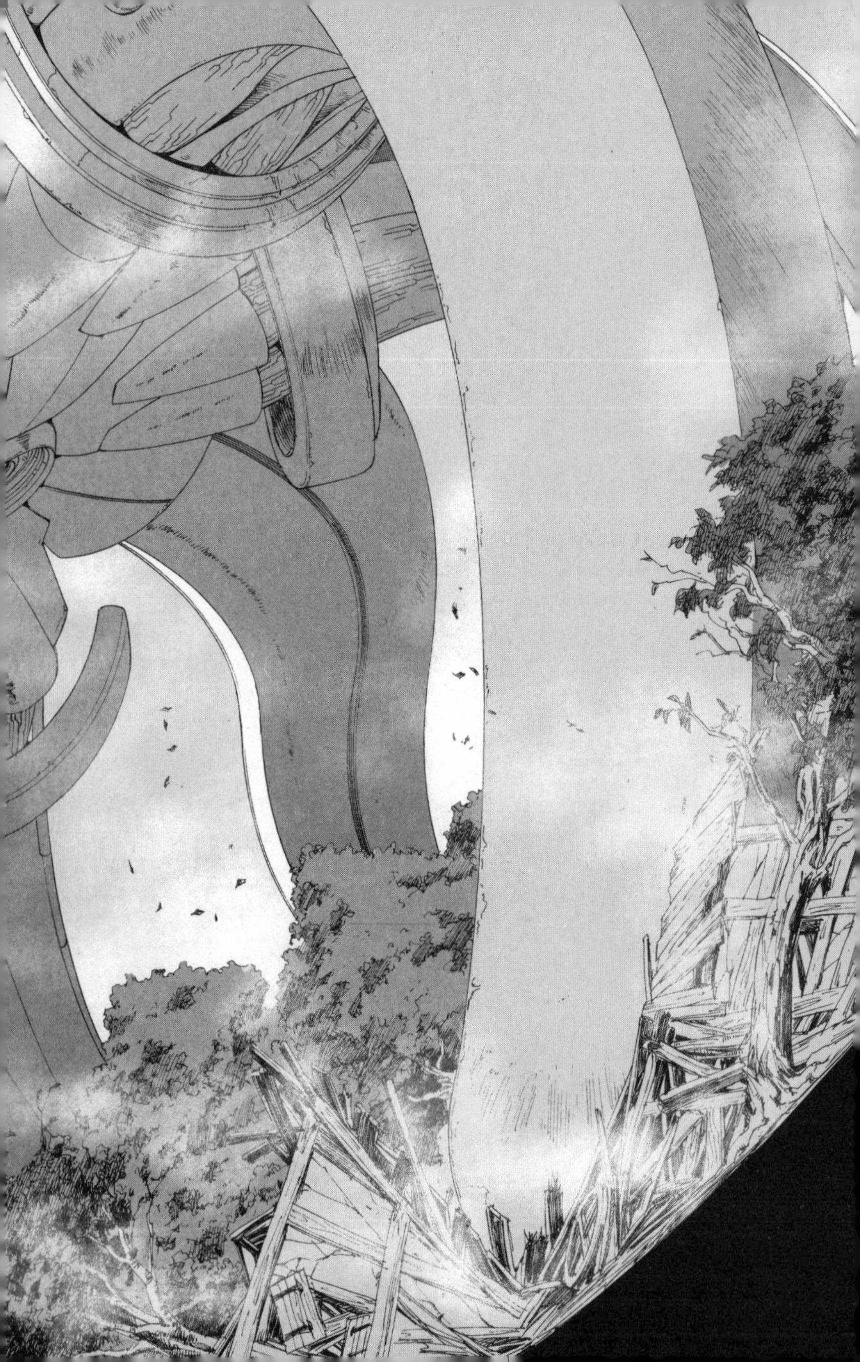

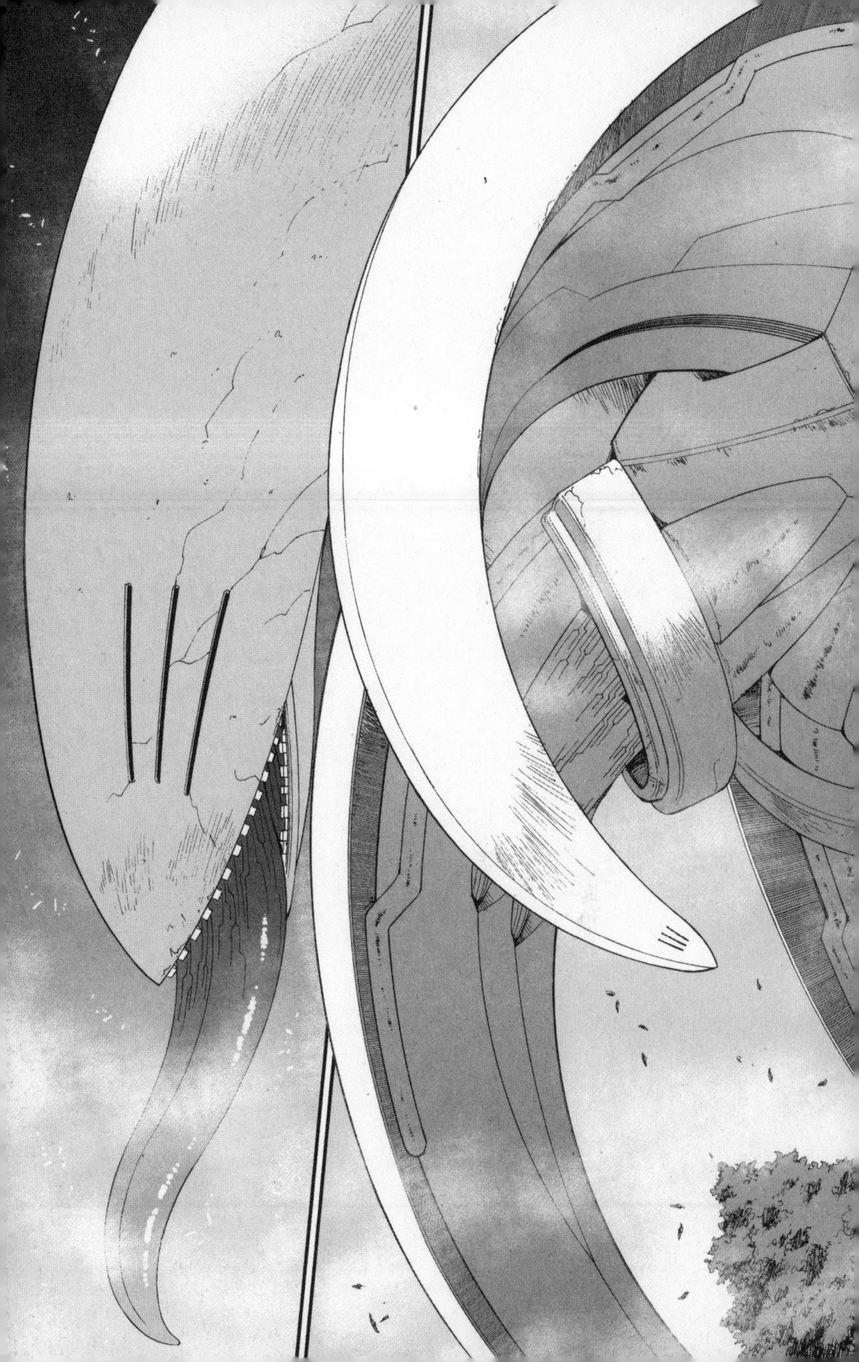

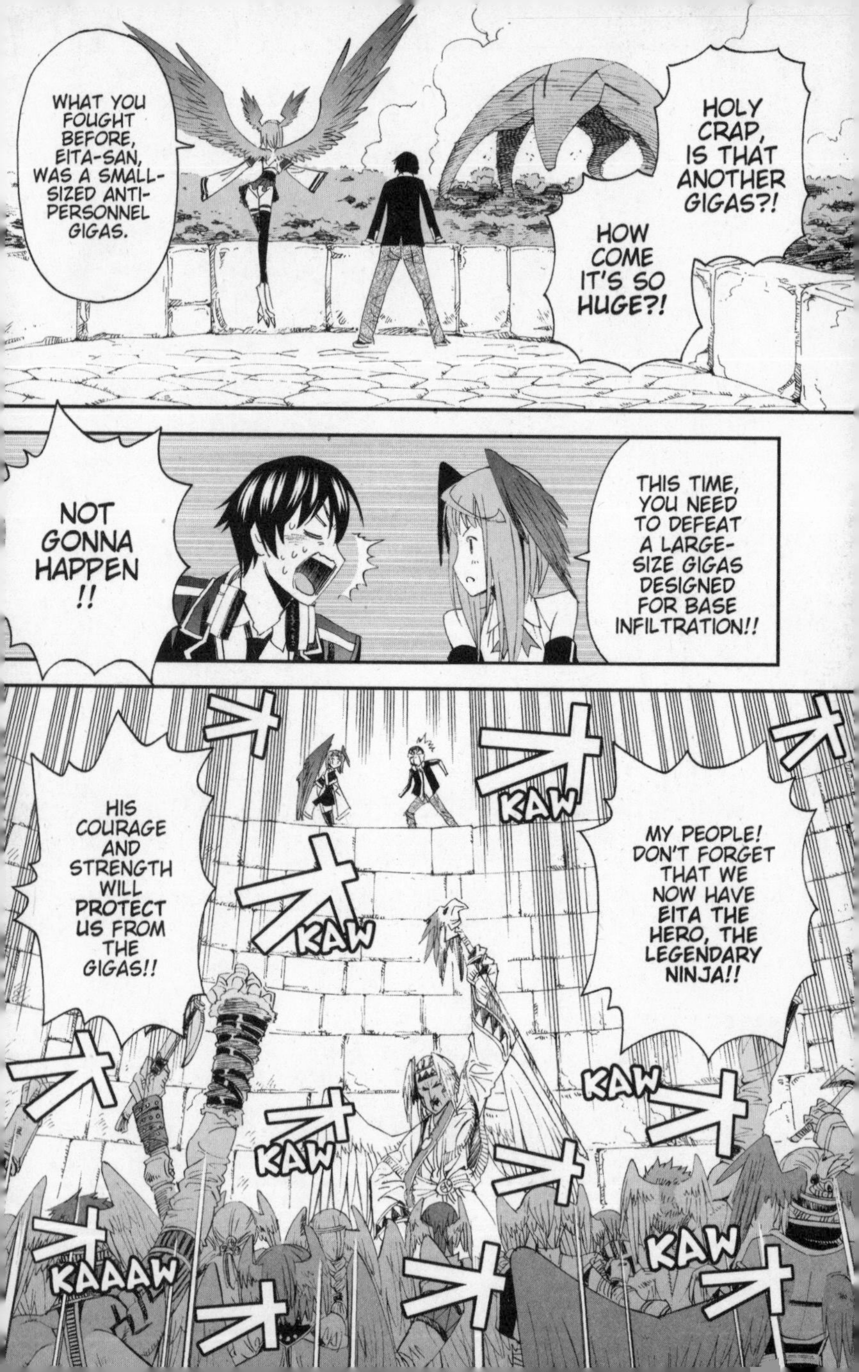
HOLY CRAP, IS THAT ANOTHER GIGAS?!
HOW COME IT'S SO HUGE?!
WHAT YOU FOUGHT BEFORE, EITA-SAN, WAS A SMALL-SIZED ANTI-PERSONNEL GIGAS.
THIS TIME, YOU NEED TO DEFEAT A LARGE-SIZE GIGAS DESIGNED FOR BASE INFILTRATION!!
NOT GONNA HAPPEN!!
MY PEOPLE! DON'T FORGET THAT WE NOW HAVE EITA THE HERO, THE LEGENDARY NINJA!!
HIS COURAGE AND STRENGTH WILL PROTECT US FROM THE GIGAS!!
KAW
KAW
KAW
KAW
KAW
KAAAW

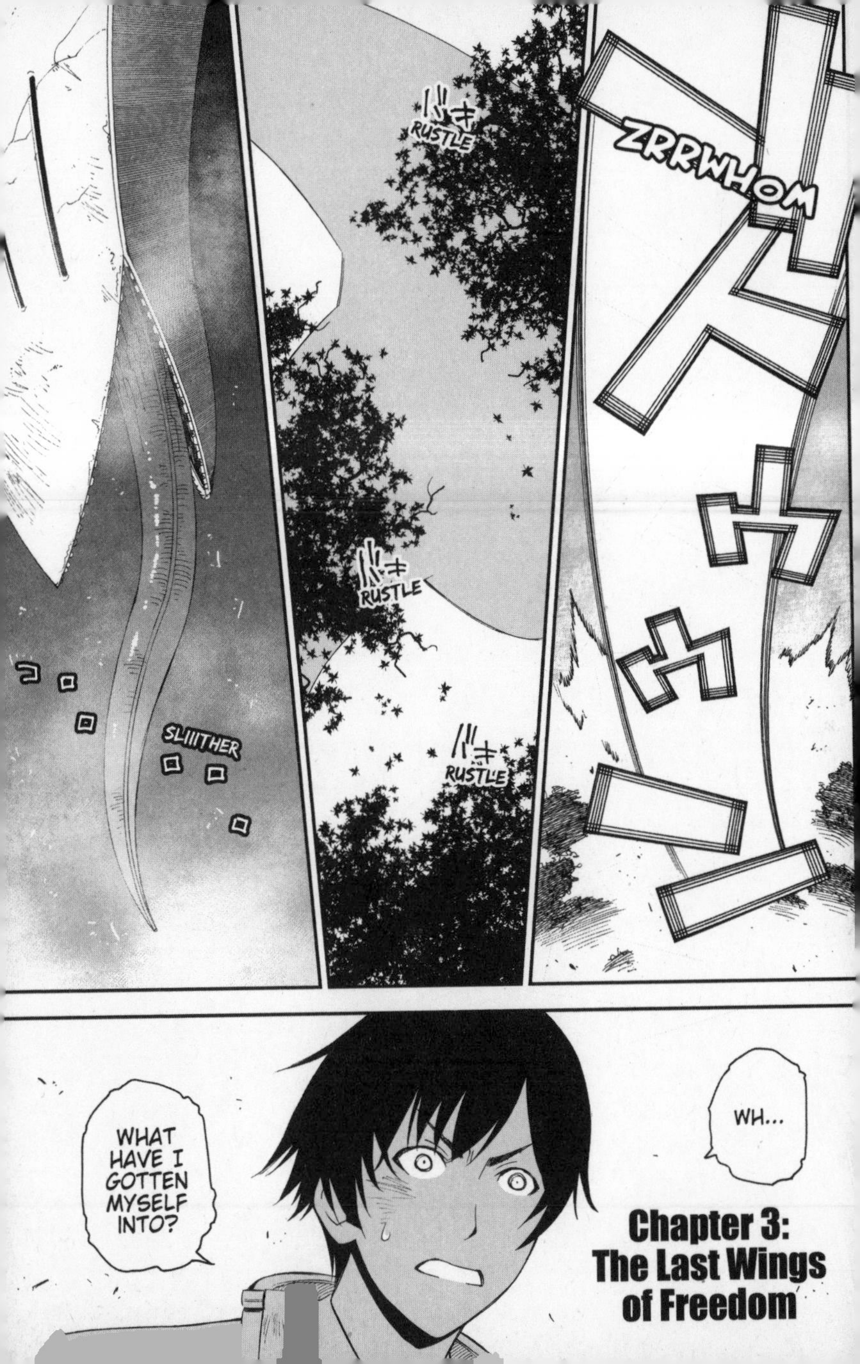
ZRRWHOM
バキ RUSTLE
バキ RUSTLE
バキ RUSTLE
SLIIITHER
WH...
Chapter 3: The Last Wings of Freedom
WHAT HAVE I GOTTEN MYSELF INTO?

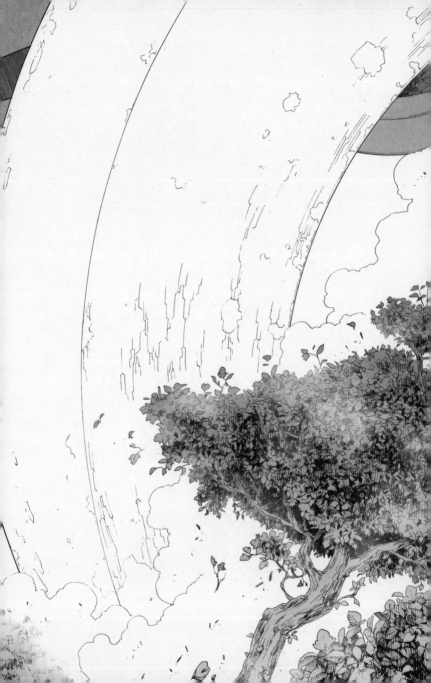

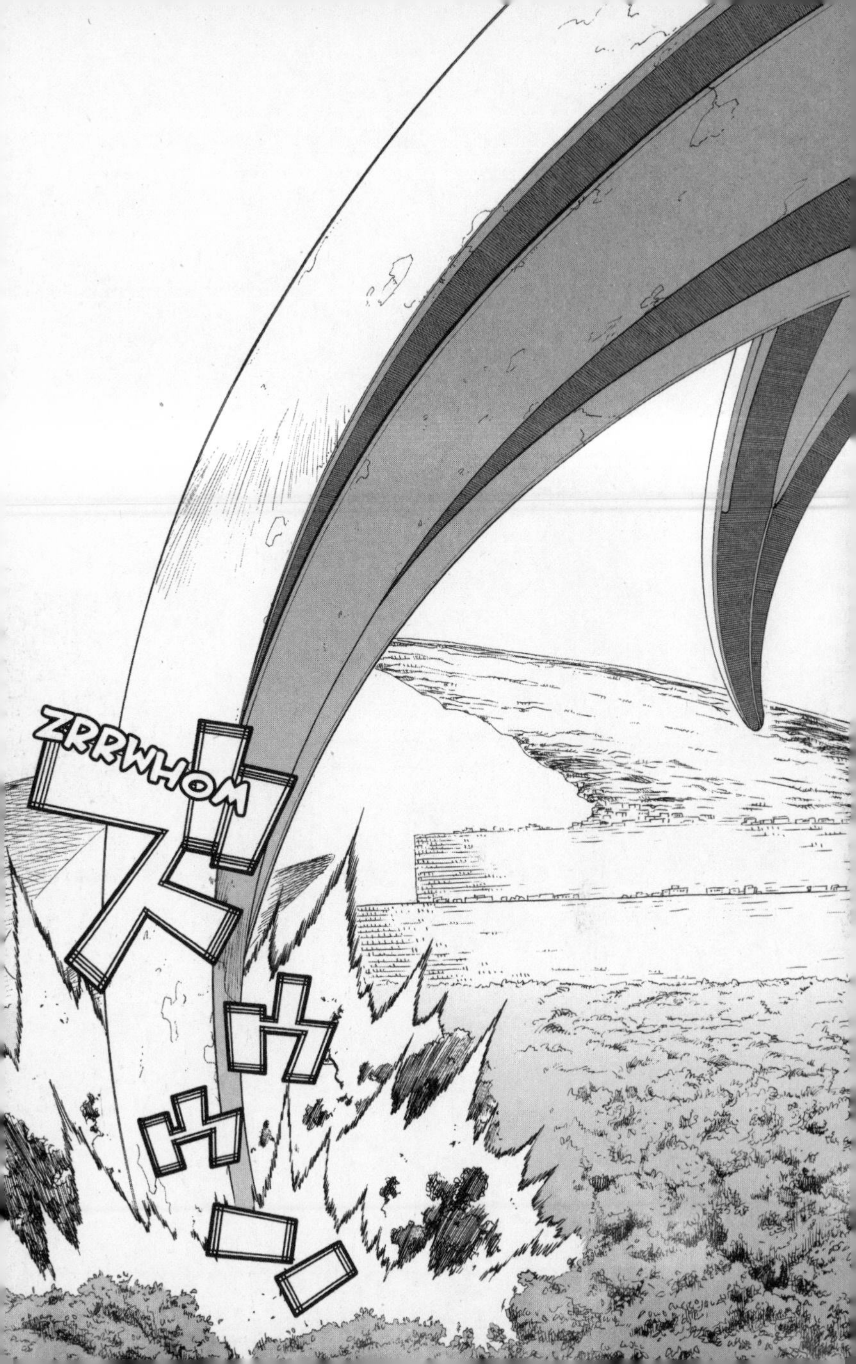
ZRRWHOM
ズドドン

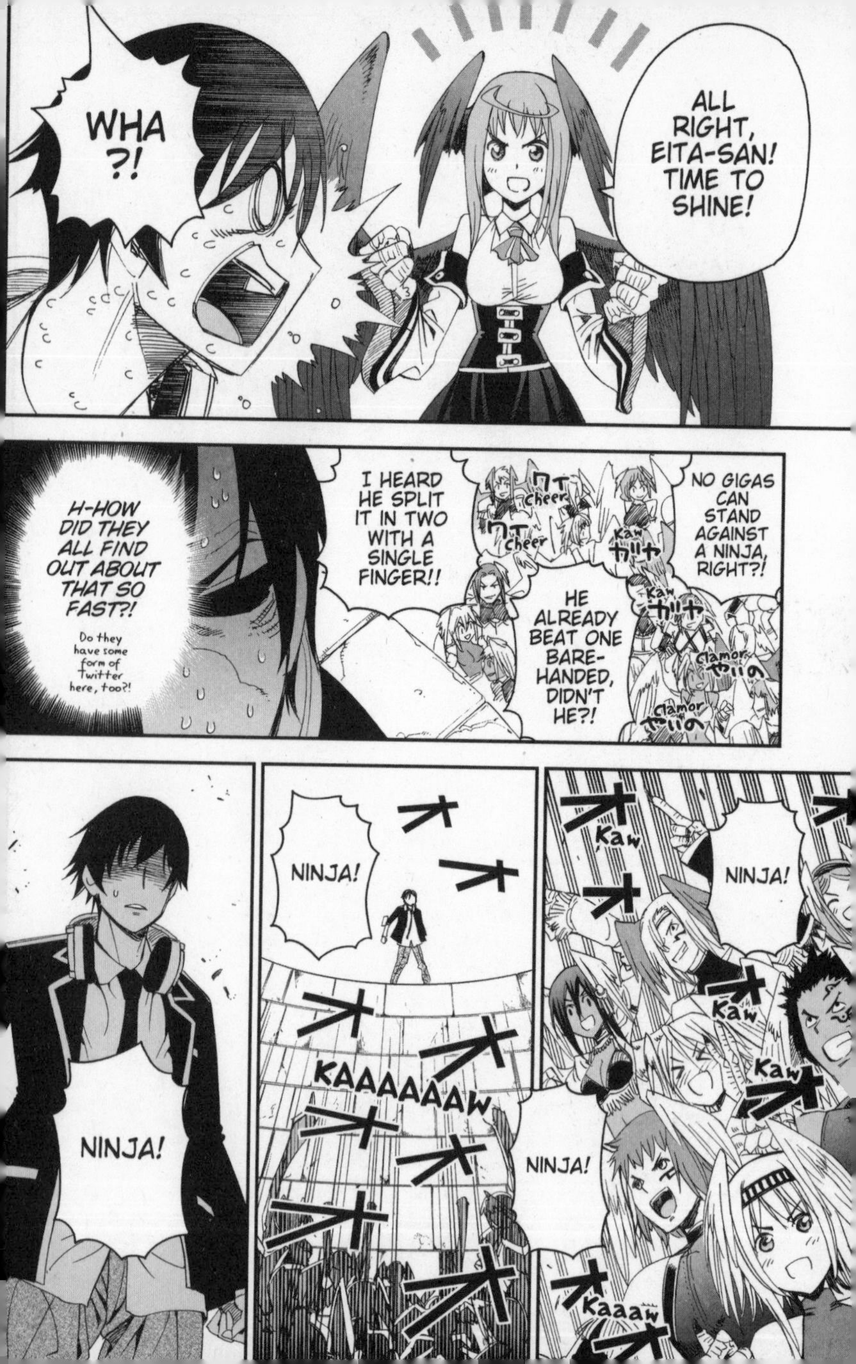
ALL RIGHT, EITA-SAN! TIME TO SHINE!
WHA ?!
NO GIGAS CAN STAND AGAINST A NINJA, RIGHT?!
Cheer
Cheer
Kaw
I HEARD HE SPLIT IT IN TWO WITH A SINGLE FINGER!!
Kaw
HE ALREADY BEAT ONE BARE-HANDED, DIDN'T HE?!
Clamor
Clamor
H-HOW DID THEY ALL FIND OUT ABOUT THAT SO FAST?!
Do they have some form of twitter here, too?!
Kaw
NINJA!
Kaw
Kaw
NINJA!
Kaaaw
NINJA!
KAAAAAAW
NINJA!

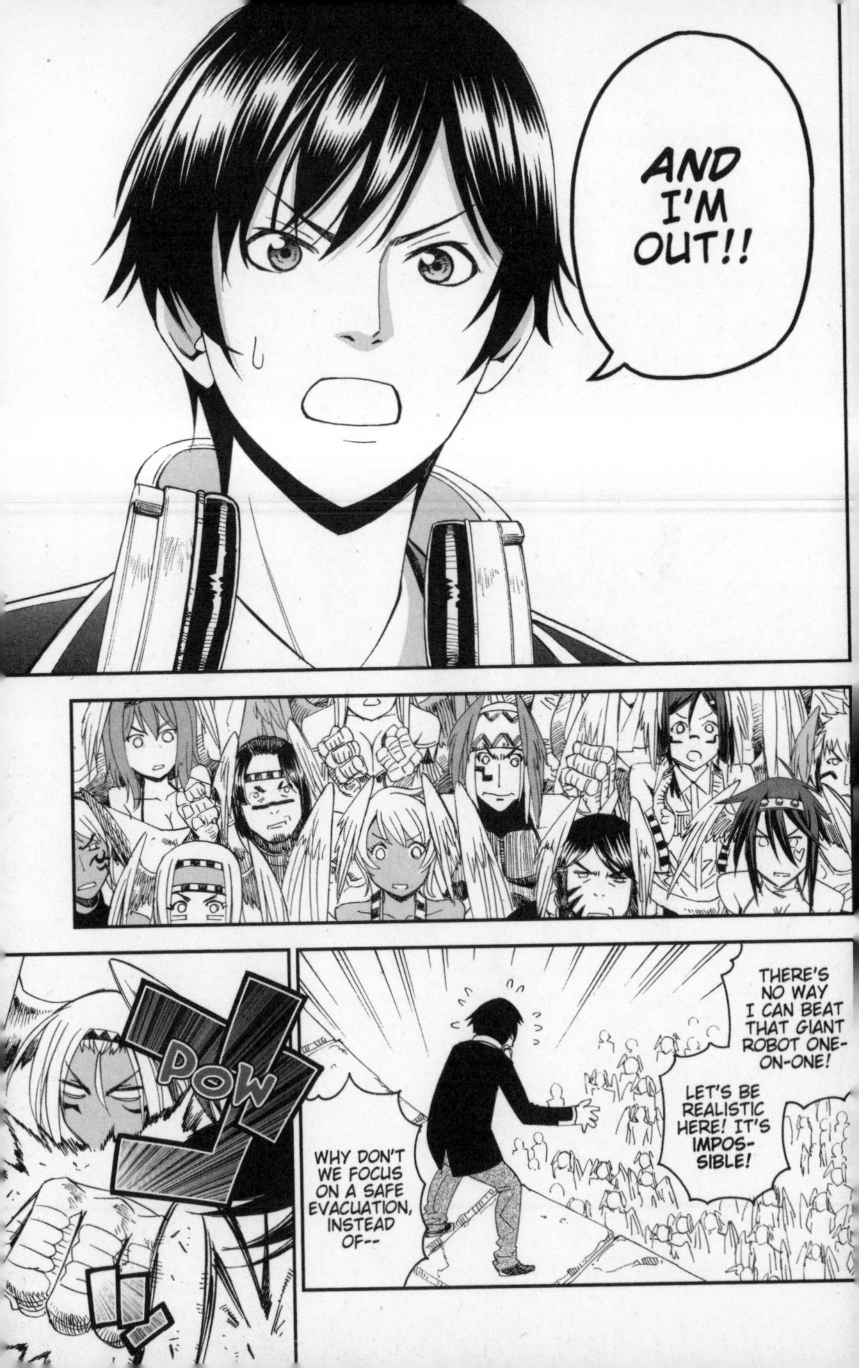
AND I'M OUT!!
THERE'S NO WAY I CAN BEAT THAT GIANT ROBOT ONE-ON-ONE!
LET'S BE REALISTIC HERE! IT'S IMPOS-SIBLE!
WHY DON'T WE FOCUS ON A SAFE EVACUATION, INSTEAD OF--
POW

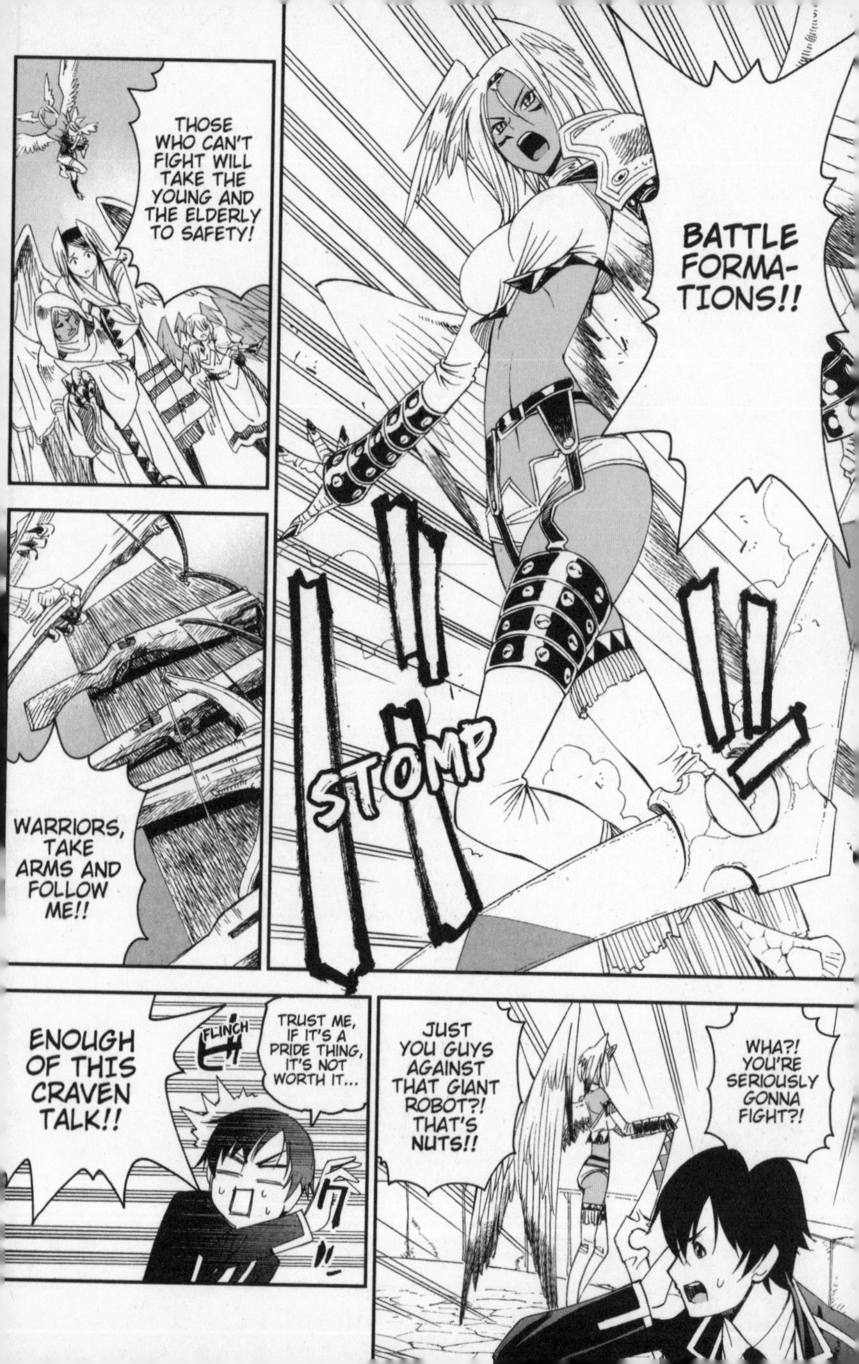
BATTLE FORMA-TIONS!!
STOMP
THOSE WHO CAN'T FIGHT WILL TAKE THE YOUNG AND THE ELDERLY TO SAFETY!
WARRIORS, TAKE ARMS AND FOLLOW ME!!
WHA?! YOU'RE SERIOUSLY GONNA FIGHT?!
JUST YOU GUYS AGAINST THAT GIANT ROBOT?! THAT'S NUTS!!
TRUST ME, IF IT'S A PRIDE THING, IT'S NOT WORTH IT...
FLINCH
ENOUGH OF THIS CRAVEN TALK!!

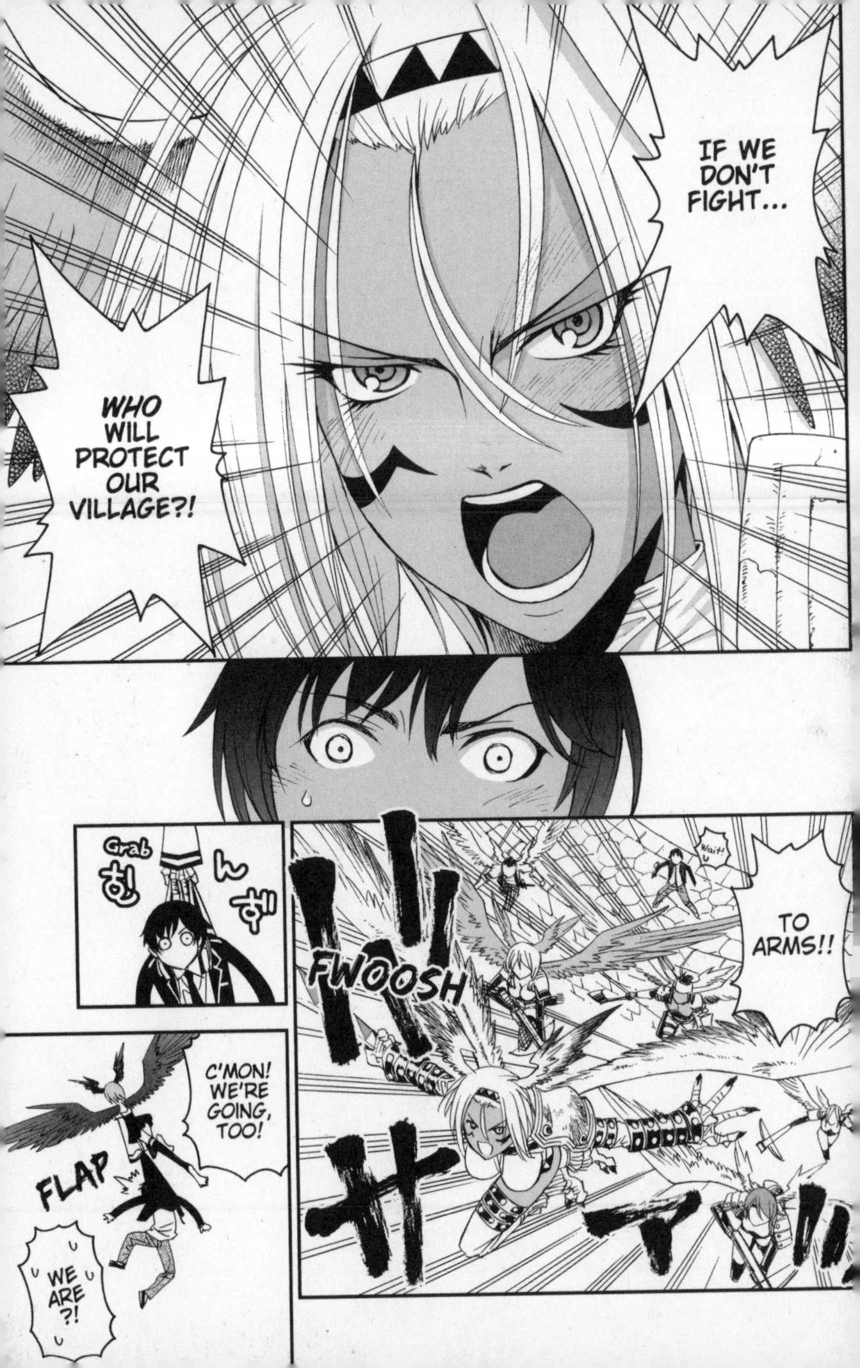
IF WE DON'T FIGHT...
WHO WILL PROTECT OUR VILLAGE?!
Wait!
TO ARMS!!
FWOOSH
Grab
むんず
C'MON! WE'RE GOING, TOO!
FLAP
WE ARE?!

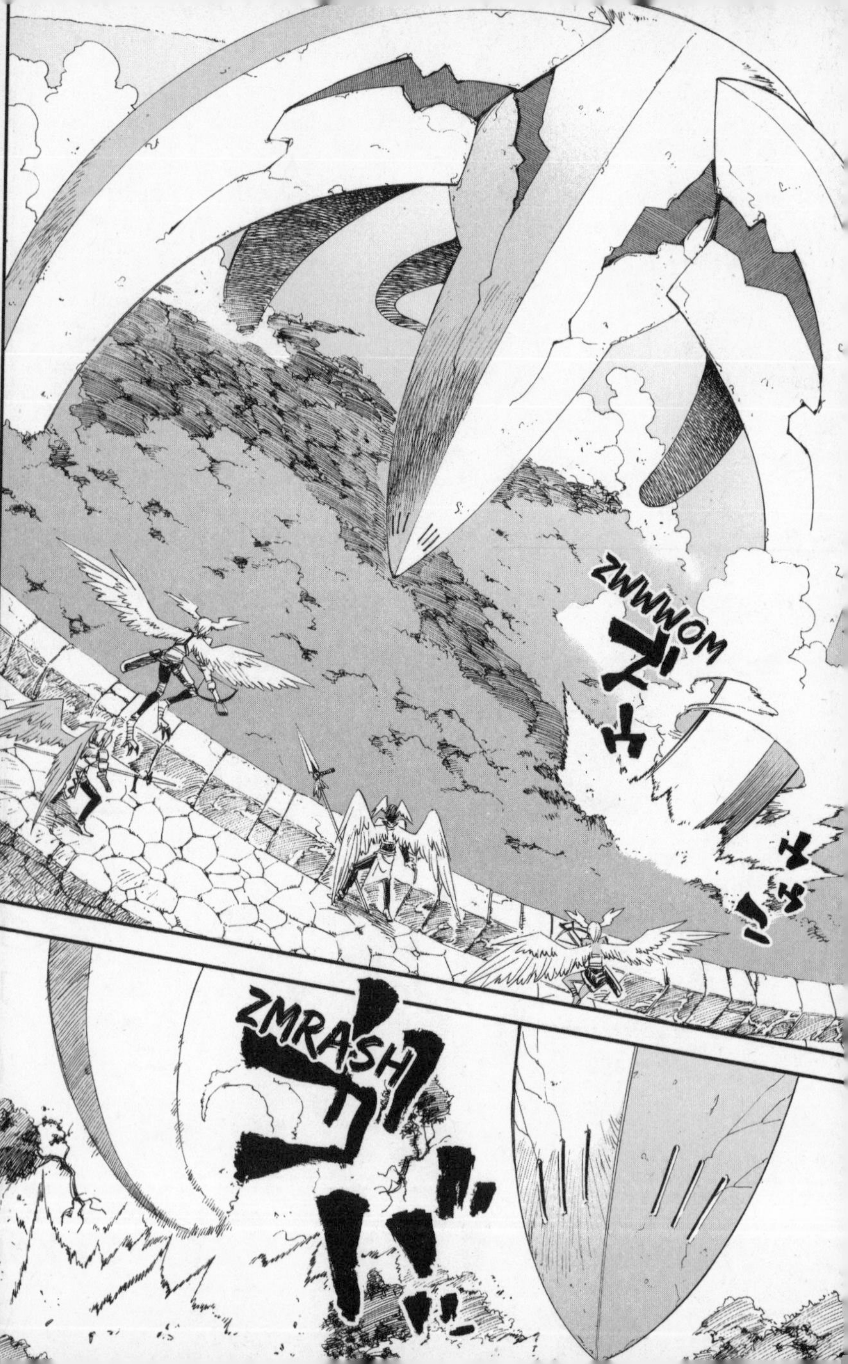
ZWWWOM
ZMRASH

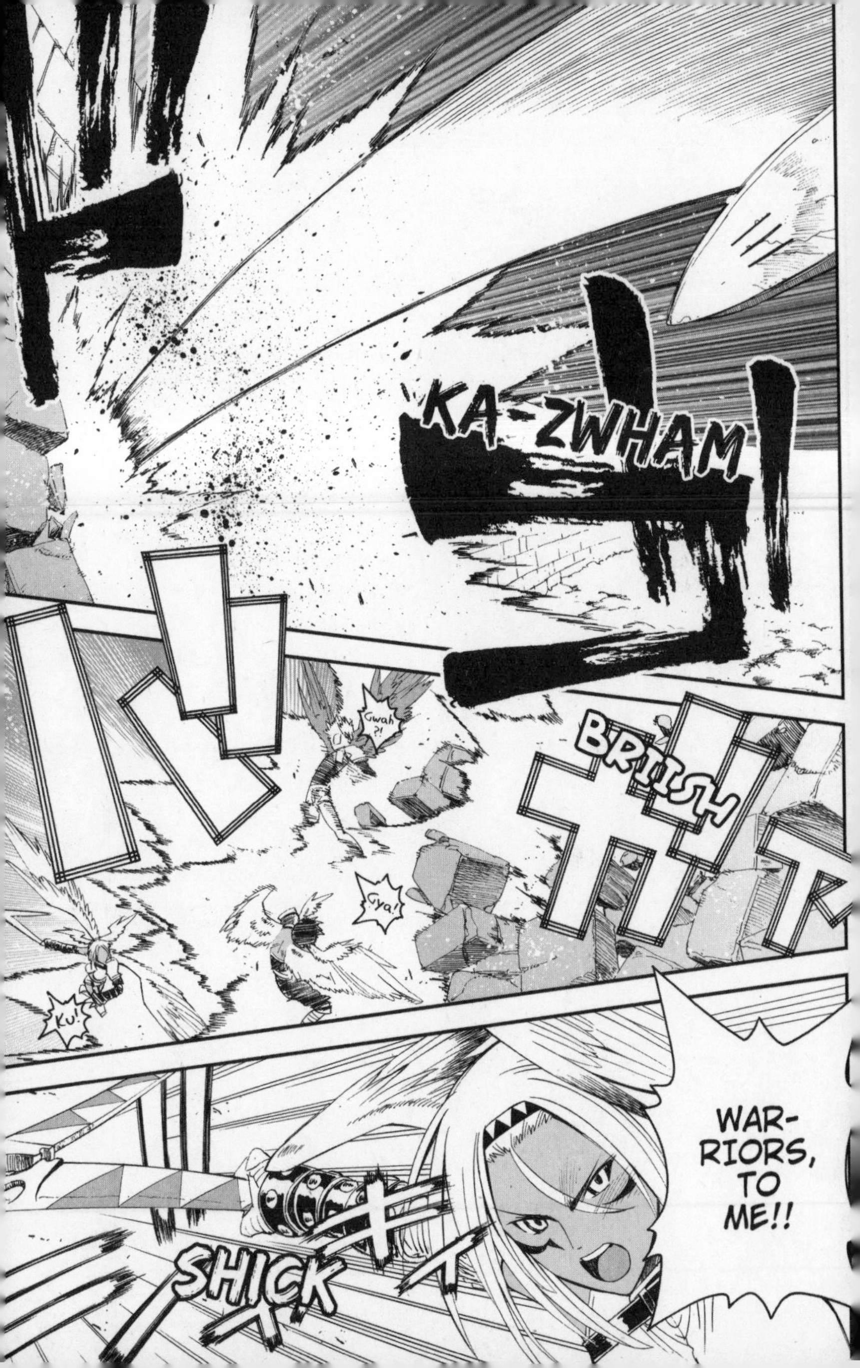
KA-ZWHAM
BRISH
Gwah ?!
Gya!
Ku!
WAR-
RIORS,
TO
ME!!
SHICK

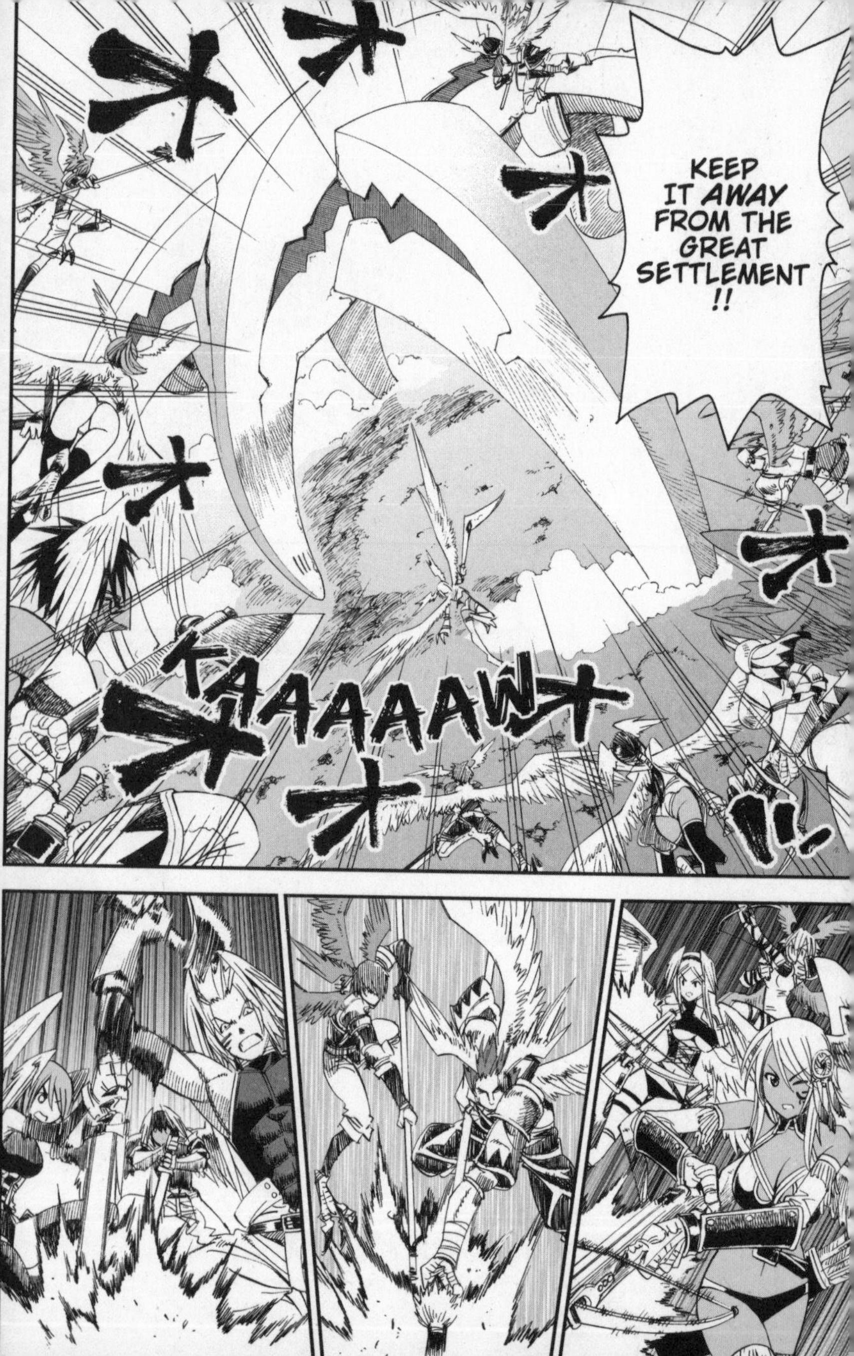
KEEP IT AWAY FROM THE GREAT SETTLEMENT !!
KAAAAAW
!!

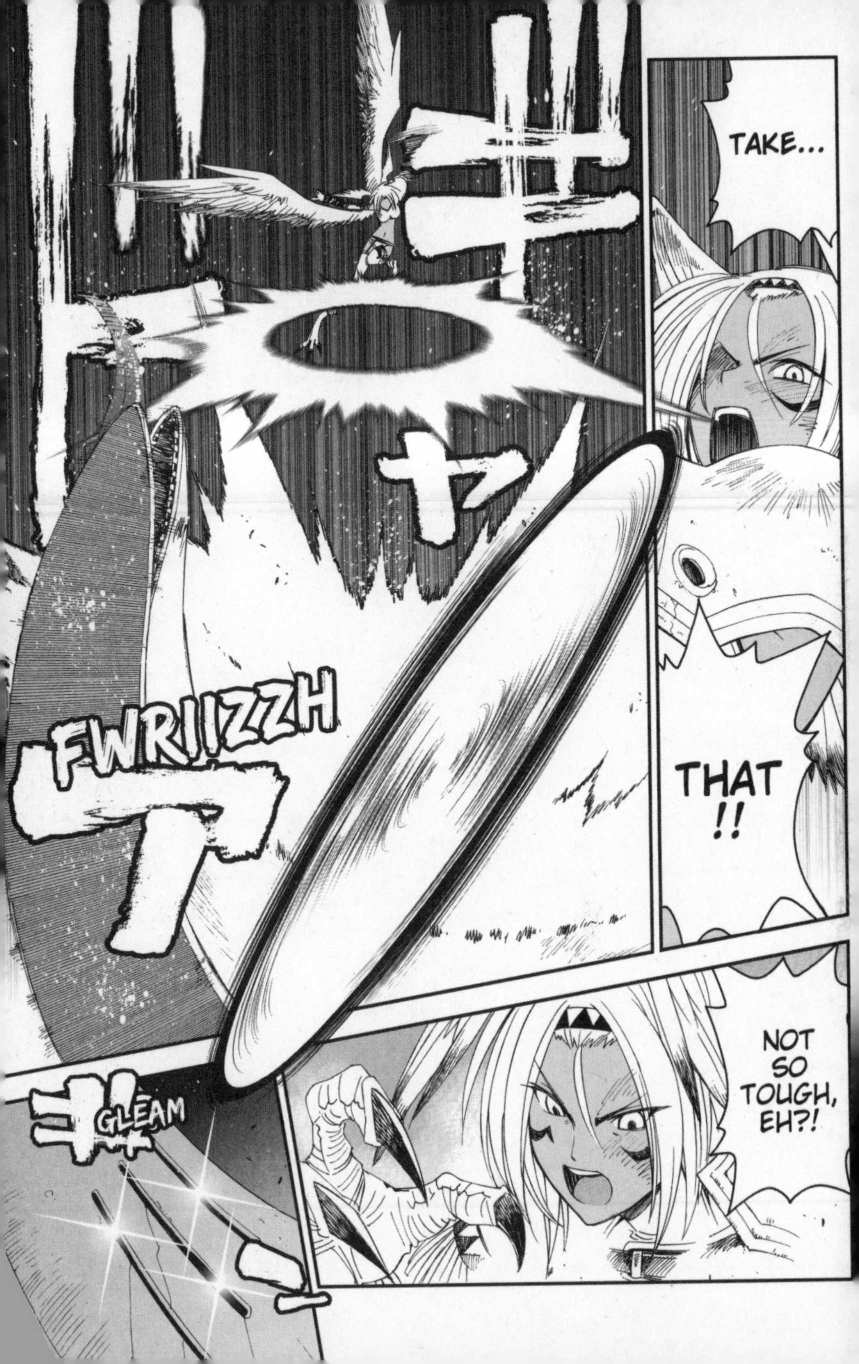
TAKE...
THAT !!
NOT SO TOUGH, EH?!
FWRIIZZH
GLEAM

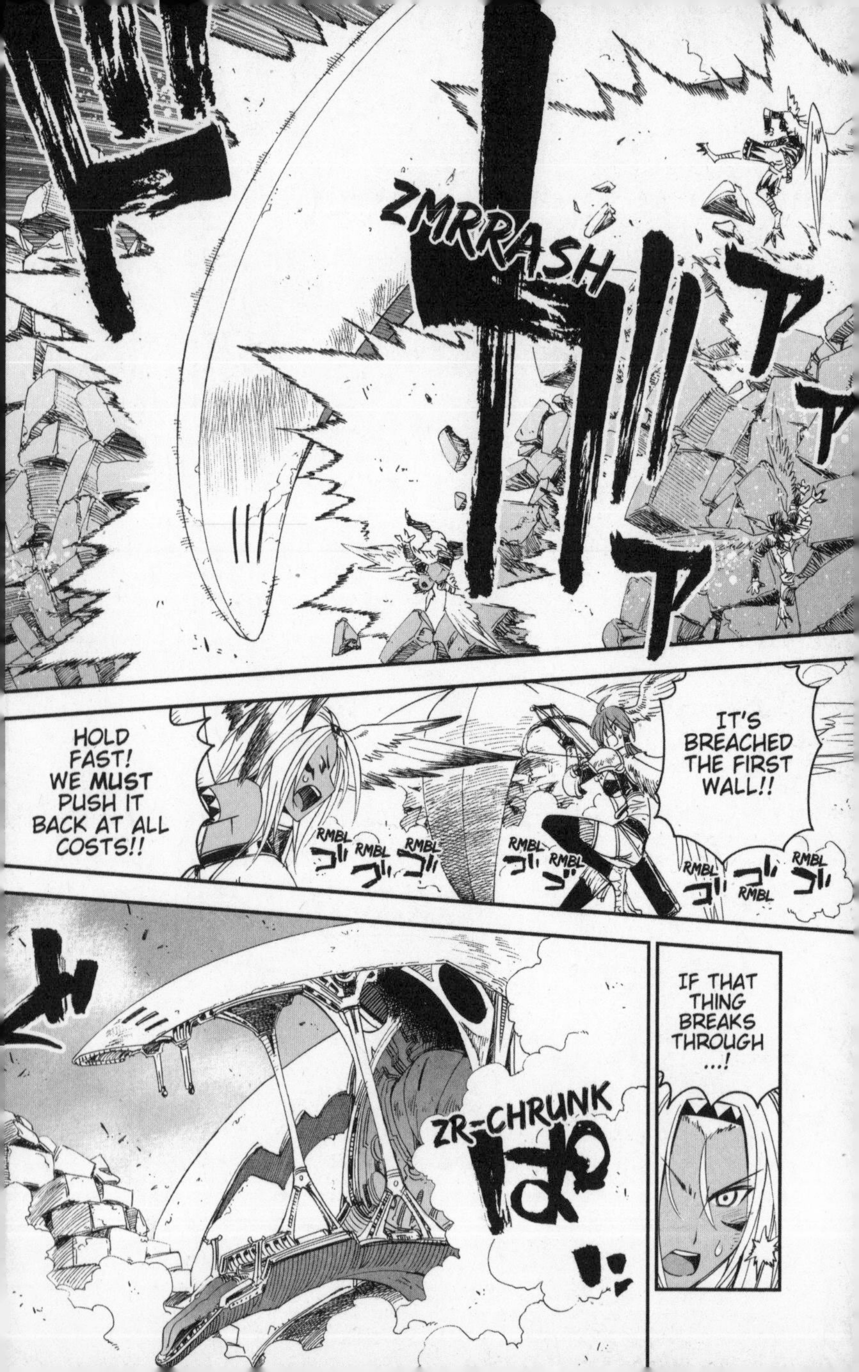
ZMRRASH
IT'S BREACHED THE FIRST WALL!!
RMBL RMBL RMBL RMBL RMBL RMBL RMBL RMBL
HOLD FAST! WE MUST PUSH IT BACK AT ALL COSTS!!
IF THAT THING BREAKS THROUGH ...!
ZR-CHRUNK

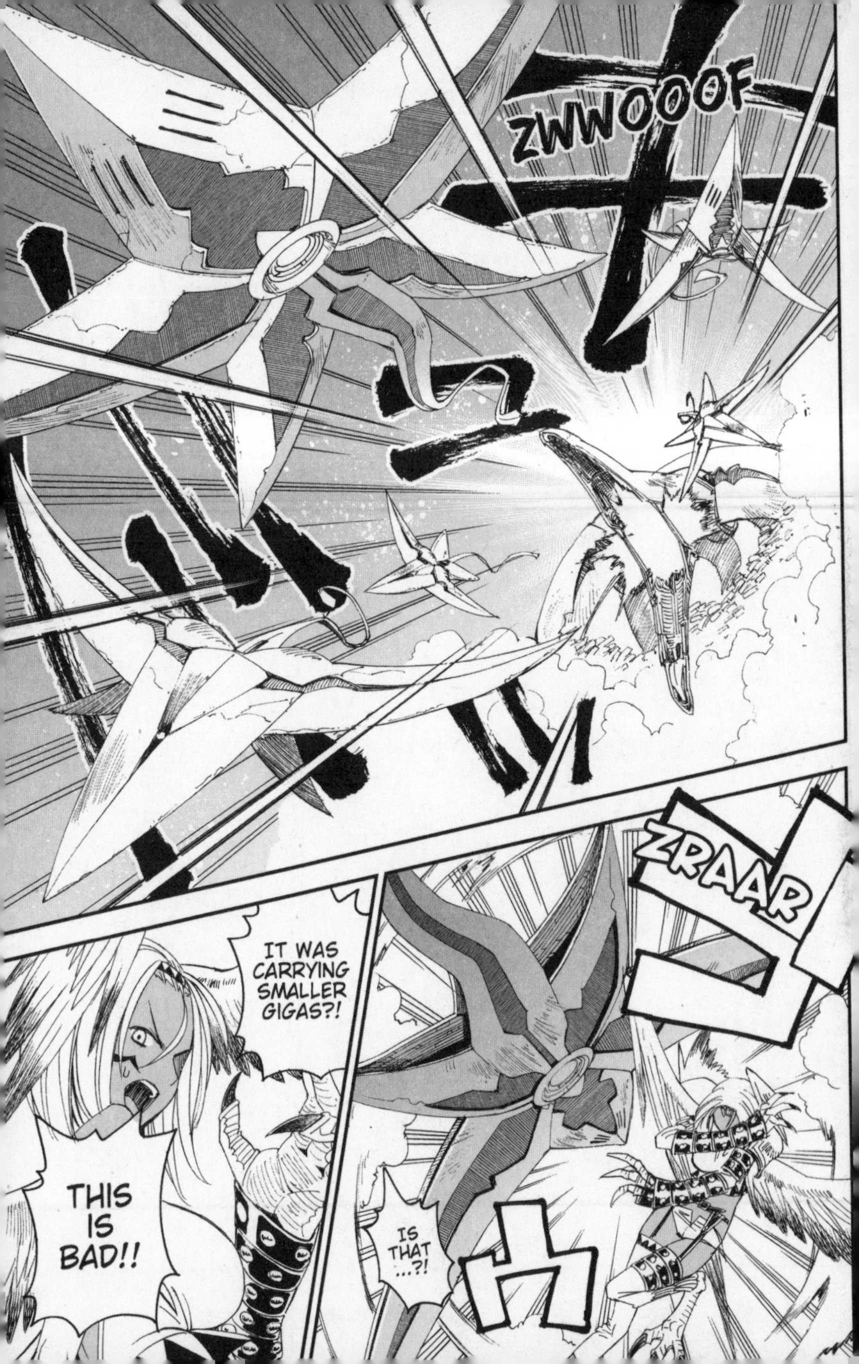
ZWWOOOF
ZRAAR
IS THAT ...?!
IT WAS CARRYING SMALLER GIGAS?!
THIS IS BAD!!

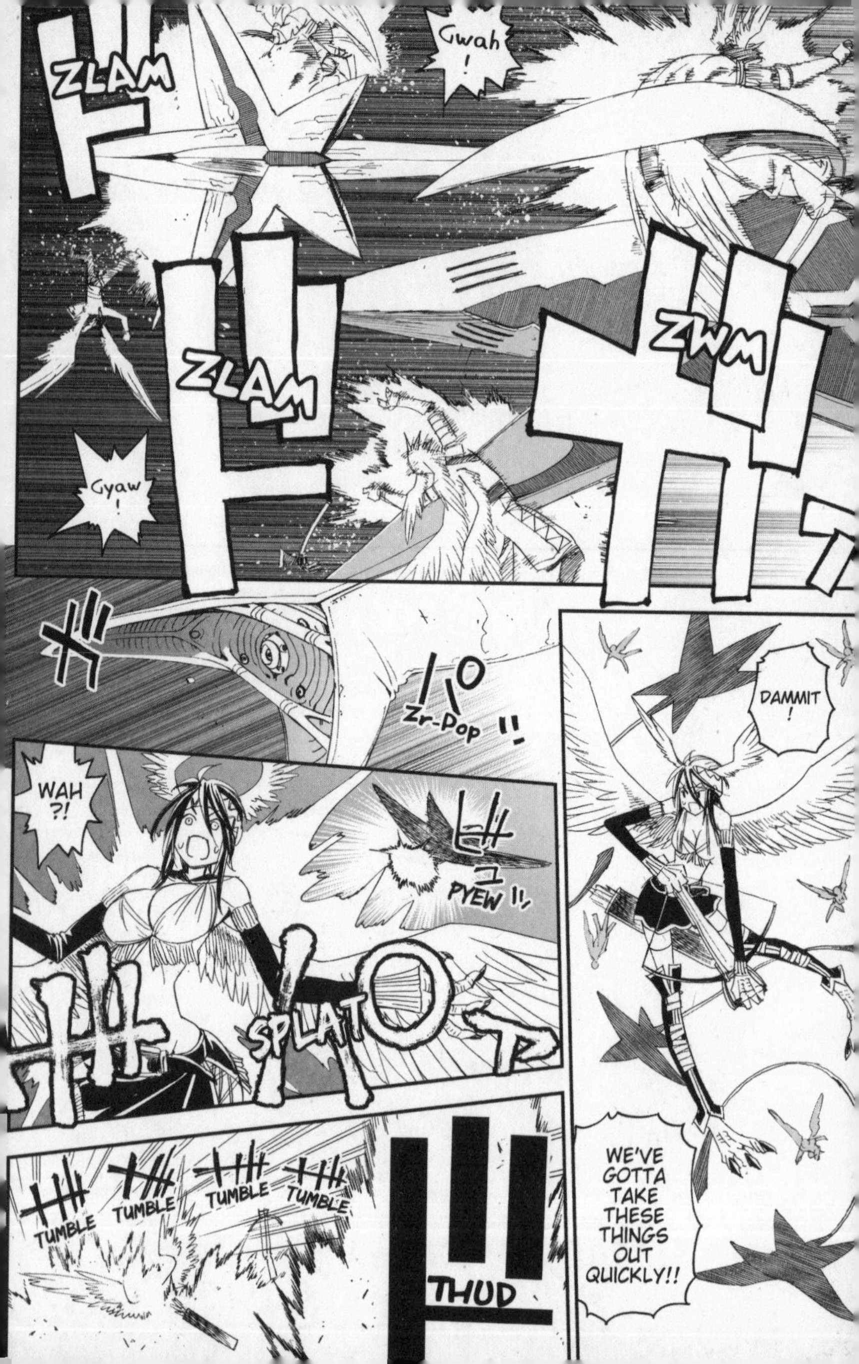
Gwah!
ZWM
ZLAM
ZLAM
Gyaw!
DAMMIT!
WE'VE GOTTA TAKE THESE THINGS OUT QUICKLY!!
Zr-Pop !!
PYEW !!
WAH?!
SPLAT
THUD
TUMBLE
TUMBLE
TUMBLE
TUMBLE

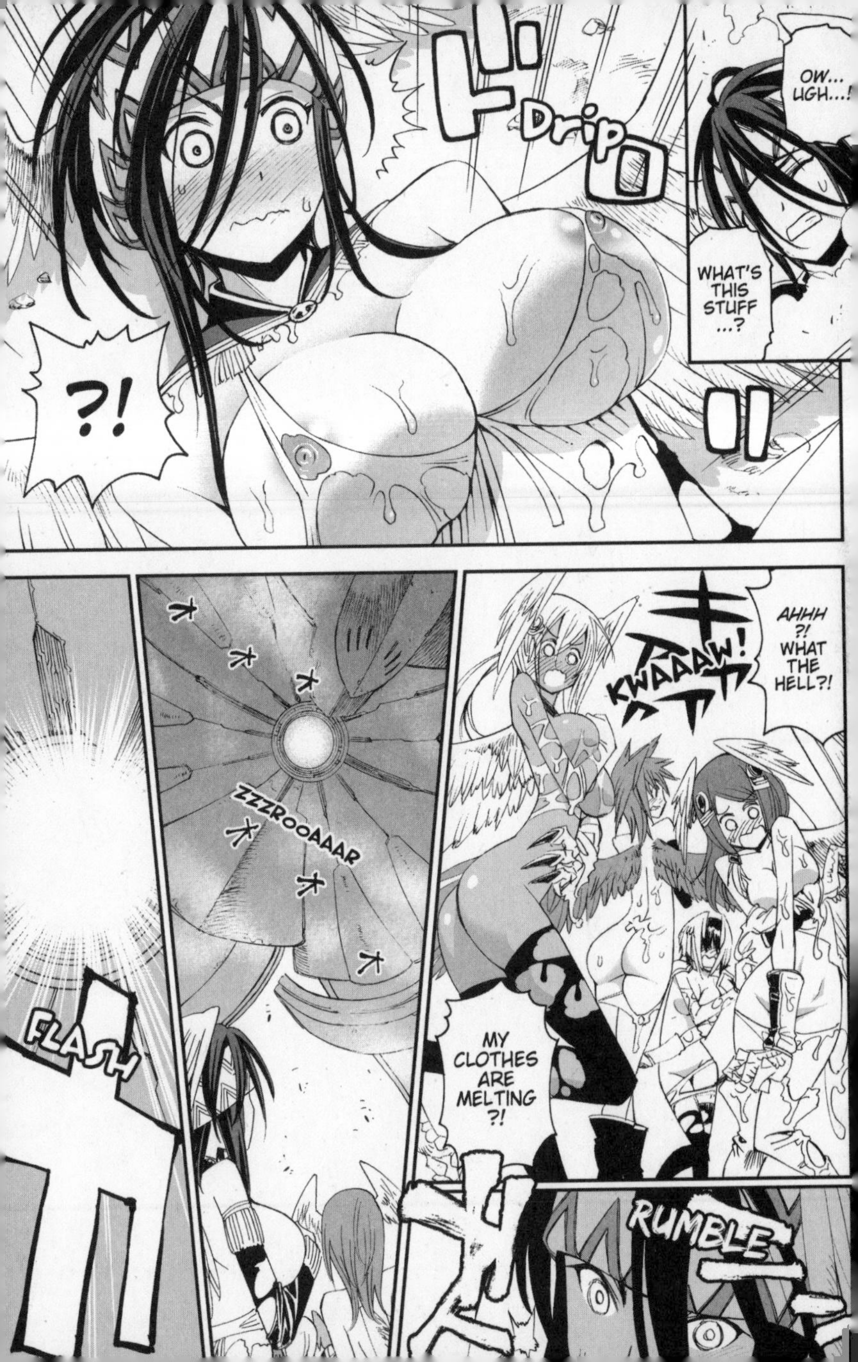

OW... UGH...!
WHAT'S THIS STUFF ...?
Drip
?!
AHHH ?! WHAT THE HELL?!
KWAAAW!
MY CLOTHES ARE MELTING ?!
ZZZROOAAAR
FLASH
RUMBLE

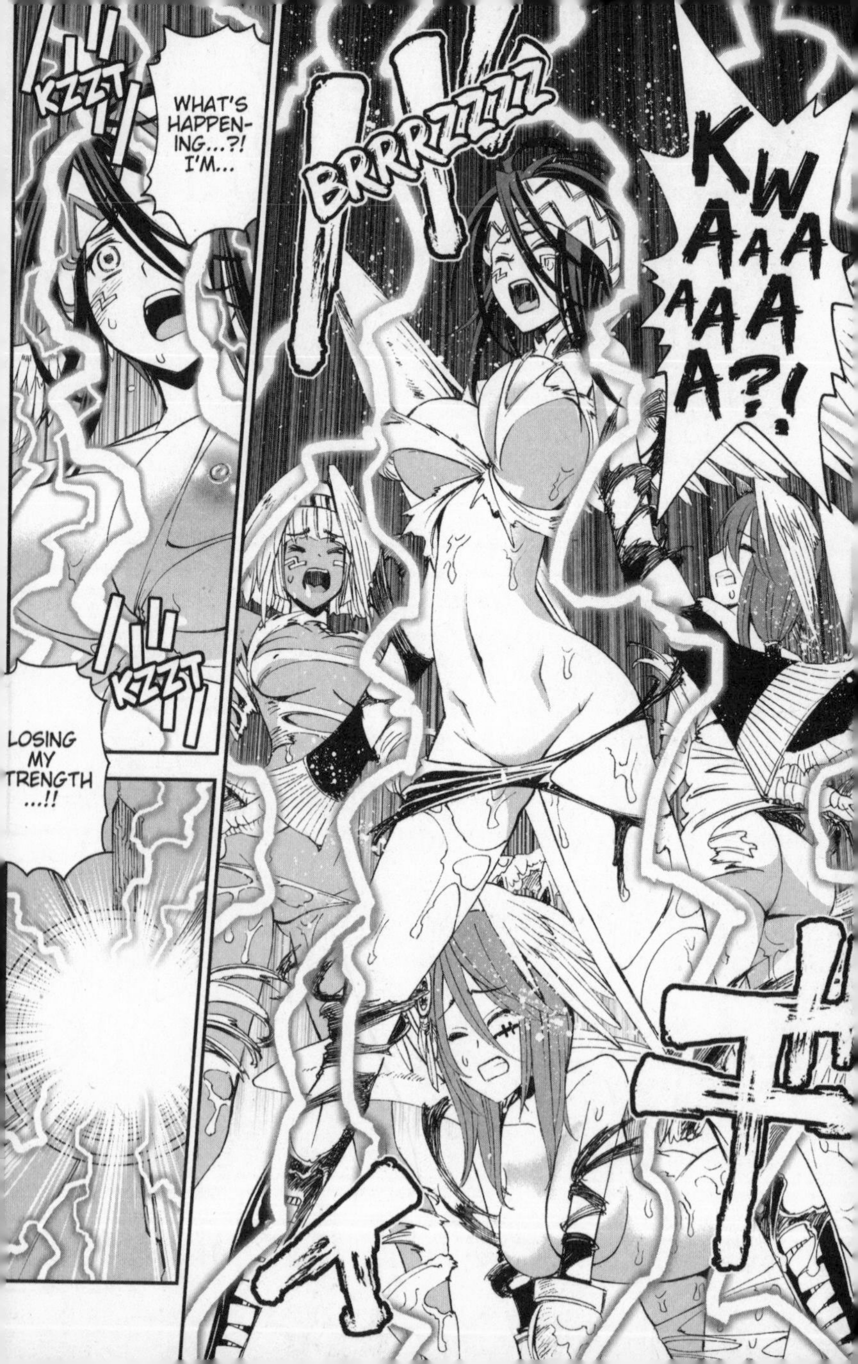
KWAAAAAAA?!
BRRRZZZZZ
KZZZT
WHAT'S HAPPENING...?! I'M...
KZZZT
LOSING MY TRENGTH ...!!

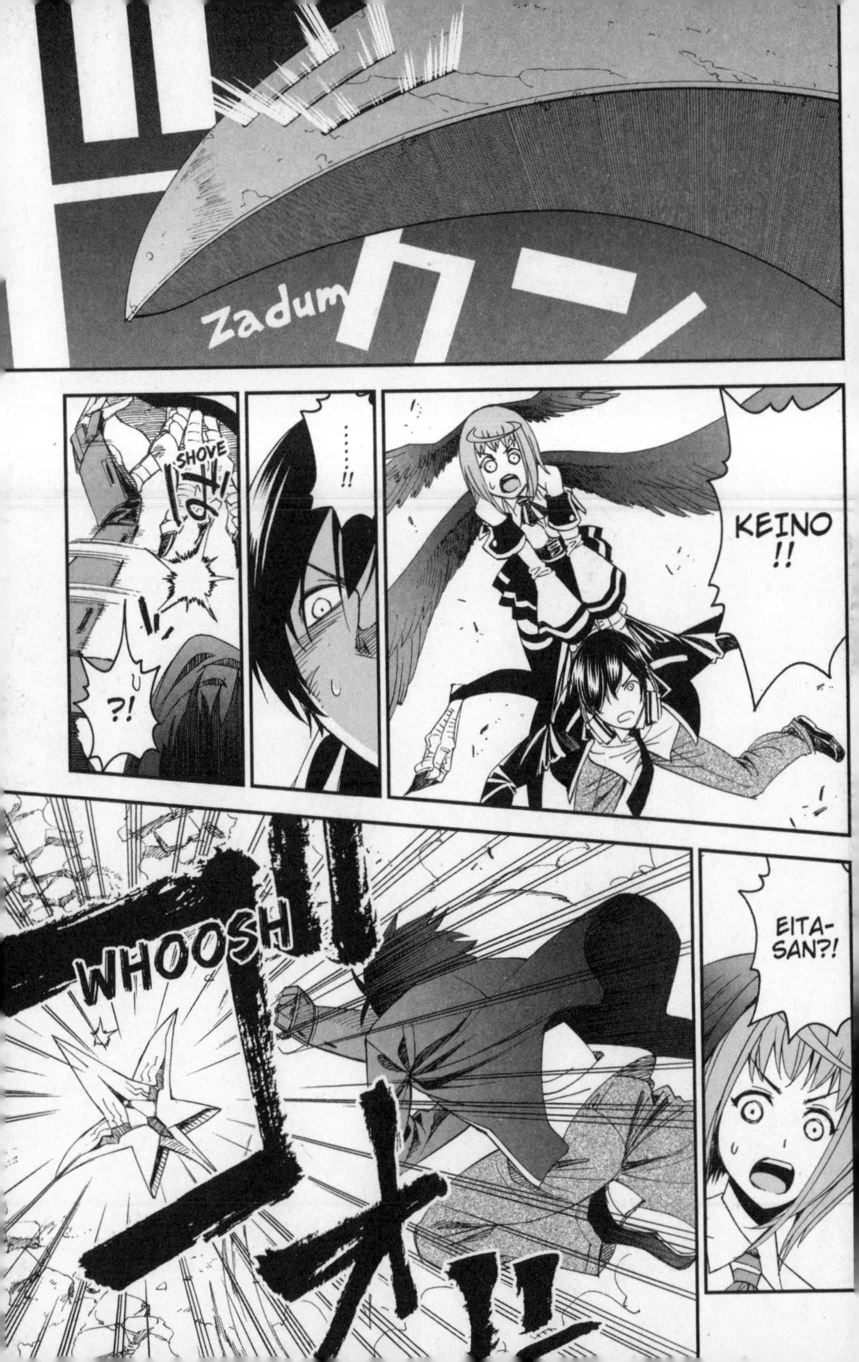
Zadum
KEINO!!
......!!
SHOVE
?!
EITA-SAN?!
WHOOSH

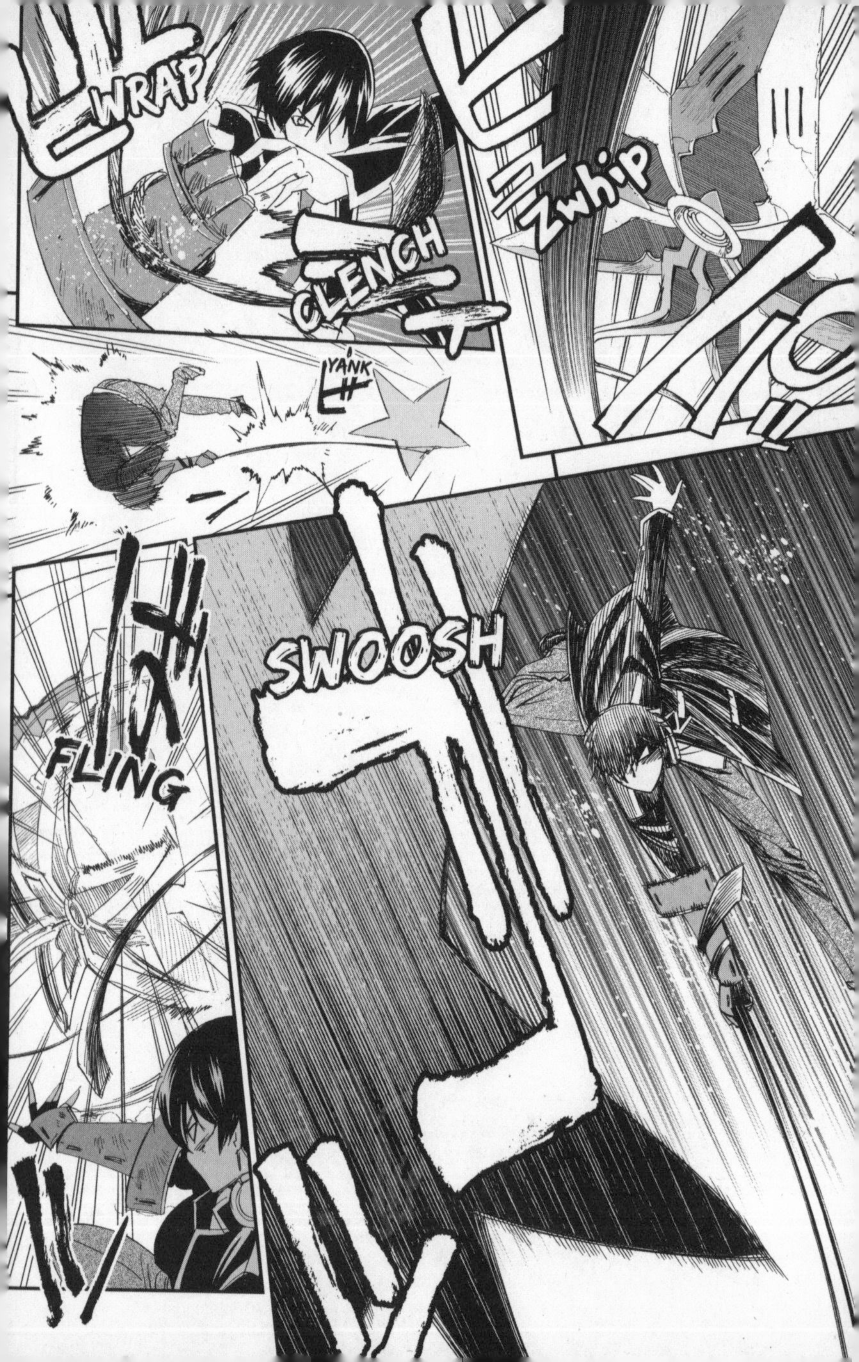
Zwhip
WRAP
CLENCH
YANK
SWOOSH
FLING

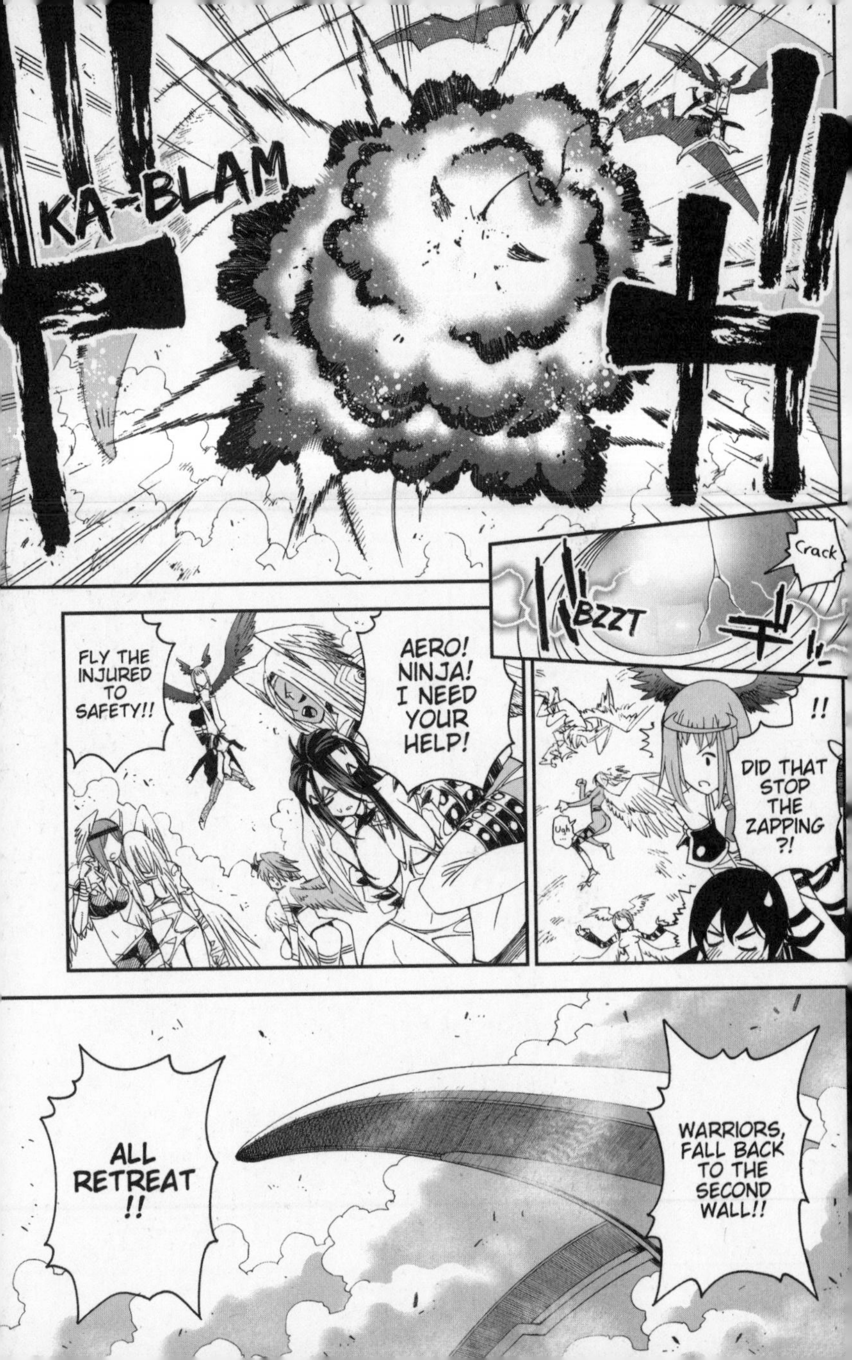
KA-BLAM
Crack
BZZT
!!
DID THAT STOP THE ZAPPING?!
Ugh...
AERO! NINJA! I NEED YOUR HELP!
FLY THE INJURED TO SAFETY!!
WARRIORS, FALL BACK TO THE SECOND WALL!!
ALL RETREAT!!

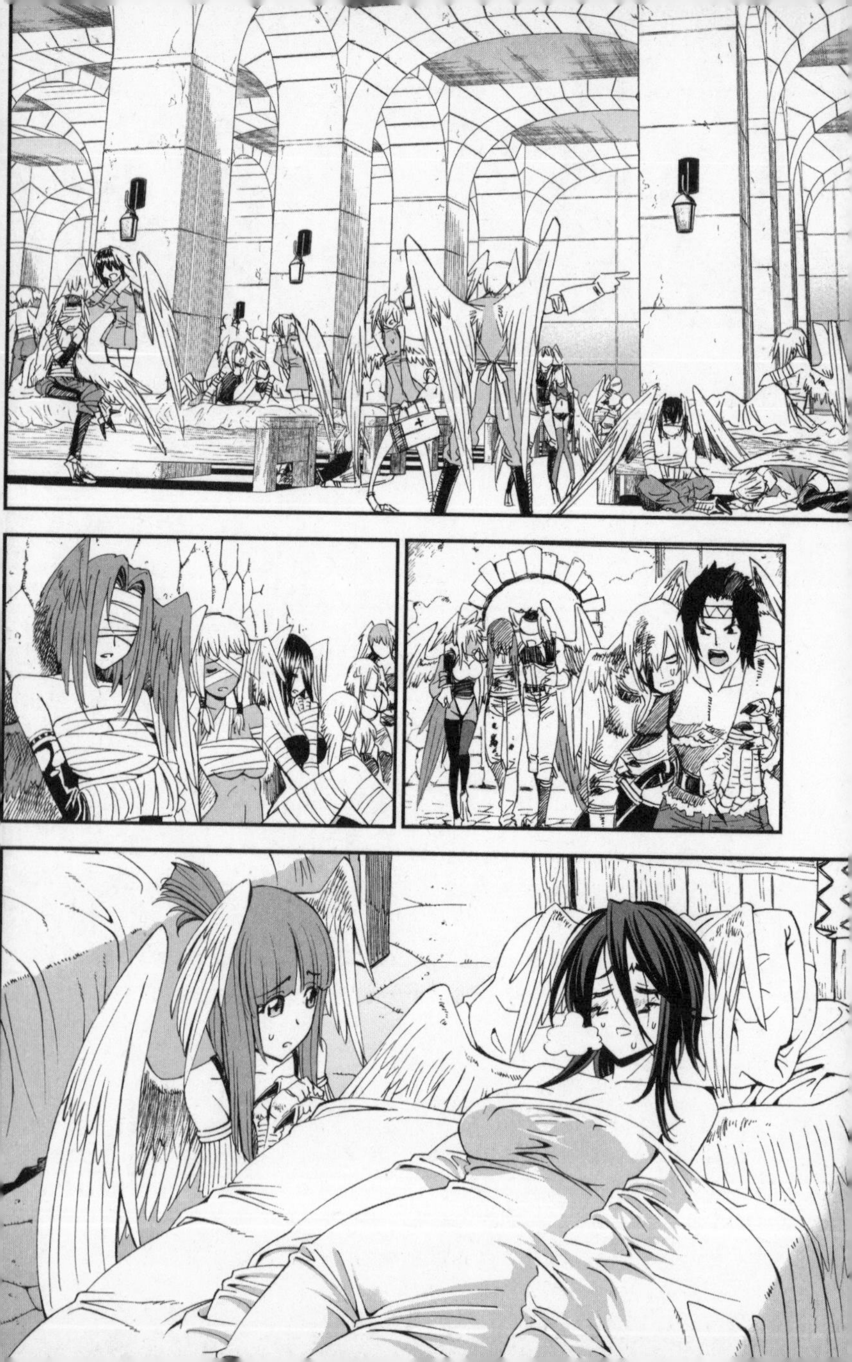

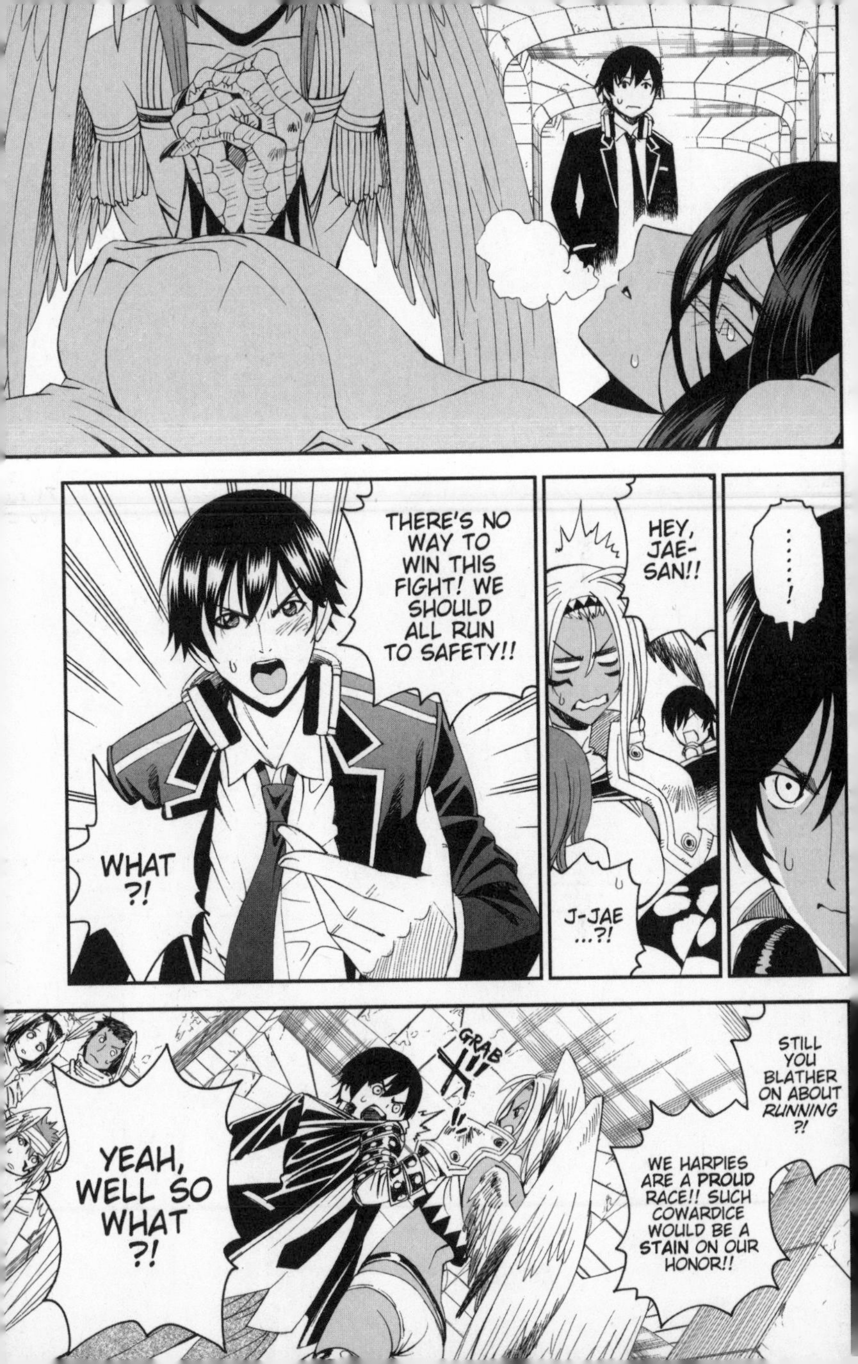
......!
HEY, JAE-SAN!!
J-JAE ...?!
THERE'S NO WAY TO WIN THIS FIGHT! WE SHOULD ALL RUN TO SAFETY!!
WHAT ?!
STILL YOU BLATHER ON ABOUT *RUNNING* ?!
WE HARPIES ARE A PROUD RACE!! SUCH COWARDICE WOULD BE A STAIN ON OUR HONOR!!
GRAB
YEAH, WELL SO WHAT ?!

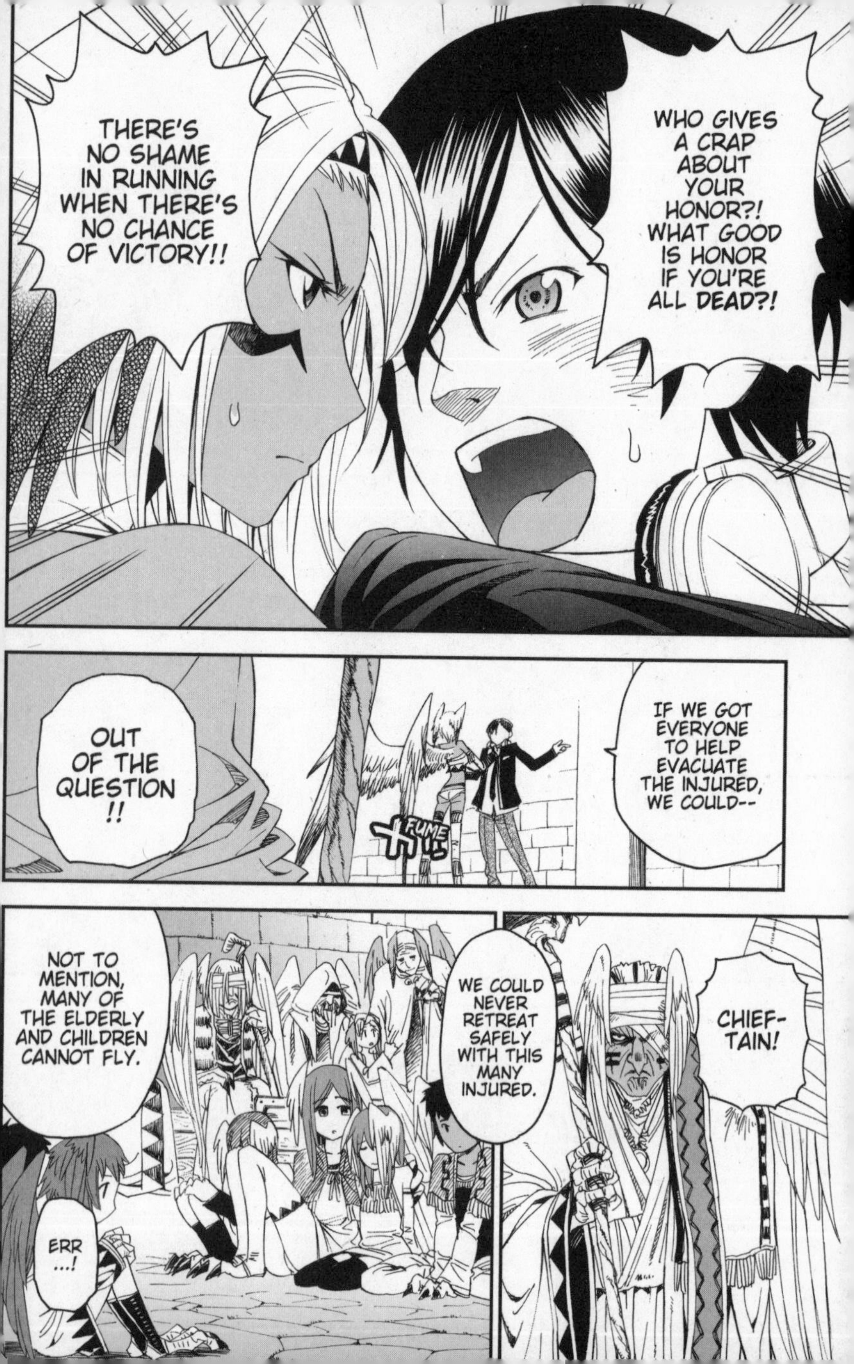
WHO GIVES A CRAP ABOUT YOUR HONOR?! WHAT GOOD IS HONOR IF YOU'RE ALL DEAD?!
THERE'S NO SHAME IN RUNNING WHEN THERE'S NO CHANCE OF VICTORY!!
IF WE GOT EVERYONE TO HELP EVACUATE THE INJURED, WE COULD--
FUME
OUT OF THE QUESTION !!
CHIEF-TAIN!
WE COULD NEVER RETREAT SAFELY WITH THIS MANY INJURED.
NOT TO MENTION, MANY OF THE ELDERLY AND CHILDREN CANNOT FLY.
ERR ...!

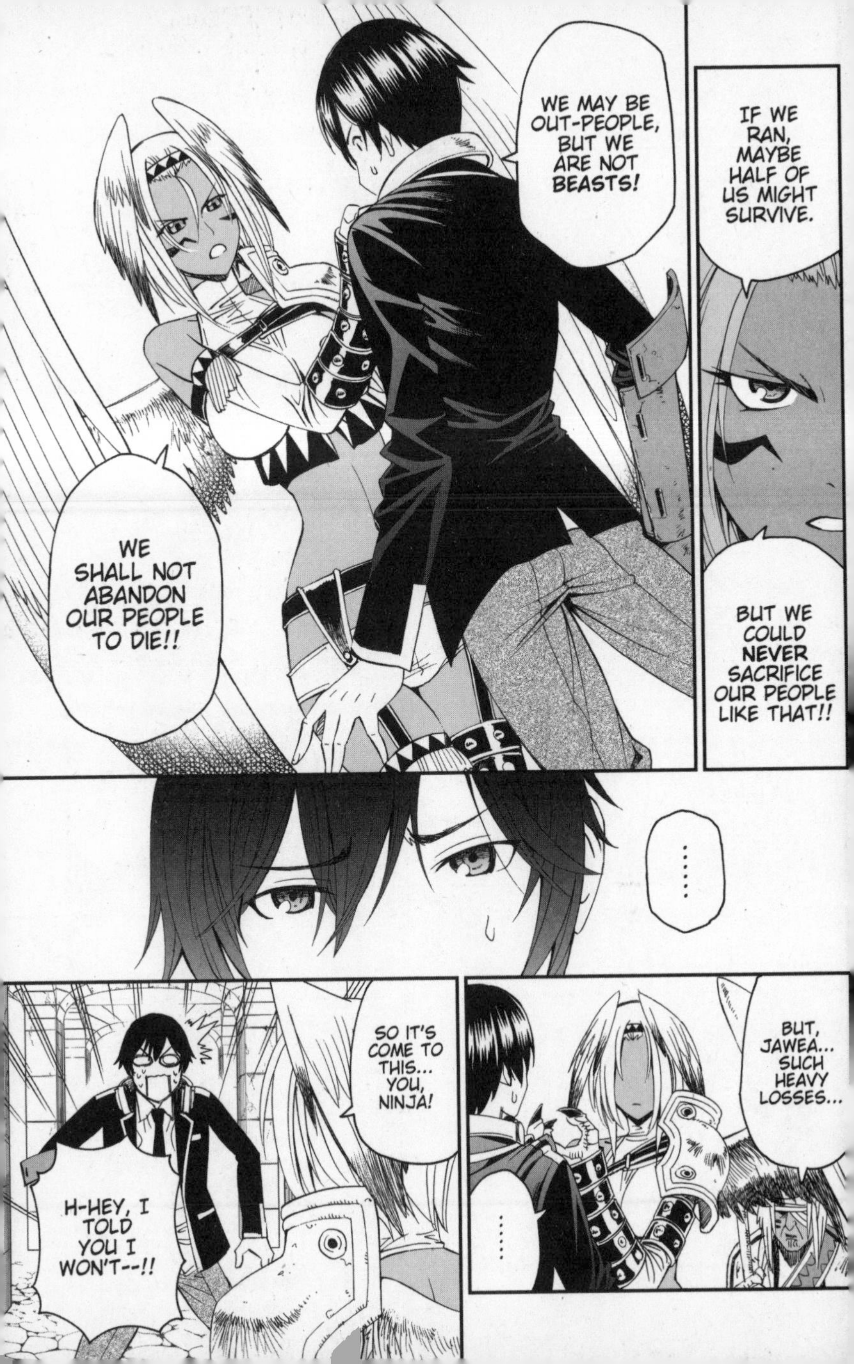
IF WE RAN, MAYBE HALF OF US MIGHT SURVIVE.
BUT WE COULD **NEVER** SACRIFICE OUR PEOPLE LIKE THAT!!
WE MAY BE OUT-PEOPLE, BUT WE ARE NOT BEASTS!
WE SHALL NOT ABANDON OUR PEOPLE TO DIE!!
......
BUT, JAWEA... SUCH HEAVY LOSSES...
......
SO IT'S COME TO THIS... YOU, NINJA!
H-HEY, I TOLD YOU I WON'T--!!

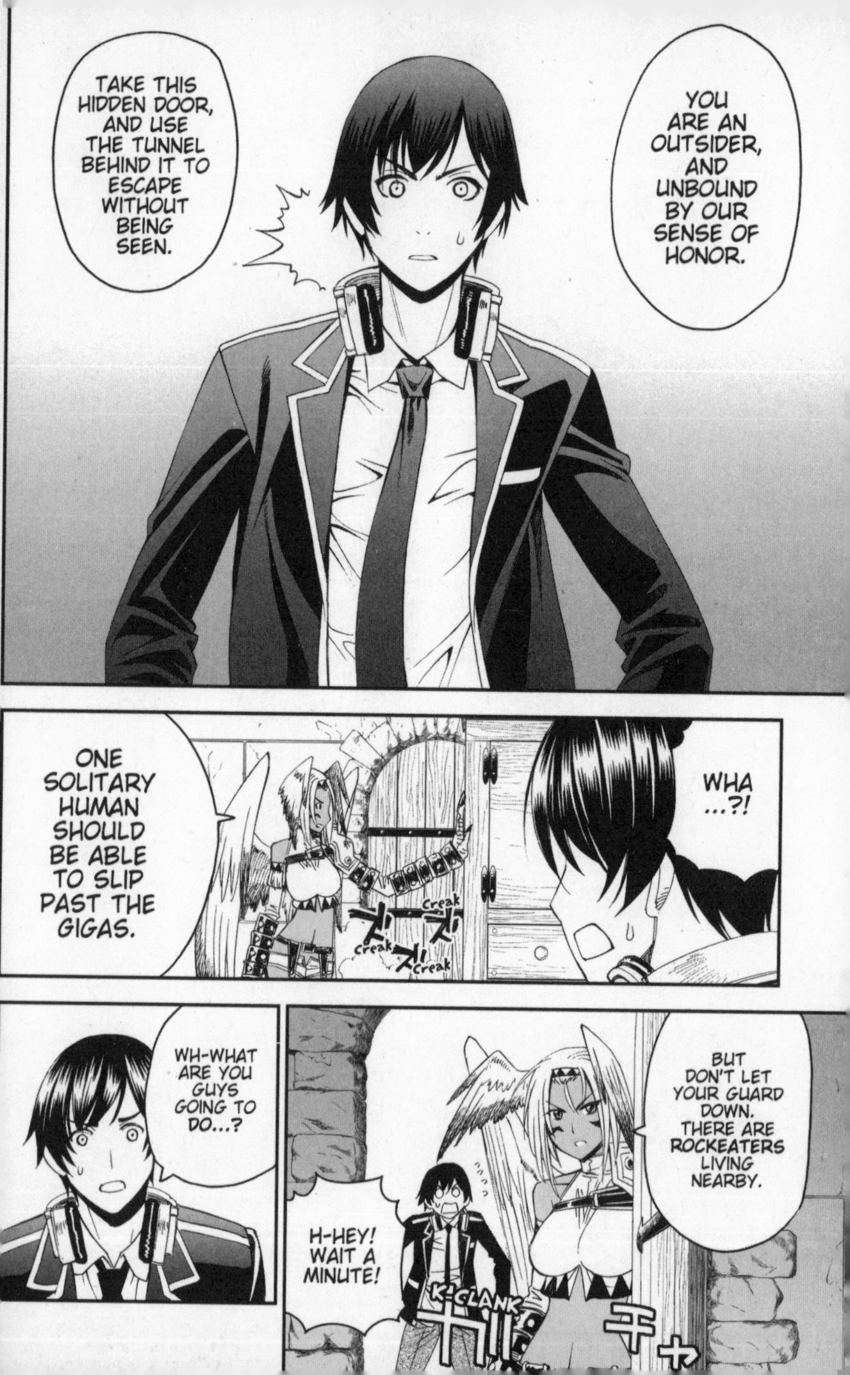
YOU ARE AN OUTSIDER, AND UNBOUND BY OUR SENSE OF HONOR.
TAKE THIS HIDDEN DOOR, AND USE THE TUNNEL BEHIND IT TO ESCAPE WITHOUT BEING SEEN.
WHA ...?!
ONE SOLITARY HUMAN SHOULD BE ABLE TO SLIP PAST THE GIGAS.
Creak
Creak
Creak
BUT DON'T LET YOUR GUARD DOWN. THERE ARE ROCKEATERS LIVING NEARBY.
H-HEY! WAIT A MINUTE!
K-CLANK
WH-WHAT ARE YOU GUYS GOING TO DO...?

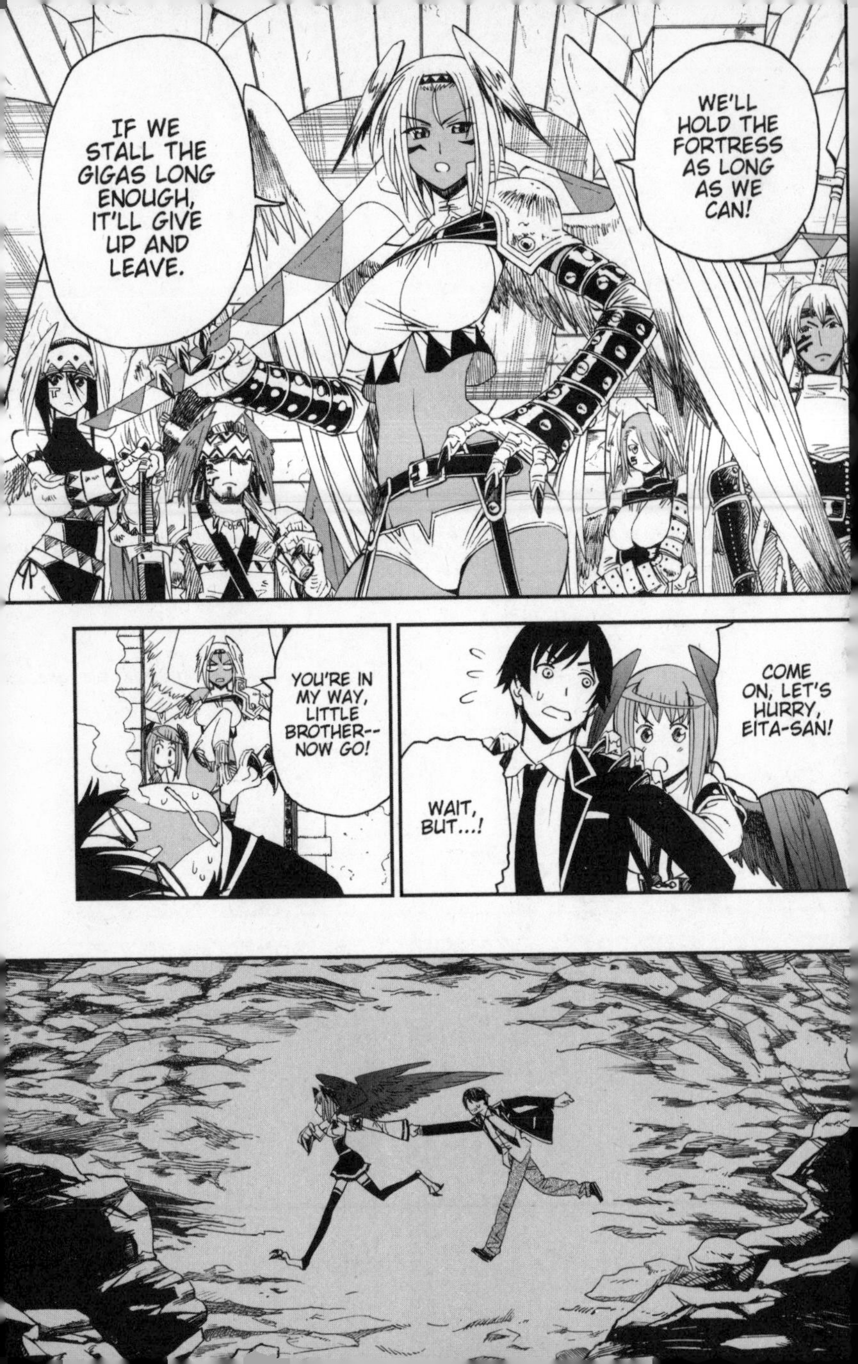
WE'LL HOLD THE FORTRESS AS LONG AS WE CAN!
IF WE STALL THE GIGAS LONG ENOUGH, IT'LL GIVE UP AND LEAVE.
COME ON, LET'S HURRY, EITA-SAN!
WAIT, BUT...!
YOU'RE IN MY WAY, LITTLE BROTHER-- NOW GO!

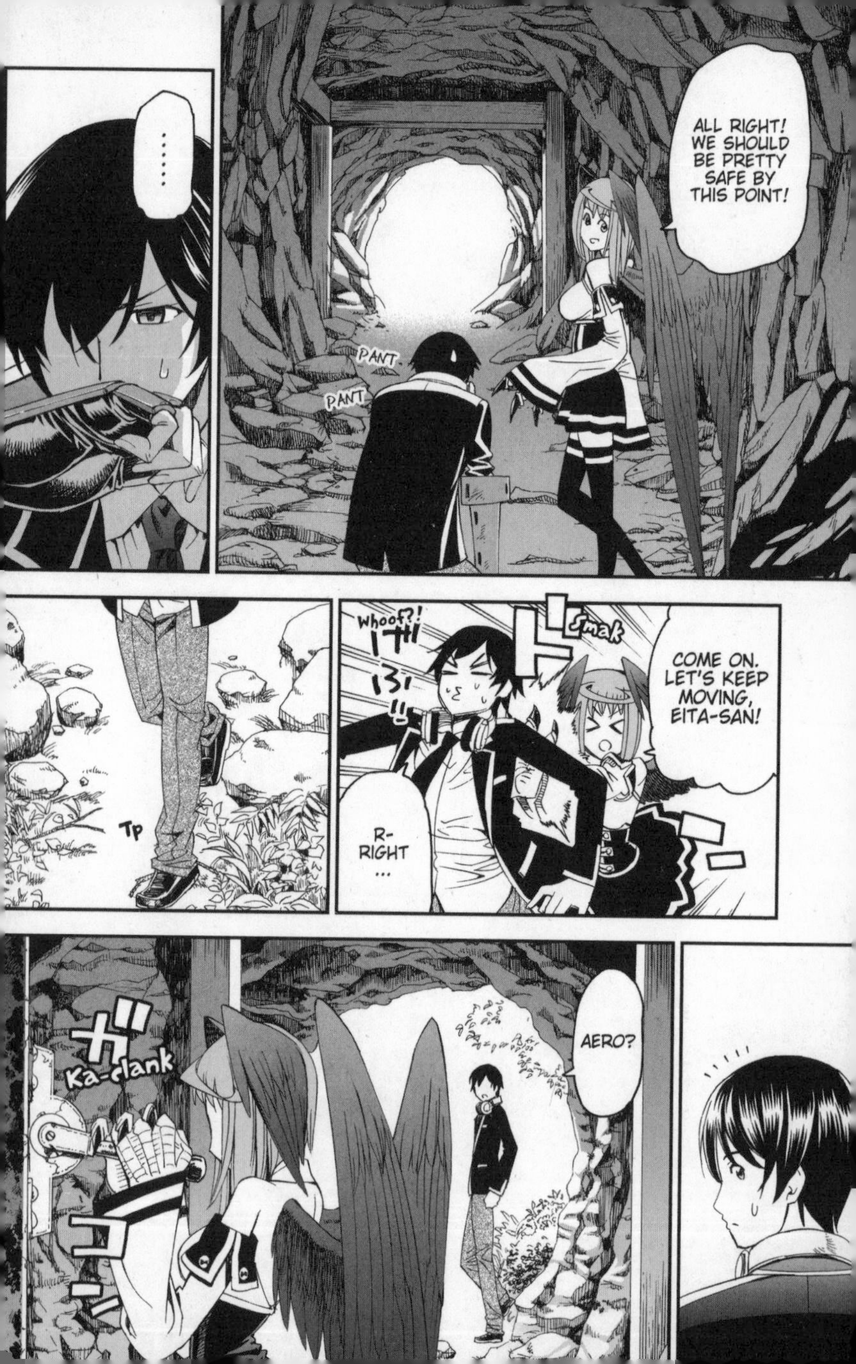
ALL RIGHT! WE SHOULD BE PRETTY SAFE BY THIS POINT!
PANT
PANT
......
Smak
Whoof?!
COME ON. LET'S KEEP MOVING, EITA-SAN!
R-RIGHT ...
Tp
AERO?
Ka-clank

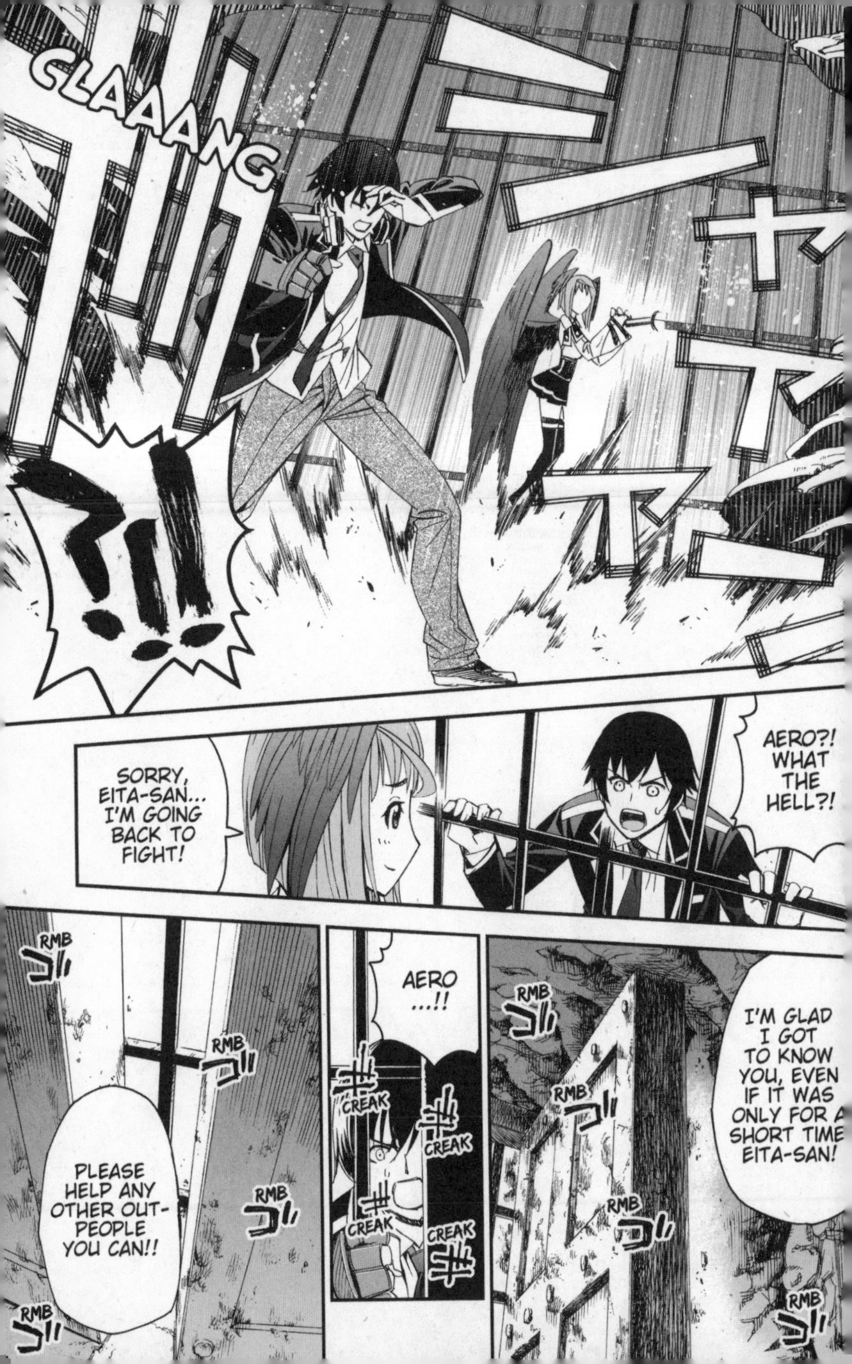
CLAAANG
?!!
AERO?! WHAT THE HELL?!
SORRY, EITA-SAN... I'M GOING BACK TO FIGHT!
RMB
I'M GLAD I GOT TO KNOW YOU, EVEN IF IT WAS ONLY FOR A SHORT TIME EITA-SAN!
RMB
RMB
RMB
RMB
AERO ...!!
CREAK
CREAK
CREAK
CREAK
RMB
RMB
RMB
PLEASE HELP ANY OTHER OUT-PEOPLE YOU CAN!!
RMB

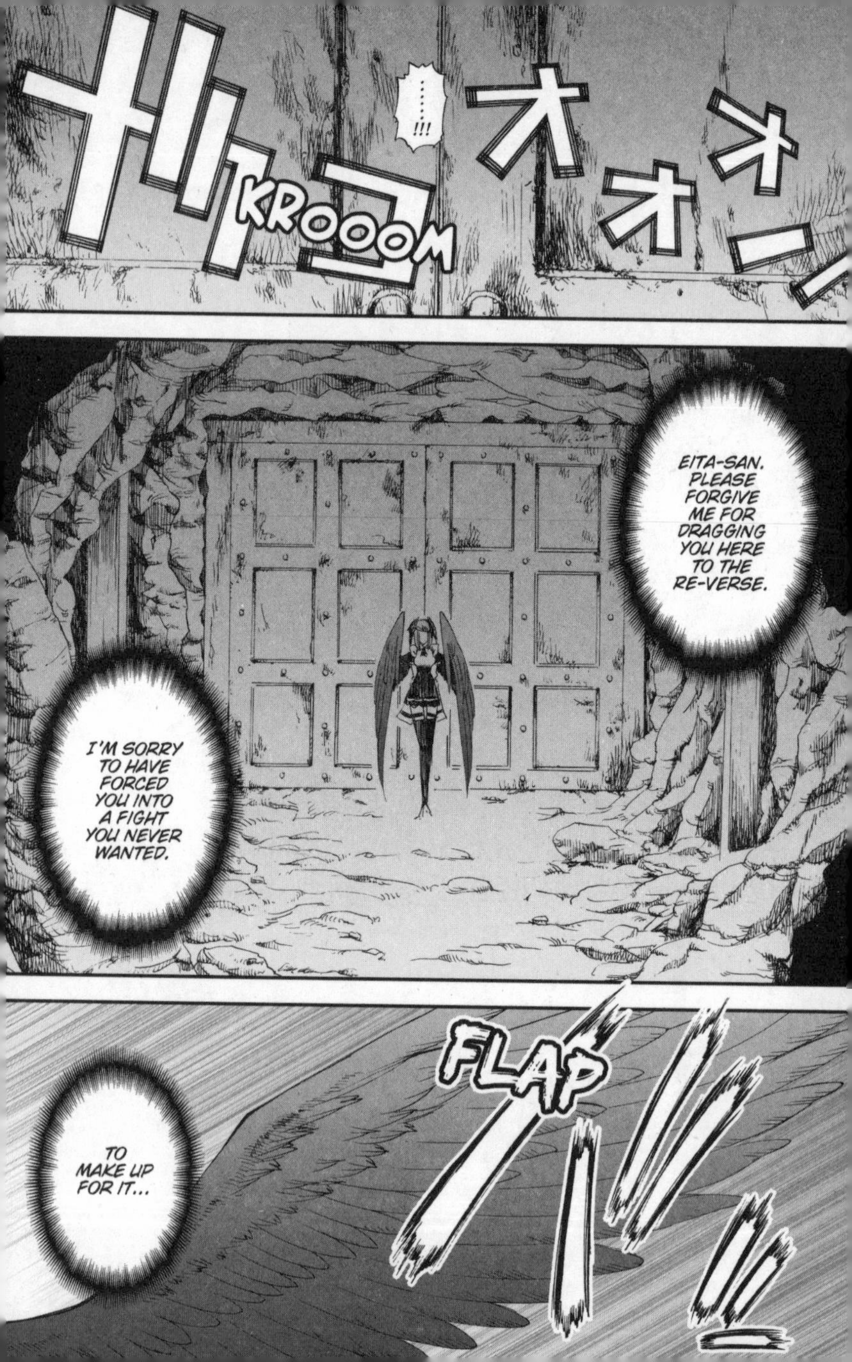

ズゴォオオン
KROOOM
......!!!
EITA-SAN. PLEASE FORGIVE ME FOR DRAGGING YOU HERE TO THE RE-VERSE.
I'M SORRY TO HAVE FORCED YOU INTO A FIGHT YOU NEVER WANTED.
FLAP
TO MAKE UP FOR IT...

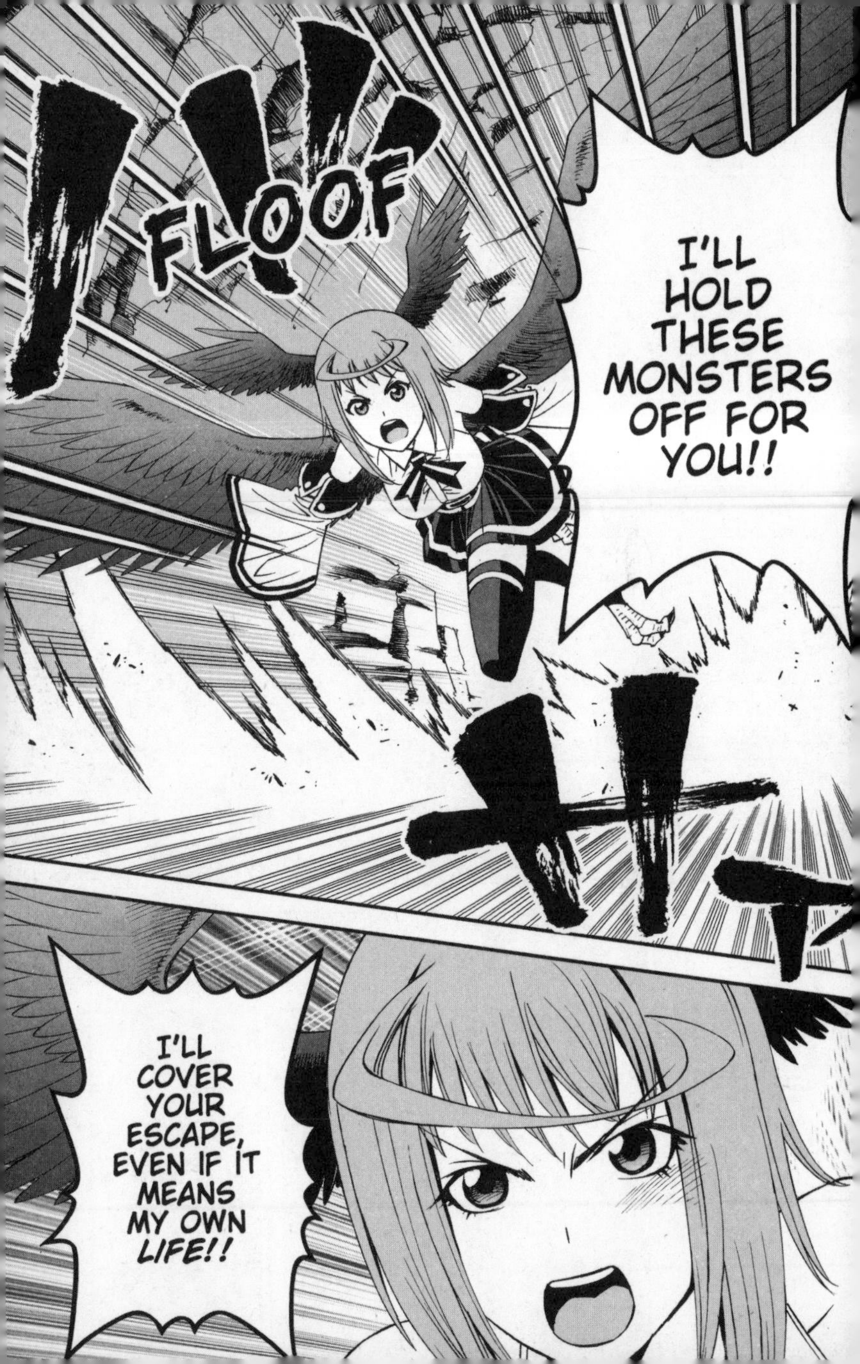
FLOOF
I'LL HOLD THESE MONSTERS OFF FOR YOU!!
I'LL COVER YOUR ESCAPE, EVEN IF IT MEANS MY OWN *LIFE*!!

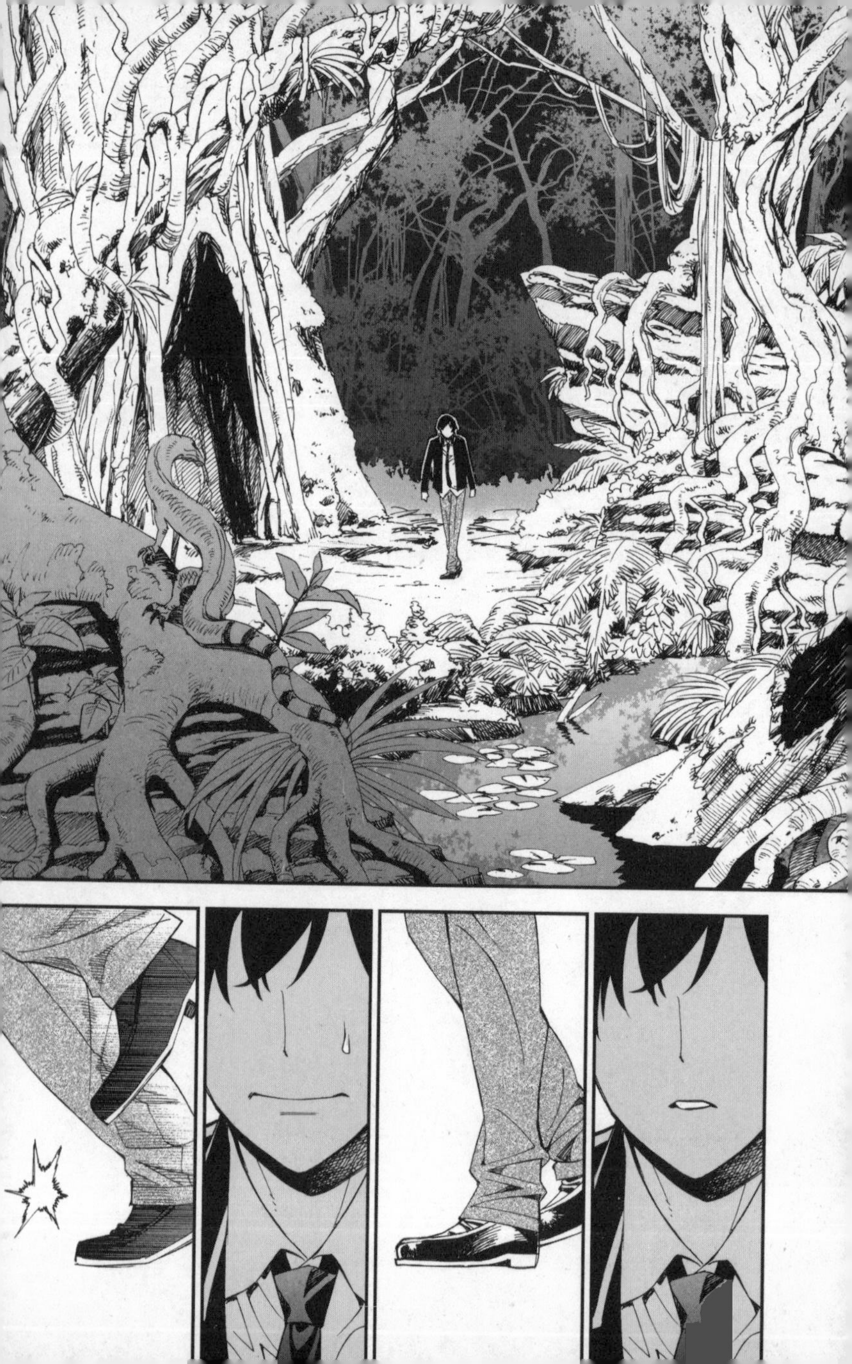

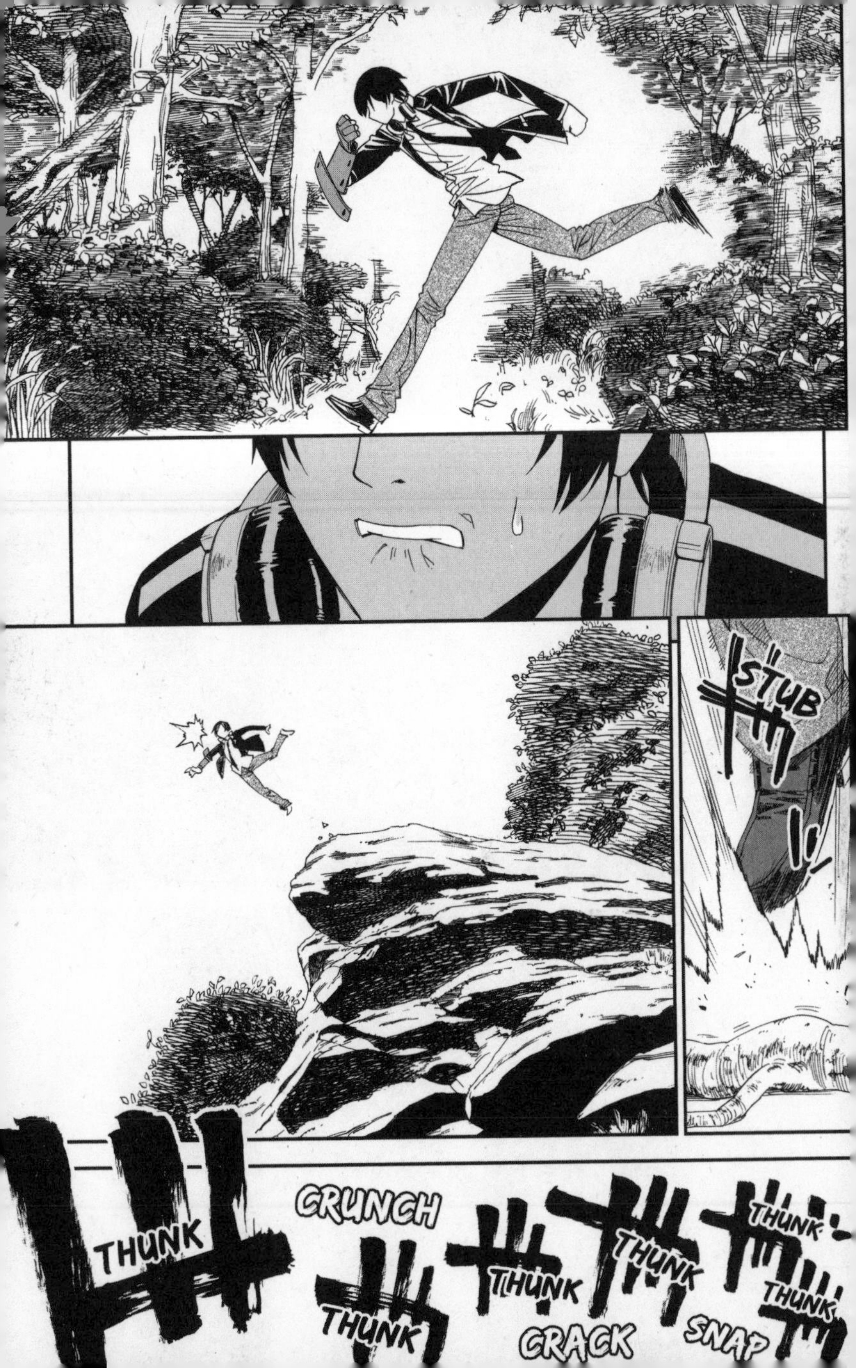
STUB
THUNK
THUNK
SNAP
THUNK
CRACK
THUNK
THUNK
CRUNCH
THUNK

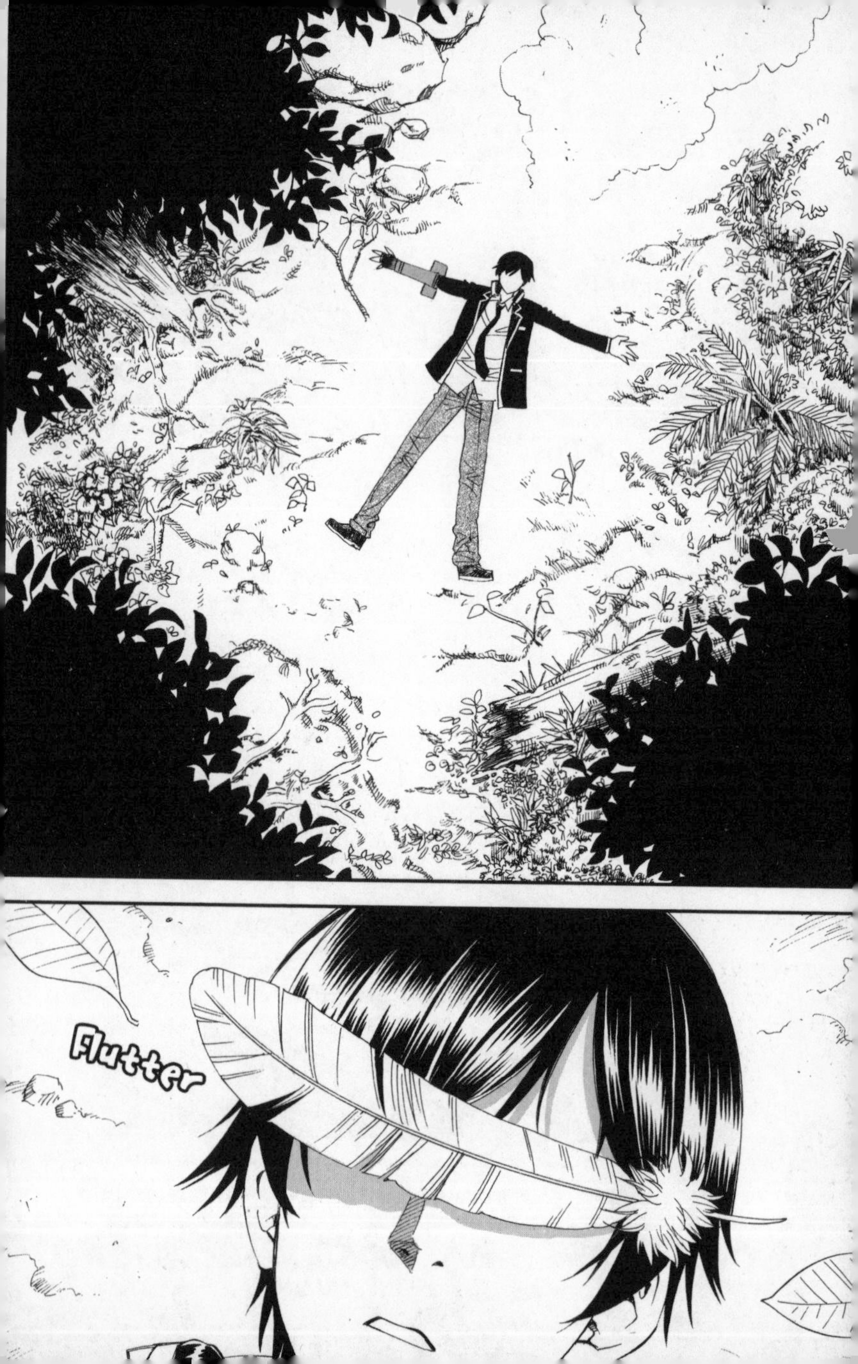
Flutter

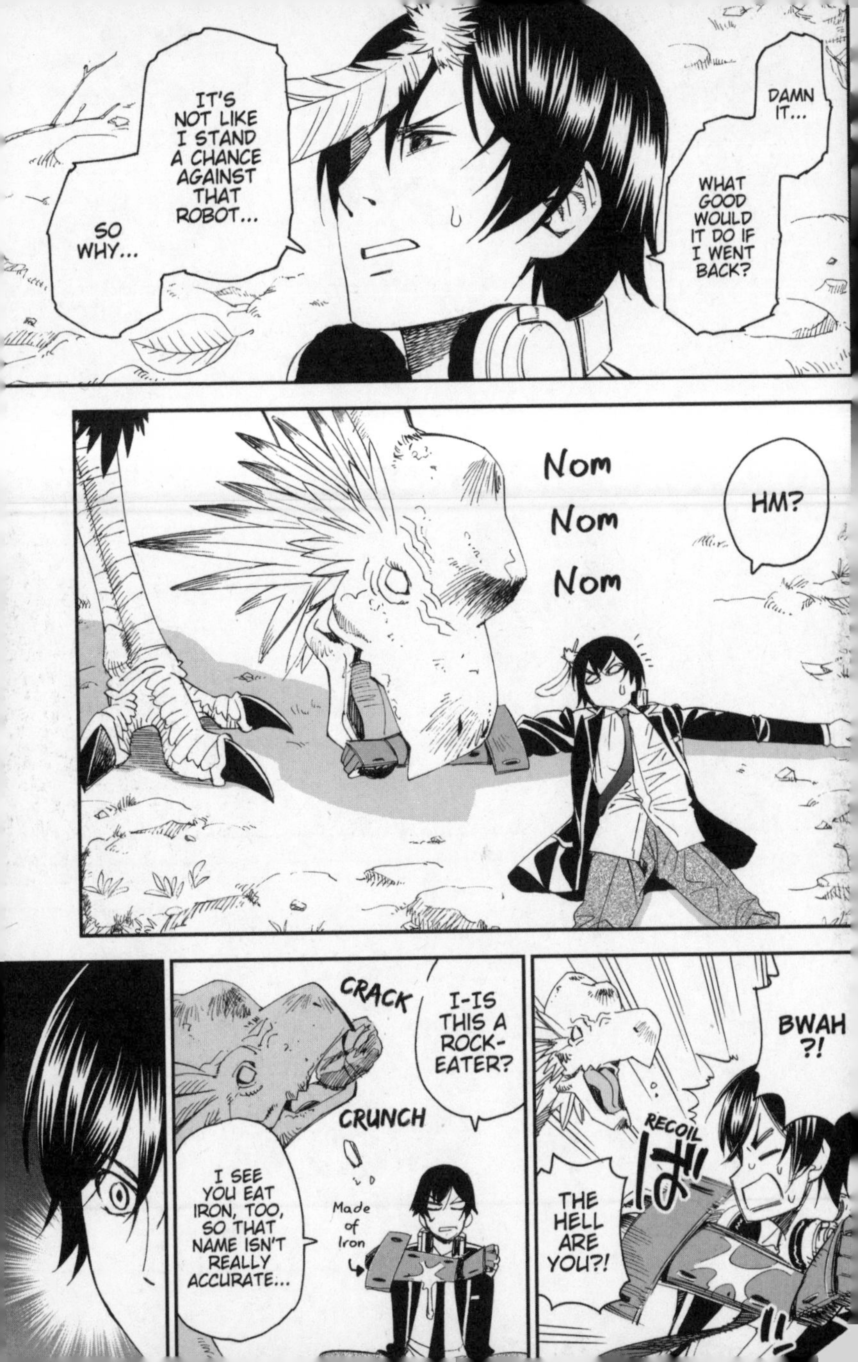
DAMN IT...
WHAT GOOD WOULD IT DO IF I WENT BACK?
IT'S NOT LIKE I STAND A CHANCE AGAINST THAT ROBOT...
SO WHY...
HM?
Nom Nom Nom
BWAH?!
RECOIL
THE HELL ARE YOU?!
I-IS THIS A ROCK-EATER?
CRACK
CRUNCH
Made of Iron
I SEE YOU EAT IRON, TOO, SO THAT NAME ISN'T REALLY ACCURATE...

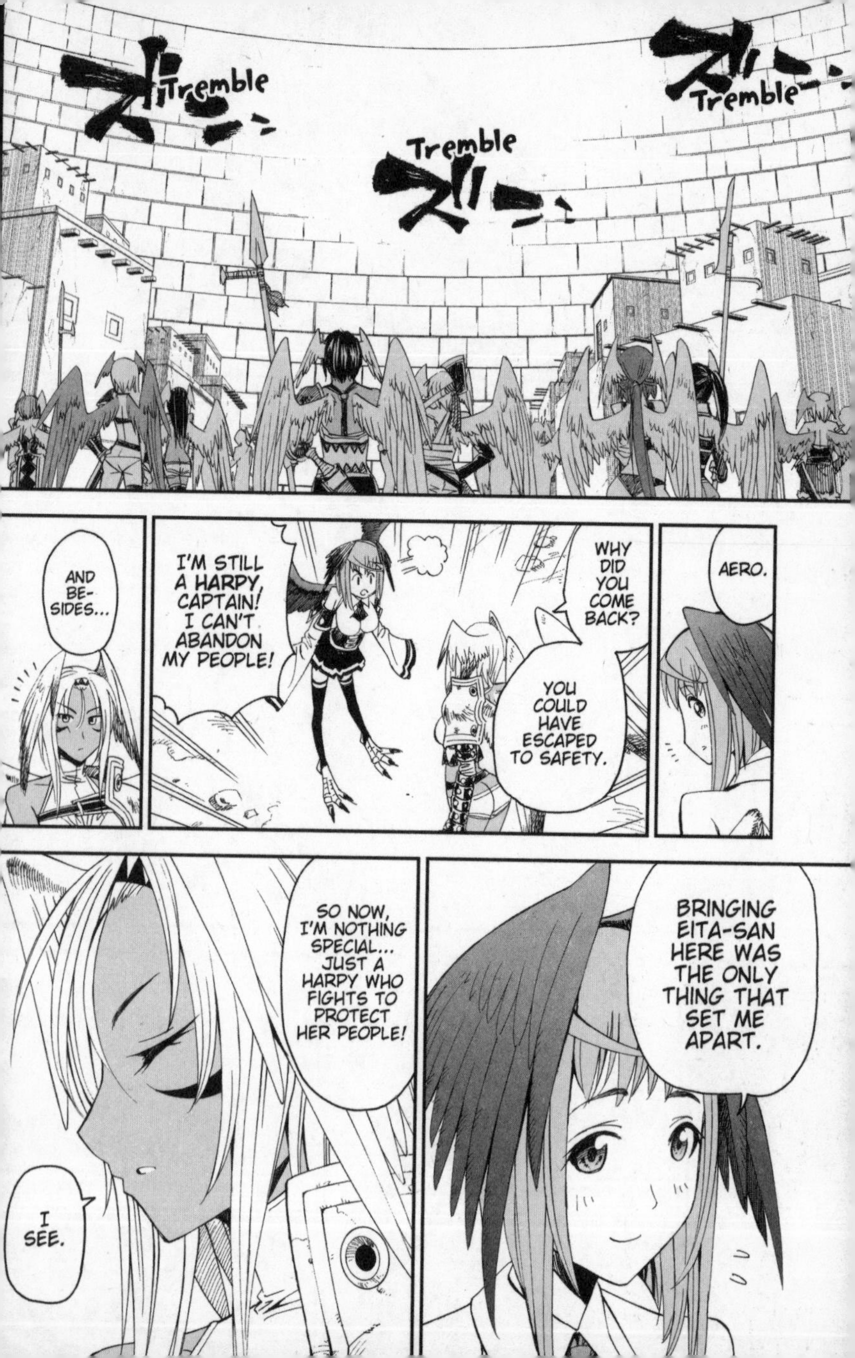
Tremble
Tremble
Tremble
AERO.
WHY DID YOU COME BACK?
YOU COULD HAVE ESCAPED TO SAFETY.
I'M STILL A HARPY, CAPTAIN! I CAN'T ABANDON MY PEOPLE!
AND BE-SIDES...
BRINGING EITA-SAN HERE WAS THE ONLY THING THAT SET ME APART.
SO NOW, I'M NOTHING SPECIAL... JUST A HARPY WHO FIGHTS TO PROTECT HER PEOPLE!
I SEE.

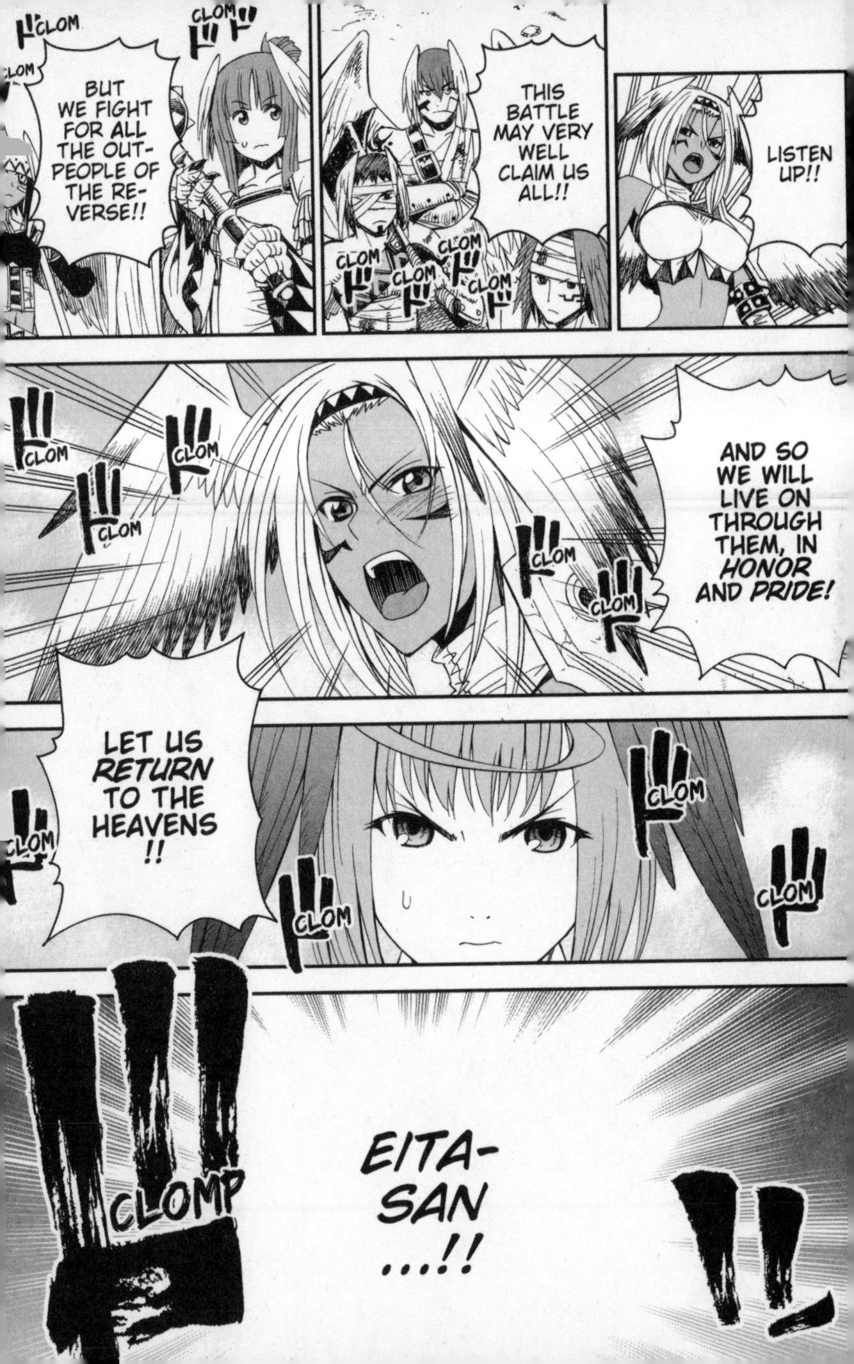
LISTEN UP!!
THIS BATTLE MAY VERY WELL CLAIM US ALL!!
CLOM
CLOM
CLOM
CLOM
BUT WE FIGHT FOR ALL THE OUT-PEOPLE OF THE RE-VERSE!!
CLOM
CLOM
CLOM
AND SO WE WILL LIVE ON THROUGH THEM, IN *HONOR* AND *PRIDE*!
CLOM
CLOM
CLOM
CLOM
CLOM
CLOM
CLOM
CLOM
LET US *RETURN* TO THE HEAVENS !!
CLOM
EITA-SAN ...!!
CLOMP

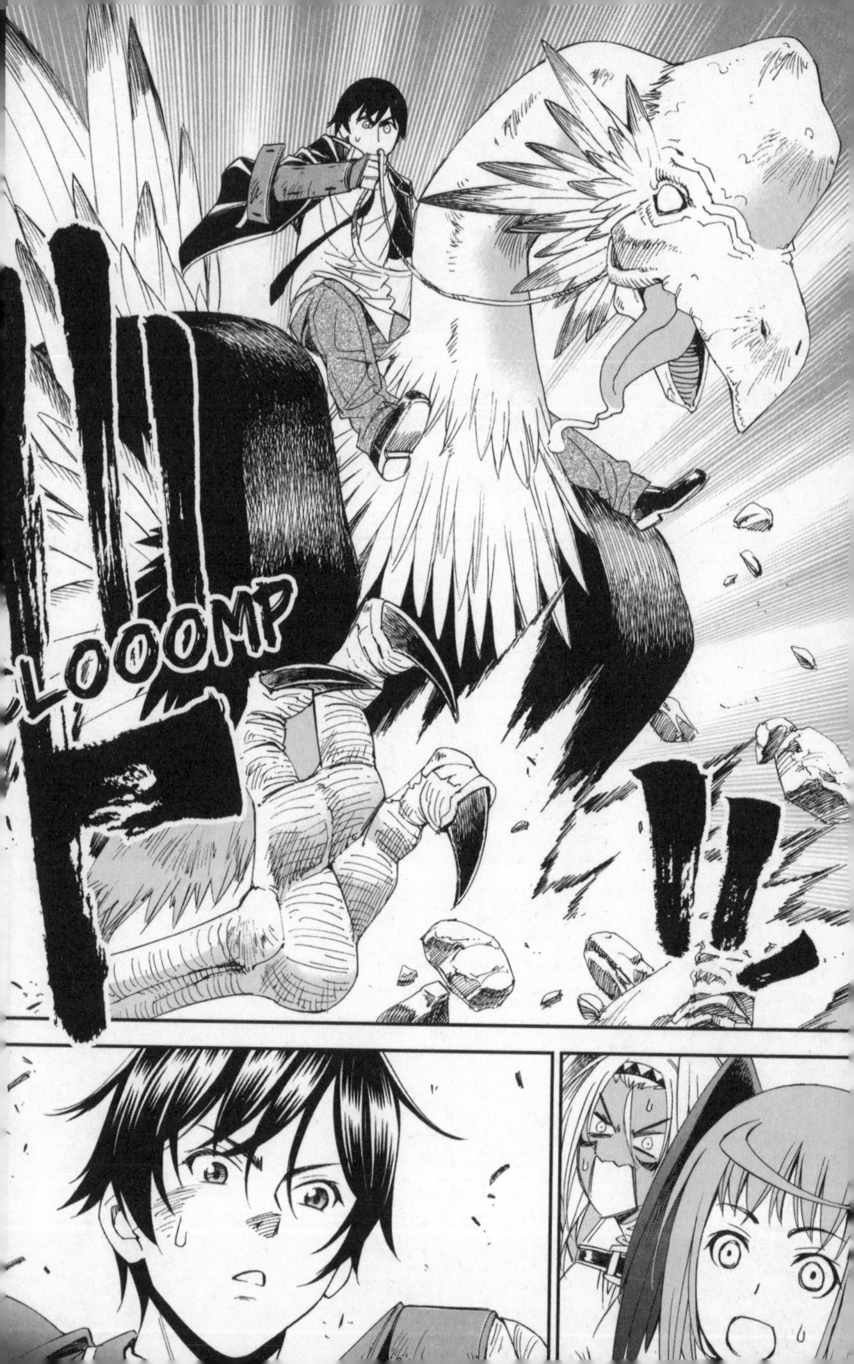
LOOOMP

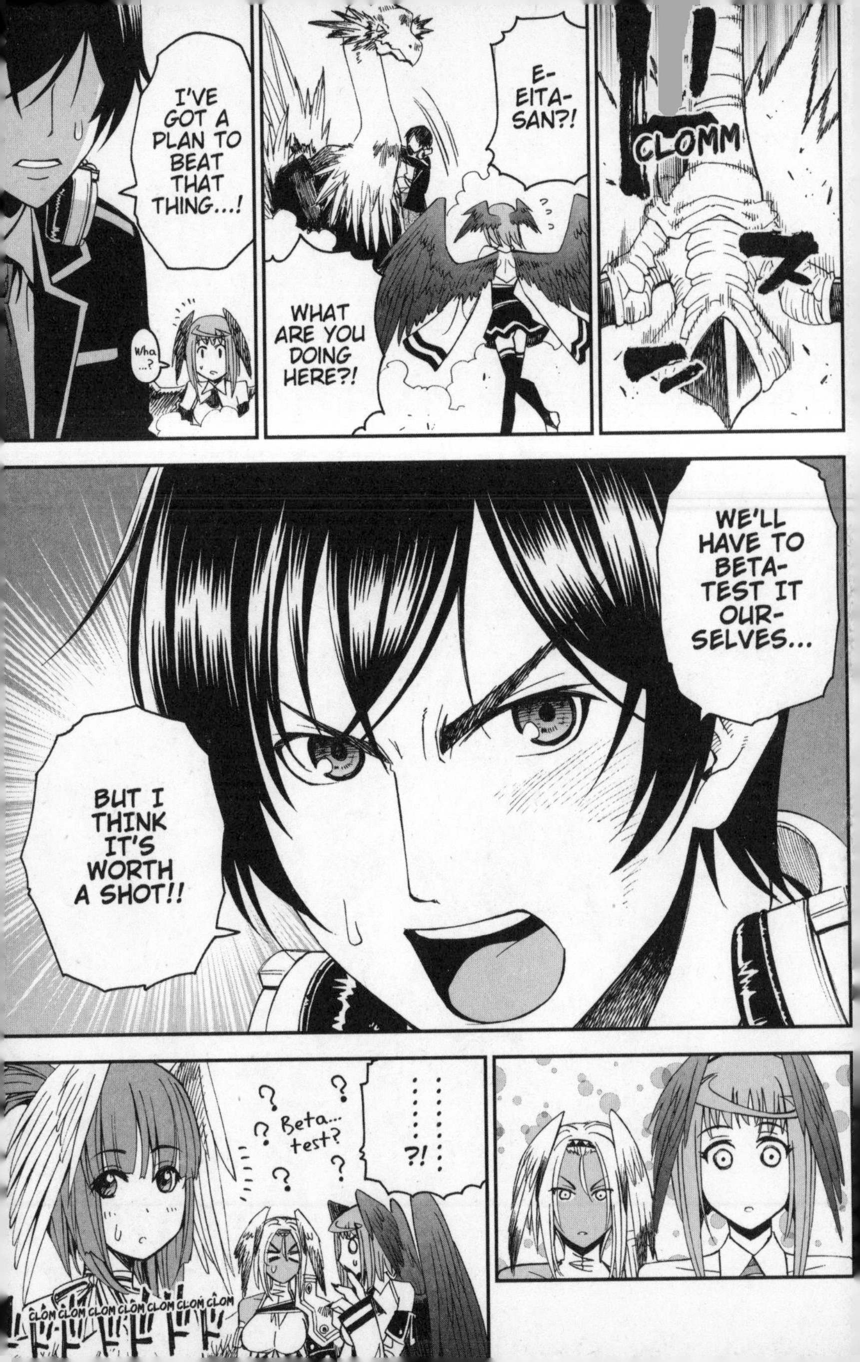
CLOMM
E-EITA-SAN?!
WHAT ARE YOU DOING HERE?!
I'VE GOT A PLAN TO BEAT THAT THING...!
Wha...?
WE'LL HAVE TO BETA-TEST IT OURSELVES...
BUT I THINK IT'S WORTH A SHOT!!
......?!
Beta... test?
CLOM CLOM CLOM CLOM CLOM CLOM CLOM

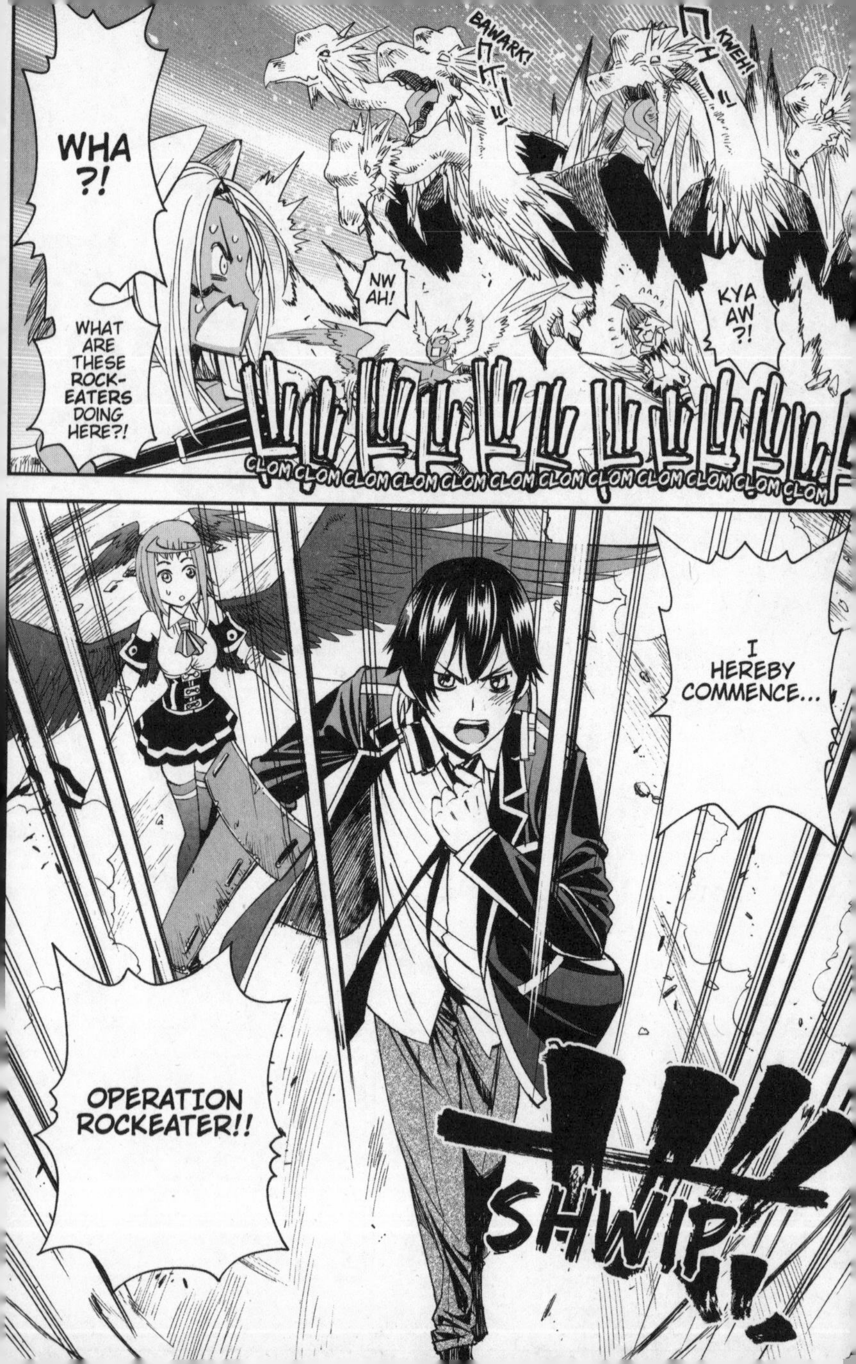
KWEH!
BAWARK!
KYA AW?!
NW AH!
WHA ?!
WHAT ARE THESE ROCK-EATERS DOING HERE?!
CLOM CLOM CLOM CLOM CLOM CLOM CLOM CLOM CLOM CLOM CLOM CLOM
I HEREBY COMMENCE...
OPERATION ROCKEATER!!
SHWIP!!

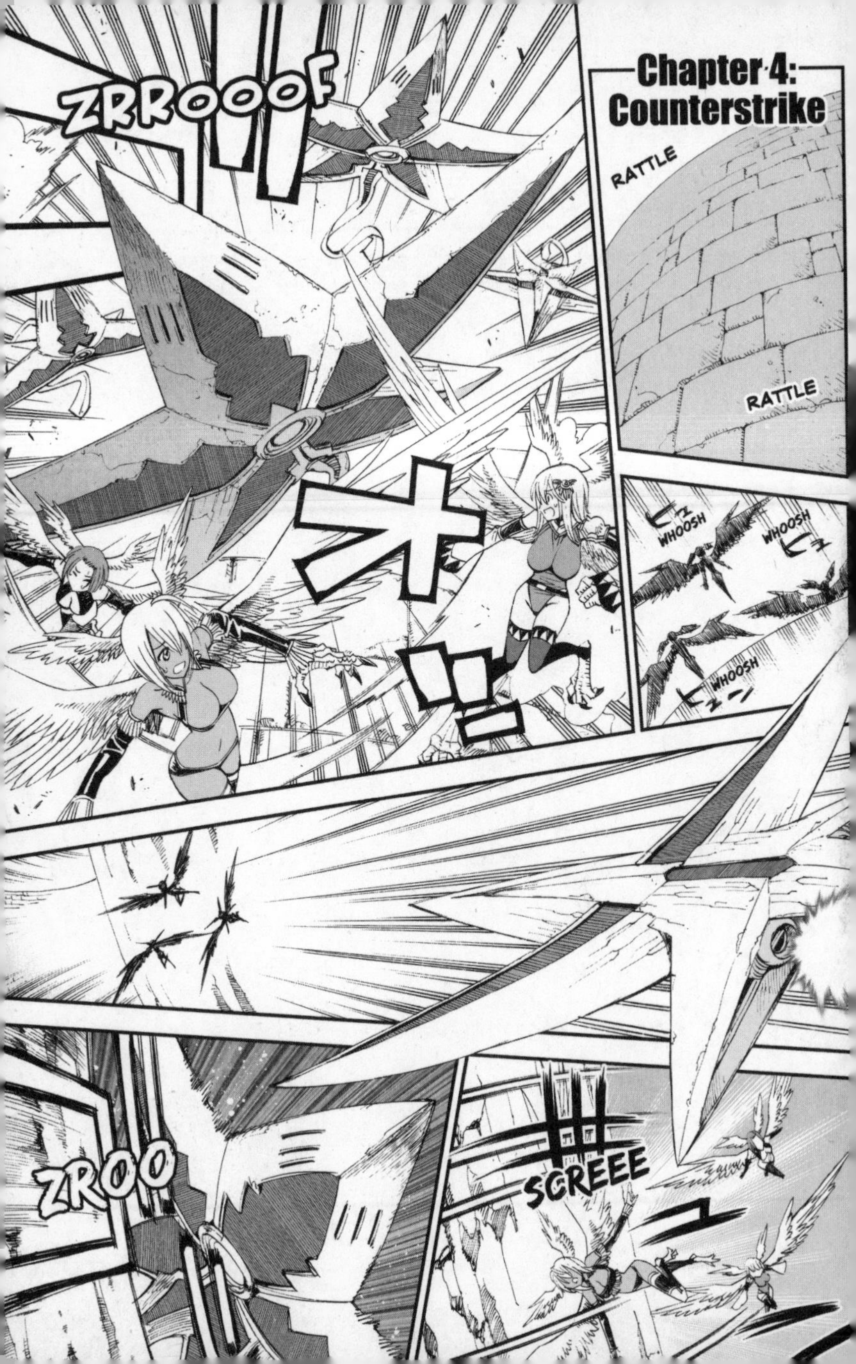
Chapter 4: Counterstrike
RATTLE
RATTLE
WHOOSH
WHOOSH
WHOOSH
ZRROOOF
SCREEE
ZROO

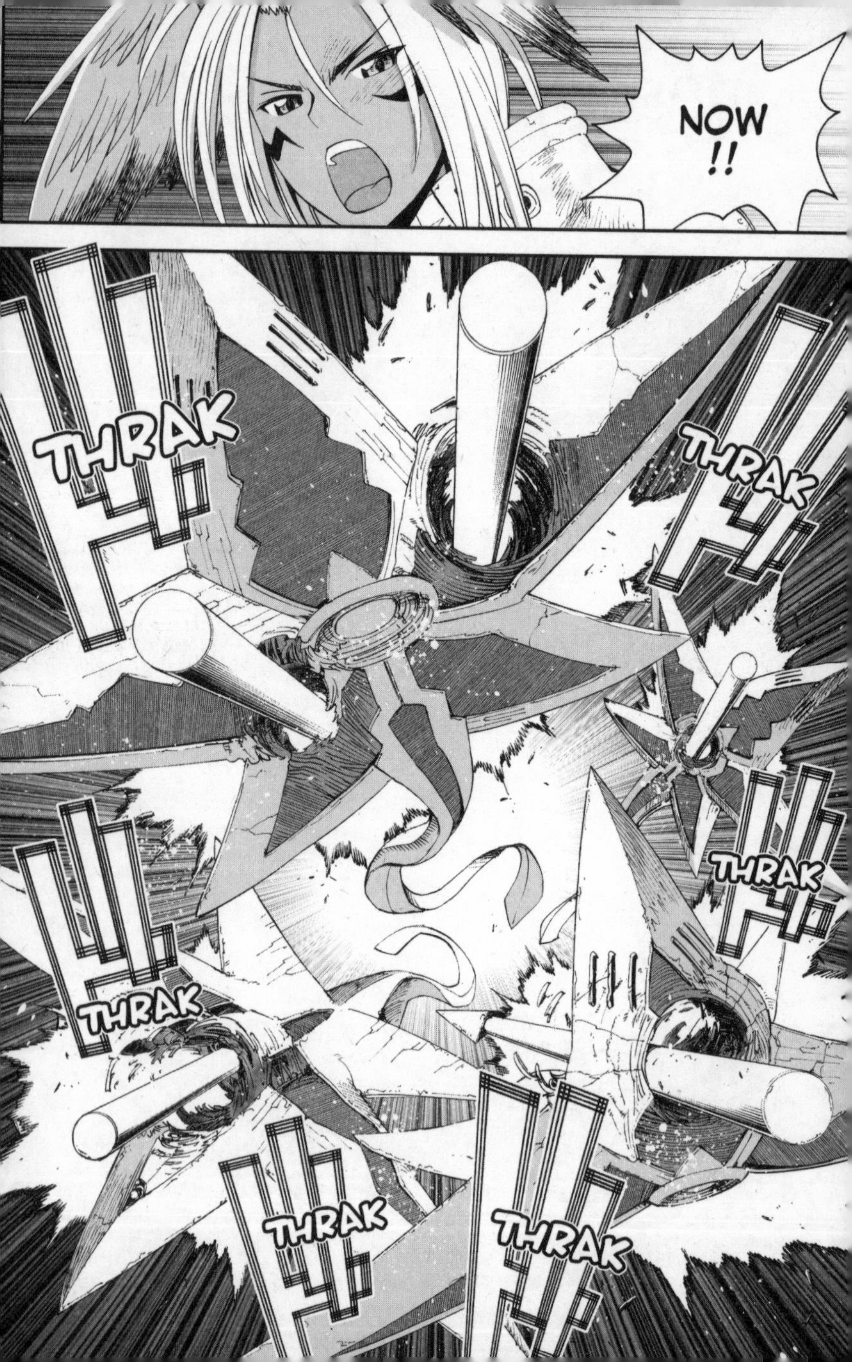
NOW !!
THRAK
THRAK
THRAK
THRAK
THRAK
THRAK

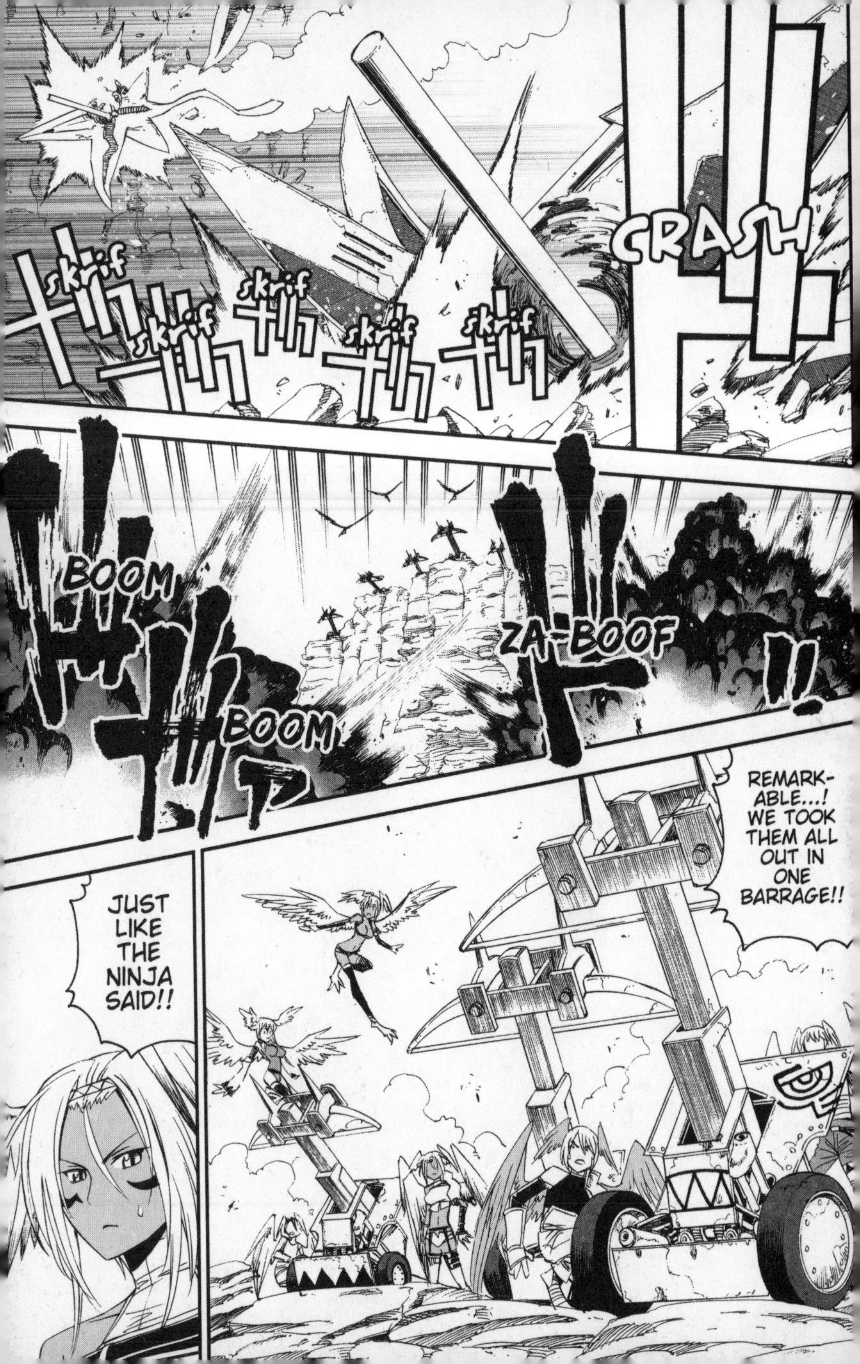
CRASH
skrif
skrif
skrif
skrif
skrif
ZA-BOOF
BOOM
BOOM
REMARK-ABLE...! WE TOOK THEM ALL OUT IN ONE BARRAGE!!
JUST LIKE THE NINJA SAID!!

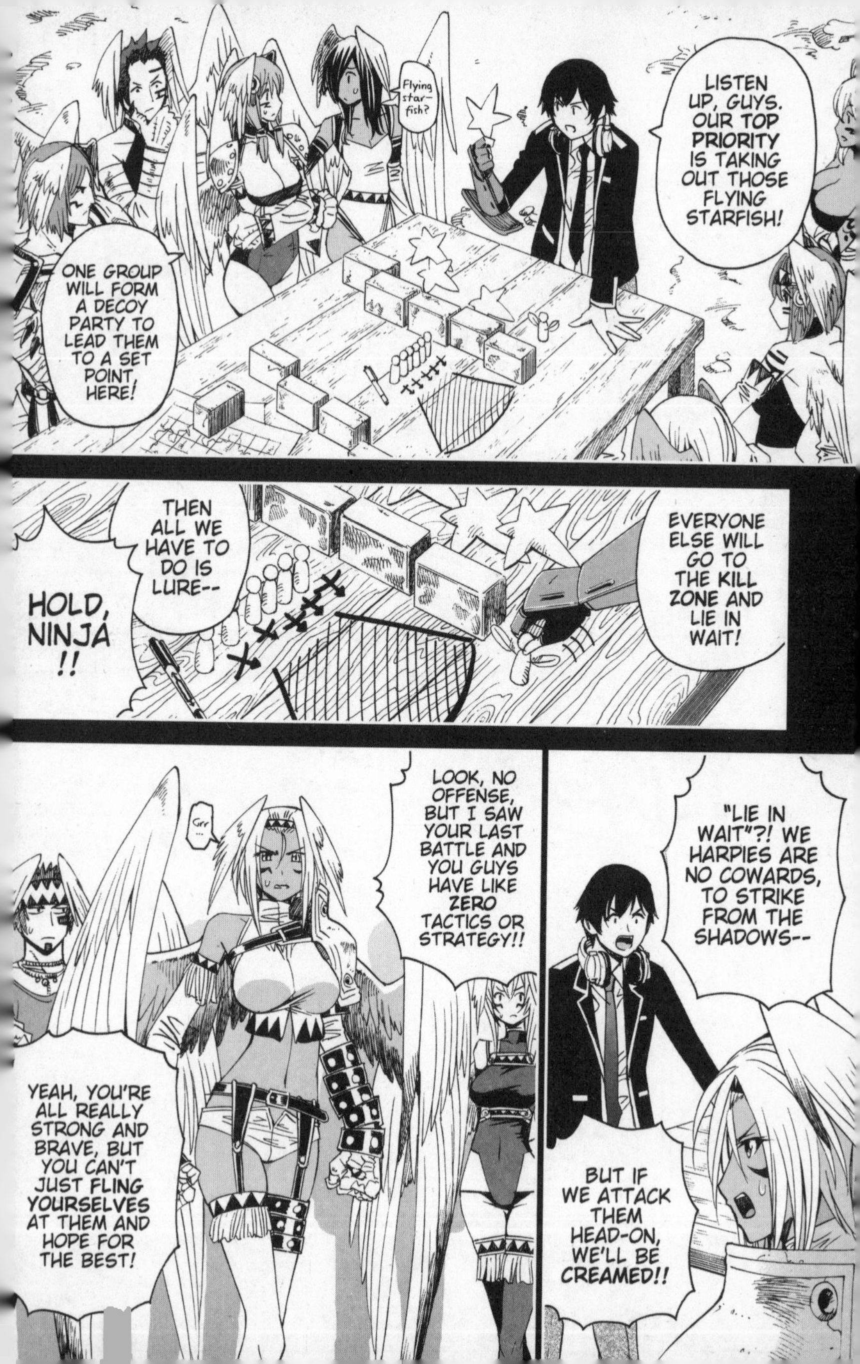
LISTEN UP, GUYS. OUR TOP PRIORITY IS TAKING OUT THOSE FLYING STARFISH!
Flying star-fish?
ONE GROUP WILL FORM A DECOY PARTY TO LEAD THEM TO A SET POINT, HERE!
EVERYONE ELSE WILL GO TO THE KILL ZONE AND LIE IN WAIT!
THEN ALL WE HAVE TO DO IS LURE--
HOLD, NINJÁ!!
"LIE IN WAIT"?! WE HARPIES ARE NO COWARDS, TO STRIKE FROM THE SHADOWS--
BUT IF WE ATTACK THEM HEAD-ON, WE'LL BE CREAMED!!
LOOK, NO OFFENSE, BUT I SAW YOUR LAST BATTLE AND YOU GUYS HAVE LIKE ZERO TACTICS OR STRATEGY!!
Grr…
YEAH, YOU'RE ALL REALLY STRONG AND BRAVE, BUT YOU CAN'T JUST FLING YOURSELVES AT THEM AND HOPE FOR THE BEST!

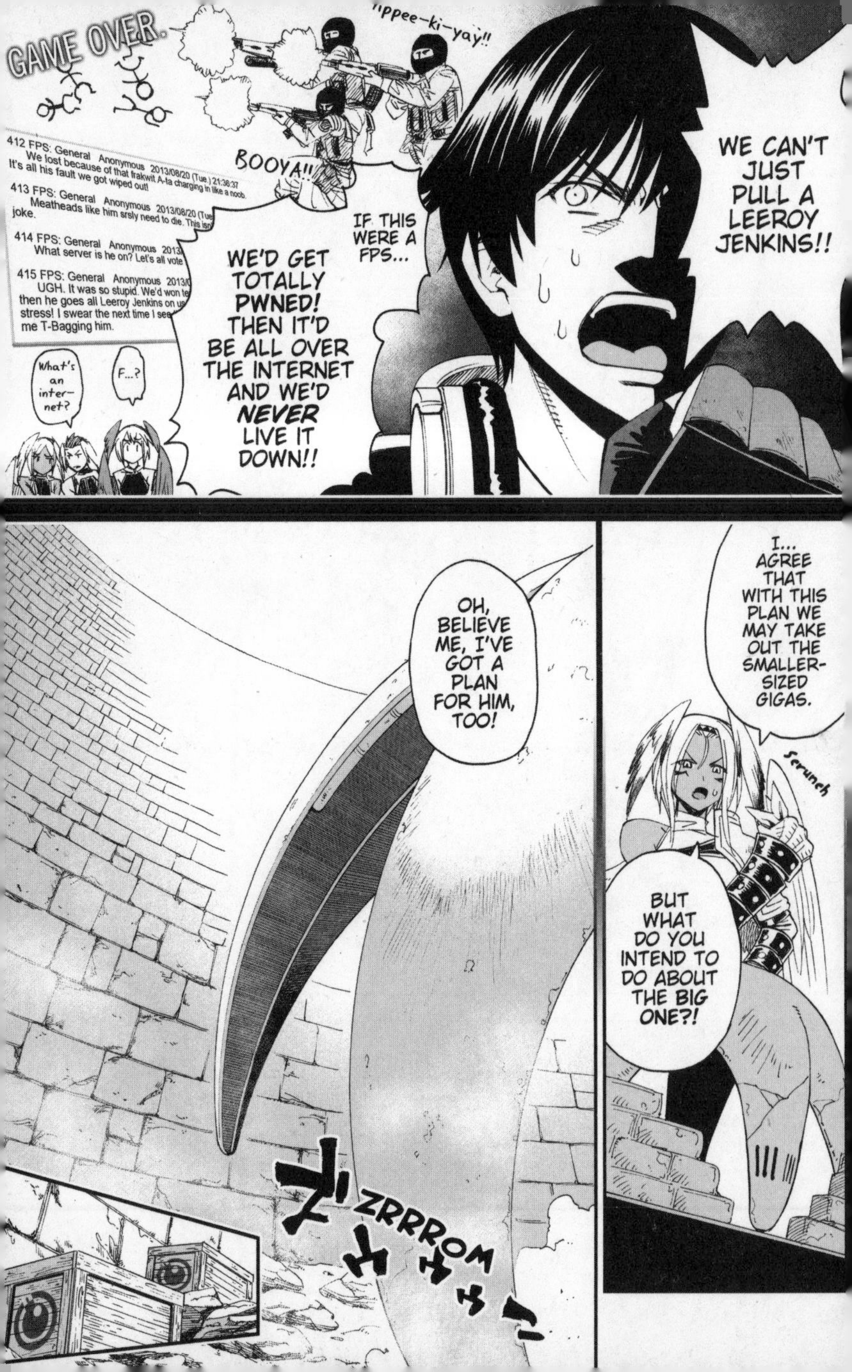
WE CAN'T JUST PULL A LEEROY JENKINS!!
ippee-ki-yay!!
GAME OVER.
IF THIS WERE A FPS...
WE'D GET TOTALLY PWNED! THEN IT'D BE ALL OVER THE INTERNET AND WE'D NEVER LIVE IT DOWN!!
BOOYA!!
412 FPS: General Anonymous 2013/08/20 (Tue.) 21:36:37
We lost because of that frakwit A-ta charging in like a noob. It's all his fault we got wiped out!
413 FPS: General Anonymous 2013/08/20 (Tue
Meatheads like him srsly need to die. This isn
joke.
414 FPS: General Anonymous 2013
What server is he on? Let's all vote
415 FPS: General Anonymous 2013/
UGH. It was so stupid. We'd won te
then he goes all Leeroy Jenkins on us
stress! I swear the next time I see
me T-Bagging him.
F...?
What's an internet?
I... AGREE THAT WITH THIS PLAN WE MAY TAKE OUT THE SMALLER-SIZED GIGAS.
Scrunch
BUT WHAT DO YOU INTEND TO DO ABOUT THE BIG ONE?!
OH, BELIEVE ME, I'VE GOT A PLAN FOR HIM, TOO!
ZRRROM

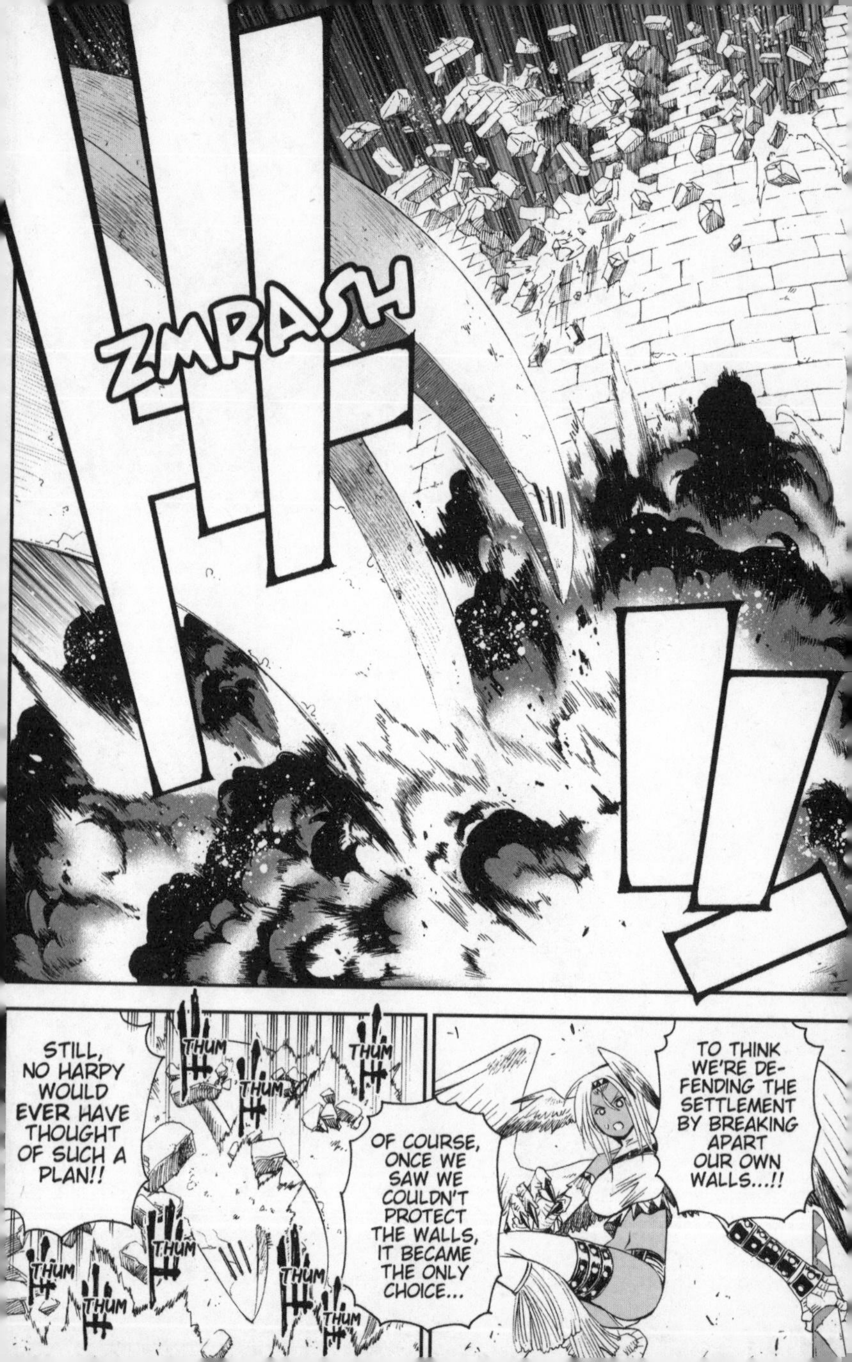
ZMRASH
TO THINK WE'RE DEFENDING THE SETTLEMENT BY BREAKING APART OUR OWN WALLS...!!
OF COURSE, ONCE WE SAW WE COULDN'T PROTECT THE WALLS, IT BECAME THE ONLY CHOICE...
THUM
THUM
THUM
STILL, NO HARPY WOULD EVER HAVE THOUGHT OF SUCH A PLAN!!
THUM
THUM
THUM
THUM
THUM

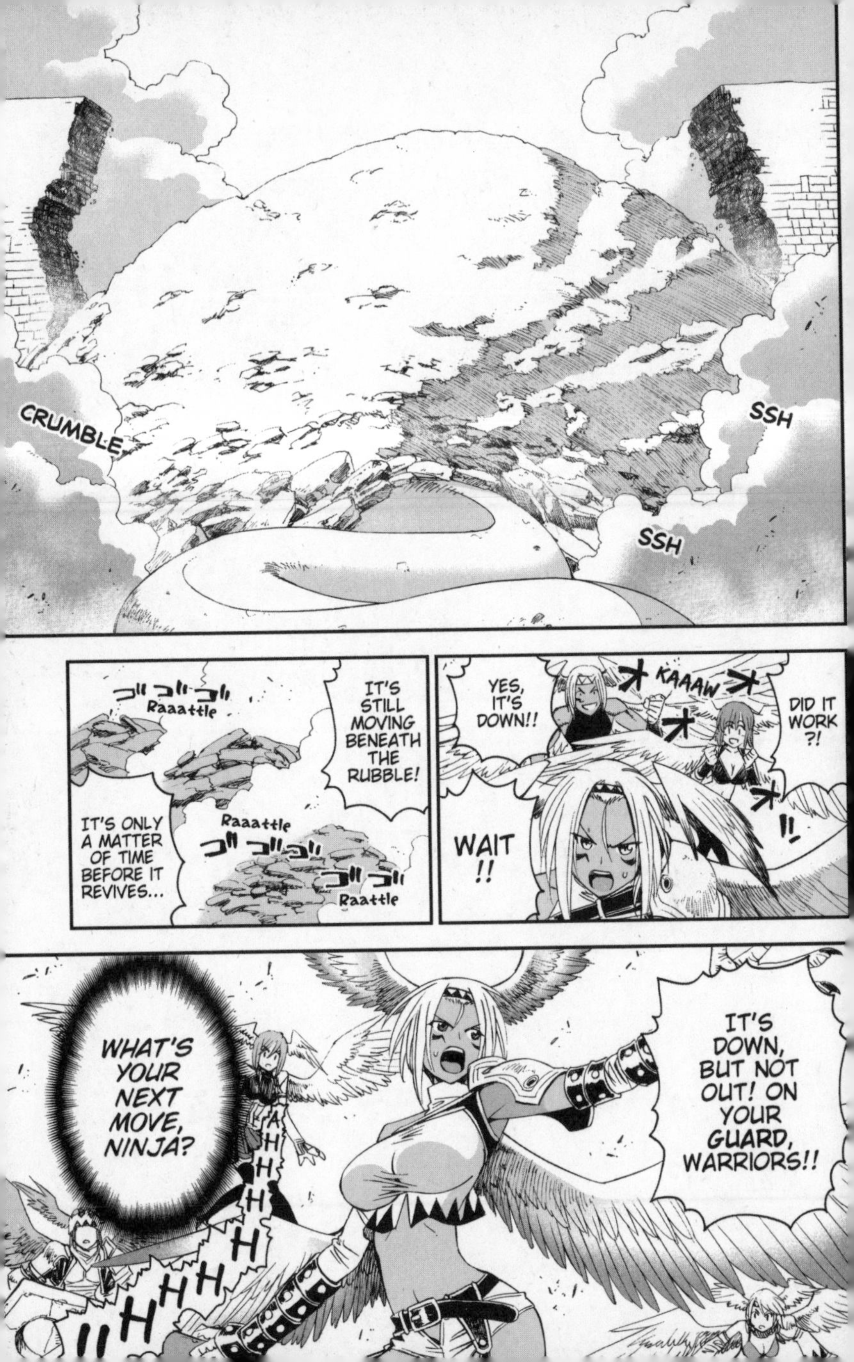
CRUMBLE
SSH
SSH
YES, IT'S DOWN!!
KAAAW
DID IT WORK?!
WAIT!!
IT'S STILL MOVING BENEATH THE RUBBLE!
Raaattle
Raaattle
Raattle
IT'S ONLY A MATTER OF TIME BEFORE IT REVIVES...
IT'S DOWN, BUT NOT OUT! ON YOUR GUARD, WARRIORS!!
WHAT'S YOUR NEXT MOVE, NINJA?
AHHHHHHHHHH!!

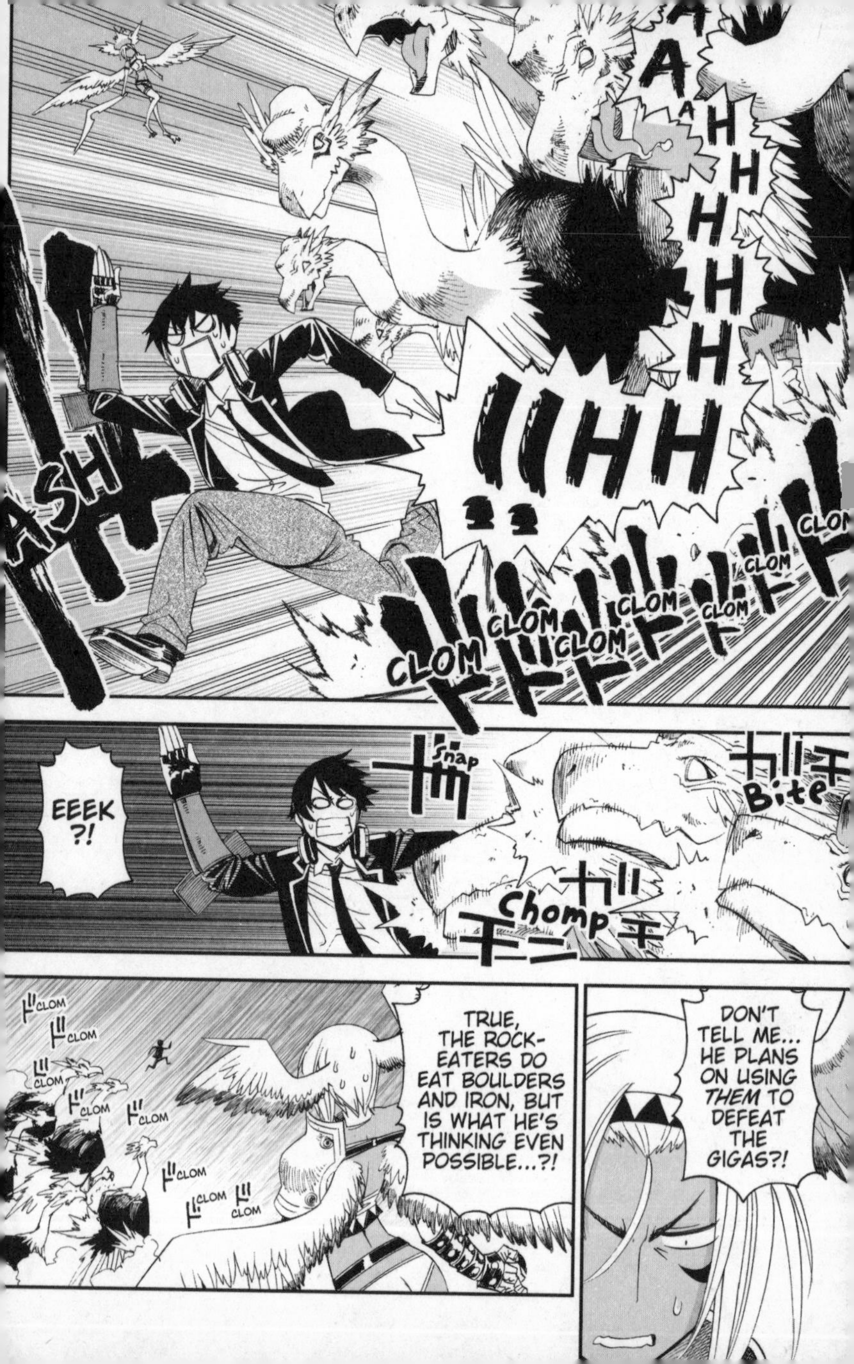
AAAHHHHHHH!!
ASH
CLOM
CLOM
CLOM
CLOM
CLOM
CLOM
CLOM
CLOM
Bite
Snap
EEEK ?!
Chomp
DON'T TELL ME... HE PLANS ON USING THEM TO DEFEAT THE GIGAS?!
TRUE, THE ROCK-EATERS DO EAT BOULDERS AND IRON, BUT IS WHAT HE'S THINKING EVEN POSSIBLE...?!
CLOM
CLOM
CLOM
CLOM
CLOM
CLOM
CLOM
CLOM

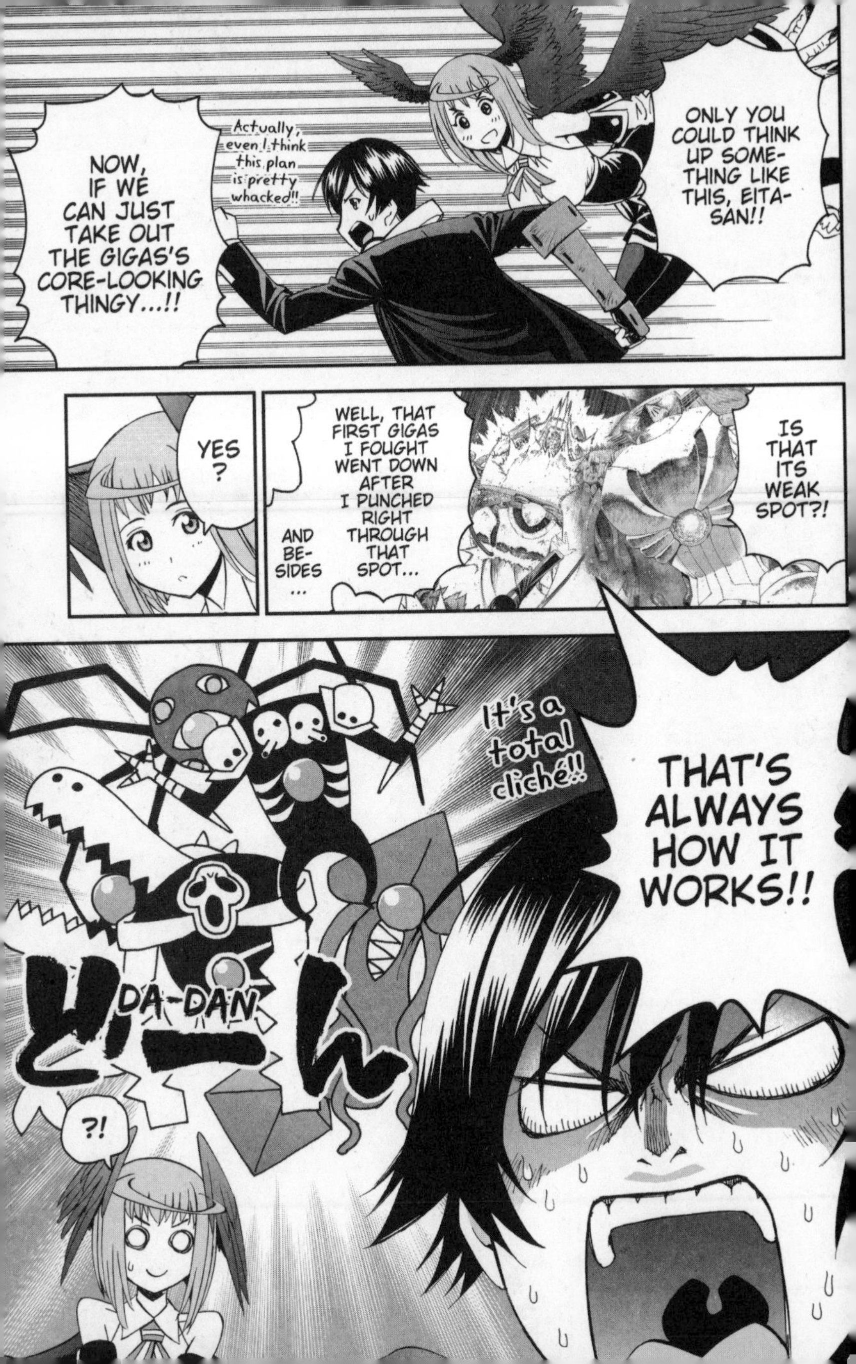
ONLY YOU COULD THINK UP SOME-THING LIKE THIS, EITA-SAN!!
Actually, even I think this plan is pretty whacked!!
NOW, IF WE CAN JUST TAKE OUT THE GIGAS'S CORE-LOOKING THINGY...!!
IS THAT ITS WEAK SPOT?!
WELL, THAT FIRST GIGAS I FOUGHT WENT DOWN AFTER I PUNCHED RIGHT THROUGH THAT SPOT...
AND BE-SIDES ...
YES ?
THAT'S ALWAYS HOW IT WORKS!!
It's a total cliché!!
DA-DAN
?!

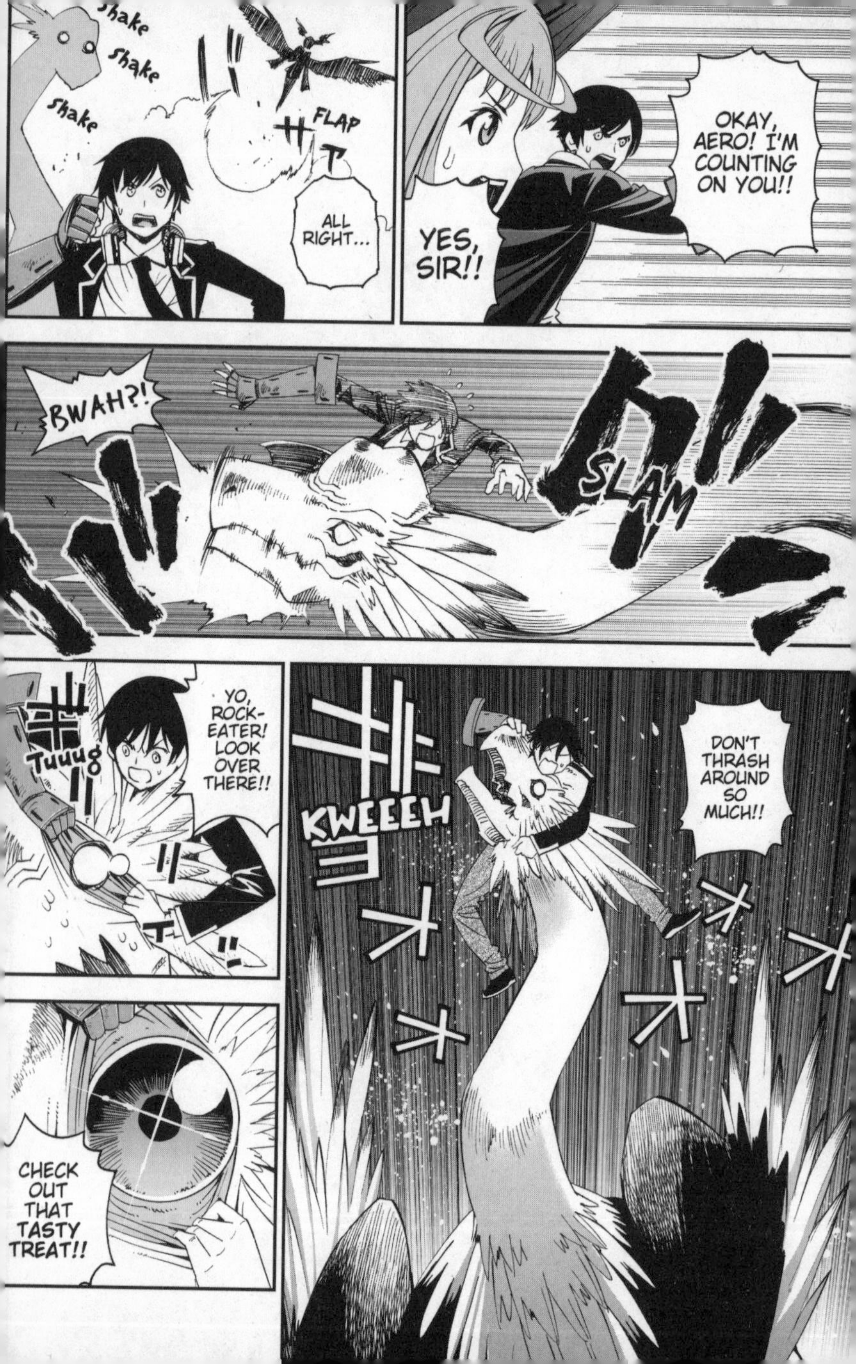
OKAY, AERO! I'M COUNTING ON YOU!!
YES, SIR!!
Shake
Shake
Shake
FLAP
ALL RIGHT...
SLAM
BWAH?!
DON'T THRASH AROUND SO MUCH!!
KWEEEH
YO, ROCK-EATER! LOOK OVER THERE!!
Tuuug
CHECK OUT THAT TASTY TREAT!!

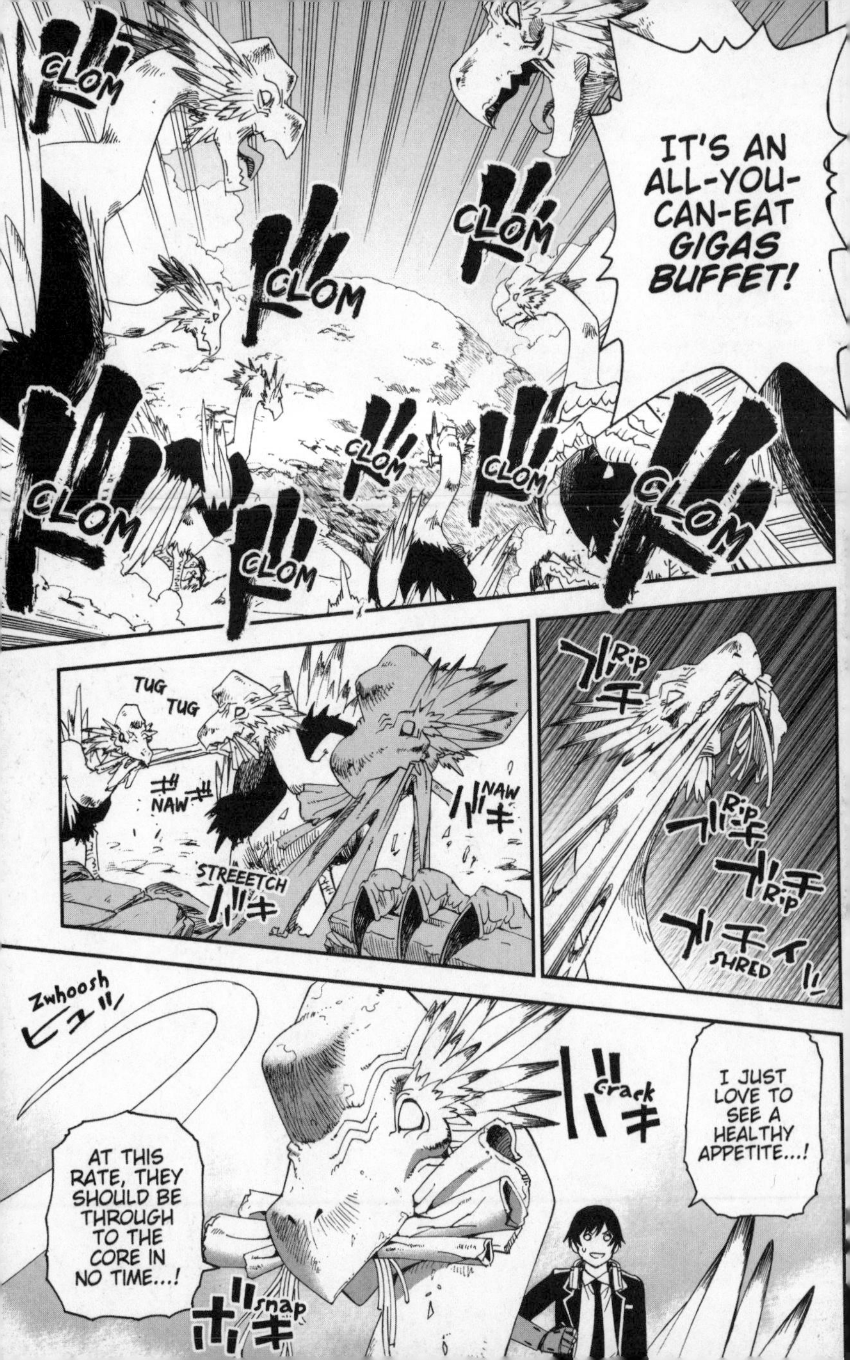
IT'S AN ALL-YOU-CAN-EAT GIGAS BUFFET!
CLOM
CLOM
CLOM
CLOM
CLOM
CLOM
CLOM
CLOM
Rip
Rip
Rip
SHRED
TUG TUG
NAW
NAW
STREEETCH
I JUST LOVE TO SEE A HEALTHY APPETITE...!
crack
Zwhoosh
AT THIS RATE, THEY SHOULD BE THROUGH TO THE CORE IN NO TIME...!
snap

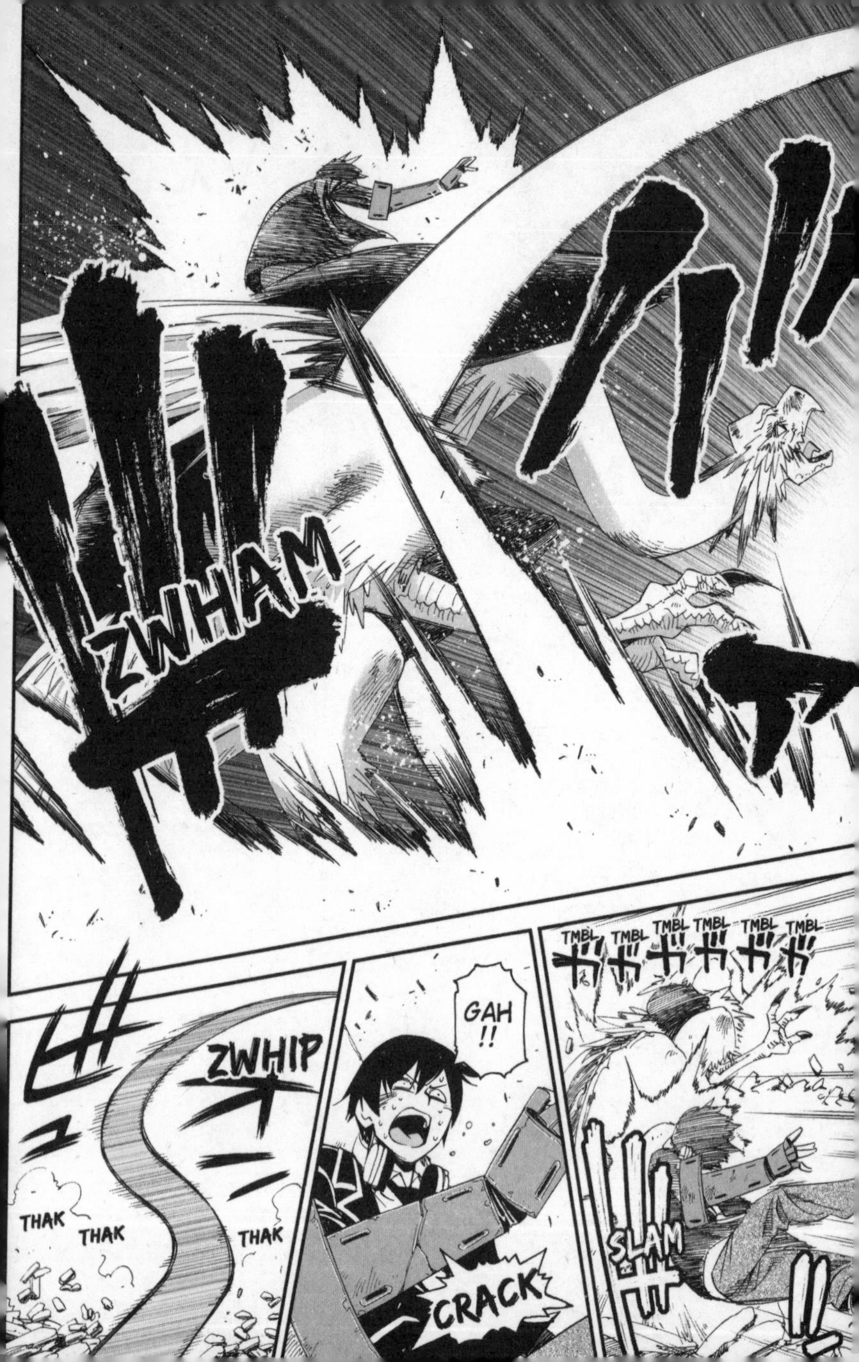
ZWHAM
TMBL TMBL TMBL TMBL TMBL TMBL
SLAM
GAH !!
CRACK
ZWHIP
THAK THAK THAK

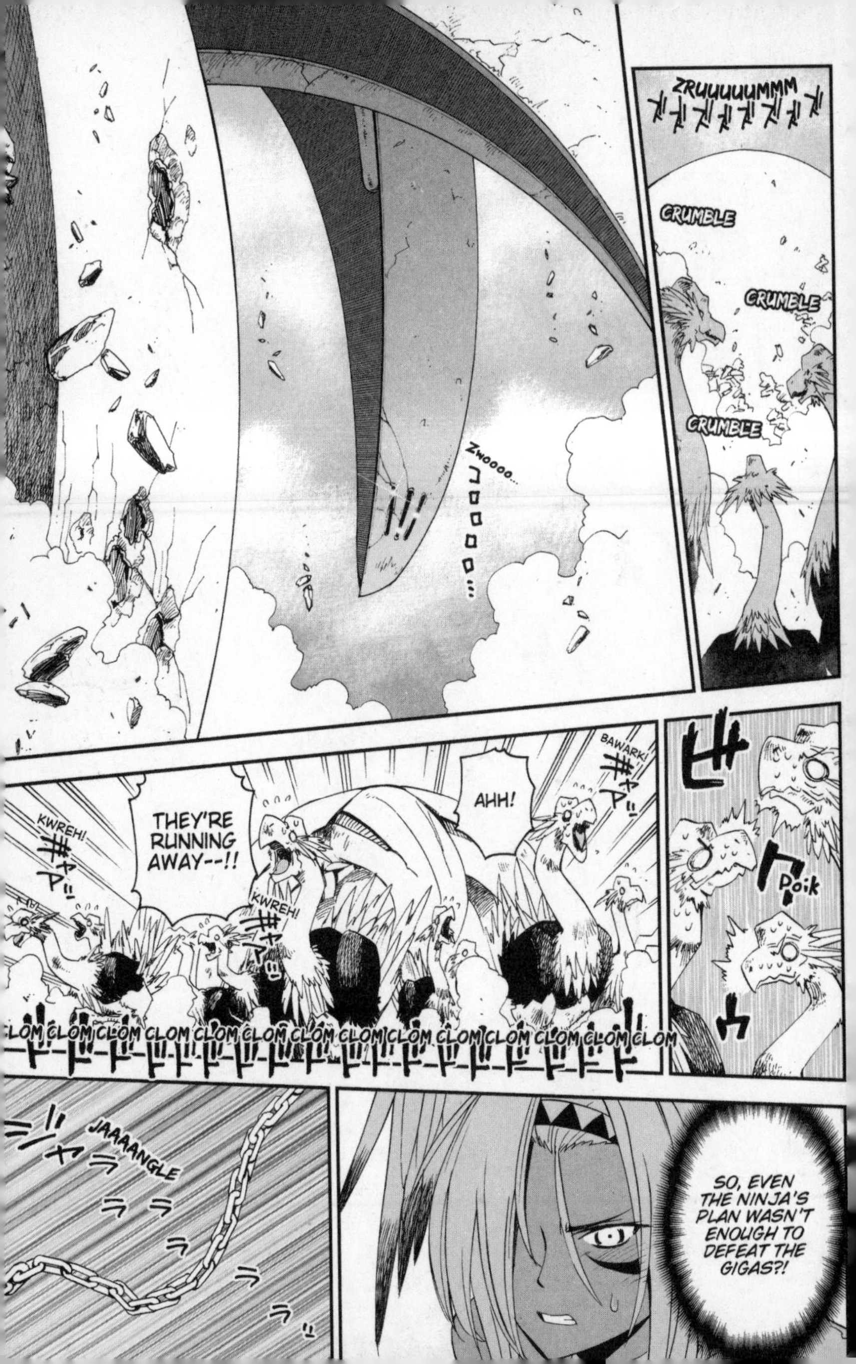
ZRUUUUMMM
CRUMBLE
CRUMBLE
CRUMBLE
ZWOOOO...
Poik
BAWARK!
AHH!
THEY'RE RUNNING AWAY--!!
KWREH!
KWREH!
CLOM CLOM CLOM CLOM CLOM CLOM CLOM CLOM CLOM CLOM CLOM CLOM CLOM CLOM
SO, EVEN THE NINJA'S PLAN WASN'T ENOUGH TO DEFEAT THE GIGAS?!
JAAAANGLE

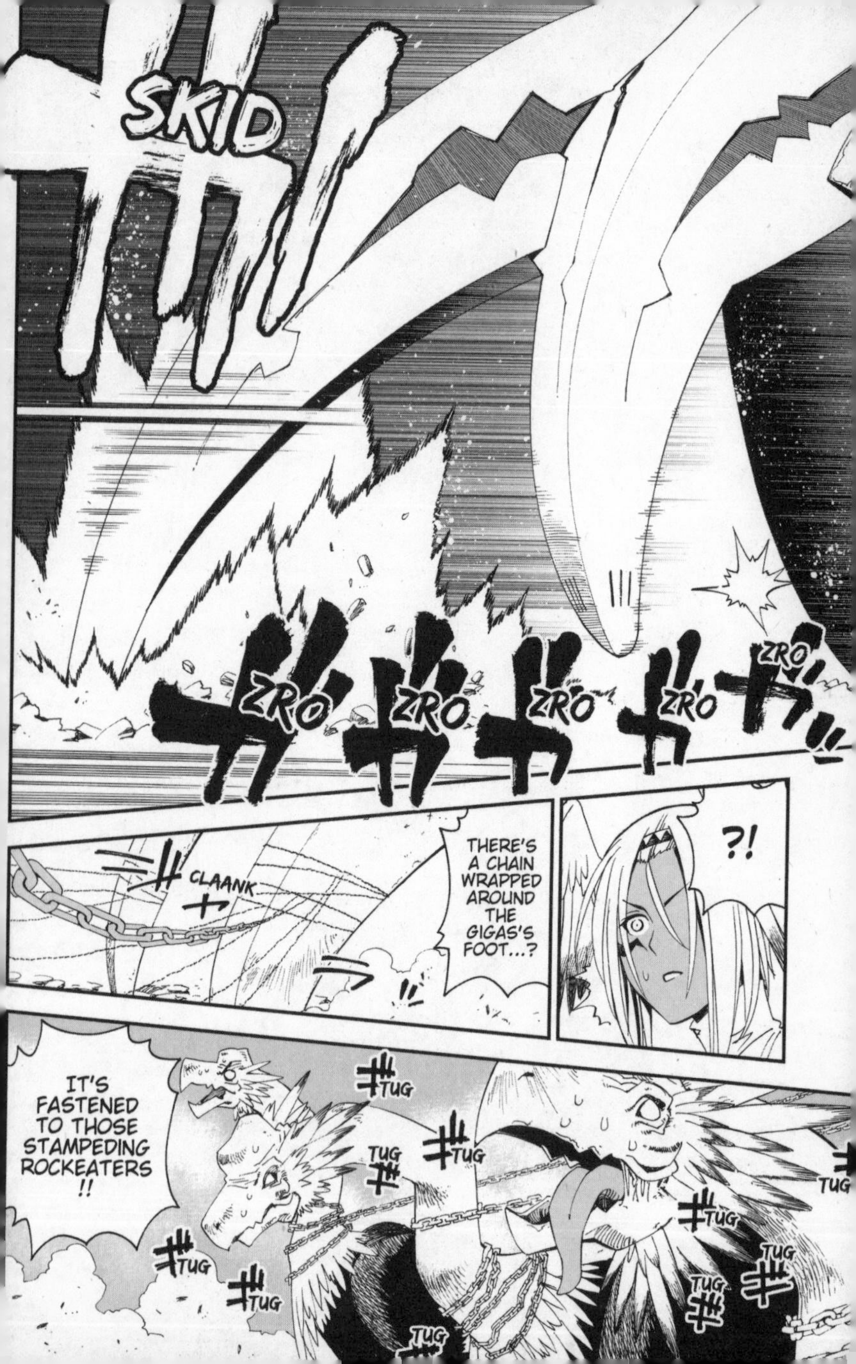
SKID
ZRO ZRO ZRO ZRO ZRO
?!
THERE'S A CHAIN WRAPPED AROUND THE GIGAS'S FOOT...?
CLAANK
IT'S FASTENED TO THOSE STAMPEDING ROCKEATERS !!
TUG
TUG
TUG
TUG
TUG
TUG
TUG
TUG
TUG
TUG

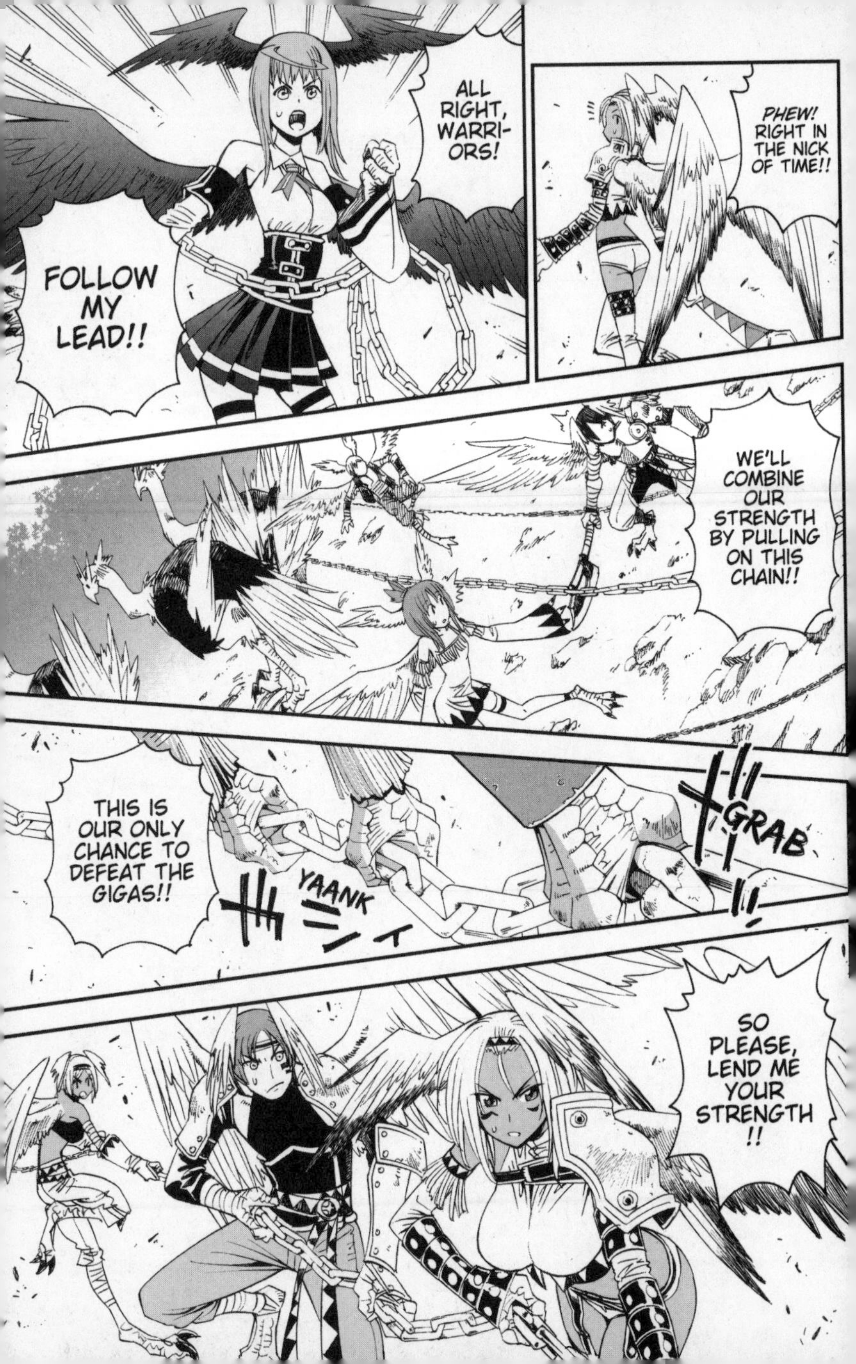
PHEW! RIGHT IN THE NICK OF TIME!!
ALL RIGHT, WARRI-ORS!
FOLLOW MY LEAD!!
WE'LL COMBINE OUR STRENGTH BY PULLING ON THIS CHAIN!!
GRAB
THIS IS OUR ONLY CHANCE TO DEFEAT THE GIGAS!!
YAANK
SO PLEASE, LEND ME YOUR STRENGTH!!

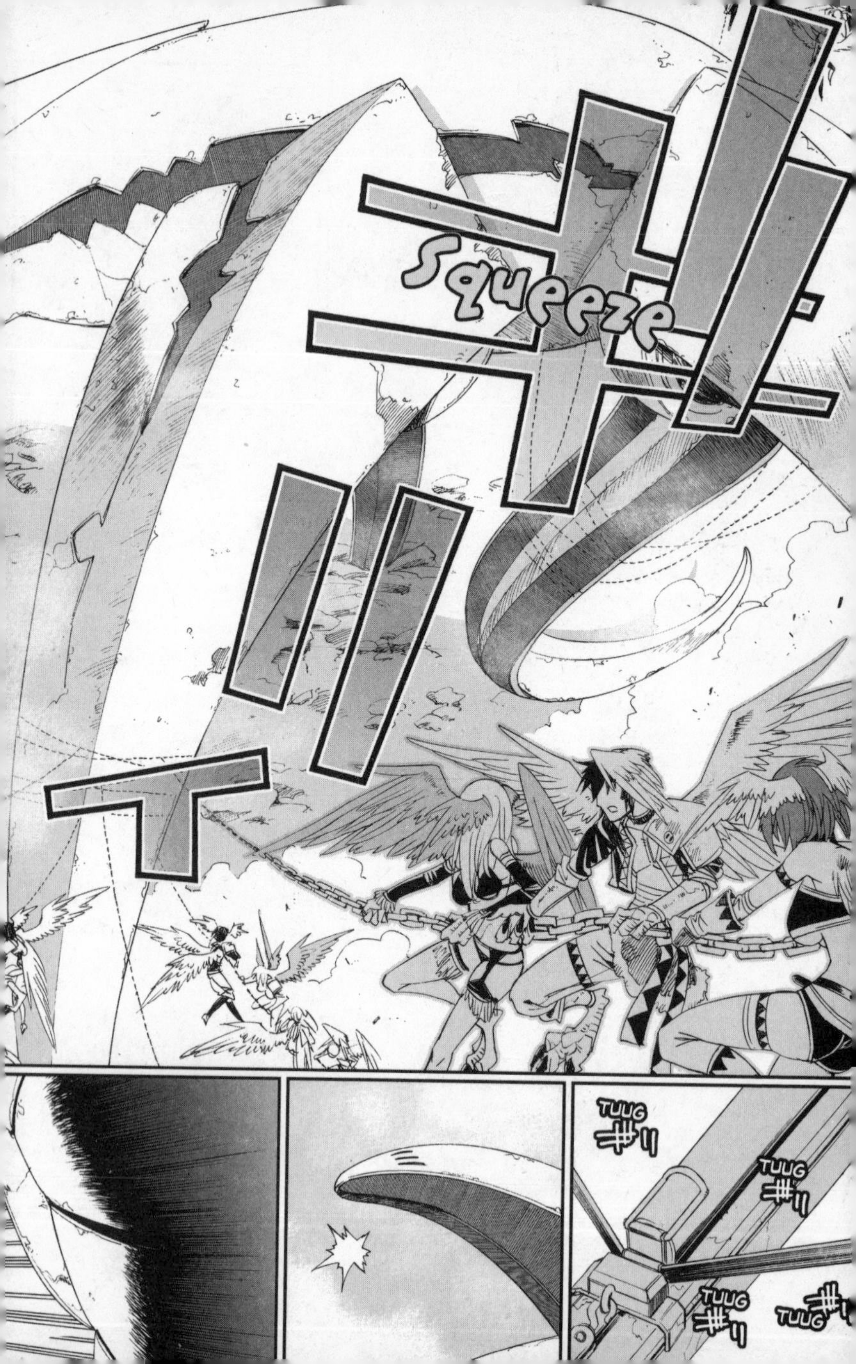
Squeeze
TUUG
TUUG
TUUG
TUUG

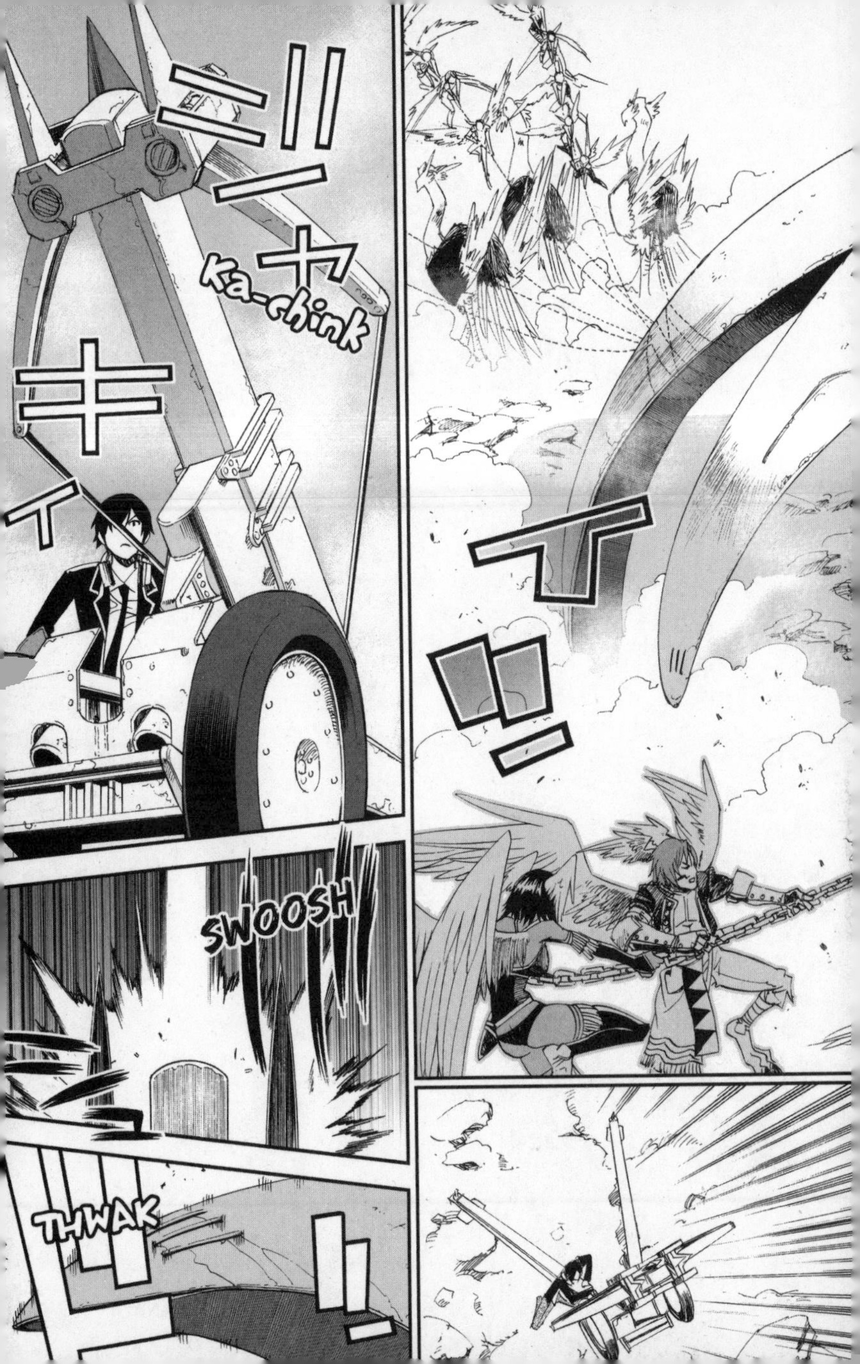
Ka-chink
SWOOSH
THWAK

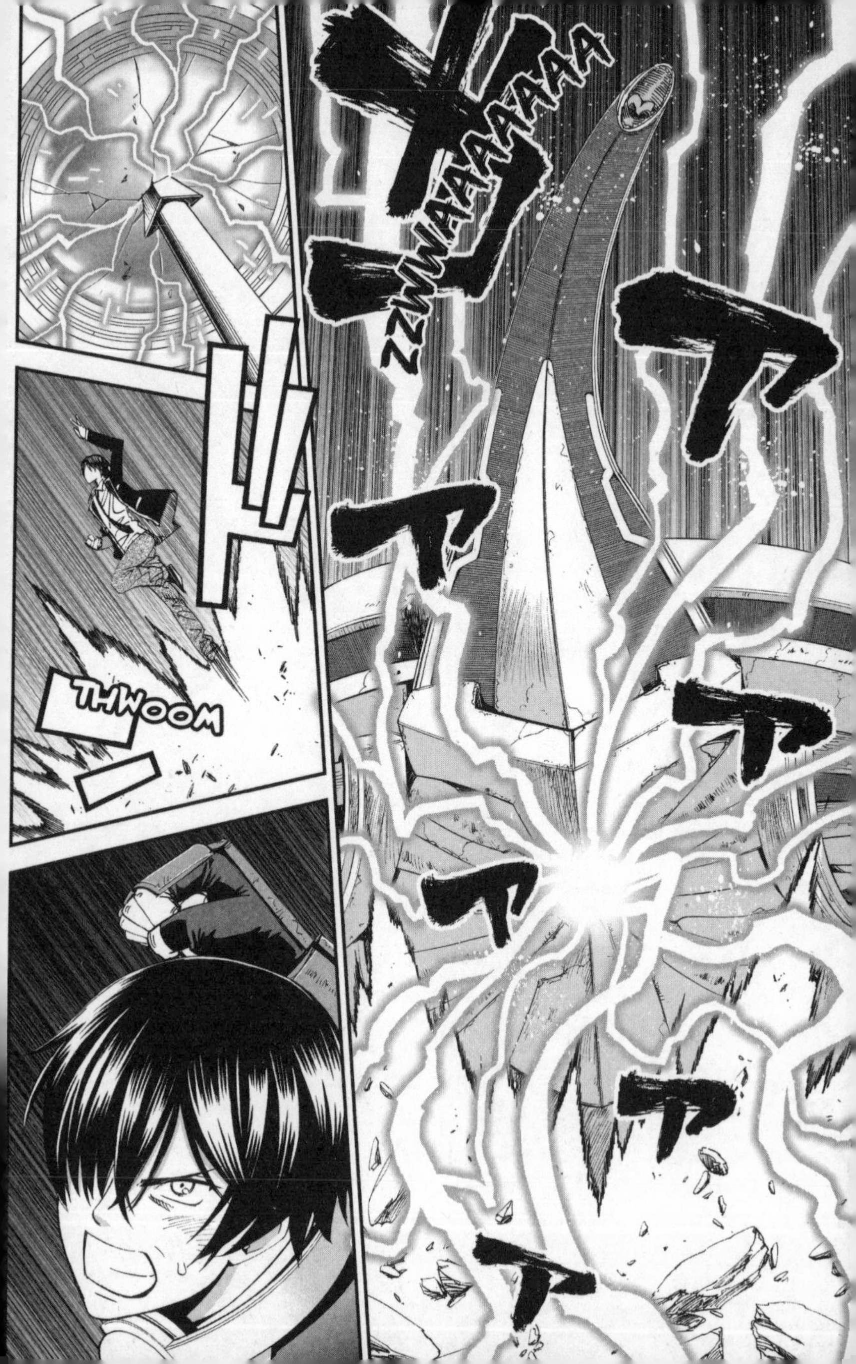
ZZWWAAAAAAAAA
THWOOM

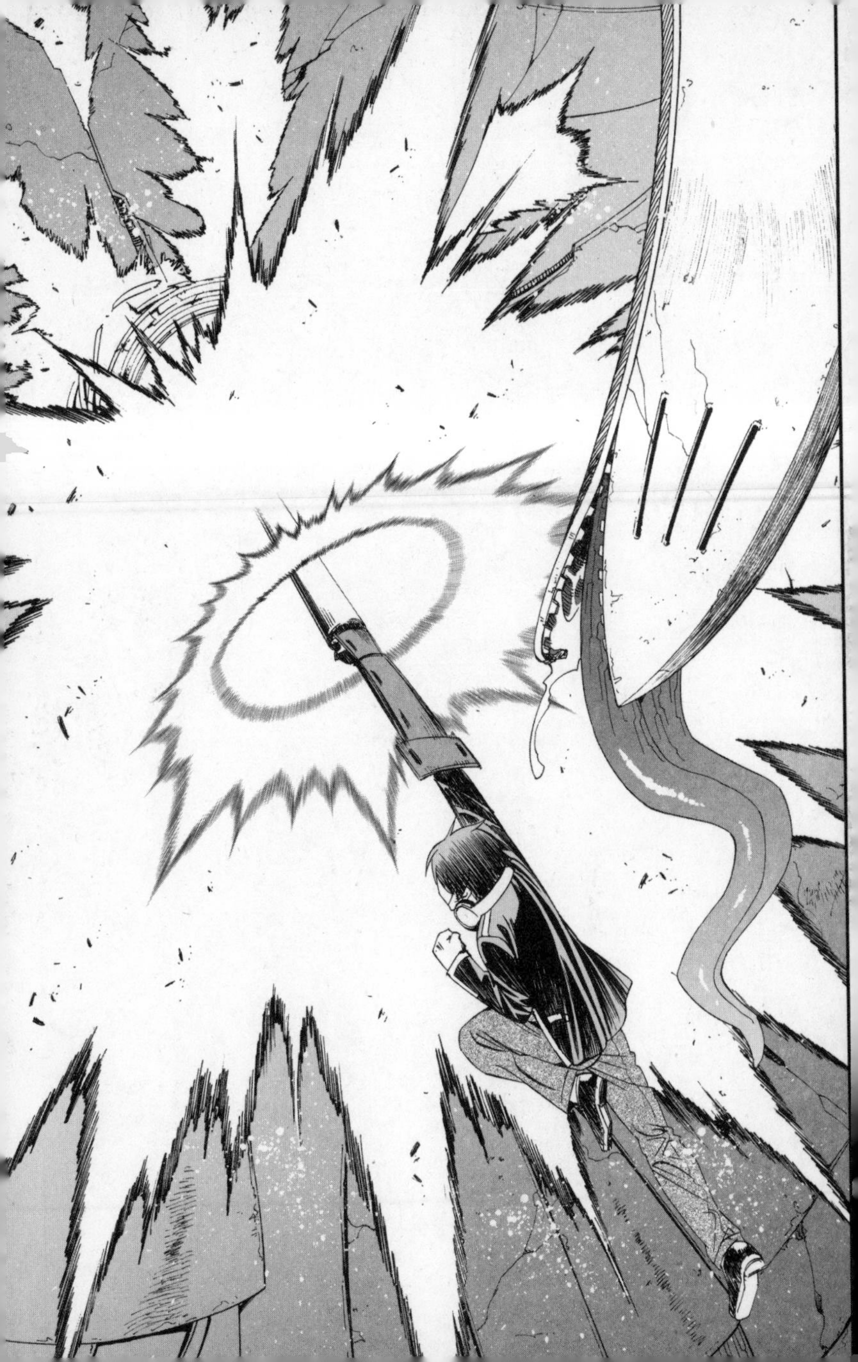

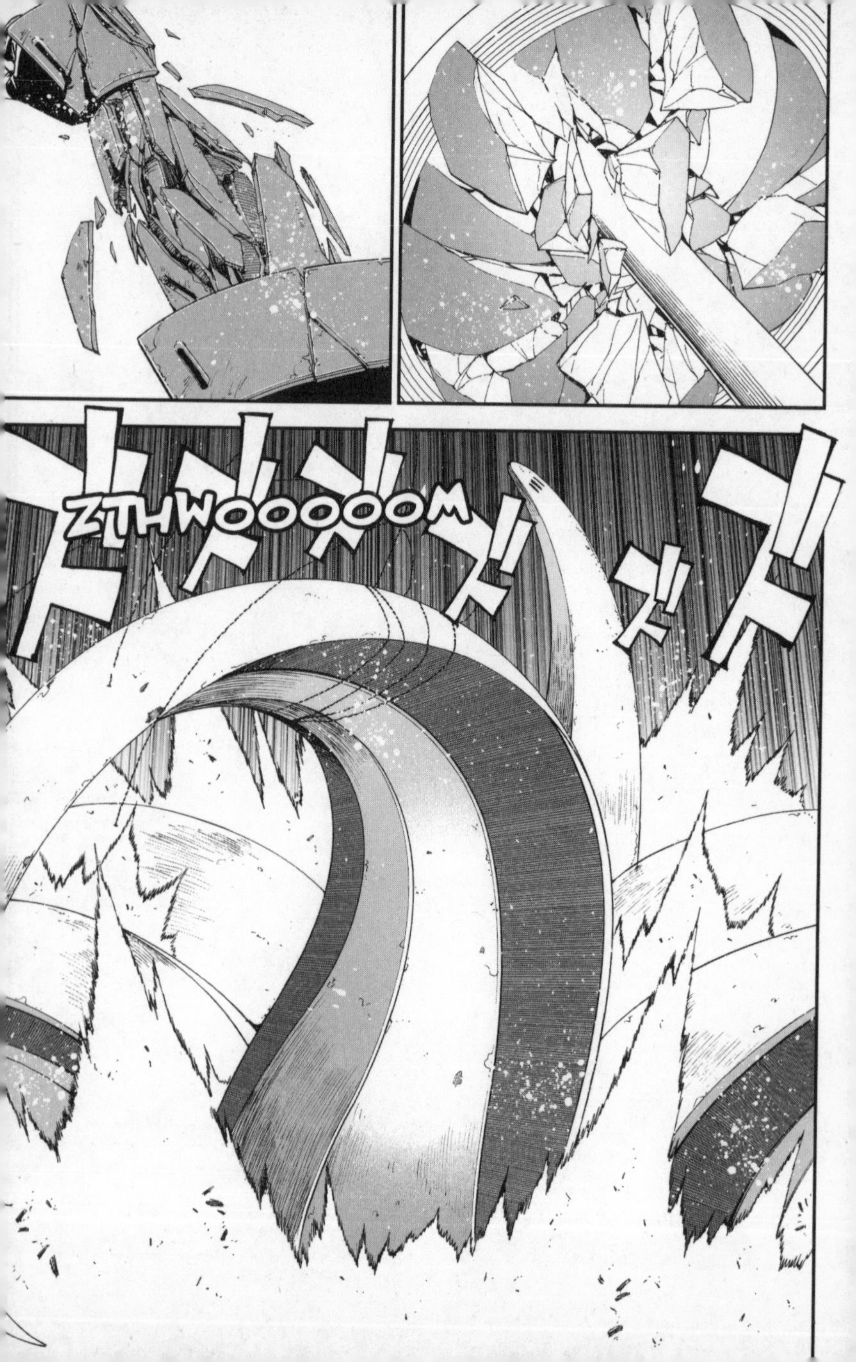
ZTHWOOOOOOM

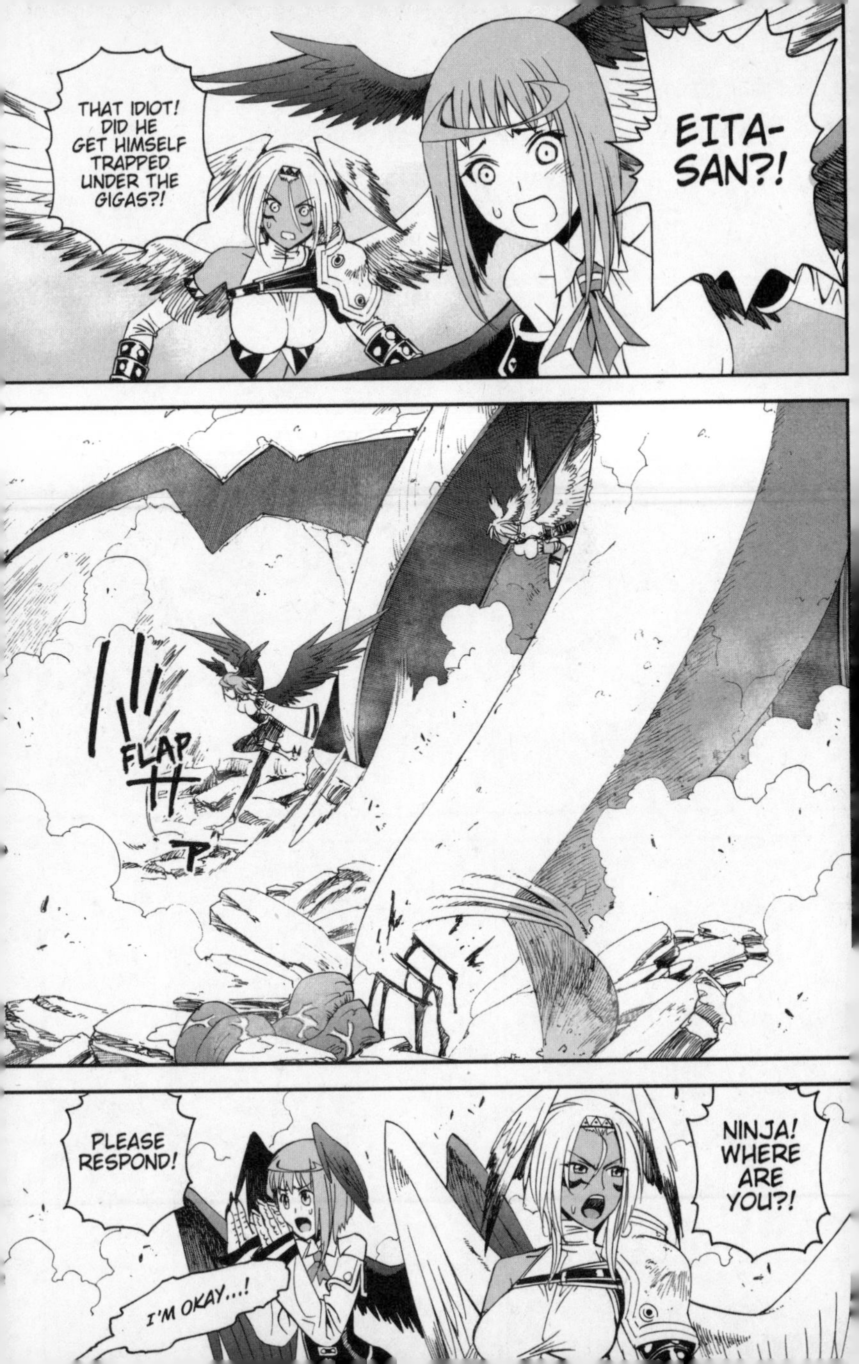
EITA-SAN?!
THAT IDIOT! DID HE GET HIMSELF TRAPPED UNDER THE GIGAS?!
FLAP
NINJA! WHERE ARE YOU?!
PLEASE RESPOND!
I'M OKAY...!

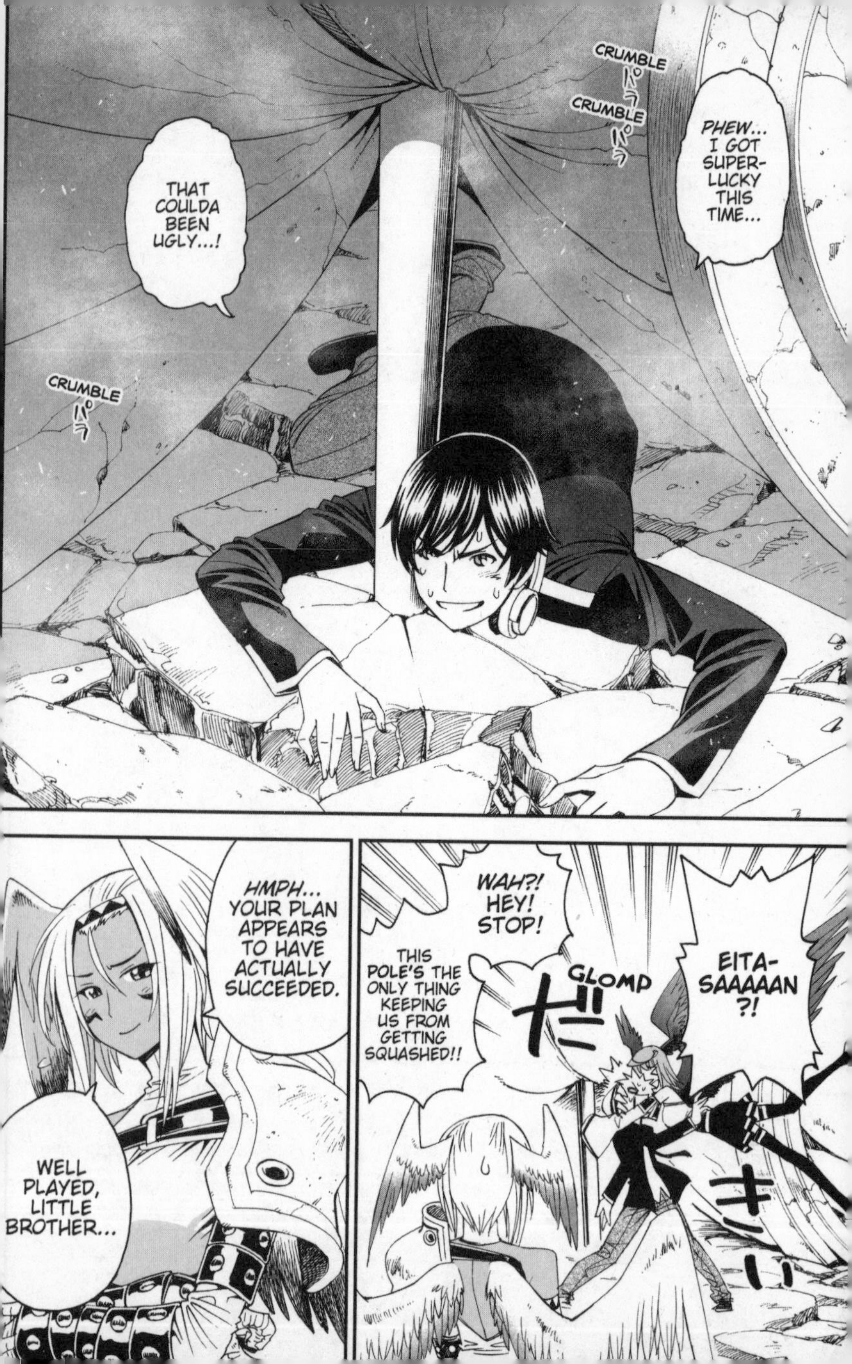

CRUMBLE
パラ
CRUMBLE
パラ
PHEW... I GOT SUPER-LUCKY THIS TIME...
THAT COULDA BEEN UGLY...!
CRUMBLE
パラ
EITA-SAAAAAN?!
WAH?! HEY! STOP!
GLOMP
THIS POLE'S THE ONLY THING KEEPING US FROM GETTING SQUASHED!!
HMPH... YOUR PLAN APPEARS TO HAVE ACTUALLY SUCCEEDED.
WELL PLAYED, LITTLE BROTHER...

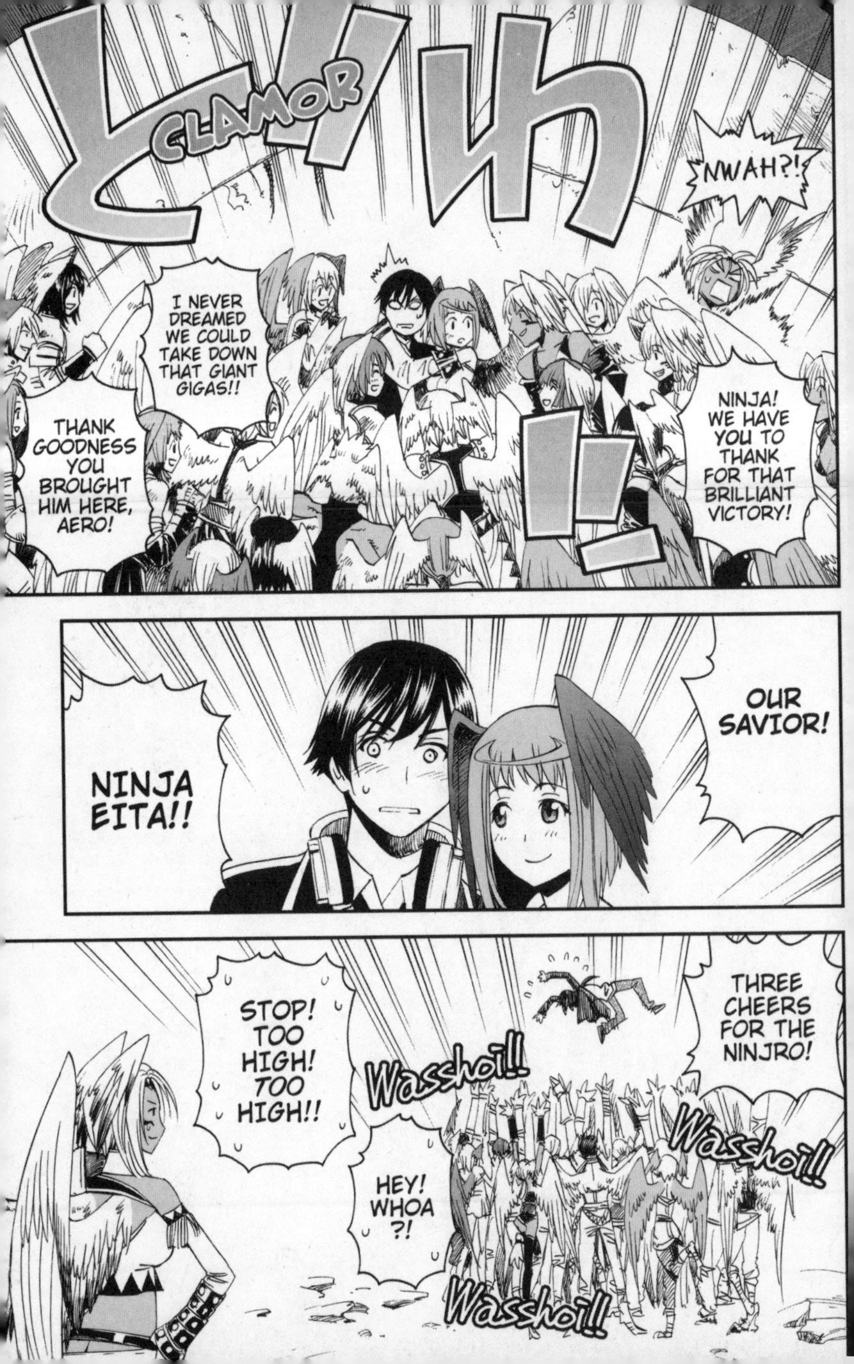
CLAMOR
NWAH?!
NINJA! WE HAVE YOU TO THANK FOR THAT BRILLIANT VICTORY!
I NEVER DREAMED WE COULD TAKE DOWN THAT GIANT GIGAS!!
THANK GOODNESS YOU BROUGHT HIM HERE, AERO!
OUR SAVIOR!
NINJA EITA!!
THREE CHEERS FOR THE NINJRO!
Wasshoi!!
Wasshoi!!
STOP! TOO HIGH! TOO HIGH!!
Wasshoi!!
HEY! WHOA?!

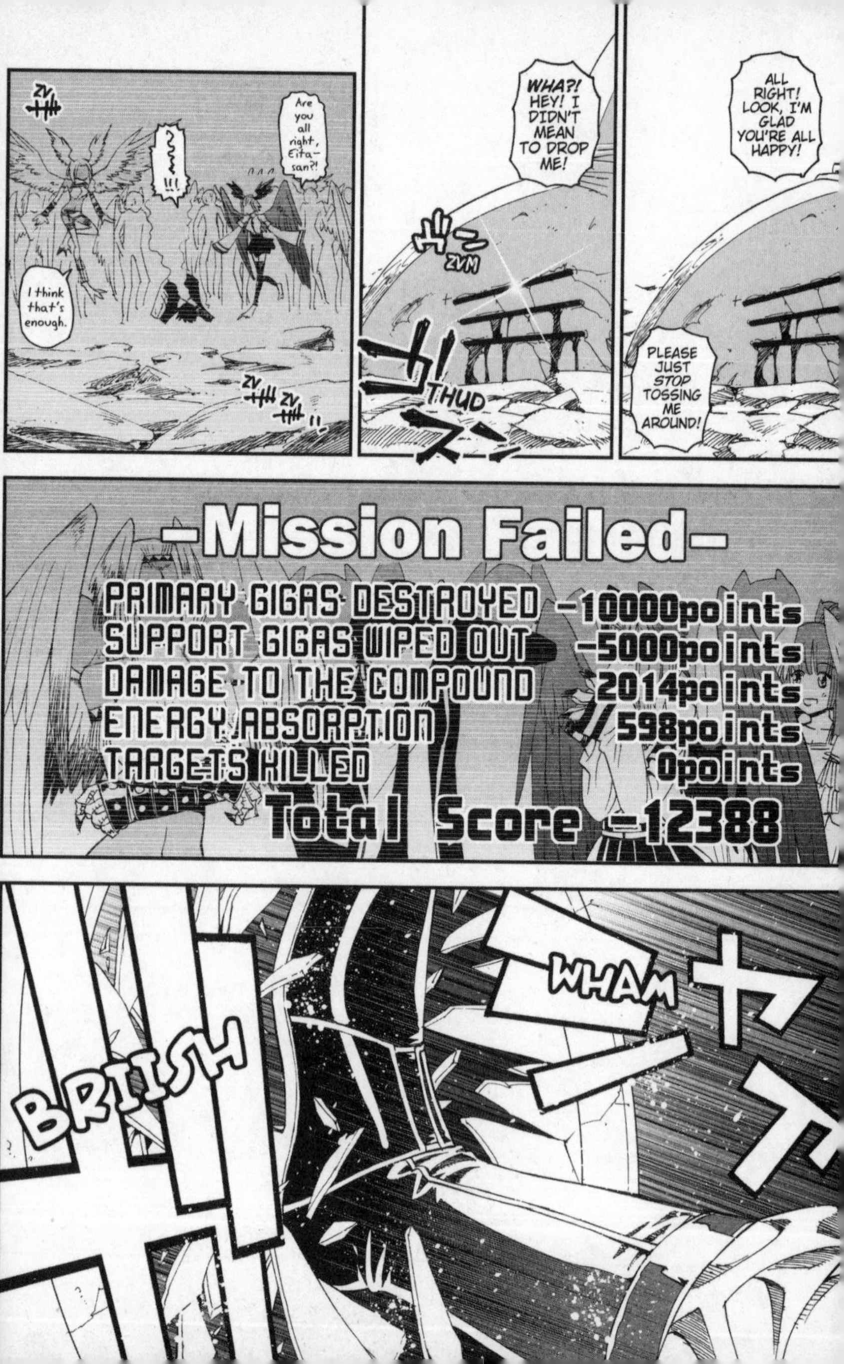
ALL RIGHT! LOOK, I'M GLAD YOU'RE ALL HAPPY!
PLEASE JUST STOP TOSSING ME AROUND!
WHA?! HEY! I DIDN'T MEAN TO DROP ME!
ZVM
THUD
ZV
Are you all right, Eita-san?!
~~~!!
I think that's enough.
ZV
ZV
-Mission Failed-
PRIMARY GIGAS DESTROYED -10000points
SUPPORT GIGAS WIPED OUT -5000points
DAMAGE TO THE COMPOUND 2014points
ENERGY ABSORPTION 598points
TARGETS KILLED 0points
Total Score -12388
WHAM
BRISH
~~~

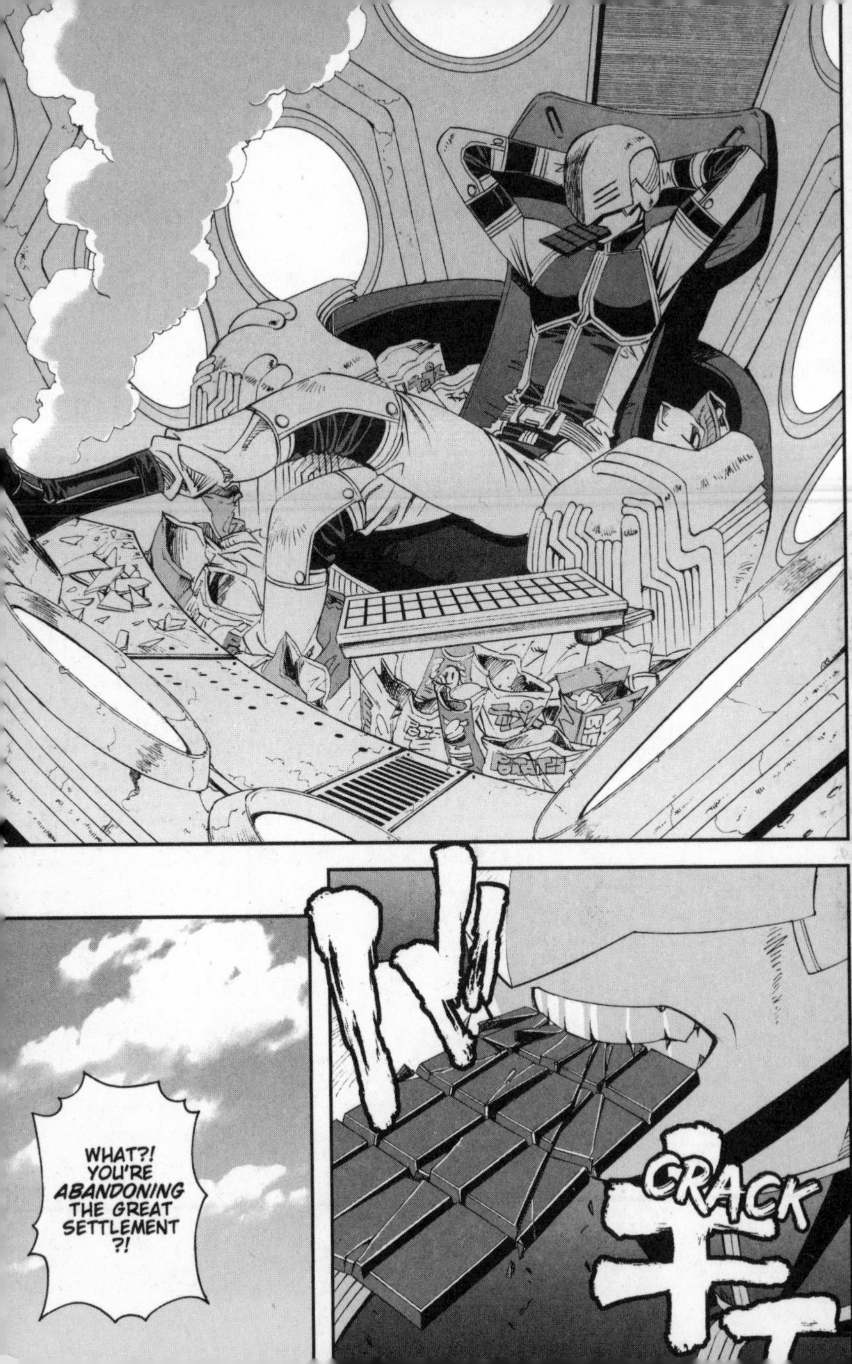
CRACK
WHAT?! YOU'RE ABANDONING THE GREAT SETTLEMENT ?!

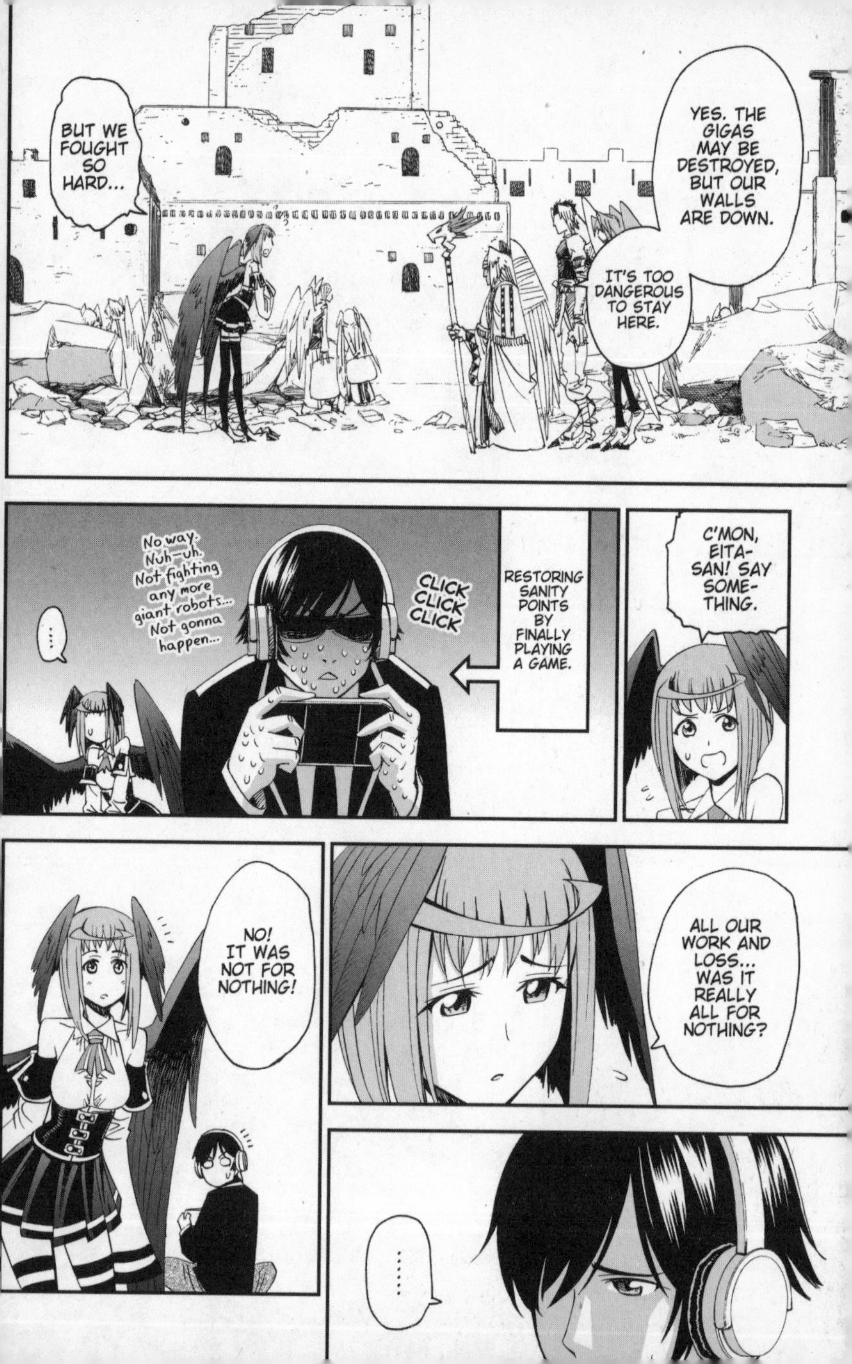
YES. THE GIGAS MAY BE DESTROYED, BUT OUR WALLS ARE DOWN.
IT'S TOO DANGEROUS TO STAY HERE.
BUT WE FOUGHT SO HARD...
C'MON, EITA-SAN! SAY SOMETHING.
RESTORING SANITY POINTS BY FINALLY PLAYING A GAME.
CLICK CLICK CLICK
No way. Nuh-uh. Not fighting any more giant robots... Not gonna happen...
....
ALL OUR WORK AND LOSS... WAS IT REALLY ALL FOR NOTHING?
......
NO! IT WAS NOT FOR NOTHING!

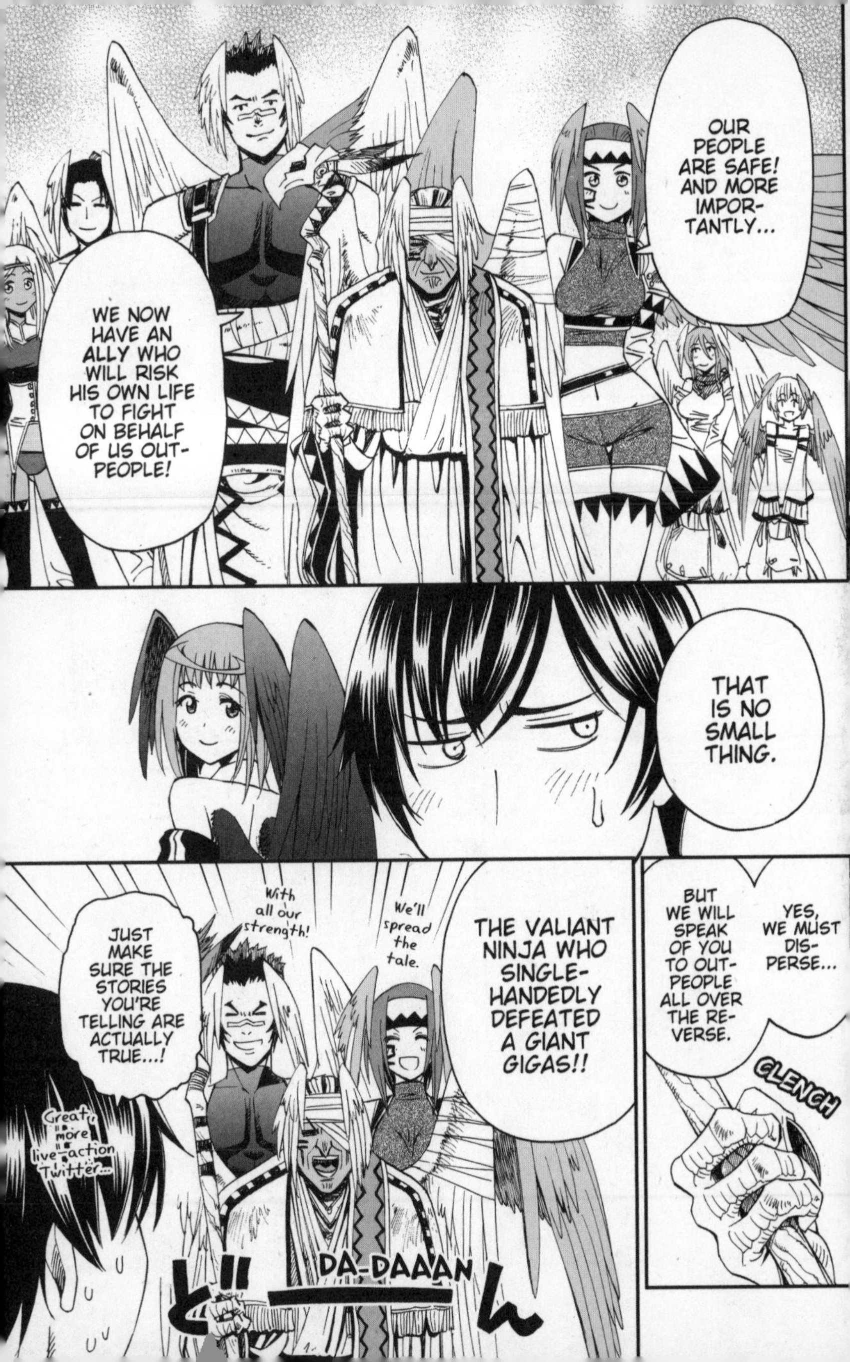
OUR PEOPLE ARE SAFE! AND MORE IMPOR-TANTLY...
WE NOW HAVE AN ALLY WHO WILL RISK HIS OWN LIFE TO FIGHT ON BEHALF OF US OUT-PEOPLE!
THAT IS NO SMALL THING.
YES, WE MUST DIS-PERSE...
BUT WE WILL SPEAK OF YOU TO OUT-PEOPLE ALL OVER THE RE-VERSE.
CLENCH
THE VALIANT NINJA WHO SINGLE-HANDEDLY DEFEATED A GIANT GIGAS!!
We'll spread the tale.
With all our strength!
JUST MAKE SURE THE STORIES YOU'RE TELLING ARE ACTUALLY TRUE...!
Great, more live-action Twitter...
DA-DAAAN

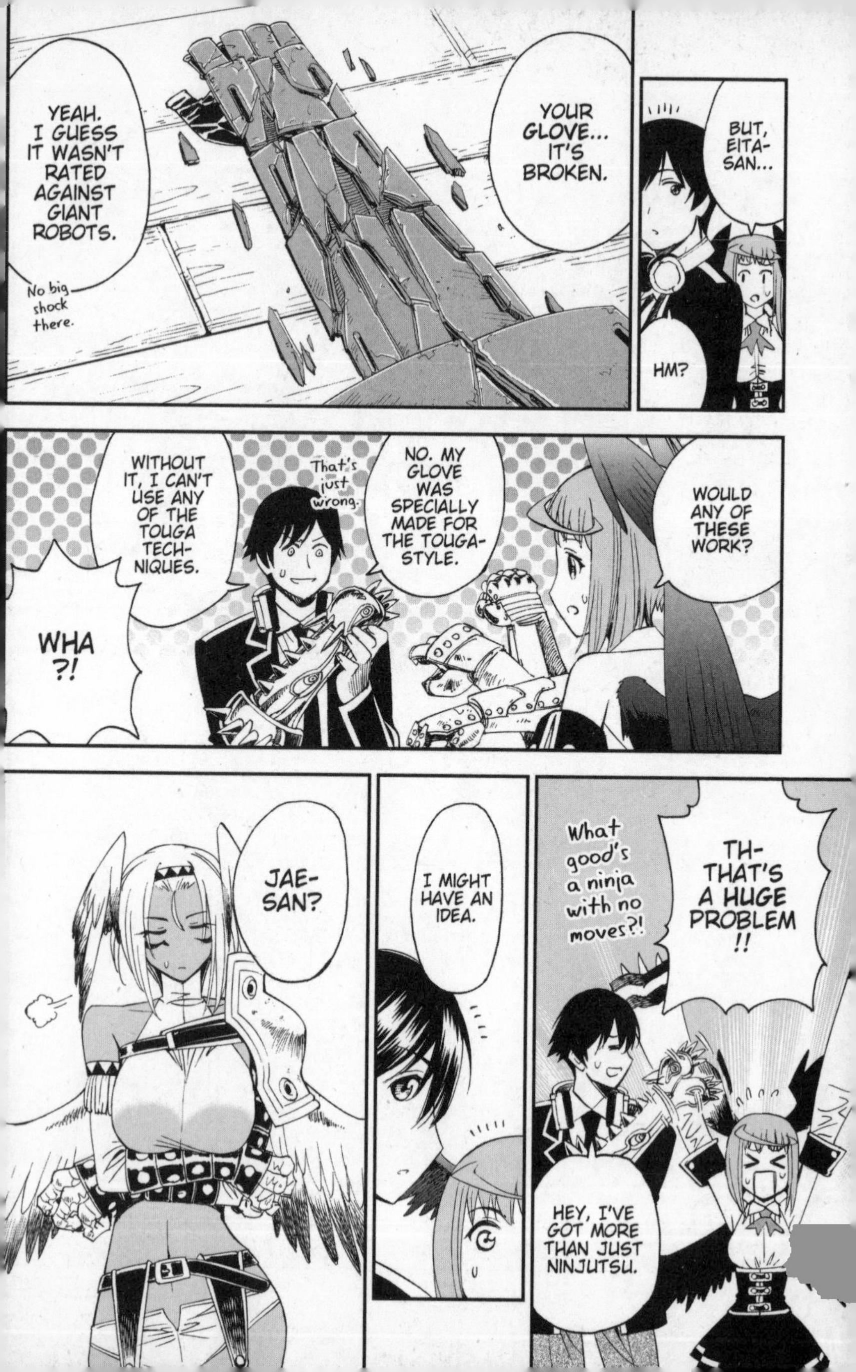
BUT, EITA-SAN...
HM?
YOUR GLOVE... IT'S BROKEN.
YEAH. I GUESS IT WASN'T RATED AGAINST GIANT ROBOTS.
No big shock there.
WOULD ANY OF THESE WORK?
NO. MY GLOVE WAS SPECIALLY MADE FOR THE TOUGA-STYLE.
That's just wrong.
WITHOUT IT, I CAN'T USE ANY OF THE TOUGA TECH-NIQUES.
WHA ?!
TH-THAT'S A HUGE PROBLEM !!
What good's a ninja with no moves?!
HEY, I'VE GOT MORE THAN JUST NINJUTSU.
I MIGHT HAVE AN IDEA.
JAE-SAN?

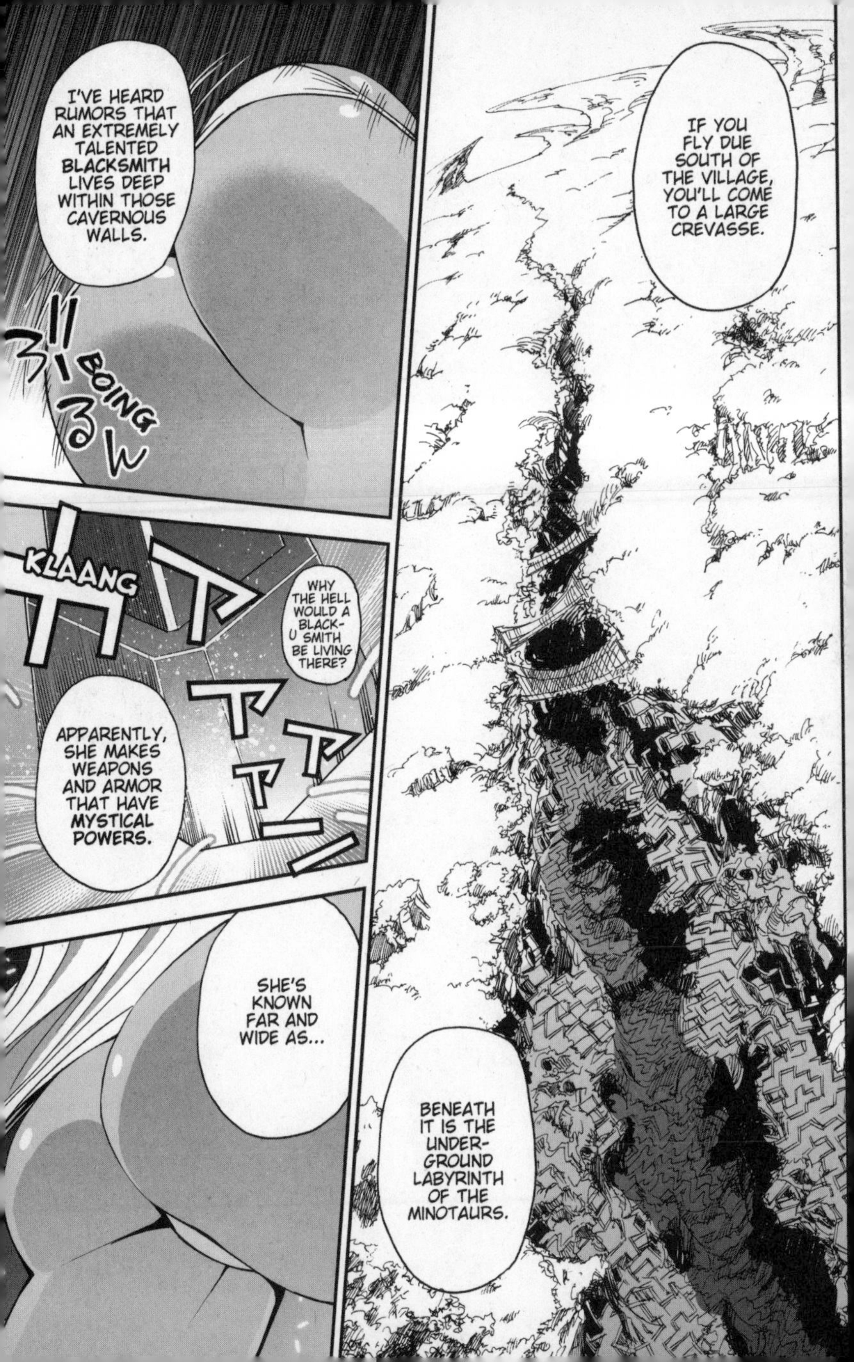
IF YOU FLY DUE SOUTH OF THE VILLAGE, YOU'LL COME TO A LARGE CREVASSE.
BENEATH IT IS THE UNDERGROUND LABYRINTH OF THE MINOTAURS.
I'VE HEARD RUMORS THAT AN EXTREMELY TALENTED BLACKSMITH LIVES DEEP WITHIN THOSE CAVERNOUS WALLS.
BOING
KLAANG
WHY THE HELL WOULD A BLACKSMITH BE LIVING THERE?
APPARENTLY, SHE MAKES WEAPONS AND ARMOR THAT HAVE MYSTICAL POWERS.
SHE'S KNOWN FAR AND WIDE AS...

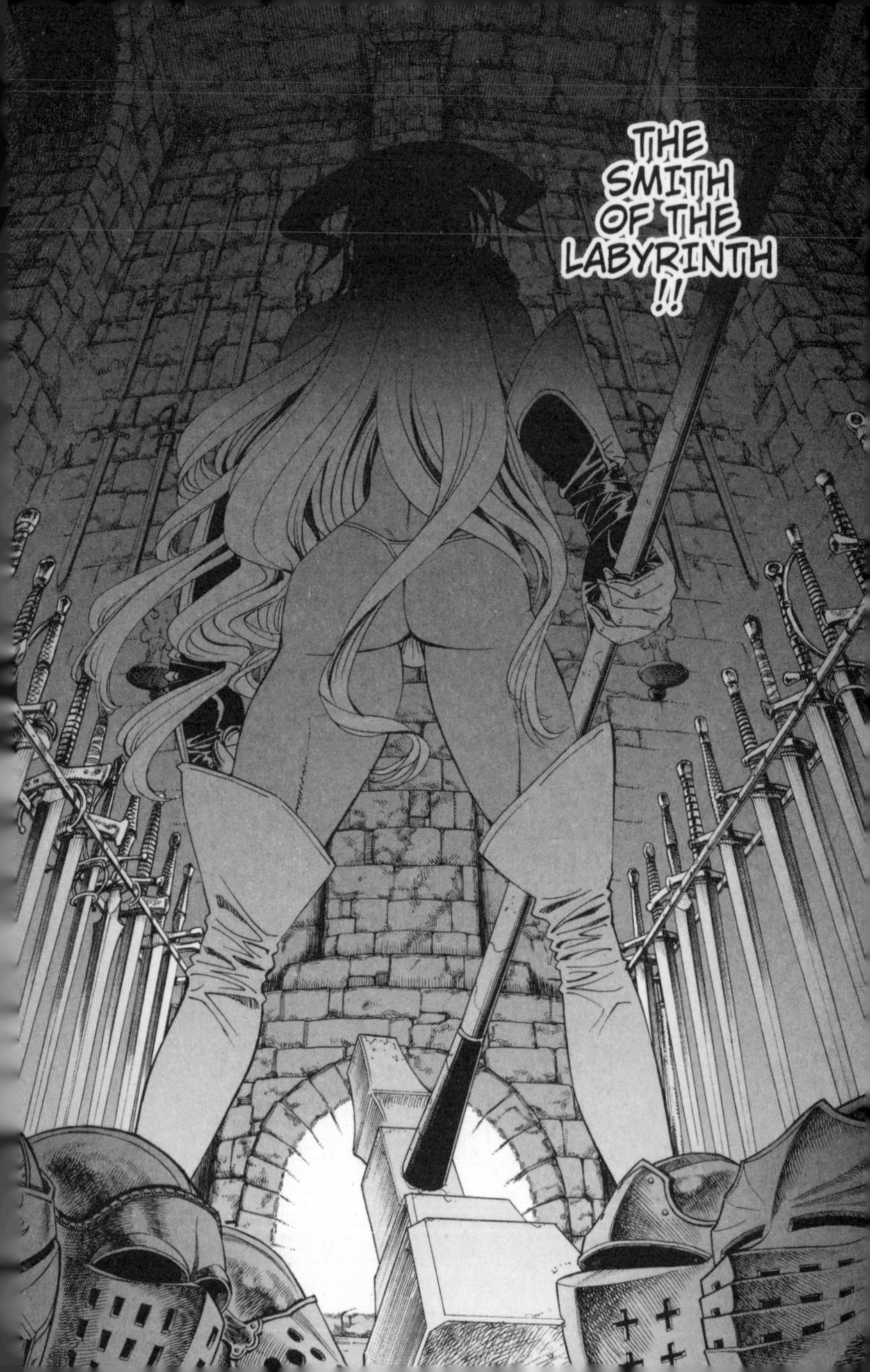
THE SMITH OF THE LABYRINTH !!

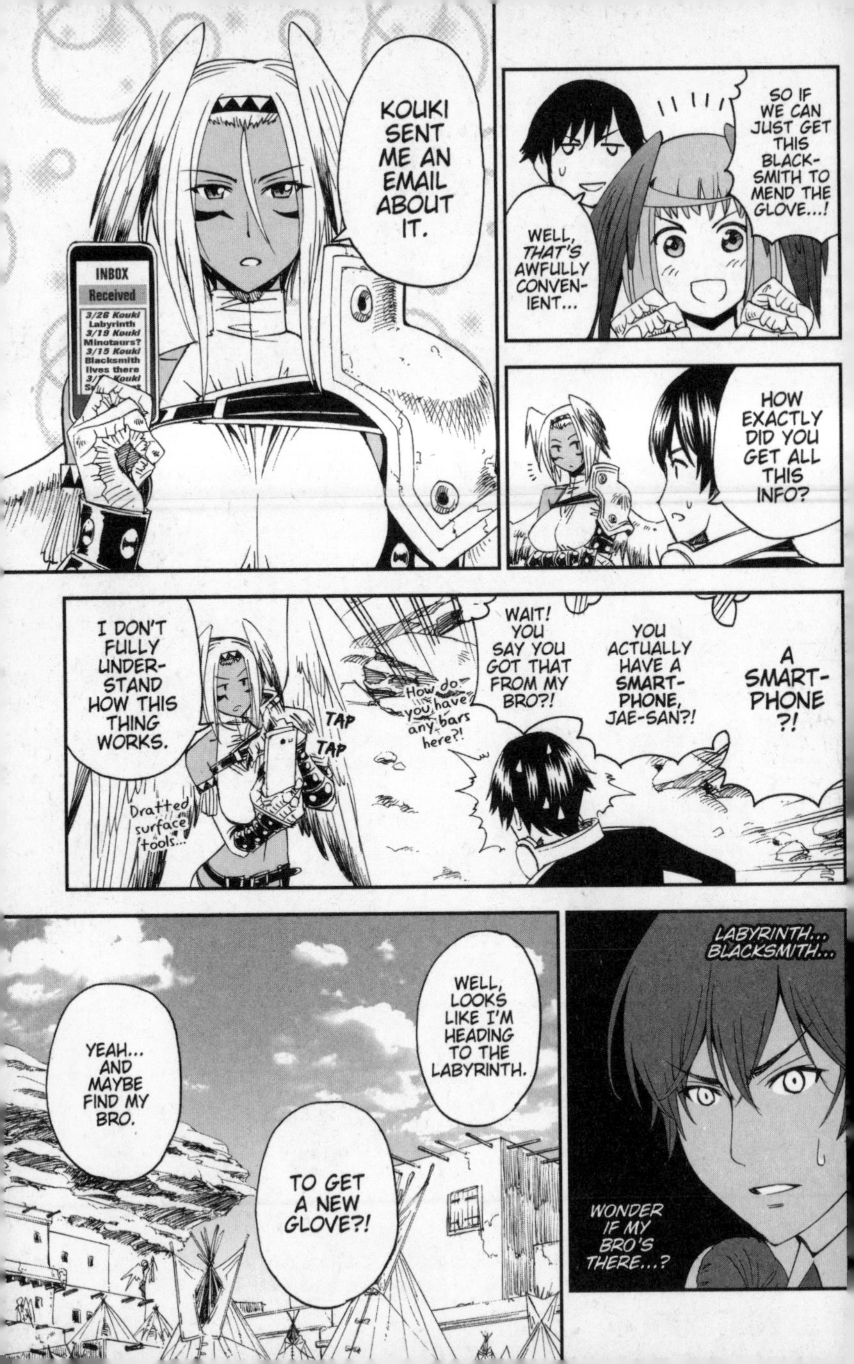
SO IF WE CAN JUST GET THIS BLACKSMITH TO MEND THE GLOVE...!
WELL, *THAT'S* AWFULLY CONVENIENT...
HOW EXACTLY DID YOU GET ALL THIS INFO?
KOUKI SENT ME AN EMAIL ABOUT IT.
INBOX
Received
3/26 Kouki Labyrinth
3/19 Kouki Minotaurs?
3/15 Kouki Blacksmith lives there
A SMARTPHONE?!
YOU ACTUALLY HAVE A SMARTPHONE, JAE-SAN?!
WAIT! YOU SAY YOU GOT THAT FROM MY BRO?!
How do you have any bars here?!
TAP
TAP
I DON'T FULLY UNDERSTAND HOW THIS THING WORKS.
Dratted surface tools...
LABYRINTH... BLACKSMITH...
WONDER IF MY BRO'S THERE...?
WELL, LOOKS LIKE I'M HEADING TO THE LABYRINTH.
TO GET A NEW GLOVE?!
YEAH... AND MAYBE FIND MY BRO.

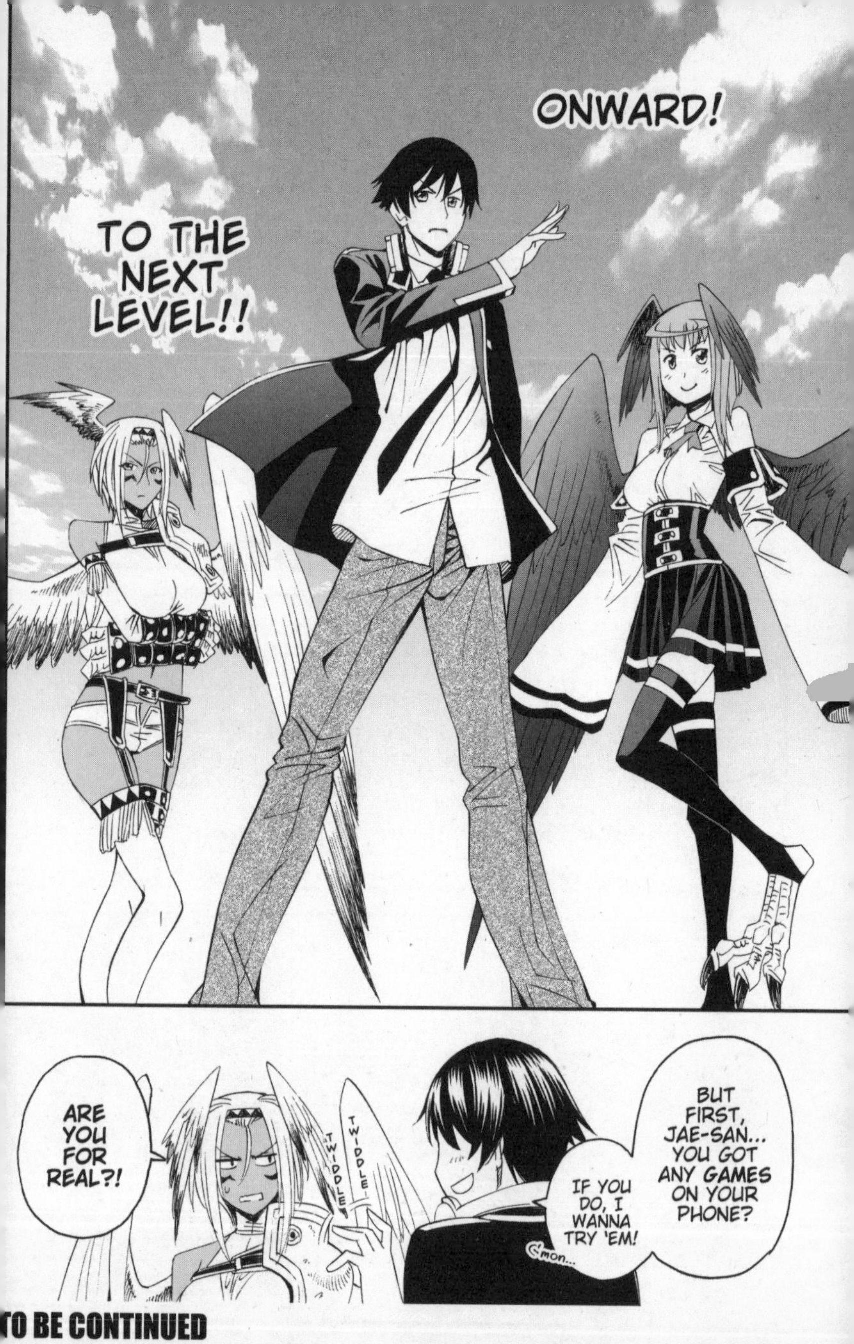
ONWARD!
TO THE NEXT LEVEL!!
BUT FIRST, JAE-SAN... YOU GOT ANY GAMES ON YOUR PHONE?
IF YOU DO, I WANNA TRY 'EM!
C'mon...
TWIDDLE
TWIDDLE
ARE YOU FOR REAL?!

TO BE CONTINUED

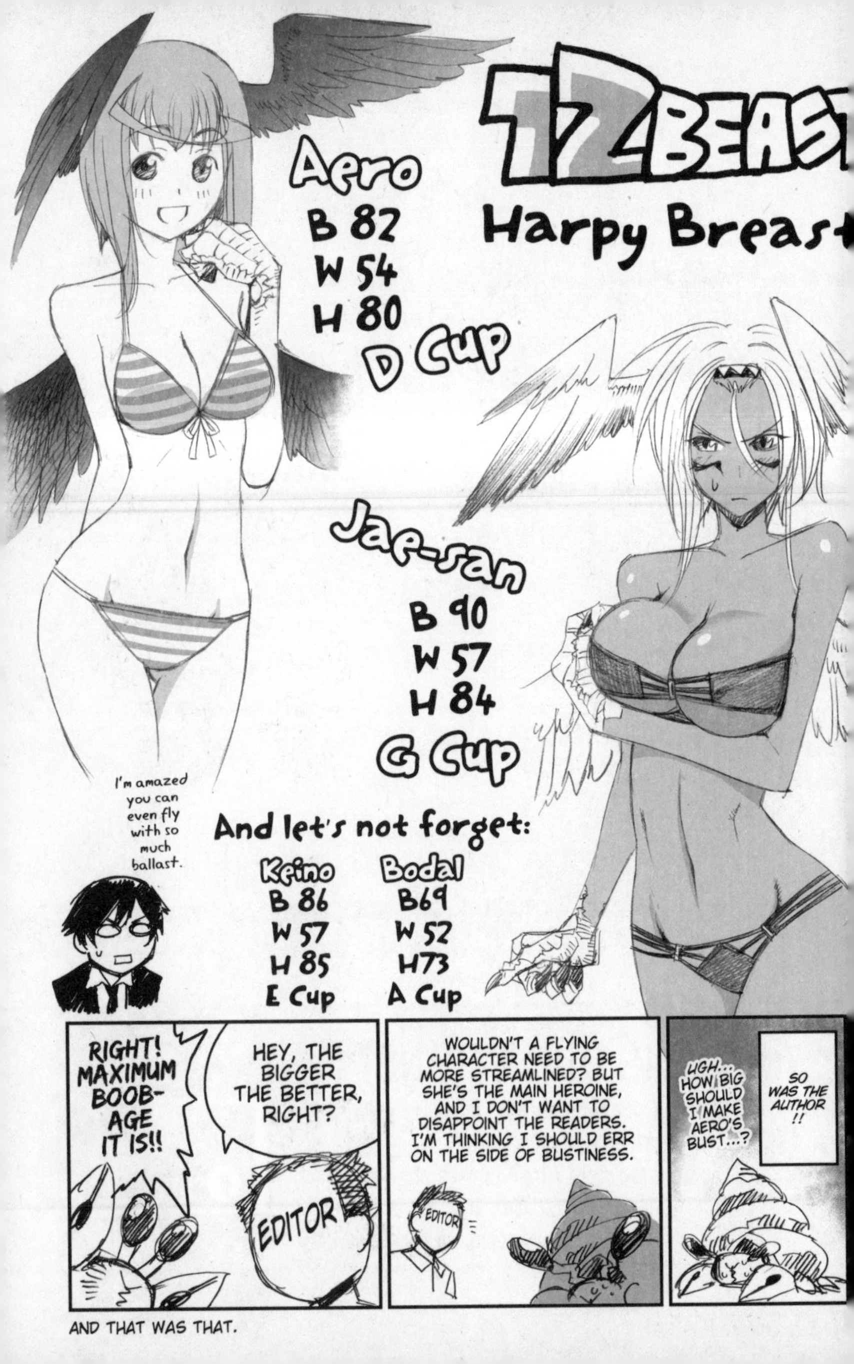

12 BEAST
Harpy Breast
Aero
B 82
W 54
H 80
D Cup
Jae-san
B 90
W 57
H 84
G Cup
I'm amazed you can even fly with so much ballast.
And let's not forget:
Keino
B 86
W 57
H 85
E Cup
Bodal
B69
W 52
H73
A Cup
SO WAS THE AUTHOR !!
UGH... HOW BIG SHOULD I MAKE AERO'S BUST...?
WOULDN'T A FLYING CHARACTER NEED TO BE MORE STREAMLINED? BUT SHE'S THE MAIN HEROINE, AND I DON'T WANT TO DISAPPOINT THE READERS. I'M THINKING I SHOULD ERR ON THE SIDE OF BUSTINESS.
EDITOR
HEY, THE BIGGER THE BETTER, RIGHT?
RIGHT! MAXIMUM BOOB-AGE IT IS!!
EDITOR
AND THAT WAS THAT.

# SEVEN SEAS ENTERTAINMENT PRESENTS

# 12BEAST

## story and art by OKAYADO    VOLUME 1

TRANSLATION
**Ryan Peterson**

ADAPTATION
**Shanti Whitesides**

LETTERING AND LAYOUT
**Ma. Victoria Robado**

COVER DESIGN
**Nicky Lim**

PROOFREADER
**Janet Houck**
**Lee Otter**

MANAGING EDITOR
**Adam Arnold**

PUBLISHER
**Jason DeAngelis**

12BEAST VOLUME 1
© OKAYADO 2013
Edited by FUJIMISHOBO.
First published in Japan in 2013 by KADOKAWA CORPORATION, Tokyo.
English translation rights arranged with KADOKAWA CORPORATION, Tokyo
through TOHAN CORPORATION, Tokyo.

Seven Seas books may be purchased in bulk for educational, business, or
promotional use. For information on bulk purchases, please contact Macmillan
Corporate & Premium Sales Department at 1-800-221-7945 (ext 5442)
or write specialmarkets@macmillan.com.

Seven Seas and the Seven Seas logo are trademarks of
Seven Seas Entertainment, LLC. All rights reserved.

ISBN: 978-1-626921-77-1

Printed in Canada

First Printing: April 2015

10 9 8 7 6 5 4 3 2 1

## FOLLOW US ONLINE: *www.gomanga.com*

# READING DIRECTIONS

This book reads
If this is your fi
reading from the
take it from the
numbered diagram here. It may seem backwards at
first, but you'll get the hang of it! Have fun!!